The Complete
Greenhouse Book

The Complete Greenhouse Book

**Building and Using Greenhouses
from Coldframes to Solar Structures**

Peter Clegg
Derry Watkins

GARDEN WAY PUBLISHING
Charlotte, Vermont 05445

Illustrations by Peter Clegg, Polly Alexander, and Robert Vogel.

Printed in the United States

Library of Congress Cataloging in Publication Data

Clegg, Peter.
    The complete greenhouse book.

Bibliography: p.
    Includes index.
    1. Greenhouses. 2. Greenhouse gardening.
I. Watkins, Derry, 1947–   joint author. II. Title.
SB415.C52   635'.04'8   78-24572
ISBN 0-88266-142-6
ISBN 0-88266-141-8 pbk.

Contents

Foreword

Across 93 million miles, the sun's energy continuously falls upon our planet's surface, its otherwise unbearable irradiation made diffuse and gentle by the earth's protective atmosphere and cloud cover. The clouds, while they may appear to block out the sun when we need it most, provide a beneficial function: they trap the earth's heat that is reradiated to the sky, thus creating at the global scale the earth's greenhouse.

Warmed by the sun, plants push out from whatever ground or rock crevice will give them hold, repeating with each seed that blooms the miracle of creation. Some plants give pleasure by their color and form; others give sustenance as fruit and legumes; and all fulfill intricate ecological roles by providing habitat for insects, by controlling moisture, and by purifying the air through photosynthesis.

But the winds blow, animals and insects forage, and the winter comes. Tilted away from the sun, the earth's surface grows still, too cold to sustain anything but dormant life. The ground is thus assigned a forced sleep, sometimes beginning too early in the fall and often lasting too late into the spring. For millennia, the hunter and the planter watched the stars and the sun journey across the skydome to learn when the spring might come. Marks were made by earth-mounds, by circles of stones, and by solar-oriented buildings that served as calendars to signal the arrival of the spring equinox and to establish the schedule for planting. The sun was so important it was called God. The calendars were so important they were made sacred. They established mankind's first scientific connection with the universe by observation and prediction.

The next most significant step to be established in the dialogue between sun and plants was to place a sheet of glass between, to protect the plant from the wind and to trap the earth's heat. The property of glass to block low-temperature reradiation from the heated ground—resulting in what is called the "greenhouse effect" and not fully understood until many centuries after glass was first made—offered the first climate control that we had over the length of the growing season.

That simple piece of glass makes the greenhouse work: It raises the temperature of the space that it encloses; it raises the capability of the greenhouse to produce, to do useful work. Thus the greenhouse takes its place beside the windmill, the waterwheel, and the solar collector plate as examples of appropriate technology that reverse "entropy" (the dimunition of work capability whenever energy is converted). These inventions take a diffuse energy form (wind, rain, and sunshine) and raise its work potential.

Enclosed in glass, the garden blooms year 'round. With insulating controls added to the glass and with thermal storage added to the interior, the greenhouse can become entirely solar heated. Attached to the house, the greenhouse becomes a "sunspace," capable of moderating the temperature and humidity of the house environment as well. Thus jointed and possibly brought into the core of the dwelling, the garden becomes the atrium, the center of family activity in all seasons.

In the Islamic culture, the garden courtyard is the symbol of paradise, walled-off from the often harsh desert surrounding and open only to the sky. In nineteenth-century England, the conservatory was the place where exotic plants were domesticated; tropical environments were thus transplanted and collected. Enclosed by the

spectacular glass and iron structures pioneered by Joseph Paxton, the public gardens civilized the outdoor climate and made the garden a place of public meeting and recreation.

These possibilities once again present themselves to us as we seek to find our place between sun and earth.

In this sensitive and intelligent book by Peter Clegg and Derry Watkins, the know-how of the architect and the gardener are combined to give the basic information required to bring to every home its solar-heated productive greenhouse. The greenhouse can sustain the life of plants and the life of the family. What follows is a remarkable book about this remarkable design technology.

DONALD WATSON
Guilford, Connecticut

ABOUT THE AUTHORS

Peter Clegg, a native of the Yorkshire Village of Saxton in England, grew up in a gardening and food-producing family, and was educated at Cambridge University where he studied architecture. He is a practicing architect in Bath, England, specializing in solar applications. He is the author of Garden Way's *New Low-Cost Sources of Energy for the Home*, first published in 1974 and now undergoing a complete revision.

Derry Watkins, his wife, a U.S. citizen, is a graduate of Radcliffe College and has worked in filmstrips and editing for several publishing firms. She is an avid organic gardener.

I

Perspective and Planning

Joseph Paxton, left, is shown in the open colonnade at the Sydenham Crystal Palace during its reconstruction in 1852. His successful design for the Great Exhibition of 1851 was the wonder of Victorian England.

1

The History of the Greenhouse

As early as the fifth century B.C., Greek writers were describing "gardens of Adonis" where exotic plants flourished. As Plato wrote, "a grain of seed, or the branch of a tree, placed in ... these gardens, acquires in eight days a development which cannot be obtained in as many months in the open." Though he implies that these gardens were not in the open air, we cannot tell whether they were actually enclosed greenhouses or were merely sheltered, well-tended gardens.

In any case, by the first century A.D., the Romans were certainly growing fruits and vegetables in simple greenhouses or coldframes. When Tiberius Caesar was ordered by his doctor to eat cucumbers (some say it was simply his imperial whim), his gardener managed to produce a cucumber every day of the year by using large pots filled with decomposing manure. The pots were covered with a transparent sheet to conserve the heat from the manure and to let in sunlight. They were wheeled outside on sunny days and kept indoors at night.

The Romans generally used thin sheets of talc or mica to cover their coldframes. But a large and elaborate greenhouse discovered in Pompeii appears to have been covered with a sort of rough glass. It contained masonry tiers to set the plants on and had a hot-air heating system running through the walls. Such a well-thought-out, heated greenhouse was not seen again until the seventeenth century. All through the Middle Ages, greenhouses appear to have been virtually unknown.

Sixteenth and Seventeenth Centuries

In the sixteenth century, traders and explorers began to bring back exotic plants that could not survive in the European climate. To look after these rare and delicate specimens, special botanical gardens were founded first in Italy, then in Holland and England.

An enormous amount of study and research went into the cultivation and description of exotic plants. Botany was just coming into being as a science. Universities, learned societies and rich amateurs competed in trying to collect all the known varieties of plants. This became increasingly difficult as more were discovered every year. (Even as late as 1722 plants were still being discovered so rapidly that when the Society of A-pothecaries was offered the Manor of Chelsea on condition that it donate fifty hitherto unknown plants to the Royal Society every year for forty years, it was easily able to do so.) By the seventeenth century, merchant ships were almost invariably commissioned to bring back rare plants from their ports of call. And by the end of the century, many privately financed expeditions were being sent forth just for the purpose of collecting new plants.

Gardening came to be seen as a respectable, scientific occupation requiring great skill. In fact, gardeners who were too successful were sometimes accused of witchcraft. Experimenting with herbs and herbal cures was an important part of every gardener's job.

In addition to their botanical and medical uses, growing exotic plants for decoration and food came into vogue among the aristocracy in the seventeenth century. Noble families began to compete with each other in cultivating unusual varieties. Oranges were the great favorites. They did not need much heat—only protection from frost—but the size of the trees necessitated the building of

Figure 1.1. A 17th-century Dutch "orangerie," a concept popular among the aristocracy. Trees were kept safe from frost indoors during winter and were moved outside in summer.

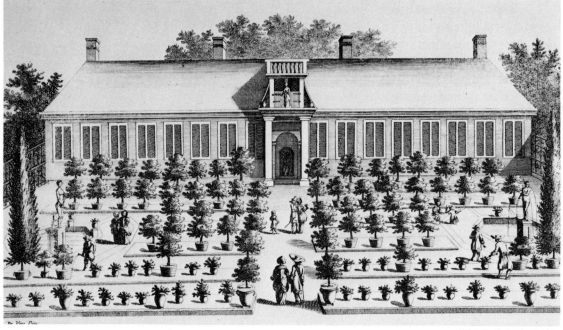

Figure 1.2. The interior of a Dutch "orangerie," with trees being moved outside. Heating stoves line the back wall.

large orangeries. Orangeries became popular throughout Europe, frequently doubling as banqueting halls during the summer when the trees were moved outdoors (Figure 1.1).

Though there were many skilled gardeners in Elizabethan times, the basic principles of plant growth were not well understood. Many of the first greenhouses were built facing north, and most had only a few small windows to let in the light. Tropical plants were brought inside to be kept warm for the winter and were carried out to be set along the garden paths during the summer (Figure 1.2). Most had little or no direct sunlight for six months of the year.

The first inventions for heating greenhouses were equally crude. Open fires, and later portable braziers filled with charcoal, were used, but both men and plants suffered from the noxious fumes given off. Moreover, the heat was unevenly distributed, scorching nearby plants while others remained cold and damp. By the end of the seventeenth century, large heating stoves with chimneys were in general use (in fact, "stove" came to be the common word for hothouse in England). Stoves eliminated the problem of smoke, but they had to be refuelled frequently and they, too, provided only a dry and localized source of heat.

John Evelyn, a 17th-century British diarist who wrote botanical tracts, is supposed to have coined the word "greenhouse," and invented one of the first hot-air heating systems. In 1691 he installed a stove in an outside wall of a greenhouse. All the air entering the greenhouse had to pass through flues over the fire. The air which fed the fire itself was drawn from the cold air at the bottom of the greenhouse, and suction from the hot chimney insured a constant flow of warm air into, and cold air out of, the greenhouse (Figure 1.3). Evelyn's ideas were well in advance of his time. He was one of the first to realize

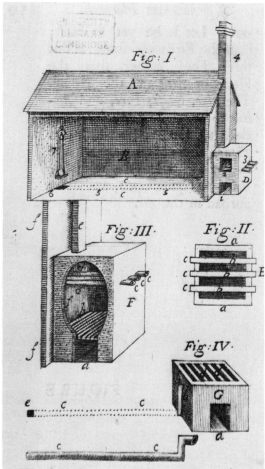

Figure 1.3. Sketches by John Evelyn, a 17th-century British botanist who is given credit for coining the term "greenhouse." His model incorporated a heating stove in an outside wall.

that plants need sunlight, and a century passed before anyone else confirmed his observation of their need for fresh air and air movement.

Eighteenth Century

By the early eighteenth century, light was generally recognized as a prime factor in healthy plant growth. People began to calculate the optimum angle for glass walls so that the least possible amount of sunlight would be reflected.

The Dutch were among the first to use large areas of glass, and they pioneered the use of sloping glass walls and of glass roofs. But since conserving heat became more difficult as the area of glass expanded, they also pioneered the use of curtains or shutters that could be drawn at night to hold the heat in. They even developed a sort of primitive double-glazing, using oil-paper inside the glass.

Two of the most famous and technically advanced botanic gardens in the world were in Holland. Leyden University had one of the earliest botanic gardens (founded in 1587), and had been responsible for many improvements in the raising of tender plants. George Clifford's famous gardens and private zoo were run by Carl Linnaeus, the great Swedish naturalist. Starting with Clifford's extensive collection of plants, Linnaeus set about the mammoth job of classifying according to strict botanical principles all the plants then known to exist.

Most greenhouses in the eighteenth century were heated with smoke flues embedded in the rear wall (Figure 1.4). The smoke from a fire below the greenhouse was directed through a complicated series of flues so that it lost as much heat as possible to the wall, which in turn gently heated the air inside. Phillip Miller, head of the Chelsea Apothecaries' Garden in the early part of the century, designed a system whereby the flues also ran through the beds so that the soil itself was warmed, just like modern electric soil-heating cables.

Around 1790, the first steam-heated systems were invented. Steam was cleaner, more efficient, easier to direct, and could achieve much higher temperatures than the smoke systems. Also, any leak in the flue was less likely to damage the plants.

The eighteenth century, "the Age of Reason," discovered almost all the principles underlying successful greenhouse gardening. The empirical experience gathered together over two centuries was systematically tested

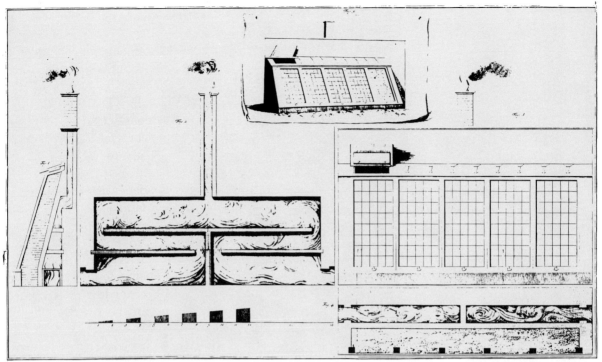

Figure 1.4. Smoke flues built into the rear wall heated most 18th-century green-houses, as this contemporary sketch indicates.

and organized by many men working in different countries. The art of growing plants gradually became a science.

Nineteenth Century

With the dawn of the nineteenth century came many new inventions, improvements in the technology of building and running greenhouses, based on the principles laid down in the previous century. Exotic plants had been grown primarily by scientists for botanical or medical purposes, but in the nineteenth century, greenhouses came to be seen as a source of pleasure and frivolous delight. In Victorian England, a greenhouse, often called a "conservatory" especially when attached to the house, became an essential decorative and recreational addition to the home of every wealthy family. It became a point of honor to have the first strawberry or the first peach of the year. Dinner parties were given in the greenhouse so that each guest could pick his dessert fresh from a nearby fruit tree.

Much experimenting was done to design greenhouses specifically suited to the needs of different plants. Wealthy landowners frequently had a dozen greenhouses, each specially heated, ventilated and lit to produce the ideal environment for growing one particular plant. A melon house, a strawberry house, a peach and apricot house, a pine pit (for pineapples), and a "conservative wall" (a south-facing, glass-covered wall) for grapes and early fruit trees would not be an unusual assortment for a country gentleman's estate.

The seventeenth-century passion for oranges had been supplanted by a passion for pineapples (frequently used as a symbol of luxury on Victorian buildings or decorative motifs) and other exotics which were more finicky and difficult to grow. Perhaps the most spectacular of these exotic plants was the giant Victoria Regia water lily. The first

Figure 1.5. This spectacular Victoria Regia, a giant water lily cultivated indoors, was depicted in this engraving in the Illustrated London News in 1849. It held the weight of Joseph Paxton's daughter.

seeds were brought to Kew Gardens in London in 1846, but the plants did not grow well. Joseph Paxton, chief gardener for the Duke of Devonshire, and already famous for his horticultural skill, built a well-heated pool in a greenhouse at Chatsworth and obtained one small plant from Kew. Within weeks the plant had grown so that the size of the pool had to be doubled. Within three months the lily had bloomed and Paxton presented the first English blossom to Queen Victoria.

Public curiosity about the Victoria Regia lily was intense. A single leaf was so large that a child could easily sit on it without being dumped into the water (Figure 1.5). Each plant produced hundreds of enormous blooms every year, and they continually outgrew the aquatic houses provided for them. The lily's popularity spread rapidly; within a few years every botanic garden in Europe had its own Victoria Regia house.

The desire to grow pineapples, Victoria Regia lilies, and other demanding plants provoked innumerable technical advances in greenhouse design and management. Patents were taken out on dozens of inventions to aid the gardener—some ludicrous, some so ingenious they are still used today. The first automatic thermostat was introduced in 1816; called the "automaton gardener," it opened or shut the ventilators in response to temperatures inside the greenhouse. The discovery that hot water would circulate by natural convection greatly simplified greenhouse heating systems.

One of the most interesting inventions was "ridge and furrow" glazing, developed by J.C. Loudon, a brilliant and inventive horticultural engineer. He capitalized on the eighteenth-century discovery that glass transmits most light when it is perpendicular to the light rays. A south-facing glass wall therefore admits most light at noon and reflects much of the morning and afternoon sunlight.

Reasoning that a more even distribution of light throughout the day would be beneficial to plants, Loudon decided essentially to fold up the glass wall in short sections so half the panes faced the morning sun and half the afternoon sun (Figure 1.6). A certain amount of light was lost at noon when the sun was perpendicular to the "ridge" between the "furrows," but he reasoned that this was probably an advantage because noon is the time when the greenhouse is most likely to overheat in any case. Ridge-and-furrow glazing is no longer considered worth the extra difficulty involved in construction, but it was widely used throughout the nineteenth century.

A great leap forward in English greenhouse technology came when the glass tax was repealed in 1845. For the first time, glass became cheap enough to be a feasible building material both for large-scale projects and for mass-producing small conservatories for the expanding middle classes. With the increased skill of glass-makers and the reduced price of glass, larger panes came into use. Previously, glazing had consisted of thousands of tiny panes of glass, but by mid-century sheets of glass up to four feet long were available.

Traditionally, greenhouses had been made of wood, but Loudon experimented with wrought-iron glazing bars to support the glass and discovered that a much thinner bar could be used, which consequently obstructed light less. Soon large greenhouses were being framed entirely in cast iron. Iron could span much larger areas than wood and was well suited to the large new panes of glass. Loudon suggested that cast iron and glass be used for all sorts of buildings besides greenhouses. In fact, he anticipated Buckminster Fuller's plan for an air-conditioned transparent dome

Figure 1.6. J.C. Loudon's diagrams show the effects of ridge-and-furrow versus flat glazing on incoming solar radiation. He utilized the discovery that glass transmits the most light when it is perpendicular to the sun's rays.

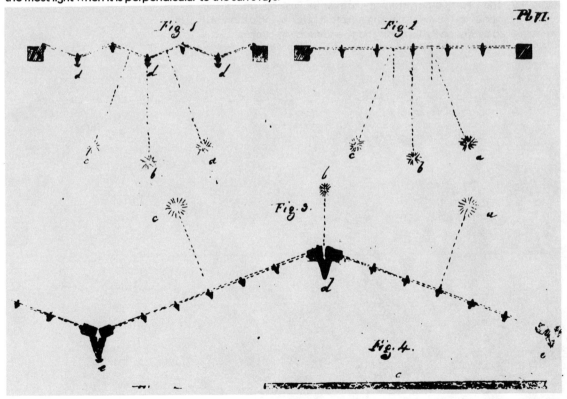

over New York City by more than 100 years when he wrote, "the most economical mode of procuring a proper temperature will be by at once covering whole towns with immense teguments of glass, and heating by steam or otherwise, the enclosed air common to all the inhabitants."

Joseph Paxton came up with the first practical application of Loudon's revolutionary ideas. In 1850 a competition was held for the best design to house the "Great Exhibition of Industry of All Nations" (a sort of early world's fair). It had to be an enormous building, one of the largest yet constructed. It had to be quick to build since there were only twelve months before the intended opening of the exhibition; and it had to be fairly inexpensive. Moreover, it had to be able to be taken down and reused elsewhere when the exhibition was over, since the site was in the middle of a public park.

Hundreds of designs were submitted, and two won special mention but were rejected by the building committee on grounds that they would take too long to build. The committee then commissioned its own architects to design a scheme to its specifications. This, too, proved unsatisfactory, but for lack of anything better was presented as the committee's final design.

Meanwhile, Paxton had begun thinking about the problem. The two special-mention entries had been cast-iron and glass buildings. Paxton had a great deal of experience with cast iron and glass, having designed and built many of the greenhouses at Chatsworth, including the Great Conservatory, then one of the largest greenhouses in the world (Figure 1.7). Though basically a curving wooden structure, the Great Conservatory was covered with Paxton's version of ridge and furrow glazing. Paxton had himself made several improvements in the techniques of greenhouse construction, experimenting with different methods in the many different greenhouses he had built for the

Figure 1.7. The Great Conservatory at Chatsworth, England, one of the world's largest greenhouses. The man standing next to it gives an indication of its size. It was designed by Joseph Paxton, using ridge-and-furrow glazing.

Duke of Devonshire. He had for many years taken an interest in the construction of iron ships, bridges and railways, so he was familiar with all the most modern technical advances in the uses of both cast iron and wood.

After visiting the site for the Great Exhibition in Hyde Park and going to see one of the newest cast-iron bridges in England, Paxton thought he had a solution to the problems of an exhibition building. On the train home, he made some quick blotting-paper sketches of his ideas, which closely resemble the final form the building took (Figure 1.8). Within a month his scheme, soon to be called the "Crystal Palace," had been submitted to the building committee, and two weeks later it was accepted.

The originality and brilliance of his design lay in its use of standard modules, mass-production techniques and prefabrication. These made possible the almost unbelievable speed with which the building was constructed, and also its remarkably low cost. It was entirely covered with glass, and most of the structural elements were cast iron, but Paxton used his own patented wooden sash bars to support

Figure 1.8. Joseph Paxton's first blotting paper sketch of the Crystal Palace was drawn while he was inspired during a train ride.

Crown copyright: Victoria & Albert Museum

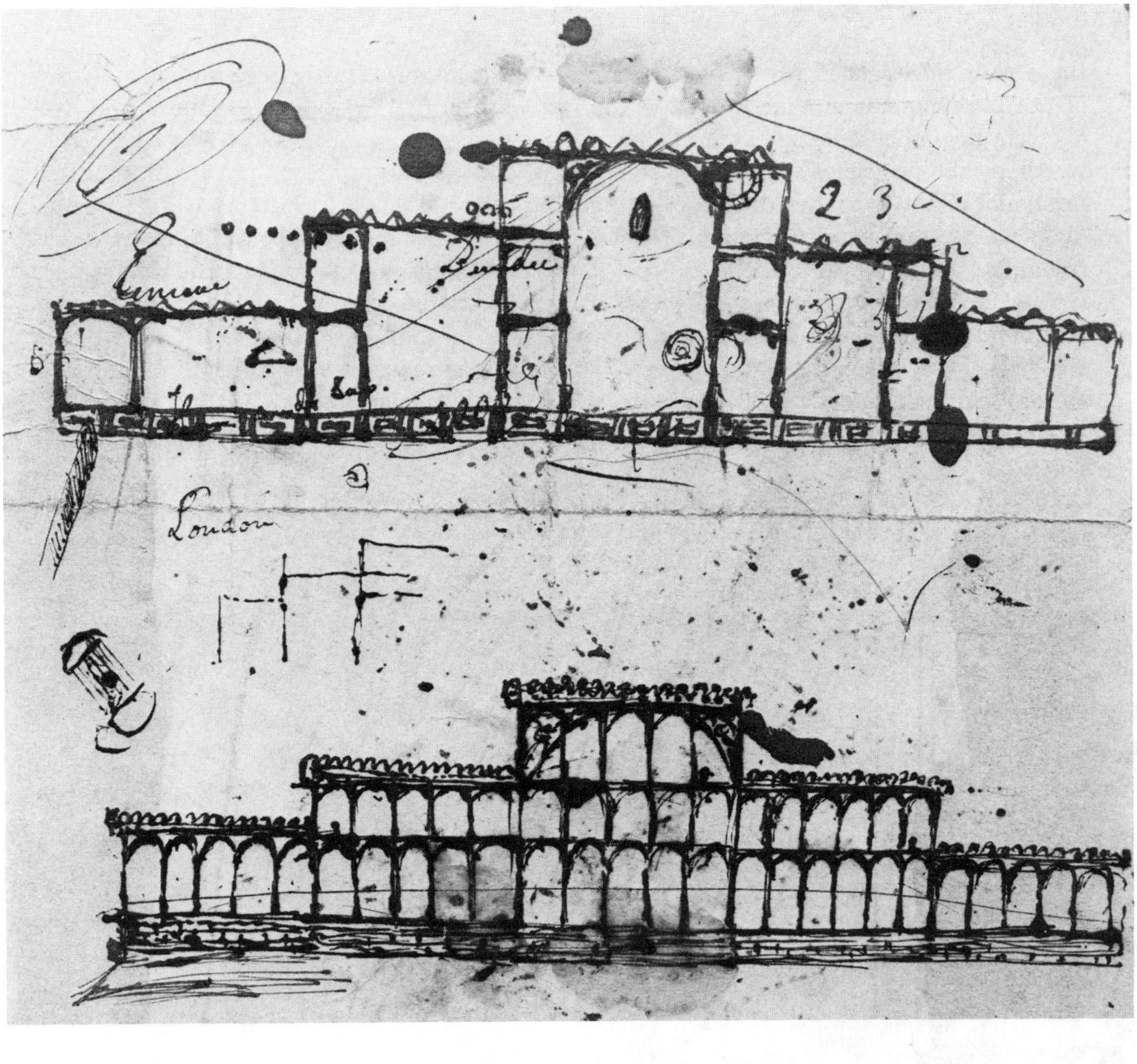

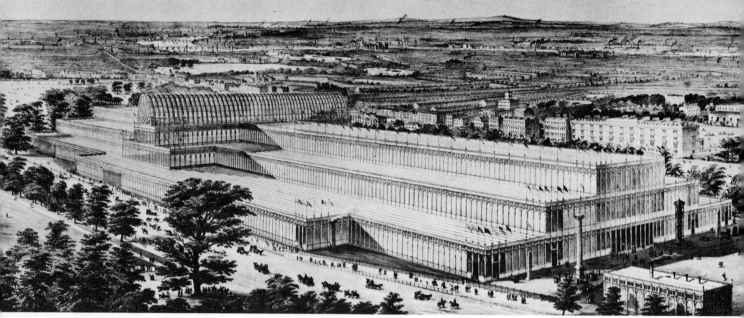

Figure 1.9. A contemporary aerial view of the massive Crystal Palace in Hyde Park, London. It covered eighteen acres and was built in only eight months.

Crown copyright: Victoria & Albert Museum

the glass in ridges and furrows. The structure of the building was similar to that of the Victoria Regia house he had built at Chatsworth, so the principles were all tested beforehand, although to the public everything about the building appeared new and revolutionary.

The Crystal Palace covered eighteen acres of ground plus five acres of balcony area. It was built in eight months and was the wonder of Victorian England in 1851, being itself the most stunning exhibit of the Great Exhibition (Figure 1.9). In 1852 it was dismantled and reconstructed with adaptations at Sydenham, several miles away, where it stood for eighty years despite predictions that the first high wind would knock it down (Figure 1.10).

To save money and building time, the Crystal Palace was built in straight lines on a rectangular plan. The only arched section was in the enormously high central hall, built to shelter the row of elm trees already growing on the site (Figure 1.11). (The sparrows enclosed along with the elm trees

Figure 1.10. The Crystal Palace at Sydenham stood for 80 years, though many predicted a big wind would blow it down. The north transept burned in 1867, so the building was no longer symmetrical.

Fox Photos Ltd.

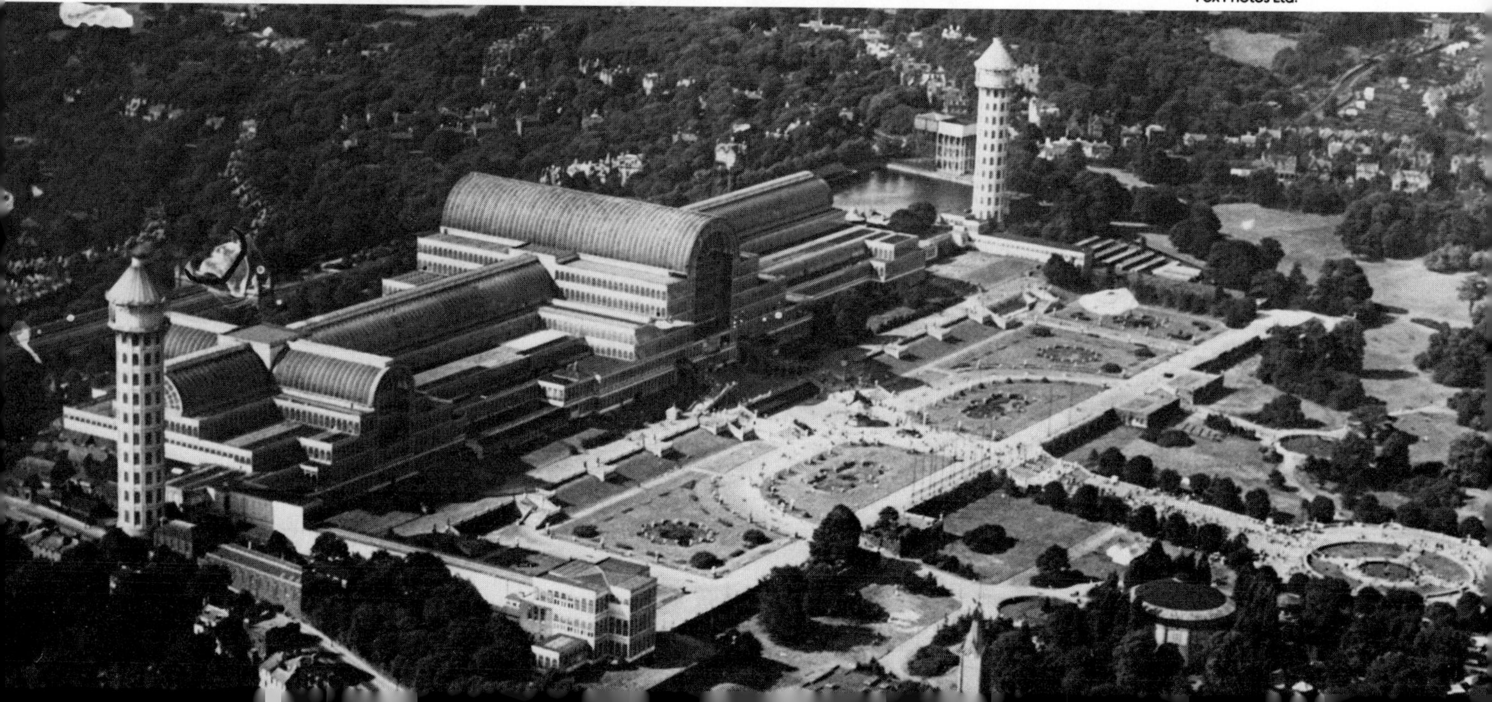

Figure 1.11. An enclosed elm tree, at left, was one of several in the central hall of the Crystal Palace.

proved a terrible nuisance, but since they could not be shot without risk of breaking the glass, they remained until the Duke of Wellington suggested hunting them with sparrow hawks.)

The Victorians loved great arching curves of glass. Most of the mid-Victorian railway stations and greenhouses were built of intersecting arches. The Palm House in Kew Gardens, which predates the Crystal Palace by a few years, is one of the most beautiful examples still standing.

In the United States, there were few greenhouses until the middle of the nineteenth century. Curvilinear greenhouses remained in style here for much longer than they did in England. Merritt's Folly, at Lyndhurst, near Tarrytown, New York, was one of the biggest and most beautiful of them (Figure 1.13). It still stands but has had an ill-fated career. For the third time since it was built in 1870, it is again derelict (though the National Trust for Historic Preservation is planning to restore part of it).

Figure 1.12. Workmen pose for a photograph while reglazing part of the Sydenham Crystal Palace in 1899. The concept of ridge-and-furrow glazing is clearly shown.

Figure 1.13. "Merritt's Folly" at Lyndhurst, near Tarrytown, New York, was one of the first giant greenhouses built in the United States, built in 1870. The National Trust for Historic Preservation hopes to restore it.

Figure 1.14. The conservatory at Enville Hall in England was one of the more elaborate and fashionable. It was torn down early in this century.

The beautiful sweeping lines of these glass buildings were not approved of by most Victorian architects. They satisfied the needs of gardeners who wanted only the maximum amount of light and the minimum amount of upkeep, but "architectural conservatories" like the one at Enville Hall (Figure 1.14) were considered much more fashionable. Later, romantic naturalism came into vogue and the structure of the greenhouse had to be disguised as part of a woodland scene.

Twentieth Century

By the turn of the century, conservatories were going out of fashion altogether. People had less time and money for cultivating exotic plants. Soon greenhouses were relegated to the kitchen garden or the occasional plant enthusiast. Many of the large and elaborate ones (including the Great Conservatory at Chatsworth) were torn down.

As domestic greenhouses have dwindled, so commercial ones have expanded. Covering acres of land, and producing tons of tomatoes or cucumbers or lettuce for the winter market, they have pushed greenhouse technology in new directions. Heating, humidifying, watering, fertilizing are all carried out automatically in many large establishments. Many no longer use soil or traditional growing techniques. The plants' needs are foreseen and accurately supplied with chemical solutions. Diseases are forestalled with chemical sprays. Built in the days of cheap energy, most commercial greenhouses are liberally heated with no provision for insulation or heat retention. They are often covered with oil-based plastic sheeting which must be replaced every few years. Consequently they are becoming increasingly expensive to maintain.

The 1960s and '70s have seen an increased emphasis on home food production as grocery prices have gone up, along with awareness of

Figure 1.15. Spectacular forms and shadow patterns can be created with glass and mullions, as demonstrated by this photo of the interior of Alton Towers, a late nineteenth-century conservatory in Staffordshire, England, which in recent years has been restored, repainted and reglazed.

the value of chemical-free food. Simultaneously, the increasing cost of fuel has encouraged work on less-energy-consuming greenhouses. The history of the greenhouse seems to be coming full circle; most domestic greenhouses today are used much as Tiberius Caesar used his—a fairly small, simple structure designed to capture the sun's warmth so that tender fruits, vegetables and flowers can be grown out of season.

Bibliography

Encyclopedia of Gardening by J.C. Loudon. London. 1822, 1835. Dated but charming compilation of gardening miscellany and Victorian taste.

The Glass House by John Hix. Phaidon Press. London 1974. $7.25. The most complete history of "the artificial climates" people have devised to protect their plants, from the Greeks, through the Victorians to present-day agri-businesses and even science-fiction visions of the future. Well written and beautifully illustrated.

The Greenhouse at Lyndhurst Prepared by Billie Sherrill Britz. The Preservation Press. National Trust for Historic Preservation in the United States, 740-748 Jackson Place N.W., Washington D.C. 1977. Paperback $5. An interesting piece of careful historical research into the building of Jay Gould's greenhouse in 1881, includes much of the original correspondence and several nineteenth-century photographs of the greenhouse in use.

Mr. Loudon's England by J. Gloag. London. 1970. A good biography of one of England's great inventor-entrepreneurs.

The Works of Sir Joseph Paxton by G.F. Chadwick. London. 1961. A fascinating biography of the architect of the Crystal Palace who began life as a gardener and went on to wealth and fame through sheer force of ingenuity.

2

Planning a Greenhouse

Choosing the location and the type of building are the two major decisions to be made in planning a greenhouse. The choice of location will be affected by the orientation, shading, wind shelter, the need for drainage or levelling, and the accessibility of various sites. The choice of type will be affected by what you can afford, whether you intend to buy a prefabricated model or build one yourself, and of course the requirements of the plants you intend to grow (see Chapters 3 and 8). Whether to build the greenhouse as a separate building, a fixed, or mobile shelter, or as a lean-to addition to your house should be given careful consideration.

Orientation

The main aim in siting a greenhouse for general use is to maximize the light, particularly in winter. This can best be achieved by a fully exposed, free-standing, glass-to-ground structure. But in most climates such a greenhouse would overheat in summer and use vast amounts of energy in winter to maintain a reasonable temperature. The building must be able to temper the extremes of climate and maintain suitable conditions for plants without relying on too much artificial energy. It must be able to make the best possible use of the sun's energy.

There has been a good deal of disagreement

about which orientation is most suitable for freestanding greenhouses. Traditionally, commercial greenhouses have tended to favor a north-south orientation to achieve even exposure throughout the greenhouse. Recent research has shown, however, that particularly in more northern latitudes (above 40°N) the overall illumination and temperature levels are higher in an east-west oriented greenhouse. As one moves south, the orientation becomes less significant from the point of view of achieving high levels of illumination, though if one of the primary aims is to maximize solar heat gain, then the east-west orientation still remains preferable. It is then possible to have a solid north wall which reduces heat loss considerably while reducing illumination levels only slightly. With a

Figure 2.1. Large, private greenhouses in the 19th century were often south-facing lean-tos, like this one from a catalog of Messenger & Co., a London distributor. They incorporated many features being revived nowadays. The rear wall was of solid and thick masonry, either part of the house or part of the garden wall. Many of these greenhouses, now more than a century old, still exist. They were designed before the age of cheap energy which existed until a few years ago. They were designed for minimum heat loss: Thick, heat-retaining masonry walls were used wherever glass was not essential; finely adjustable ventilating equipment avoided unnecessary heat loss while maintaining good ventilation for plants; blinds were lowered to insulate all glass areas on cold nights. This one was called a "forcing house" and was about 12 feet wide.

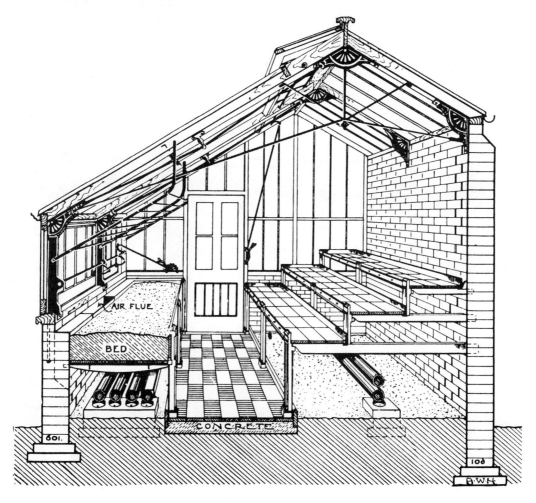

bright white-painted wall, or a reflective foil surface, the actual illumination on sunny days would be increased.

Lean-to greenhouses automatically have a solid rear wall and should be attached to a south-facing wall of the house. South or southeast exposures are ideal; southwest exposures can create problems of overheating.

A southwest-facing greenhouse receives a maximum exposure to direct sunshine at the time of day when the outside air temperature is also hottest (mid-afternoon). At that time the sun is low enough to penetrate the vertical wall and sloping glass roof with maximum intensity. A southeast exposure, on the other hand, is more beneficial because the plants get a boost of welcome sunlight and warmth early in the day when the air temperature is not so high.

Shelter

Most greenhouses overheat in summer unless they are partially shaded. Shelter from trees can be used to advantage to provide shade during summer. This is particularly true of deciduous trees which conveniently lose their leaves in winter when their shade is no longer wanted. But be sure that there are no evergreen trees or buildings south of the greenhouse to provide unwanted shade in winter when the sun is low.

Trees can also provide useful windbreaks which reduce the heat loss from the greenhouse in winter and therefore cut energy consumption. The average heat loss through a glass wall increases by as much as 50 percent when the wind blows across it. This is because a major factor in the rate of heat loss (U value) is the speed of the air moving across the glass. Thus it is worth choosing a site for a greenhouse that, though exposed to sunlight, is sheltered from winds. Trees and hedges form the best kind of windbreak since they absorb the force of the wind in their branches. Walls and impenetrable foliage tend merely

to deflect the wind, causing it to gust and actually increase its force. If you want to construct artificial windbreaks, use slat-type wooden fences, or snow fences, which do not form an impenetrable barrier. A good windbreak will provide shelter over a distance of about ten times its height, before the wind picks up its previous speed again. Lean-tos will not necessarily be protected since the turbulence and suction in the wake of the house is often just as strong as the wind force on the side facing the wind.

Site Drainage and Levelling

A sloping site for a greenhouse will provide you with more construction problems than a flat one, but it can also provide some advantages. On one hand, sinking half the greenhouse into the hillside reduces heat loss since the exposed area of the greenhouse is reduced, and the earth itself is a fairly good insulator. On the other hand, a lot more excavation is required, together with careful construction of retaining walls (of compacted earth or concrete) and attention to drainage on the uphill side of the site. To minimize excavation, work on the cut-and-fill principle, using any excavated earth to build up part of the foundation platform (Figure 2.2). It is important to insure that the built-up part of the platform is well compacted, not likely to erode and cause subsidence.

Drainage is a particular problem on the uphill side of the greenhouse. Both surface and subsurface water must be intercepted and prevented from flooding the greenhouse. Subsurface drainage can be provided by using four-inch perforated plastic piping. Groundwater will seep into this and can then be directed into a storm sewer or a drywell or at least diverted to where it will not harm the greenhouse.

Surface water (mostly rain) can be collected in a drainage gutter at the bottom of

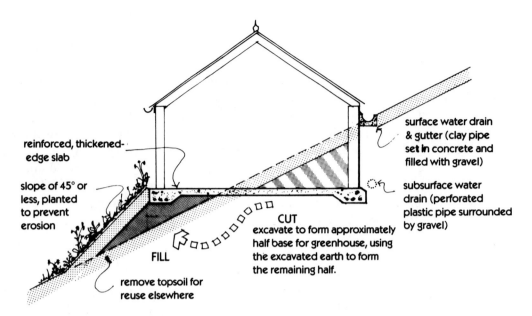

reinforced, thickened-edge slab

slope of 45° or less, planted to prevent erosion

FILL

remove topsoil for reuse elsewhere

CUT
excavate to form approximately half base for greenhouse, using the excavated earth to form the remaining half.

surface water drain & gutter (clay pipe set in concrete and filled with gravel)

subsurface water drain (perforated plastic pipe surrounded by gravel)

Figure 2.2. The cut-and-fill principle was employed in this design, which utilizes a bank of earth to reduce heat loss from the wind, and to provide natural insulation. It requires a gutter for drainage.

the uphill side of the building. This should consist of a concrete trench, or else half-round pipes set in concrete, laid to slope around each end of the building. It should be filled with gravel to allow the water to seep through and prevent the gutter from clogging up with eroded earth.

Rainwater from the roof must be disposed of with any greenhouse. There are two alternatives: either a gutter at eaves level or a drain at ground level.

If you use a gutter, you can collect the water in a rainbarrel (an old oil drum will do) for use inside the greenhouse. This is the most ecologically sound idea since the rain is that which would have watered the plants now growing there. And rainwater is generally better for plants than the chlorinated supply from a central system (which is lethal for some ferns and sensitive plants) and it is supplied free of charge. If you cover the barrel with a lid to prevent evaporation, your plants could probably survive most of the year on collected rainwater with help from a hose occasionally. A rainbarrel avoids the trouble of installing a central supply of water, which

can be costly. If you don't want to use a rainbarrel, you will have to direct the water into a storm sewer or drywell.

Without a gutter, you must provide adequate drainage around the greenhouse to protect the earth on each side of the building from erosion. For a small greenhouse, drainage is not absolutely essential, but a larger building collects a lot of water, and it is necessary to protect the earth around the foundations. A muddy area around the greenhouse is useless and unsightly, and it can damage the foundations. The simplest solution is to dig a trench about six inches deep and eight inches wide and fill it with gravel, which absorbs the impact of the water and then allows it to drain away or evaporate. Water dripping from the eaves onto clean gravel will not cause mud splashing or erosion. With large buildings it is worth constructing a proper channel from half-round earthenware pipes set in concrete and leading to a storm sewer or drywell. With small buildings, if you do not provide any drainage, remember that the soil next to the greenhouse may be subject to torrents of rain, so plant accordingly.

Benches and Staging

If you intend to use the greenhouse primarily for plants, and the space you can afford to build is limited, planning the greenhouse should be given careful consideration.

A lot of space can be taken up by pathways. Staging or benches can also be disruptive since they limit one's reach, whereas with ground beds, providing you are reasonably careful about where you put your feet, you can tend larger beds from the same path. In greenhouses which are primarily used for rearing seeds for transplanting outdoors, it is useful but not essential to be able to get a garden cart inside. This requires at least one main path the width of your cart (probably at least two feet). Subsidiary paths can be much narrower (down to one foot). Remember that many plants suffer from being continually brushed against.

Lean-to greenhouses afford space for pot plants and seedflats along shelves at the back, and lower and larger ground beds at the

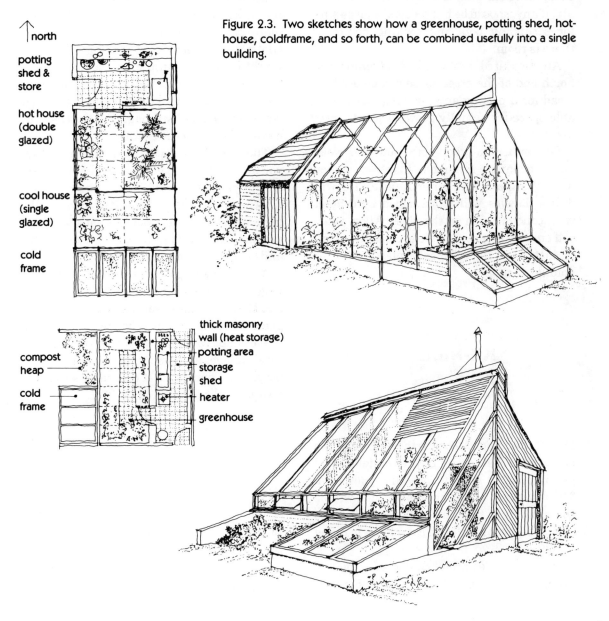

Figure 2.3. Two sketches show how a greenhouse, potting shed, hothouse, coldframe, and so forth, can be combined usefully into a single building.

north

potting shed & store

hot house (double glazed)

cool house (single glazed)

cold frame

compost heap

cold frame

thick masonry wall (heat storage)
potting area
storage shed
heater
greenhouse

front. If you do use staging, make sure you also make use of the area underneath it, for shade-loving plants, storage of pots and tools, or even growing mushrooms.

Hanging baskets can provide additional growing space for many flowers and vegetables. Suspended in full sunlight, fruiting vegetables such as tomatoes will grow well. Remember, though, that all hanging baskets tend to dry out more easily.

Part of the greenhouse should be reserved as a workbench for potting plants or transplanting seedlings. This area requires careful planning, with space for tools, pots, seed flats, and soil. This is where the water supply, if any, should be located, and a large sink for scrubbing pots and soaking plants, if there is room.

An insulated timber shed adjoining the north end of the greenhouse can be used instead for a potting area, leaving more valuable space for actually growing plants (Figure 2.3).

Remember to give both you and your plants adequate headroom. Plants grown too near the glass will suffer from cold downdrafts. Leaves will be damaged by contact with condensation on the glass. Allow yourself enough room to be able to clean the glass, or install an inner layer of plastic film for double glazing.

Kit-Built or Individually Designed?

One of the major decisions to be made at the outset is whether to buy a prefabricated greenhouse or design and build your own. The major influences on this decision will be the amount of time and money you have to spend, and your skill and confidence in doing it yourself.

Many so-called prefabricated greenhouses are in fact "pre-cut." All frame members are cut to size and you have to fabricate the structure yourself and then glaze it. The process can take a lot longer than the few hours some manufacturers claim, particularly when you run into hard-to-follow instructions, or find you have a crucial part missing and have to write back to the manufacturer. There are also normally delays associated with foundations. Any greenhouse sturdy enough to warrant a decent foundation is going to cost you extra time and money preparing the site before you actually start to erect the greenhouse. You should budget for this in making out your costs.

Be sure of what you are getting when you buy a kit. Some manufacturers sell a complete package including heating and ventilating equipment, and staging which you might be able to build more easily yourself. Others advertise at deceptively low prices and you will find yourself paying double what you originally thought by the time you have added in all the extras.

The other problem with kit building is that you are unlikely to get exactly what you want at the price you want it; a custom design, whether you build it yourself or hire a builder, is more likely to produce a satisfying end product, though it may cost you more time and perhaps more money.

A lot of savings can be made using salvaged materials and second-hand timber, and there are many sources of do-it-yourself plans which if not entirely suitable, you can often adapt to your own situation. Agricultural colleges are a good place to start looking for plans. There is a list of further sources at the end of the chapter.

Lean-to or Detached?

It is worth spending some time considering the advantages of having a greenhouse attached to your house. Lean-tos are easier and cheaper to build because one wall already

No. 509.—Winter Garden erected for the Rt. Hon. Sir Edward Clarke, P.C., K.C., Thorncote, Staines.

Architect: J. H. Eastwood, Esq., Cheniston Gardens, Kensington, W.

No. 510.—Interior of the above Winter Garden.

14

Figure 2.4. A page from the nineteenth-century catalog of Messenger & Co. Ltd. shows the elegant interior and exterior of a wealthy man's "conservatory" or "winter garden."

exists. They are easier to heat because one wall is warmed by the heat of the house. Indeed, in many areas a well-designed solar greenhouse can contribute to the heating of your house through the winter. They are easier to service because water and electricity are available from the existing supplies in the house. Some people will prefer to have their flowers, herbs and vegetables within easy reach of the house; some will prefer the greenhouse to be more a part of the garden.

If you have an appropriate situation for a lean-to, a wall with a south or southeast exposure, consider the many advantages. A lean-to greenhouse need not be merely a tacky little box which you buy prefabricated and stick on the outside of your house to provide shelter for pot plants. If it is carefully designed it can enhance both the beauty and the usefulness of your home.

Glass doors between the greenhouse and your living room will provide a permanent way of displaying your plants and make your living room appear much larger, while preserving a separate environment for the plants. Alternatively, the greenhouse itself could be treated as a separate room, not only for plants but for people. It could be a sun room for spring and fall, those times when, in temperate climates at least, the sun is most desirable. In England during the nineteenth century, the lean-to greenhouse or "conservatory" became a vital necessity for every wealthy home. It was a place for breakfast in the morning sun, or soirees with candlelight flickering over the plants (Figure 2.4).

A glass house is still a cheap way of providing a sheltered living space, or play space for children, even though it may only be usable at certain times of the year. Now that energy is becoming more expensive and fossil fuels less abundant, we should be thinking in terms of using some areas only at certain times of the day or year. It makes sense to heat only the parts of the house that are in use, and to respond to climatic changes by living outside in summer and retreating into snug, easily heated and therefore small rooms in winter. The intermediate seasons,

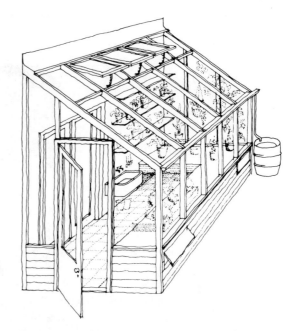

Figure 2.5. A typical lean-to greenhouse, attached to a house. While not "solar" in nature, it saves heat by acting as a buffer between indoors and outdoors in winter.

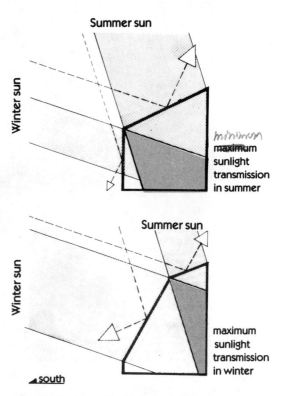

Figure 2.6. The effect of different inclinations of glazed walls and roofs on the transmission of sunlight at different times of the year. Light striking glass at an acute angle is reflected; the more acute the angle, the greater the percentage of light reflected.

spring and fall, are often the times when the intermediate environment of the unheated glass house comes into its own.

Building a lean-to greenhouse will decrease the winter heat loss from your house. The intermediate enclosure, even if it is unheated, reduces the rate of heat loss by providing a kind of buffer zone. The temperature in the "conservatory" will float somewhere between the inside room temperature and the outside air temperature. For instance, on a cold winter's night, if the temperature inside the house is 68°F and the outside temperature is 32°F, the temperature in the lean-to might average around 40°F. Since the rate of heat loss from the house is directly proportional to the temperature difference from one side of the wall to the other, this amounts to a reduction in heat loss (and therefore in energy consumption) of about one-third.

Besides reducing direct heat loss through the walls, a conservatory can also collect and store heat during the day to provide a supply of heat which can be used to warm the house, or to maintain a reasonable temperature in the greenhouse overnight, thus reducing dependence on conventional heating sys-

tems. To operate efficiently as a solar collector, the conservatory must have some kind of heat storage (which could be as simple as a thick masonry wall) and insulating shutters or curtains to insure that the stored heat is not wasted at night. Insulation and storage systems will be dealt with more extensively in Section IV.

The standard prefabricated lean-to consists simply of a glass wall and a sloping glass roof (Figure 2.5). The pitch of the roof is normally determined by headroom requirements inside, and by the most convenient height for attaching the ridge of the roof to the house. Upstairs windows can present a problem in this respect. It is often the case that a lean-to will admit more sun than you require in summer, and in winter the roof will reflect a lot of the incoming radiation (Figure 2.6). Lean-to solar greenhouses are designed to maximize heat gain in winter and minimize overheating in summer.

If you are interested in using the greenhouse as part of your living area it is worth considering a more permanent and integral home extension. This could be a sunroom, or even an enclosed porch, which provides you

Figure 2.7. A combination sunroom and trellised patio gets maximum sun in winter, yet can be shaded with foliage in summer.

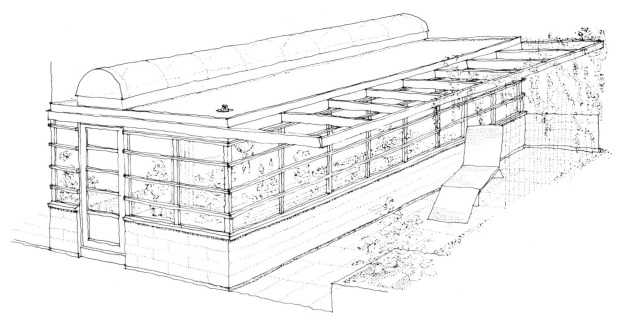

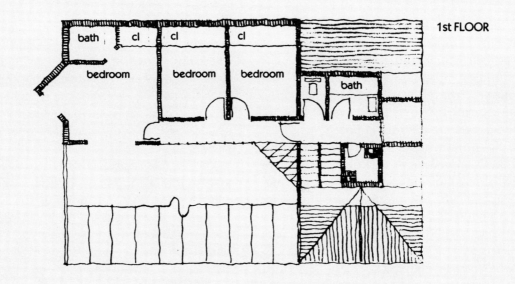

1st FLOOR

bath | cl | cl | cl

bedroom | bedroom | bedroom

bath

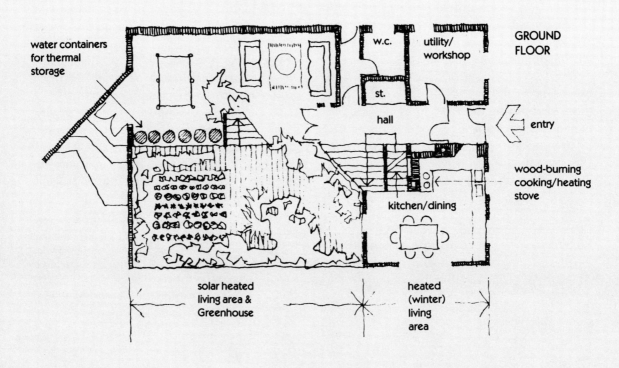

water containers for thermal storage

GROUND FLOOR

w.c. | utility/ workshop

st.

hall

entry

wood-burning cooking/heating stove

kitchen/dining

solar heated living area & Greenhouse

heated (winter) living area

HALF BASEMENT

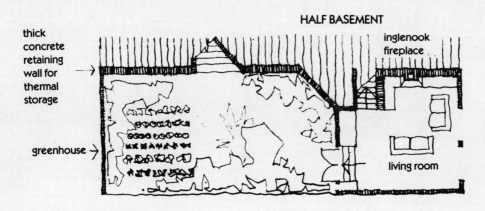

thick concrete retaining wall for thermal storage

inglenook fireplace

greenhouse

living room

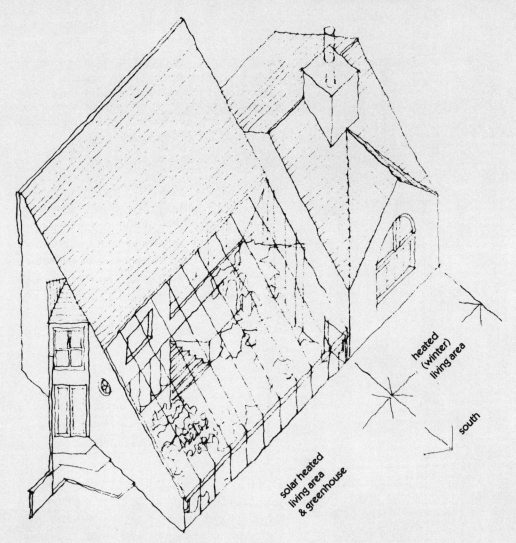

heated
(winter)
living area

south

solar heated
living area
& greenhouse

Figure 2.9. How a large greenhouse area could be integrated into the design of a simple home in a temperate or cool climate. Each room relates to the conservatory in one way or another. The conservatory is a large unheated space that unites all other rooms, which are smaller heated areas. It has sliding shutters that are hauled up into the roof space when not needed. On hot summer days or sunless winter days, the shutters might be partly closed. Thermal storage is provided in concrete floors (paved with bricks or quarry tiles) and in additional water containers at the rear of the greenhouse portion. Further examples of "sunspace" architecture are discussed in Chapter 15.

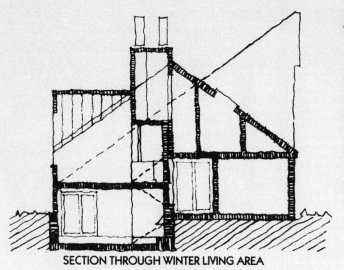

SECTION THROUGH WINTER LIVING AREA

insulating shutters counterweighted in attic slide between glazing bars to provide shade in summer & insulation in winter

bedroom

SECTION THROUGH SOLAR HEATED LIVING AREA

Arkitektur Magazine

Figure 2.8. A luxurious interior environment can be created under the glazing of a greenhouse. This is a sunroom and swimming pool in a solar-heated house in Kokkedal, Denmark, in which the pool's water acts as a heat accumulator. A heat pump retrieves the heat for distribution inside the house.

living space on more than one level. An enclosure such as this provides space for a winter vegetable garden or swimming pool (Figure 2.8) as well as a focus for other rooms in the house. In colder regions, a conservatory makes an ideal extra living space which need not be heated other than by the sun, and provides a kind of intermediate environment which you use as and when the weather permits.

Free-standing Greenhouses

If you are intending to build a free-standing greenhouse, an initial question to consider is whether you need a permanent structure, complete with staging, and heating and ventilating equipment, or whether a simpler structure more like a large coldframe for your vegetables would be more appropriate.

The former normally requires more investment, but you end up with a building that will last for many years in which you ought to be able to grow vegetables and exotic flowers all year round. The latter is cheaper to build, can be lightweight and is useful for extending the growing season in your vegetable garden, starting off plants earlier in spring and extending the summer for fruiting vegetables into the fall.

An even-span free-standing greenhouse (Figure 2.10) is what most people think of when the word "greenhouse" is mentioned. It is a simple glass shed, rectangular in plan, designed primarily for growing pot plants and seedlings on "staging" (benches and shelves set at convenient working height) exposed to light from all directions. It fits

with extra living space as well as a plant room. It could be designed and built to fit in sympathetically with your house and need not look like an attached greenhouse at all. By using a combination of vertical glazing and skylights, a sunspace can create a suitable area for houseplants and vegetables, which, though admitting less light than a standard lean-to greenhouse, is easier to insulate and heat. The combination of a sunroom and a trellised patio (Figure 2.7) provides you with a space that is likely to receive maximum direct sunlight in winter, and yet can be shaded with overhanging foliage (such as wisteria, passion flower vines and honeysuckle) in summer.

More ambitious sunspaces can take in the whole south side of a house and produce extra

conveniently into tight sites (units are available as small as six feet by four feet) and, if built on solid base walls, it wastes little space around it, since plants can be grown directly up against the exterior of the walls.

A "dutch" greenhouse (like an even-span greenhouse with sloping glass walls, see Figure 2.11) is not very suitable for use with staging since the walls are slanted. It is better suited to growing crops directly in the ground because it covers a greater area at ground level. Dutch greenhouses were developed with a view to covering the greatest ground area with the lightest, strongest kind of frame while allowing adequate headroom for tending the plants. The splay sides add considerably to the structural rigidity of an even-span greenhouse. It is for this reason that many prefabricated greenhouses have slightly splay sides.

The original dutch greenhouses had removable side sashes which could either be opened for ventilation or removed entirely during hot weather. These movable windows are known as "dutch lights."

Both the standard even-span model and dutch-light version are designed primarily to maximize illumination on the plants. The recent concern for energy conservation has led

Figure 2.10. A free-standing unit, what most people tend to think of when the word "greenhouse" is mentioned.

to the development of "solar" greenhouses which are concerned with collecting and storing solar heat, while maintaining adequate levels of illumination throughout the heating season. Ironically, these new developments have produced greenhouses which closely resemble the old "three-quarter span" lean-tos that were common in England and America in the last century. The three-quarter span provided the good ridge ventila-

Figure 2.11. A "dutch" greenhouse has splayed sides—good for structural rigidity and providing increased ground planting area.

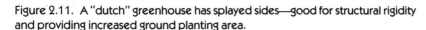

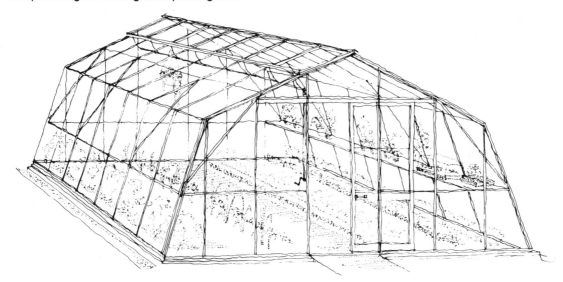

tion possible with an even-span model, as well as the solid insulated north wall which cut down very little on light and provided a masonry heat "sink" for storing solar energy. If the north-facing roof and the rear portion of the sidewalls were also insulated, the three-quarter span lean-to would provide an efficient shape for a solar heat trap (Figure 2.12).

A good solar greenhouse requires a considerable amount of thought in the design and construction. The building must be well insulated and tightly built. It will have to be custom-designed to fit a given location, and though the effort involved may be considerable, the result is likely to be an efficient greenhouse which uses little or no auxiliary energy and yet provides suitable growing conditions for most of the winter months.

The development of plastic films as greenhouse coverings has led to the design of much cheaper and simpler greenhouse structures where the aim is to provide a transparent shelter for plants grown directly in the ground. Simple rigid frameworks to support plastic film can be made from timber vaults, steel or aluminum ribs or even semi-rigid polyethylene tube or metal conduit. These are lightweight, cheap and easy both to con-

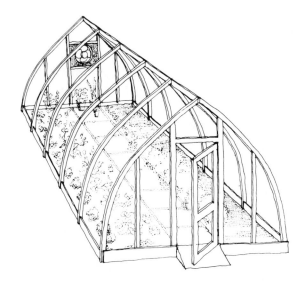

Figure 2.13. A "Gothic arch" design, suitable for do-it-yourself fabrication, was developed at Virginia Polytechnic Institute.

struct and dismantle. The "gothic arch" design, developed at Virginia Polytechnic Institute, is one of the designs more suitable to do-it-yourself fabrication (Figure 2.13).

The stability of the shape combined with the lightness of the plastic covering make arched greenhouses relatively mobile. A small quonset model (Figure 2.14) could easily be moved from crop to crop in a winter vegetable garden by two or three people. A lightweight structure such as this might require a few bricks to rest on, but no elaborate foundations. It would, however, need to be tied down to stakes driven into the ground to prevent it from blowing over in high winds.

The main difficulty with plastic film greenhouses (apart from the deterioration of the material itself) is the provision of adequate ventilation, particularly in summer. The standard solution is to install a fan at one end to suck the air out from the ridge of the building, but this entails some extra expense, both in capital and in running costs.

A simple plastic-covered structure used as a cold frame for hardening off transplants, or for speeding up germination of seeds planted outside can be a useful addition to a garden. Being a simple structure to build, it would be

Figure 2.12. A three-quarter lean-to model, an efficient shape for a solar heat trap—if the north side of it is insulated.

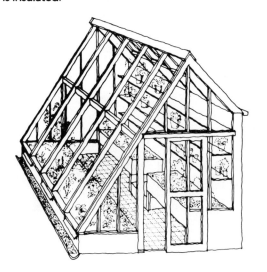

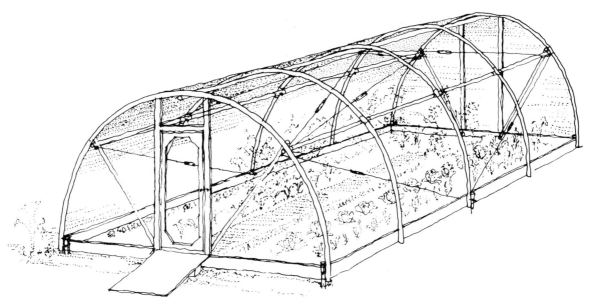

Figure 2.14. A small quonset model can be moved easily, requires no elaborate foundation—just enough stability so it won't be blown away.

Figure 2.15. The first prefabricated, mass-produced mobile greenhouse in England was this simple A-frame design. It was developed in 1860 by Sir Joseph Paxton, who was better known for his larger glass buildings, including the 1851 Crystal Palace in London, described in Chapter 1. Paxton's A-frame design was portable and could easily be dismantled for transportation. It consisted simply of a kit of panels which leaned against each other at angles of 30, 45 or 60 degrees. An ingenious system of hardware attached the ridges, and between each panel ran a full-height ventilator which served to link the panels together. The ends also came in prefabricated sections which were interchangeable for the 30- and 60-degree models. The inherent flexibility and mobility of the system made it popular with the new suburban middle class in Victorian England. Greenhouse horticulture had previously been limited to the rich who could afford custom-made designs.

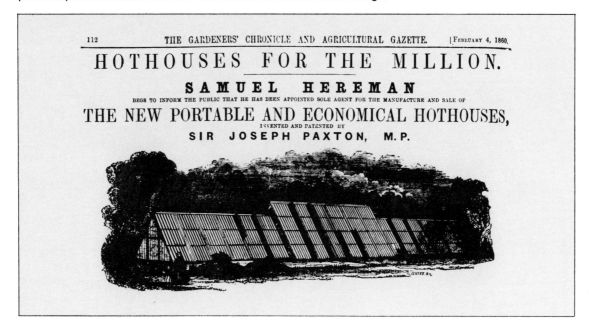

an ideal stepping stone toward the construction of a more permanent solar greenhouse, and could introduce you, not only to the skills of building, but also to the benefits of growing plants in greenhouses.

Sources

The Cooperative Extension Service at your state university usually has plans of greenhouses which can be built cheaply and easily. Some of the better do-it-yourself plans are listed below:

"A Gothic Greenhouse for Town and Country Houses," Publication 487, from the extension Division, Virginia Polytechnic Institute and State University, Blacksburg, Virginia 24061.

"The Cornell 'Twenty-one' Plastic Greenhouse," $2 from the Department of Vegetable Crops, Cornell University, Ithaca, New York 14850

"Build a Greenhouse this Weekend," using a timber frame and Filon fiberglass panels. Free from Filon Corp., 12333 South Van Ness Avenue, Hawthorne, California 90250.

"A Portable Plastic Greenhouse" and an "A" frame greenhouse are two of many blueprints available from the Agricultural Engineering Department, University of Connecticut, Storrs, Connecticut.

PREFABRICATED GREENHOUSE
MANUFACTURERS AND SUPPLIES:

Aluminum Greenhouses Inc., 14615 Lorain Avenue, Cleveland, Ohio 44111

E.C. Geiger, Box 285, Harleysville, Pennsylvania 19438

Lord & Burnham, Irvington, New York 10533

Maco Products, Box 3312, Salem, Oregon 97302

National Greenhouse Company, Box 100, Pana, Illinois 62557

J.A. Nearing Company, 10788 Tucker Street, Beltsville, Maryland 20705

Redfern Greenhouses, Mt. Hermon Road, Scotts Valley, California 95060

Peter Reimuller, Greenhouseman, Box 2666, Santa Cruz, California 95060

Sturdi-Built Manufacturing Company, 11304 S.W. Boones Ferry Road, Portland, Oregon 97219

Texas Greenhouse Company, 2717 St. Louis Avenue, Fort Worth, Texas 76110

Turner Greenhouses, Box 1620, Goldsboro, North Carolina 27530

3

The Greenhouse Environment

The essential elements of a successful greenhouse environment (in fact, of any successful gardening, but they are easier to control in a greenhouse) are heat, humidity, ventilation, and light.

Different plants need different environments. Some like it hot, damp and shady, others cool, dry and sunny. You will be restricted mostly to plants that like the same sort of environment, though a single greenhouse can provide quite a wide range of conditions if well arranged. Careful consideration of each plant's requirements should be given before deciding where to put it. The hottest, driest spots will be near the roof (or heater), and the coolest, dampest places under the benches along the north wall.

With judicious misting, ventilating, heating, shading, or extra lighting, a few plants not well suited to the general environment of your greenhouse can be kept healthy, but they will require extra work and should be limited in number.

A plant's needs for heat, humidity, light and ventilation are all closely interrelated. Generally, the hotter a greenhouse is kept, the more humidity and light it will require. Ventilation helps to regulate heat and humidity and supplies fresh air the plants need.

Heat

Plants have definite temperature requirements; temperatures beyond their limits generally cause serious growth or disease problems. The night temperature of a greenhouse dictates what plants can be grown in it. Thus greenhouses generally are classified according to their minimum nighttime temperature.

In this discussion we will distinguish among "hot," "warm," "cool," and "cold" greenhouses, though as a practical matter it will become clear that the choice for most amateur gardeners is between "warm" and "cool," depending on what you want to use it for.

A "hothouse" is kept at a minimum temperature of 60°F. or more. A "warm" greenhouse must be kept at 50°, which means heating at night and during cloudy or very cold days in winter. A "cool" greenhouse is heated only when there would otherwise be danger of frost inside; it aims at a minimum temperature of 40°. A "cold" greenhouse (this includes coldframes and portable cloches) is not heated at all; it relies only on heat received from the sun during the day and drops below freezing at night.

Hothouses are expensive to run because large amounts of fuel are required to maintain such high temperatures. They are really only useful for tropical plants and for propagating on a large scale. Most seeds and cuttings require a significantly higher temperature (usually about 70°F.) to do well than do mature plants of the same species. A small propagating case—a sort of mini-greenhouse with an additional source of heat, to be described later in the chapter—is a satisfactory substitute for a hothouse if you have only a few plants that require a great deal of heat (see Figures 3.1 and 3.2). Because hothouses are an expensive and specialized hobby, we will deal with them only briefly here. Good

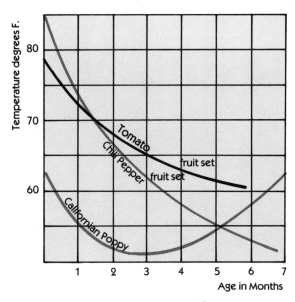

Figure 3.1. Significantly higher temperatures are required for most seeds and cuttings than for mature plants of the same species.

insulation, carefully sealed joints and heat-conserving designs must be incorporated in a hothouse, given the present cost of heating fuels. It may be worth sacrificing a certain amount of sunlight and installing artificial illumination to supplement the natural light if this will keep the heating costs down. Insuring adequate ventilation and maintaining correct humidity is more crucial in a hothouse, and automatic sensoring equipment is generally necessary.

Warm greenhouses are the kind most people imagine when they hear the term greenhouse. They have the characteristic warm, moist feeling, full of the rich scent of flowers and bare earth. Almost all plants—except for the extremes of tropical and alpine plants—will grow well in a warm greenhouse. Many would also grow satisfactorily (though a bit more slowly) in a cool greenhouse. African violets, gardenias, most orchids, tomatoes and melons in winter, and many other plants require the extra heat of a warmhouse. A warm greenhouse can be fairly expensive to operate, but a wide range of plants can be grown, and many propagated at night temperatures of 50° to 60°F.

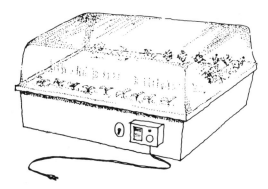

Figure 3.2. A commercial propagating case, of a type that can be purchased. It has an off-on switch and a heat control.

Actually, the distinction between "hot" and "warm" fades in practice when you operate the greenhouse different ways for different seasons. In early spring and summer, when starting flower and vegetable plants, you would probably want to keep a minimum nighttime temperature of 60°F. But in midwinter, when you are just holding plants over to spring, the temperature might be allowed to drop to 45°.

A cool greenhouse is in many ways the ideal choice for the amateur, especially if it is equipped with a propagating case in which

---

WHEN IT'S TOO HOT

If your greenhouse gets too hot to grow anything in during summer, it can be used for drying fruits and vegetables harvested out of doors. Simply clean the food, cut it into small pieces, blanch it for three or four minutes, place it on trays (best made of plastic screening or cheesecloth) and leave it in your hot greenhouse.

One or two vents should be left open for some air circulation. If you want to go into food drying in a big way, partition off the south side of the greenhouse (because a smaller space will heat up faster) and screen the vents to keep out bees and flies.

---

extra heat and humidity can be given to seeds and cuttings. Most plants with which the amateur is familiar can be grown in a cool greenhouse, which can be operated at much lower cost than a warmhouse. Early evening is usually the best time to supply the extra heat needed to keep the temperature above freezing.

Most houseplants and vegetables will grow well in a cool greenhouse, though they may not flower or fruit without extra heat. Bonzais, cacti and many plants that need a cold but frost-free, semidormant period to flower the following year will winter over well in a cool environment. These are also the ideal conditions for forcing spring bulbs like narcissus and crocus to bloom during the long, dreary winter months.

A cold greenhouse—that is, unheated—is one in which only hardy plants will survive the winter. Alpine plants like saxifrages, dwarf conifers, hardy bulbs and shrubs, are best suited to this kind of greenhouse because, while they can withstand freezing, they need protection from wind and extremes of temperature. Good ventilation is needed during the day, and shade in summer, because alpine plants cannot take high temperatures or stale air.

In cold climates, an unheated greenhouse cannot be used for nonhardy plants until spring has arrived. Then, with the stored warmth of the sun it becomes a good place for getting an early start on annual flowers and vegetables. With the addition of a heated propagating case that is somewhat insulated by the surrounding greenhouse, it can meet the needs of anyone interested in a greenhouse primarily to improve an outdoor garden.

A cold greenhouse is the cheapest and simplest kind, both to build and to operate. The most common is probably a *coldframe*—simply a glass-covered box for growing seedlings and then hardening them off, ready to plant out in the garden. (See Chapter 14.) Even half a cider jug covering a parsley plant counts as an unheated greenhouse. Mobile coverings for a single plant or a row of plants are called *cloches*, and are useful in the garden in spring to protect young plants from damage by either frost or animals. A glassed-in sunporch also makes a good, large, unheated greenhouse. Solar greenhouses usually fall into the category of either cool or cold, depending on how well designed they are and what the climate is like.

Any greenhouse can be heated less, to accommodate less-heat-loving plants, but it would be wasteful to build a greenhouse with all the heating equipment and extra insulation needed by a hothouse and then use it only for starting vegetables in the spring. Equally, it would be wasteful to try to heat an alpine house, designed for maximum ventilation, sufficiently to grow orchids. You should consider exactly what plants you want to grow before building a greenhouse.

Probably you will have to devote as much time and trouble to ventilating and shading in summer to prevent excess heat as you will spend on heating in winter. Many plants do better outdoors in partial shade in summer than they will do in the hot, confined atmosphere of the greenhouse. And where summers are hot, it may be as well to leave the greenhouse empty for a month or two—though with sufficient ventilation and shading, temperatures can be kept down to a reasonable level.

As mentioned before, you can take advantage of seasonal variations. In summer, thanks to the heat of the sun, every greenhouse automatically becomes a warmhouse. With good ventilation it becomes an excellent place for growing eggplants, peppers, melons, okra and other plants that might not get enough heat outdoors for their best growth. And if you wished to grow a few heat-loving plants in winter without a hothouse, they could be grown in the greenhouse during the summer and brought indoors to a sunny windowsill when it becomes chilly. An insulating shade or shutter on the window to protect them at night might be all that would be necessary. Alternatively, they could be overwintered in a propagating case, if it were large enough.

To get an extra early start on seedlings, a cold greenhouse could be heated for just a few months a year. Some people divide their greenhouses into two sections with a thin curtain, keeping one side at quite a high temperature and relying on the heat passing through the curtain to prevent freezing on the other side. This technique presents difficulties with air circulation, but it is a clever way of growing plants with different requirements in the same greenhouse.

Soil temperature is almost as important as air temperature. It determines the rate at which roots develop and the rate at which they can take up water and nutrients. Because the soil is dark and moist, it absorbs and retains quite a bit of the sun's heat, so it is usually several degrees warmer than the air. Thus many plants can withstand sudden drops in air temperature, even to below freezing, without harm. For maximum growth the soil should be between 65 and 70°F., especially for young plants. Older plants can be "hardened off" (gradually accustomed to cooler temperatures) so that they will grow well with a soil temperature of about 50°F. If a minimal amount of heat is to be supplied to the greenhouse, it should be applied to the soil for best results.

Humidity

The amount of humidity needed is closely related to the temperature. A chilly greenhouse must be relatively dry to discourage several plant diseases (see Chapter 9). The warmer the air, the more water it can contain. When cool air is warmed, its relative humidity (the actual amount of water in the air compared to the total possible amount) decreases. It will therefore tend to absorb water from the things around, and plants will be dried out. So when the temperature in-

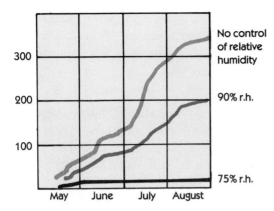

No control
of relative
humidity

90% r.h.

75% r.h.

300

200

100

May   June   July   August

Figure 3.3. Relative humidity and its effect on plant diseases. The figures at left indicate the number of tomato plants infected.

creases, you should increase the humidity, too. Hosing down the paths, spraying the plants, and limiting ventilation are the easiest ways to raise the level of humidity.

When hot, humid air is cooled (for example, at night, in contact with the inside surface of the greenhouse) it is no longer able to hold so much moisture, and water droplets condense out onto the glass, pots, benches, and even plants. Drops of condensation on plants during cool nights can be harmful, damaging leaves and encouraging fungus diseases. If possible, the greenhouse should be designed to shed condensation rather than to let it drip. A steep slope on the glass will help, but any irregularity such as a sash bar or a bit of dirt will encourage the formation of drips. An anticondensation film sprayed on the glass helps to prevent water from forming into droplets, and also prevents the glass from fogging up on cold days.

Ideal relative humidity varies with the season, but in general, for most greenhouses, is about 60 percent. An ordinary house is drier, probably about 30 percent. On a foggy day the outdoor humidity may be as high as 95 or 100 percent, but unless it feels very damp outdoors, you can usually expect ventilation to reduce humidity in the greenhouse. Excessive humidity is usually more of a problem than excessive dryness. Most disease organisms need a relative humidity of

70 percent to survive, while your plants will be quite happy with 40 percent if they have an adequate water supply to their roots.

WATERING

Watering your plants will, of course, increase the humidity of the air as water in the soil evaporates. But plants should not be watered just to raise the humidity level. Overwatering leaches out nutrients and may cause the soil to become waterlogged, depriving the roots of the oxygen they need and promoting disease. Allowing the soil to dry out between waterings encourages vigorous root growth. The one exception is for plants in soilless composts, which must be kept evenly moist.

When to water. The art lies in knowing just when a plant needs more water. The simplest test is to press the soil gently with your fingertip; if it feels dry, the plant probably wants more water. A good test with a clay pot is to feel the bottom of the pot; as long as that is moist, the plant has sufficient water. Clay pots can also be rapped with the knuckles—dry pots are supposed to give off a hollow ring and wet ones a dull thud, but it is difficult to decide on that basis alone.

A wilting plant is not necessarily asking for more water. It may be complaining of trouble with its roots due to damage by pests or disease. Or, on sunny winter mornings, the cold soil may be preventing the roots from taking up the moisture fast enough to replace the water the leaves are losing to the sun-warmed air.

Every plant uses water at different rates, depending on its species, the stage in its life cycle, the time of year, the weather, and the kind of pot it is in, among other things. Plants from dry climates tend to use less water and prefer generally drier conditions. Many plants have a dormant period in which they need to be left completely dry. When forming flower buds or fruits, most plants need more water than usual. In winter, when they are less active, plants use less water, but on sunny days they will use more.

How much. As difficult as discovering *when* a plant needs water is figuring out *how much* it needs. The soil in each pot should be dry before watering, and thoroughly saturated after. The time-honored formula is to water until some water appears from the hole in the bottom of the pot. The water should sink into the soil almost immediately (if not, your soil mix probably needs more sand and organic matter to make it drain better), but it can take several minutes to find its way out the drainage holes. So you must go back to check each plant, pouring off any excess and re-watering those that have not let any water through.

If the pots are set on a bed of gravel or on slats, you can let the excess drain into that, saving you the work of going back to check and adding some humidity to the air as the water evaporates. But you must be sure you are watering thoroughly enough. An approximate guide is to leave half an inch between the top of the soil and the top of the pot—filling that space with water is sufficient for most plants. It is a good idea to check your watering habits occasionally by putting saucers under the pots and seeing if a bit of water leaks out. If none appears, you are not watering enough (or else the drainage holes are blocked and need cleaning). If more than a few tablespoonsful collect in the saucer, you are overwatering (or else the soil has shrunk away from the sides of the pot, letting the water rush straight through. In this case a second watering should wet the mass of the soil, but the plant should really be repotted in better soil with more organic matter.)

Beds of earth in solid staging are watered much like pots—until they begin to drip. Ground beds are more difficult to judge, but less susceptible to extremes of wetness and dryness thanks to their mass. To check on the amount, try digging up a trowelful of soil a few hours after you have watered. If the soil is thoroughly moist six or seven inches down, you have given it enough. Make sure that the beds are dry half an inch below the surface before rewatering.

Watering from above. The most common way to water plants in a greenhouse is with a watering can. Ideally, the can should come with two roses—a fine one that can face upwards to give a gentle rain for seedlings, and an ordinary rose for watering solid beds. Standard garden watering cans are not very satisfactory for watering any but the largest pot plants, because the rose sprinkles water over too wide an area, and without the rose too much water rushes out. Special watering cans with long, narrow nozzles for reaching individual pots at the back of the staging are useful.

A *hose* is a common alternative to the watering can. It saves time filling and carrying cans, but you must be careful to use only a gentle flow of water. Spray attachments are a help.

Watering from below. Probably the best way to water pot plants is from below. Set the pot in a tub of water and soak for several hours, keeping the water level about halfway up the pot. When the soil glistens, remove the pot and let it drain for a few hours before setting it back in place, unless a gravel bed or slatted staging allows it to drain in place. Watering from below is a messy, time-consuming business, but it insures that both pot and soil are thoroughly saturated.

Newly potted plants—especially those in clay pots—benefit greatly from being soaked. Seed flats and cuttings are also best watered from below to disturb the soil as little as possible. Some special plants like African violets and cyclamen, which are fussy about water on their leaves, or on the growing point of the bulb, do better if regularly watered from below. All plants in pots will appreciate being watered from below every few months even if you can't be bothered to do it every time they need watering. A large sink, or a galvanized tub, or an old bathtub are best for soaking pots. The more you can soak at one time, the more efficient the operation becomes.

To avoid problems of deciding when and how much to water, you can let the plant take up water at its own rate. If you insert the end of a cotton wick half an inch into the drainage hole of each pot when planting, you can put the other end of the wick in a bucket of water, and by capillary action the plant will absorb the water it needs. Provided the bucket is kept full, the plant will never go without. This is an excellent system for those who want to go away and leave the greenhouse unattended periodically. But it is a bit messy looking and is a nuisance if you want to take blooming plants indoors for display. You can buy automatic watering systems, which are more elaborate versions of capillary action (see Chapter 6).

It is always better to water in the morning so the leaves have a chance to dry off during the day, and so the humidity given off by the damp soil occurs in the hottest part of the day. Do not water on cloudy days if you can avoid it, because the humidity will already be higher than usual and the plants will be using less water during the day.

In winter, it is well worth using warm water early in the morning to heat up the cold soil so the plant can make use of every bit of sunlight. If you have no hot water supply in the greenhouse, leave buckets of water out overnight to warm up at least to the greenhouse temperature.

Rain water is ideal for watering, but if it cannot conveniently be collected, tap water will do. Very hard water can cause problems for some plants, but water softeners should not be used because they sometimes contain harmful chemicals. If the water is heavily chlorinated, it is a good idea to leave it standing in a bucket or watering can overnight so the chlorine can evaporate.

Ventilation

Both temperature and humidity are immediately affected by ventilation. An increase in ventilation will lower the temperature and generally will lower the humidity as well, unless the weather is extremely wet.

Plants need fresh air to replenish their supplies of carbon dioxide and oxygen. They use a bit of oxygen all the time, day and night, for respiration, but they use a great deal of carbon dioxide during the day for photosynthesis. Except under very cold or very cloudy conditions (when the carbon dioxide level is sufficient) giving extra CO_2 helps the plant to use the available light and heat more efficiently. The atmosphere was much richer in carbon dioxide when prehistoric plants came into existence, so it is not unnatural that their descendants should prosper when given extra CO_2.

In winter when vents are closed most of the day to conserve heat, the CO_2 level can fall well below even the .03 percent found out of doors. And short days make efficient use of existing light vital in winter, so enriching the atmosphere with carbon dioxide is worthwhile on sunny days (Figure 3.4). A .1 percent carbon dioxide level is probably a good

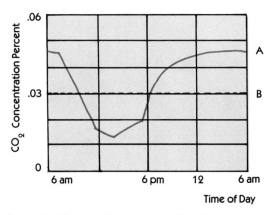

Figure 3.4. The variation in carbon dioxide concentration throughout the day: (A) inside the greenhouse, and (B) outside.

figure to aim for; if the level got as high as .2 percent it might be harmful.

Burning natural gas and melting dry ice are both good sources of CO_2, but in many ways the most satisfactory solution is keeping a compost heap in the greenhouse. A well-made compost pile releases a significant amount of CO_2 and quite a bit of heat as well. Moreover, it will benefit from protection in winter and will provide you with excellent potting soil in a few months. It will happily simmer away in a dark corner under a bench, requiring only to be turned every few weeks. When the temperature in the heap begins to drop, it is time to start the next heap.

Plants need fresh air every day. It is better to supply some extra heat in winter and open the vents for a short while each day than to be too energy-conserving and keep the greenhouse closed up tight.

Ventilation should be provided whenever the temperature gets too high, as at midday, or whenever you want to reduce the humidity, as in later afternoon to replace hot, humid air so that excess condensation does not form when the greenhouse cools overnight.

Natural ventilation (as opposed to fan-driven) is usually sufficient if there are vents on both sides of the roof so the air movement across the ridge draws the air out of the greenhouse. Vents should be opened away from the wind to avoid drafts and the possibility of damage to hinges in sudden gusts. Ventilation is improved if there are some vents at ground level as well, so the natural convection of hot air rising pulls cooler air from below; but by the same token this is extremely heat-consuming if you are trying to heat the space. Lean-to greenhouses, or those provided with insufficient opening vents (usually an area equivalent to at least a fifth of the floor area is recommended) should

Figure 3.5. A plastic ventilating tube system is located just under the gable of this free-standing plastic-covered greenhouse. The holes provide uniform air distribution from a 1/2-h.p. electric fan in the wall.

have an exhaust fan at one end to pull out stale air.

Fans. Plants need a bit of air movement as well as fresh air to stimulate sturdy growth. If the air is still, a layer of stale air accumulates around each leaf as it uses up the elements it needs and gives off its waste products. Air movement stirs up the stale air, bringing fresh supplies of CO_2 and oxygen and taking away the excess humidity given off by the plant. So when vents must be closed for long periods of time, it is useful to have a small ceiling fan to circulate the air inside. Figure 3.5 shows a fan-tube ventilation system in a plastic-covered greenhouse.

Plastic-covered greenhouses usually have more problems with ventilation than glazed greenhouses because they are more airtight, and less accidental ventilation (called *infiltration*) occurs at the joints. Different glazing materials and their advantages are discussed in detail in Chapter 5.

Light

An increase in light level will usually cause a plant to grow faster and bloom sooner, but too much light will burn the leaves. The optimum amount of light varies enormously with different species and at different stages in the life of the plant. Seedlings can usually make more efficient use of more light than mature plants. Fruiting and flowering plants generally require more light than foliage plants. Many vegetables that grow well in a warm greenhouse over the winter will not set fruit until the days get longer and brighter unless extra light is provided. Within the range acceptable to a particular plant, an increase in light level should be accompanied by an increase in temperature, humidity and carbon dioxide so the plant can make the best use of the light. (Figures 3.6 and 3.7.)

Most plants need to be acclimated gradually to changes in light level. Taking even the

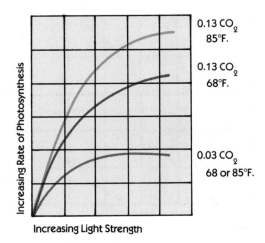

Figure 3.6. Photosynthesis increases with more carbon dioxide and temperature as well as light.

most sun-loving plant from under the bench and putting it in full sun is likely to result in a miserable, sunburned plant.

If you want to increase the amount of light available on cloudy winter days, begin gradually with the artificial light source well above the plant. To supplement natural daylight effectively, you will need a lamp that gives off a wide range of the spectrum. Ordinary light bulbs and cool-white fluorescent

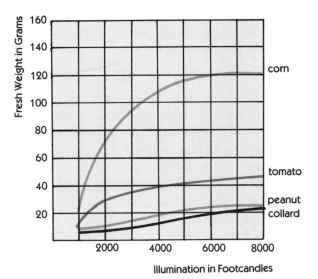

Figure 3.7. The effect of light levels on plant growth. More light generally makes a plant grow faster, though there are limits beyond which light is unneeded and may even be harmful.

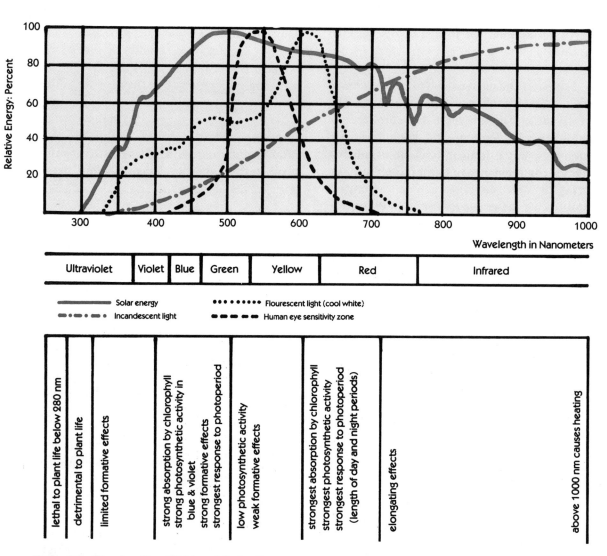

Figure 3.8. Wavelengths of light and their effect on plant growth.

tubes each give off only a limited range of the spectrum but together they provide a good mixed light for plant growth (ideally, the ratio should be 300 watts of flourescent light to every 100 watts of incandescent). Full-spectrum lights which simulate sunlight are made especially for plant growing, but are quite expensive (Figure 3.8).

The number of hours of daylight affects the blooming schedule of some plants as strongly as the intensity of light affects others. Christmas cactus, chrysanthemums and poinsettias in particular are induced to bloom by strict adherence to a set number of hours of light and of darkness. Most other plants are indifferent to the number of hours of light, provided they get sufficient quantity. For them, fifteen hours of weak light will do as well as eight hours of strong light.

Propagation

A greenhouse is a great help in propagating plants. The controlled temperature and humidity levels encourage even the most reluctant cutting to put out roots, and nearly 100 percent of your seeds should germinate if planted properly.

Both seeds and cuttings should be started in a moist, warm, sterile medium. Any good greenhouse soil with an extra handful of sand or vermiculite can be used. It is a good idea to sieve the soil to remove any large lumps. The smaller the seed, the finer the texture of the soil should be. Pasteurization is not strictly necessary but it is usually recommended to reduce the incidence of damping-off disease. On the other hand, if you are not in a hurry, you can sow more seeds a few weeks later in case the first lot do not do well. Most seed is, after all, very inexpensive. The second time around it would obviously be sensible to pasteurize the soil to prevent a second failure. Because they have no roots yet, seeds and cuttings do not need any nutrients, so sand, peat or vermiculite are all acceptable growing media. But in a few weeks the new plants will need either feeding or transplanting if soil is not used. Soilless mixtures for starting seeds or cuttings (usually half peat and half sand) are available commercially or can be made up at home (see Chapter 7). They are lighter in weight than soil and are easy to use. Wet them thoroughly before using, or else the peat will resist watering later. Pouring boiling water on peat, soaking it overnight, or sprinkling it while stirring constantly are the favored methods of wetting peatmoss.

Sowing. Seeds should be sown thinly in a greenhouse—more thinly than in an outdoor garden. Virtually all seeds are likely to germinate, and they can become vastly overcrowded before they are big enough to transplant. If this happens, you can cut off every other seedling at soil level, then transplant some as soon as they have their seed leaves. Hold seedlings by a leaf rather than by the stem to avoid permanent damage.

Fine seeds should be sprinkled over the surface of the soil and lightly pressed in, not covered. Larger seeds should be sown to twice their own depth. Sowing seeds in rows makes weeding and transplanting easier, especially if you are not sure how to distinguish the seed leaves from weeds (though if the soil is adequately pasteurized, there should be no weeds). But broadcasting the seeds is easier with those that are so fine they are difficult to sow thinly in rows.

Some seeds need light to germinate; others require complete darkness. Seed packets are often uninformative, so it is wise to consult a good gardening encyclopedia before planting. All seeds should be given good but indirect light as soon as they have germinated, and within a few days most should be put in full sunlight.

Cuttings. Cuttings should be taken with a sharp, clean knife, then pressed firmly into a hole in the rooting medium and left for a few weeks in a warm, humid atmosphere with good light. Some cuttings will root in plain water, which should be changed every few days. Dipping the cut end in rooting hormone encourages the plant to put out roots more quickly. Hardwood cuttings generally take longer to root than soft cuttings from new growth. Most plants will root better in summer when there are ample food supplies stored in the leaves.

The easiest way to tell if a cutting has rooted is simply to wait until it starts to grow again, putting out new leaves, but if you are in a hurry to know, give a gentle tug. To be doubly sure, pull one up, and if it has put out roots from a half to one inch long, you can assume the others of the same species have also rooted, and are ready to be transplanted or grown in full sunlight.

PROPAGATING CASE

Both seeds and cuttings need a constant temperature of around 70°F. and a high degree of humidity. A plastic bag or a sheet of glass placed over the seedbed or cuttings (but not touching the plants or soil) will help. But a propagating case—a sort of miniature greenhouse with an additional source of heat—provides the ideal warm, humid atmosphere needed.

A propagating case is quite simple to build. Make a large box about ten inches deep, with a glass or plastic lid that can be propped open at different angles. The bottom of the box should have a waterproof tray at least a half inch deep so the flats of seeds or cuttings placed in the tray can be watered from below. Flats (shallow boxes, usually about two inches deep and a foot long by two feet wide) or individual pots (used for starting large, fast-growing plants or those that dislike being transplanted) are then placed in the trays and the whole case is placed over a gentle source of heat. Soil-warming cables in the bench below the propagating case are the most usual form of heat. An electric lightbulb suspended above the plants is enough heat for a small case, but bottom heat gives better results.

More elaborate propagating cases can be made or purchased. These have sloping covers (often shaped like an even-span greenhouse) which shed the condensation that inevitably accumulates. They often have automatic thermostats to regulate heat and humidity, and they usually have an internal source of heat.

Figure 3.9. Two types of propagating cases that can be made easily by the do-it-yourselfer. In one, a fiberglass sheet is arched to form a transparent cover; in the other, a plastic sheet is merely stapled to a cover frame. Both are based on the coldframe principle, but are for use inside a greenhouse for finely controlling the environment to grow seedlings or cuttings.

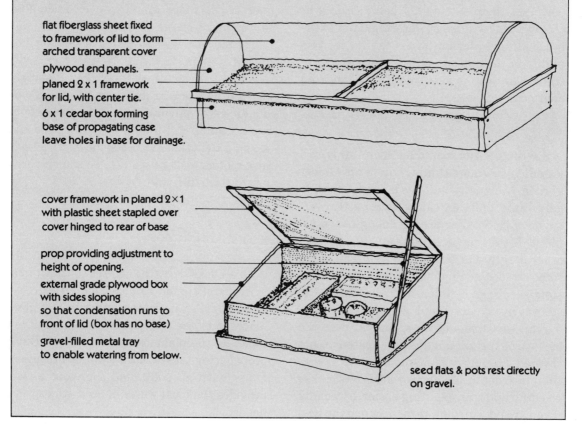

flat fiberglass sheet fixed
to framework of lid to form
arched transparent cover

plywood end panels.

planed 2 x 1 framework
for lid, with center tie.

6 x 1 cedar box forming
base of propagating case
leave holes in base for drainage.

cover framework in planed 2×1
with plastic sheet stapled over
cover hinged to rear of base

prop providing adjustment to
height of opening.

external grade plywood box
with sides sloping
so that condensation runs to
front of lid (box has no base)

gravel-filled metal tray
to enable watering from below.

seed flats & pots rest directly
on gravel.

Without automatic controls, a propagating case must be carefully tended. On warm days, it should be left partly open so heat does not build up. Excess condensation should be wiped from the cover periodically. If mold begins to form, keep the lid open for several hours to allow the surface of the soil to dry and the mold to disappear.

Always water seeds and cuttings from below to avoid disturbing the fine new roots or splashing the leaves (which would encourage rot). If the surface appears to be drying out before the bulk of the soil has thoroughly drained, spray it lightly with tepid water. Ideally, only warm water (65°F.) should be used for watering so the temperature of the soil is not lowered. Because the growing medium was thoroughly moistened before the seeds or cuttings were planted, and the propagating case has a humid atmosphere, it is not likely to need watering again until the plants have rooted and are a bit sturdier.

When the seeds have sprouted or the cuttings rooted, the lid of the propagating case should be opened for a few hours a day to reduce humidity. In a few days, you can move the new plants to a warm, draft-free part of the greenhouse. Continue to water from below by soaking them for several hours in a pan of water whenever the soil appears dry. As soon as the plants are touching leaves with their neighbors, they should be transplanted to individual pots or larger boxes so both leaves and roots have plenty of room to grow. Once the roots are well established,

Figure 3.10. Peek inside the polyethylene sheets and you'll find a misting system, in this case continually moistening beds of chrysanthemum cuttings. The plastic enclosure keeps the humidity extremely high inside. Water in the form of fine mist sprays from the overhead tube, and in this system, the mister runs on a time clock, turning on for a few seconds at a time every few minutes.

MISTING

Fine, constant misting (Figure 3.10) is a sophisticated alternative to a propagating case. Constant misting prevents the leaves from drying out and encourages rapid rooting of cuttings. Many plants that are otherwise impossible to propagate by cuttings will root rapidly this way. Warm soil, good drainage, and automatic control of the water flow in the mister are all needed for success. Seeds can be raised under an automatic mister, but they do no better than they would in a propagating case. Cuttings are an easier and more certain form of propagation with a mister. An automatic system should be available in the $50 to $100 range.

place in full sunlight. Young plants respond even more to good light, warmth and extra carbon dioxide than do mature plants, so it pays to give them the best conditions you can.

Always make changes in humidity, heat, and light intensity gradually. Any sudden shock will set the young plants back and make them susceptible to disease. Every transplanting is a shock, so they should be moved to their final quarters as soon as possi-ble. If they are to be grown outside, moving them to a coldframe and opening the lid a little more each day will help to adjust them gradually to outdoor conditions.

Plants in a greenhouse should be inspected frequently for infestations of insects or disease. A discussion of the various pest and disease problems and what to do about them will be found in Chapter 9.

References and Sources

The Complete Book of the Greenhouse by Ian Walls. Ward Lock Ltd., London. 1973. $5.95. Thorough but rather technical English manual on growing crops in large greenhouses. Stresses flower production but also good on tomatoes. The author believes in chemical fertilizers and pesticides.

The Complete Handbook of Plant Propagation by R.C. Wright. Macmillan. 1975. $12.95. A complete and useful guide, from germinating seeds to grafting apples, including all sorts of flowers and vegetables. Tells how to harvest and store your own seeds and how to take difficult cuttings in a mist propagator.

The Food and Heat Producing Solar Greenhouse by Rick Fisher and Bill Yanda. John Muir Publications, Santa Fe, New Mexico. 1976. Paperback, $6. Has a good sensible chapter on how to use a small unheated greenhouse for home food production. Derived mainly from experience with solar greenhouses in the Southwest.

Greenhouse: Place of Magic by Charles H. Potter. E.P. Dutton & Co. Inc., New York. 1967. Paperback, $3.95. A good all-around book on using a greenhouse. Lots of information on different varieties of flowers, but nothing on growing vegetables indoors. Recommends chemical fertilizers and pesticides.

Growing Food and Flowers in Containers by Ted Flanagan. Garden Way Publishing, Charlotte, Vermont. 1973. Paperback, $3.95. A handbook for those with limited space. Not too detailed but is a good introduction to bottle gardens and other containers indoors.

In Your Greenhouse with Percy Thrower. Hamlyn, London. 1963, 1972. Excellent detailed information on how to grow many varieties. Good simple advice on using your greenhouse. Well illustrated.

Making Things Grow Indoors by Thalassa Cruso. Alfred A. Knopf, New York. 1969. Paperback, $4.95. The best all-around book on houseplants. Useful, though not written specifically for greenhouses. No information on fruits and vegetables. Excellent advice on enjoying and caring for potted plants.

Organic Gardening Under Glass by George and Katy Abraham. Rodale Press, Emmaus, Pennsylvania. 1975. $8.95. A good all-purpose book on runnning a greenhouse without resorting to artificial .fertilizers and pesticides. Information a bit spotty, but includes sections on many exotic fruits and vegetables you might not otherwise think of growing.

Building and Using Our Sun-Heated Greenhouse by Helen and Scott Nearing. Garden Way Publishing. 1977. Paperback, $6.95; hardcover, $11.95. An endearing book by two pioneers of the back-to-the-land homesteading movement in the United States. Describes their extremely simple greenhouse that adjoins a stone wall near the coast of Maine, and their frugal growing techniques.

Seeds and Cuttings by H. Peter Loewer. Walker and Company, New York. 1975. Paperback, $3.95. A small book full of useful information on plant propagation. Clearly written and well illustrated but lack of an index is a problem.

The Solar Greenhouse Book, edited by James C. McCullagh. Rodale Press. 1978. Paperback, $8.95. Mostly about design and construction, but includes three chapters on using a solar greenhouse and cites much first-hand experience. Emphasis on organic techniques and winter vegetables.

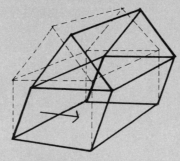

Problem
wind force on gable
end of greenhouse

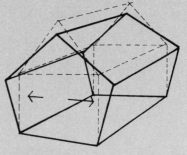

Problem
wind force on side
of greenhouse

Problem
excessive load on roof,
eg. from snow.

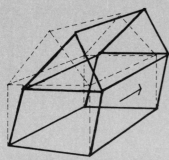

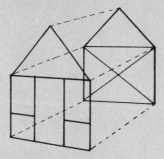

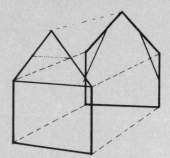

Solution:
Either A: Diagonal bracing along
length of building using one member capable of acting in tension &
compression or two diagonal tension members (ties).
Or B: Rigidfy side wall with additional framing or siding.

Solution:
Either A: Diagonal bracing with one
strut (compression & tension member) or two ties (act in tension
only—these could be simple wires.
Or B: Rigidify end walls with additional framing with rigid joints.

Solution:
Either A: Rigidify framework joints
at eaves with triangular bracing or
gussets.
Or B: Tie together the longitudinal
walls with a tension member to
prevent walls moving outward.

II

Mechanics
and
Paraphernalia

4

Construction Details

This chapter is about various construction techniques and materials necessary for building a greenhouse. Some information is very basic, and will be superfluous for those with building experience. We have tried to give several alternative ways of approaching construction details for each particular stage in the building of a greenhouse, together with some idea of the advantages and disadvantages of each. We hope that once you are armed with this technical information, it will broaden the range of different greenhouse buildings you might construct.

Principles and techniques are more important, we think, than providing a complete construction manual for any one particular form of greenhouse. Two major elements of greenhouse construction are dealt with in the following order: (1) foundations and base walls and (2) structure and framing. A third, glazing, will be covered in Chapter 5.

Foundations and Floors

Before beginning excavation for the foundations it is important to know the exact size and location of the proposed greenhouse. Once this has been determined and there are a few simple drawings, or at least some definite ideas to follow, the process of setting out the site can be begun. The position of the greenhouse is likely to be related in some way to an existing straight line. It may be a boundary line, an existing building or a north-south axis. This line should be used to establish one edge of the greenhouse. Then mark the two corners on that edge and measure right-angles at each corner to two of the other edges. Measure along each of these edges and establish the third and fourth corners of the building. Then begin to check dimensions. Initially setting out is a matter of trial and error but there are a number of useful tricks that can make the process easier. To measure right angles, use a large builder's square (Figure 4.1) which you can make yourself out of bits of 1 inch x 4 inch lumber, or use the 3-4-5 principle. This involves measuring three feet from the corner along one edge and marking that point. Then measure four feet along the other edge and mark that point also. The distance between the two points should, by Pythagoras's age-old theorem, be five feet. Any inaccuracy must be corrected. The corners of the building, once established, should be marked with stakes driven into the ground, and nails driven into the top of each stake. For nonrectilinear buildings more geometrical work is nec-

essary but the same principles can be followed. For L-shaped buildings, the plan can be divided into two rectangles and set out accordingly.

BATTER BOARDS

Once the corners of the building have been marked with posts, set up "profiles" (otherwise called "batter boards") beyond the corners of each building, so that when the corner posts are removed for excavating the foundations, the corners of the building can still be located. Profiles (Figure 4.2) consist of 1 inch x 6 inch horizontal boards nailed to stakes which are driven into the ground about two feet beyond the corner posts. To insure that these boards are all horizontally aligned, use a straight-edged board and a spirit level. Twine or strong string is then stretched taut between boards as shown so that the intersections of the string mark the position of the corner posts below. Saw cuts are then made in the profile boards to mark the position of the string should it break during excavation work. The original corner posts can then be removed, and marks on the profile boards

Figure 4.1. The first step in setting out a foundation is to mark the corners, doublechecking its squareness.

Setting Out: 1

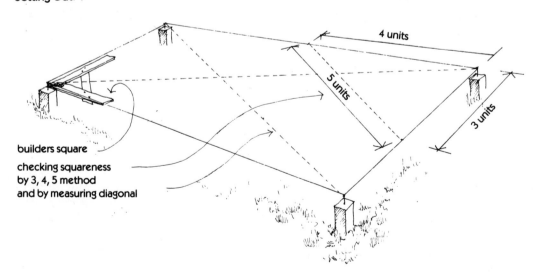

builders square

checking squareness
by 3, 4, 5 method
and by measuring diagonal

4 units

5 units

3 units

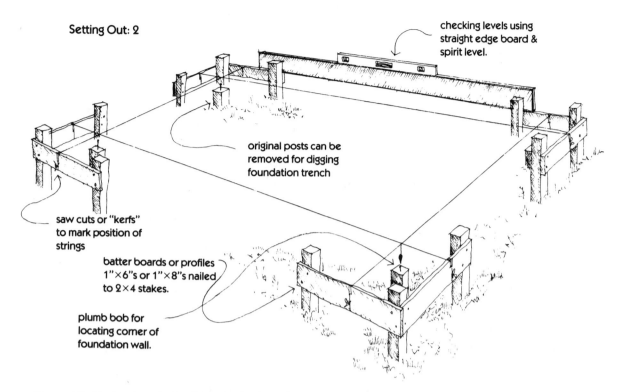

Setting Out: 2

checking levels using straight edge board & spirit level.

original posts can be removed for digging foundation trench

saw cuts or "kerfs" to mark position of strings

batter boards or profiles 1"×6"s or 1"×8"s nailed to 2×4 stakes.

plumb bob for locating corner of foundation wall.

Figure 4.2. Next, set up batter boards, also known as profiles, a short distance away so the string or twine intersections mark the exact locations of the corners.

provide an easy reference for the corners of the building. It is useful also to have the profiles serve as a "site datum," a fixed horizontal level to which all other vertical measurements can be related. This makes it easy, for instance, to see how much the site needs to be leveled, and to measure depths of foundations and footings.

FOOTINGS

The purpose of a foundation, of course, is to anchor the building securely to the ground. The footing, at the base of the foundation, acts as a kind of pad to prevent the structure from sinking into the ground. The strength and depth of foundations and footings depend on soil conditions, as well as the weight of the building above. A densely compacted clay or rocky subsoil will provide a firmer base than a sandy subsoil, which requires a deeper or wider foundation. Generally, for a lightweight building such as a greenhouse, the

foundation and footing can be accommodated in one simple concrete base to which the wall above can be anchored (Figure 4.3). For very light plastic film structures, cedar or redwood stakes driven into the ground will provide sufficient anchorage. And for more elaborate schemes in which the greenhouse forms an extension to an existing house, or is heavier than the usual type of lightweight glass structure, a proper foundation wall and footings would be more suitable (Figure 4.4).

In this case a deep trench is dug to below the frost line (check local building practice) and a concrete footing is cast at the bottom of the trench. The footing should be as deep as the width of the foundation wall and at least twice as wide. A suitable mixture for foundation concrete is 1,2,6—that is, one measure (by volume) of cement for every two measures of sharp sand and six of gravel or "aggregate" (pebbles up to 1 inch diameter). The constituents should be mixed dry on a clean flat surface. Add water gradually until the concrete is liquid enough to "flow" fairly eas-

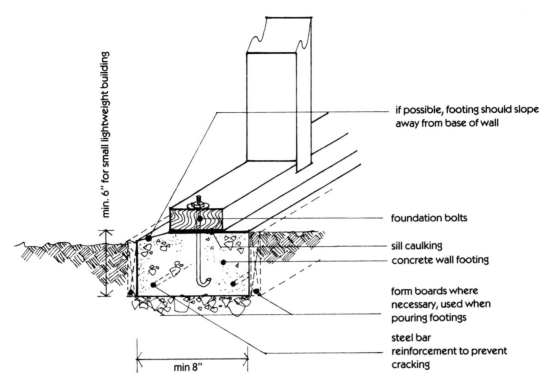

Figure 4.3. Simple concrete wall footings for lightweight building and good soil conditions.

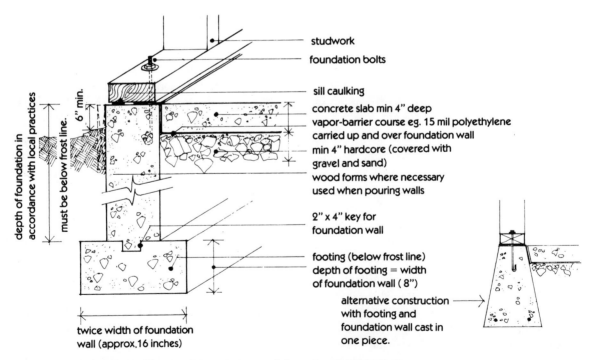

Figure 4.4. Complete footings and foundation wall for a heavyweight greenhouse, with vapor-barrier concrete floor. This type of construction is suitable for use where the greenhouse forms part of the dwelling.

ily when shoveled along the trench. For large foundations, it might be advisable to hire a small concrete mixer. These are easy to run and save a lot of back-breaking work. For even greater speed, when more than 3 cubic yards of concrete is required, consider buying ready-mixed concrete. But be sure to calculate exactly the right amount required, and have everything ready when the truck arrives. Excess concrete sets rapidly, and is troublesome to dispose of. It should be "tamped" with a large wooden post to release the air trapped in the mixture and to insure a denser and stronger footing. Tamping is done by striking the surface of the wet concrete mix with a large flat-ended object, over and over again.

FOUNDATION WALL

Once the footing has set hard (in one or two days) the foundation wall can be constructed above it. This can be made of concrete as shown in the illustration, or of concrete blocks, preferably hollow ones, filled with concrete. For additional strength and protection against frost and subsoil movement, vertical reinforcement rods can be placed in the cavities. Again, it is wise to inquire about local building practice.

The wall should extend above the surrounding ground level by about 6 or 8 inches, and if a cast concrete wall is used, this will

Figure 4.5. A concrete retaining wall cast with movable forms.

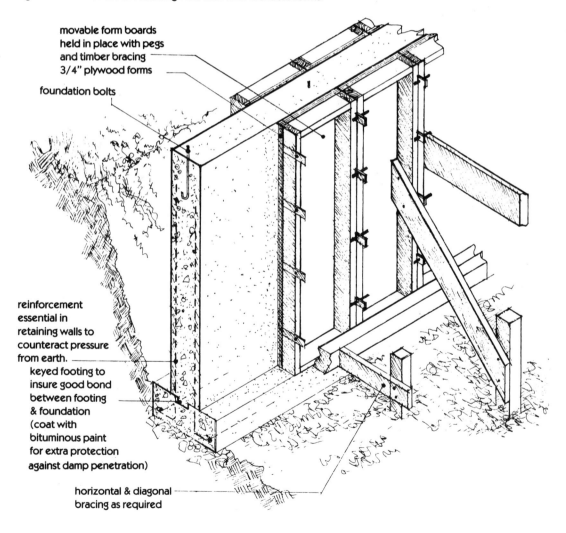

movable form boards held in place with pegs and timber bracing
3/4" plywood forms
foundation bolts

reinforcement essential in retaining walls to counteract pressure from earth.
keyed footing to insure good bond between footing & foundation (coat with bituminous paint for extra protection against damp penetration)

horizontal & diagonal bracing as required

entail the use of some kind of forms to keep the concrete in place while it sets. In areas of clay soils it may be possible to use mounded earth as a form, but the earth might easily collapse into the concrete when pouring the wall. So it is generally easier and safer to use wood. Wooden forms, also known as *shuttering*, can be knocked together from leftover 2 x 4s and cheap grade (½ to ¾ inch) plywood. It must be well braced against the surrounding ground to avoid a disastrous collapse when the wall is poured. Figure 4.5 shows a system of movable lumber forms for a foundation retaining wall (where the outside ground level is above internal floor level). The wooden panels can be used over and over again (they should be oiled to stop the concrete from sticking) and the jointing system allows the forms to be dismantled and rebuilt easily.

The top of the foundation wall should have foundation bolts or "anchor" bolts cast into it. These are used to fix the wooden or metal structure of the greenhouse to its concrete base. Make sure they are positioned correctly and will not sink into the concrete while it is still too liquid. Proper foundation bolts are hook-shaped or bent, but steel nuts with large washers will do just as well.

CONCRETE FLOOR

If the greenhouse is to have a concrete floor it can be cast at the same time as the foundation walls. In this case a thickened-edge slab construction (Figure 4.6) should be used. Preferably, the whole floor slab should be cast in one piece to minimize the risk of cracking. It should be at least 4 inches thick, resting on another 4 inches of "hardcore" (bits and pieces of broken brick, stone and concrete) and gravel. It is wise but not absolutely necessary to reinforce the slab with steel mesh and reinforcing rods, to prevent cracks from occuring due to settlement or uneven loads on the structure. When casting a thickened-edge slab, set up wooden forms all the way around the outside of the base to contain the liquid concrete and act as a guide for leveling off the top of the slab. The edge of the forms should be perfectly level and horizontal. Pour the concrete and use a straight-edged board spanning from one side of the slab to the other to tamp down the mixture.

DAMPPROOFING

If the greenhouse is to be an integral part of the house, it should be constructed to the same standards of dampproofing. This means that in a concrete floor a vapor barrier (a layer of tarred paper, roofing felt or thick polyethylene sheet) is required. It is said that good-quality, well-mixed, and well-tamped concrete is in itself adequate moisture proofing. It would certainly be worth taking the risk on this if the greenhouse was not to be part of the living room of the house but merely an intermediate space between inside and out. But if complete dampproofing is necessary, it is as well to follow established procedure. The vapor barrier can either be incorporated on top of the layer of hardcore (which should be leveled off with sand so that the rough edges of bricks and stones do not puncture the sheet), or on top of the concrete itself, which should then be covered with an additional 1½ inch or more of *screed*. A screed is a finishing layer of concrete consisting of sharp sand and cement in the ratio of thre to one. Any joints in the vapor barrier should be lapped, and around the edges of the slab it should be carried up into the walls to provide a completely sealed building.

Normally, however, the penetration of moisture will not be a problem. For most greenhouses used specifically for plants, a concrete floor is a disadvantage since it eliminates the use of the ground for planting, and even if this is not envisioned at the outset, it may be desirable later, and concrete floors are difficult to get rid of. For more temporary floors in plant greenhouses, gravel is suitable

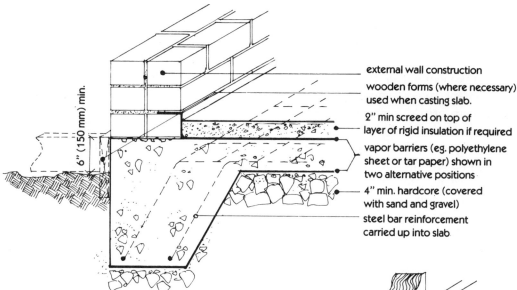

external wall construction

wooden forms (where necessary) used when casting slab.

2" min screed on top of layer of rigid insulation if required

vapor barriers (eg. polyethylene sheet or tar paper) shown in two alternative positions

4" min. hardcore (covered with sand and gravel)

steel bar reinforcement carried up into slab

6" (150 mm) min.

Figure 4.6. An integral slab and foundation (thickened-edge slab) with a moisture-proofed concrete floor. This is suitable for use where the greenhouse forms part of the dwelling. The post foundation shown is for use with lightweight timber buildings and suspended floors.

and inexpensive. Second-hand bricks, set in sand or ashes, provide a relatively hard-wearing and attractive flooring for those parts of the greenhouse, such as paths, where bare earth is not required.

Base Walls

Any greenhouse designed to minimize the use of "artificial" energy sources is unlikely to be completely glazed. As mentioned previously, fully glazed greenhouses tend to be thermally inefficient, and the use of base walls (from ground to bench height), at least on the north side of the greenhouse, will reduce heat loss from the building. Bricks and blocks provide cheap, strong walls, and are easy to work with, despite the tendency of most self-builders to be more at home with wood. Blocks are easier to lay than bricks for someone who is inexperienced, and they gen-

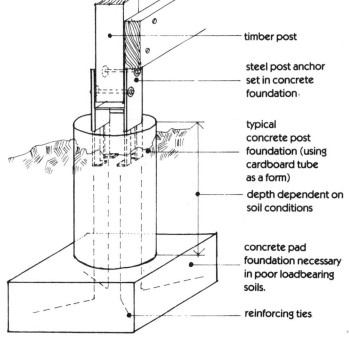

timber post

steel post anchor set in concrete foundation

typical concrete post foundation (using cardboard tube as a form)

depth dependent on soil conditions

concrete pad foundation necessary in poor loadbearing soils.

reinforcing ties

erally provide better thermal insulation. The same principles apply to working with either, and a small amount of practice and a lot of patience will soon provide the necessary skills for laying a simple base wall for a greenhouse. The important points to remember are as follows:

1. Mix a good, clean mortar, and use it "fresh." Four or five parts of "soft" sand

("soft" refers to the texture of the sand, more gritty sand for use in concrete is referred to as "sharp") to one of cement, by volume, should be thoroughly mixed, dry, on a large sheet of old plywood or concrete slab. By increasing the cement content, you can make the mortar harder and more brittle, more waterproof, and stronger, but more likely to crack. More sand makes a more plastic mortar, which allows more movement in the wall without cracking. Add clean water to the dry ingredients, mixing continuously until the mortar is as liquid as is consistent with holding the mark of a bricklaying trowel. It is a good idea to add hydraulic lime to make the mortar more workable, and adhere more easily to the bricks. Lime, like portland cement, is a binding agent and if used, it should be substituted for part of the cement content of the mixture. It is possible to use a mortar of sand and lime only—all mortars were like this until about 60 years ago—though for external conditions it is better to take advantage of "modern" developments in building technology, and use cement. Keep mixing and turning over the mortar from time to time to improve its workability, and add water if it is in danger of setting too quickly. Too much water, however, reduces the final strength of the mix.

2. To lay blocks on a concrete foundation wall or footing, first dampen the surface of the concrete to prevent the mortar mix from drying out too fast and losing its adherence. When laying hollow blocks as a base wall, or a foundation wall below ground, bolts or short metal rods can be set in the concrete footing so they will stick into the hollows of the blocks and can be bedded in. This will give a particularly good connection between the concrete base and the block wall.

3. There are many different patterns or "bonds" for laying bricks or blocks. The essential thing is to avoid having one vertical mortar joint directly above another. Figure 4.7 shows some of the different bonds used for laying brick walls of one or two bricks' thickness.

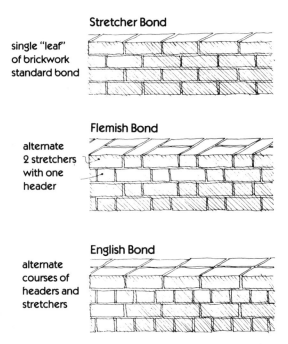

Figure 4.7. Some different types of "bonds" used in laying bricks or blocks. There are many other possible patterns, but the point of all is to avoid having one vertical joint over another.

4. Measure the length of the brick wall from outside corner to outside corner. That length should be as near as possible to a multiple of the combined length of one brick and one mortar joint, to avoid using half bricks and quarter bricks that destroy the bond pattern and weaken the wall. To a certain extent, it is possible to fudge the spacing of the bricks by increasing or decreasing the size of the mortar joints. Ideally these should be ⅜ inch wide. Standard bricks are 2½ by 3¾ by 8 inches long, so in setting out the bond, an average length of 8⅜ inches should be allowed for each brick-plus-mortar joint. For concrete blocks the nominal size includes the dimension of the mortar joint, so if you buy a 16-inch block you will find that it only measures 15⅝ inches, allowing ⅜ inch for the vertical mortar joint. It is therefore slightly easier to figure out the number of blocks you will need in each course. Increasing or decreasing the width of the joints slightly can add as much as 4 inches to a twelve-foot long brick wall. Lay out the first course (horizontal row) of bricks without mortar to establish

the proper spacing and then go back and set them in mortar.

5. When laying a brick or block, first make a "bed" of mortar for it on the wall below. With the back of the bricklaying trowel, spread some mortar on one end of the brick to be laid so you make one vertical joint every time you lay a brick. Put on more mortar than is required, tap the brick into position, using the handle of the trowel, and thereby squeezing out the excess mortar. Scrape this off with the trowel and throw it back into the mortar mix.

6. Always start at the corners of the wall and work toward the middle. Lay three courses at each end, checking that each brick is plumb (aligned vertically with the ones below) and level horizontally with the corresponding course at the other end of the wall. Attach a piece of string to two long nails or pegs and tap these into the mortar joints at each end, with the string taut (Figure 4.8). With the string acting as a horizontal guide it is then relatively easy to lay the intermediate bricks.

7. To cut bricks, you can use the sharp edge of a good quality forged steel bricklaying trowel, or the back of a bricklaying hammer, chipping away along the line where you want the brick to split. This is a skill that may not come easily and a heavy hammer and a wide-bladed masonry chisel may prove to be easier. Some lightweight concrete blocks can be sawed with an old crosscut saw (do not use your best wood saw), but most types are best cut with a hammer and chisel.

8. Finish or "point" the mortar joints on the side you are working on as you go along. At the end of each course, go around and point up the other side. The mortar will not set hard for an hour or so, and the finished pointing can be left until later provided you scrape off all the excess from the joints. Mortar joints can be finished flush with the outside of the brickwork or indented with the point of the trowel to form a "V" or "weathered" joint (Figure 4.9). For appearances sake, particularly if you are an amateur and happen to have a lot of mortar on the finished surface of the bricks, go over the brickwork with a wire brush and a bucket of water when

Figure 4.8. Some rules to follow when laying a brick or block wall.

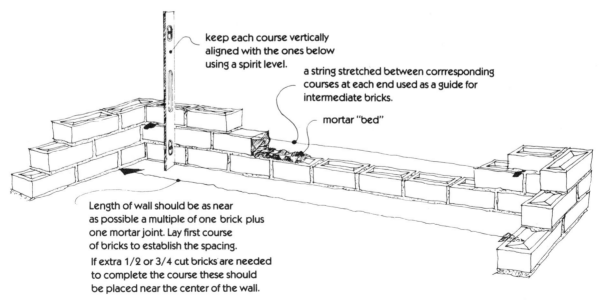

keep each course vertically aligned with the ones below using a spirit level.

a string stretched between corrresponding courses at each end used as a guide for intermediate bricks.

mortar "bed"

Length of wall should be as near as possible a multiple of one brick plus one mortar joint. Lay first course of bricks to establish the spacing.

If extra 1/2 or 3/4 cut bricks are needed to complete the course these should be placed near the center of the wall.

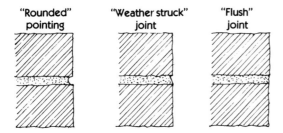

"Rounded" pointing   "Weather struck" joint   "Flush" joint

Figure 4.9. Good, clean joints improve the overall appearance of brickwork. The rounded pointing is made with an old broom handle, the others with the tip of a pointing trowel.

the mortar is half hard, a few hours after the pointing has been done.

Structure and Framing

The most common materials used for the structural skeleton of a greenhouse are wood and aluminum. Wood is easier to work with and readily available, but requires care and maintenance; aluminum is virtually maintenance-free. Aluminum, unlike steel, does not "rust," but forms a thin layer of aluminum oxide on the outside surface that prevents further oxidation, while slightly detracting from the appearance of the material. Most prefabricated aluminum greenhouses have an "anodized" finish that remains a bright silver color provided it is not scratched. Aluminum is particularly suitable for prefabricated greenhouse kits, but not for more original personalized designs. Prices of wood and aluminum greenhouses are similar, and often the choice of basic structural material comes down to one of personal preference and aesthetics.

The prospective greenhouse builder should consider other materials before making up his mind. Kits are now available that use polyethylene tube bent into arch forms as the supports for a skin of plastic film. Many different kinds of greenhouses have been built using metal tubing (electrical conduit is ideal —cheap, lightweight, and strong) and standard angles, joints and connectors.

Metal tubes make suitable structures for domed greenhouses. Domes have received perhaps more than their due share of publicity ever since Buckminster Fuller invented, or, more correctly, discovered geodesics. The dome is a beautiful shape, but one should consider the advantages of a conventional horizontal-vertical building before embarking on a more ambitious multifaceted structure. Contrary to popular conception, true geodesics require structural members of many different lengths and complicated structural joints. They can also cause agonizing problems when it comes to fitting doors (which are most convenient as seven-by-three-foot vertical openings), and meeting the ground (which is, by nature, horizontal). Before getting carried away by the vision of an easy-to-build crystaline dome greenhouse, think through all the structural problems, and read one or two of the standard texts such as Lloyd Kahn's *Domebooks* Numbers 1 and 2.

Deciding upon the structure of a greenhouse requires a knowledge of some basic structural principles. First, a greenhouse—though it may be a lightweight structure—could easily double its weight with a snow load, and second, in many areas, it can be subject to immense wind loads. It must, therefore, be completely rigid. Many aluminum framed greenhouses available in kit form only become rigid when the glass is in place. This seems to be asking a lot of ⅛-inch-thick greenhouse glass. Rigidity is best achieved within the structure itself by the principle of triangulation. A simple post-and-beam structure will tend to distort under horizontal wind loads, causing great stress at the joints, which will eventually give way. Figure 4.10 shows how a simple greenhouse structure must be braced to meet various loads. Without any triangular bracing in the structure, it is possible to make the greenhouse more rigid by careful detailing of the

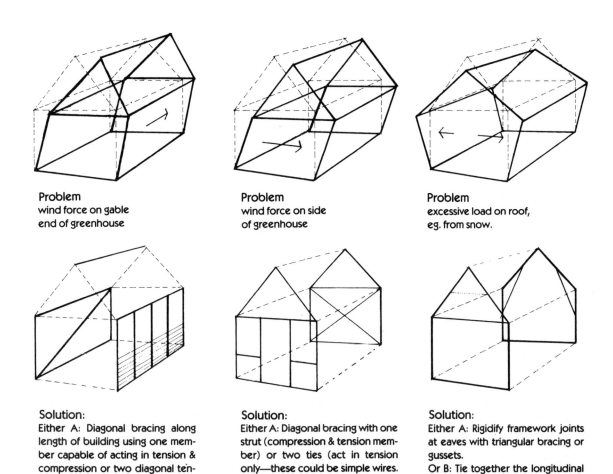

Problem
wind force on gable
end of greenhouse

Problem
wind force on side
of greenhouse

Problem
excessive load on roof,
eg. from snow.

Solution:
Either A: Diagonal bracing along
length of building using one member capable of acting in tension &
compression or two diagonal tension members (ties).
Or B: Rigidfy side wall with additional framing or siding.

Solution:
Either A: Diagonal bracing with one
strut (compression & tension member) or two ties (act in tension
only—these could be simple wires.
Or B: Rigidify end walls with additional framing with rigid joints.

Solution:
Either A: Rigidify framework joints
at eaves with triangular bracing or
gussets.
Or B: Tie together the longitudinal
walls with a tension member to
prevent walls moving outward.

Figure 4.10. How a simple greenhouse structure must be braced to accommodate various loads and pressures.

joints. Figure 4.11 shows various methods of jointing in timber to give increasing strength and rigidity. It is worth noting that, with two connectors at any one joint, one is in effect setting up a miniature triangulated structure. The farther apart those connectors, the more rigid the structure, until with a plywood gusset joint one is in effect incorporating a piece of diagonal bracing.

JOINTS

All joints should be carefully considered in any greenhouse design. The joints are usual-ly the most expensive and certainly the most time-consuming parts of any structure. This is one reason why wood remains the most popular material for self-building work. The flexibility of a material that can be sawed, chiseled, glued and nailed, is attractive. Aluminum is the easiest of metals to work with, but allows much less room for error (since the structural members are much smaller). Detailing must be precise, and one is limited to using either nuts and bolts or rivets. Anticipating the fact that most people who design and build their own greenhouses will use wood, the following section is concerned in greater detail with that material.

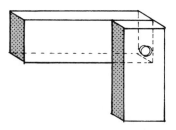

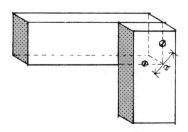

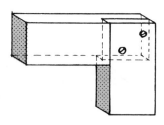

Pin joint made with single dowel or bolt. Has no rigidity.

Lapped joint for maximum rigidity must be glued and screwed (or bolted). Rigidity depends upon area of two timbers in contact and upon distance between fixings, (a). The greater this distance, the stronger the joint

Half-lapped joint. When well made this joint is stronger than a lapped joint because of the greater surface area in contact. Should be glued and screwed (or doweled if appearance is a major factor). A simple, easily constructed joint (no chiselling).

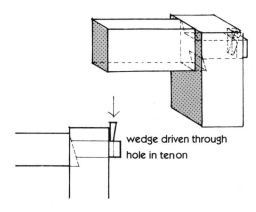

wedge driven through hole in tenon

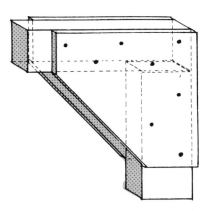

"Tusk" tenon joint —one of many variations on mortise and tenon joints, once the mainstay of carpenters and joiners. A well-made joint requires a lot of patience but achieves great strength and rigidity by using a simple wedge driven through the tenon. No glue; no simpler variations on the mortise & tenon principle are suitable for door & window frames.

Gusset joint. Plywood gussets glued to each side of the two pieces of timber and nailed (or screwed). The larger the area of the gusset the stronger the joint, until eventually the gusset becomes the cladding of the structure (note that timber cladding reduces the need for rigid joints).

Figure 4.11. Timber jointing techniques, increasing in strength from left to right. The framing diagram for timber greenhouses shows the approximate sizes of glazing bars and the structural bracing required for stability.

TIMBER SIZES

One of the most basic decisions in constructing a wooden greenhouse is the size of structural members to use. It is, of course, possible to calculate the load on each particular member and work out the exact minimum safe dimension of the piece of lumber required to carry that load. More than likely, however, one's decisions will be based on rough esti-

mates and experience of other structures. Take a look at some of the prefabricated greenhouses for sale and make a note of the sizes of studs and rafters and the spacing between them, in relation to the size of the greenhouse. A company selling prefabricated greenhouses will not want to put any more expensive bits of timber into them than is necessary, so you will be able to get some idea of the minimum size of the timber struts you will need.

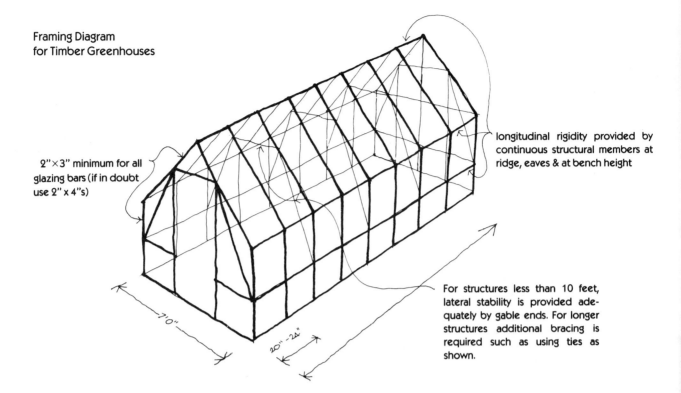

Framing Diagram
for Timber Greenhouses

2"×3" minimum for all glazing bars (if in doubt use 2" x 4"s)

longitudinal rigidity provided by continuous structural members at ridge, eaves & at bench height

7'0"

20"-24"

For structures less than 10 feet, lateral stability is provided adequately by gable ends. For longer structures additional bracing is required such as using ties as shown.

To add to these investigations, here is our own rough guide for the sizing of structural members needed for conventional timber-framed greenhouses. For rafter spans of up to seven feet, it is possible to get away with using 2 x 3s though 2 x 4s would give more room for error and provide a structure that you could climb over and swing from without worrying.

For small spans such as this, enough lateral rigidity would be provided by the joints in the woodwork and by the end walls, though for greenhouses of more than about ten feet long, some internal rafters should be reinforced with ties. For spans greater than about seven feet, the roof should be reinforced with ties at every rafter.

Longitudinal rigidity in a small structure is provided by the ridge beam and the wall plate at the eaves, provided that both are tied to the studs and rafters with secure joints. Additional bracing (as shown in Figure 4.11) would provide additional strength in areas where strong winds are common.

Stresses on the whole structure are greatly increased in areas of high wind or snow loads,

and it is always wise to increase the size of structural members to cope with the most severe loads. Using 2×6s throughout provides a much more solid structure, less likely to flex and thereby weaken at the joints. When using panes of glass that are larger than usual, it is necessary to increase the size of the studs accordingly.

Spacing of studs and rafters largely depends on what kind of covering material you use. Most materials require support at least every two feet, though plastic films and flat fiberglass sheets can take longer spans, being more flexible. Greenhouse glass comes in standard widths from 10 inches to two feet, with 20 inches and two feet being the most common.

Remember to take into account the width of studs and rafters as well as the glass when calculating the spacing between structural supports. For instance, 20-inch pieces of glass will fit between two-inch studs spaced every 22 inches if the glass fits between the studs, or every 21 inches if the glass fits into ½-inch rabbets cut into the studs.

QUALITY OF WOOD

Choose carefully the quality of wood used in any greenhouse. Whatever kind of lumber is used, it should be free from cracks; it should be straight, not warped; and it must be well seasoned, not green. If second-hand material is used, it should be substantially free from active woodworm, dry-rot and fungal attacks; and it is not a bad idea to treat all timber with a fungicide before using it.

Of various kinds of wood available, most hardwoods are expensive as well as being difficult to work with. Standard dimensional lumber (usually Douglas fir), available at any lumber yard, is often adequate, though individual pieces should be checked for straightness, lack of knots and shakes, or cracks along the grain. Western red cedar "heartwood" (cut from the center of the tree trunk) and California redwood are more expensive, but have the distinct advantage of being highly resistant to all forms of decay and fungal attack. They are therefore virtually maintenance-free because they do not require painting or coating with preservatives.

EXTERNAL FINISH

Also to be considered before buying lumber is the quality of the external finish. If a paint finish is anticipated, planed timbers should be used, since rough-sawed timber does not take paint well. If only a preservative will be used, then rough-sawed timber will provide an adequate surface because preservatives actually permeate the wood instead of forming a protective layer on top of it. In most climates, repainting will be necessary every three or four years to maintain a good finish, while preservatives last much longer. There are many kinds of wood preservatives on the market, but you must avoid those based on pentachloraphenol or creosote, which are poisonous to plants when they leach into the soil. All copper-based preservatives such as copper napthenate are suitable. Check ingredients on the label before buying.

Even if you intend to paint the greenhouse, you should still treat the wood with a preservative first. The paint provides a water-repellent layer—a smooth surface that water will run off—and when white paint is used, the amount of light admitted to the greenhouse is increased significantly. Wood preservative underneath paint prevents the timber from rotting should repainting be neglected.

Painting a greenhouse properly can be a laborious task. Because it is so easy to get a satisfying visual result quickly with a can of paint, it is all too easy to do a job that will only last a few months without showing signs of weathering. A strong exterior finish on woodwork requires a priming coat, at least one undercoat, and a thin top coat, preferably of high-gloss, oil-based paint. Before starting, fill all cracks and knots, and sand down any rough grain. A real old-time professional would sand down between coats too, so an even and smooth series of layers is built up on the wood. Thick coats of paint will tend to blister and crack more easily. And paint the structure before glazing to avoid all the finicky edges with the glass. When repainting, use a thin sheet of cardboard as a mask while painting around the glazing.

For a natural wood finish on softwood, you can use an external quality polyurethane gloss varnish on top of timber coated with preservative. The polyurethane, like paint, forms a strong water-repellent outer skin. And with several coats it is possible to build up a glass-like finish on the outside of the wood.

Paint and varnish decay because of constant temperature changes, causing expansion and contraction and eventually separating the layer of paint from the wood below, causing cracking. This is unavoidable. Wood begins to rot when moisture collects in various cracks and crevices and cannot dry out.

This is avoidable by designing the building carefully so it sheds water at every junction. Here are some useful waterproofing points to remember:

1. Make sure that every junction of two materials, from ridge, to eaves, to window sills, to base walls, and foundations is designed to shed water, not collect it or channel it into the building.

2. All horizontal joints exposed to the weather should be avoided. However tight they appear, they are natural places for water to collect. Where they are inevitable (e.g., at eaves or window sills) they should be protected by overhangs and "drips" (grooves which prevent the water from running back into the joint—see Figure 4.12).

3. Never expose end grain timber to the outside, particularly in exposed places. The only place where this is permissible is under sheltered eaves.

4. Give extra coats of preservative, polyurethane varnish or paint to all particularly exposed places, but do not just put more paint on; build up protection with several thin layers.

Figure 4.12. Details of a timber-framed glass greenhouse showing weatherproofing at typical junctions.

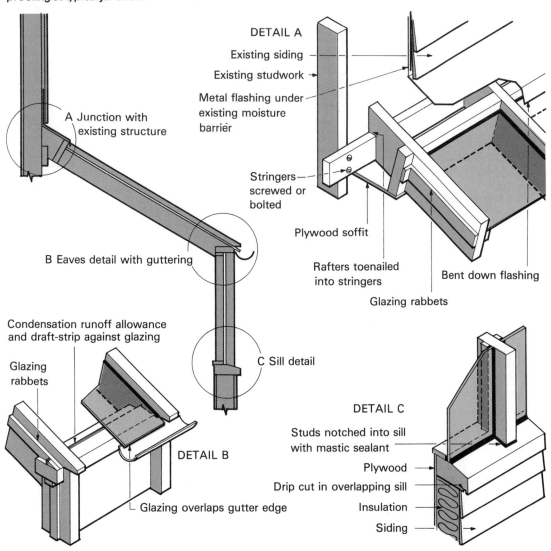

DETAIL A
Existing siding
Existing studwork
Metal flashing under existing moisture barrier
A Junction with existing structure
Stringers screwed or bolted
Plywood soffit
Rafters toenailed into stringers
Bent down flashing
Glazing rabbets
B Eaves detail with guttering

Condensation runoff allowance and draft-strip against glazing
Glazing rabbets
C Sill detail
DETAIL B
Glazing overlaps gutter edge

DETAIL C
Studs notched into sill with mastic sealant
Plywood
Drip cut in overlapping sill
Insulation
Siding

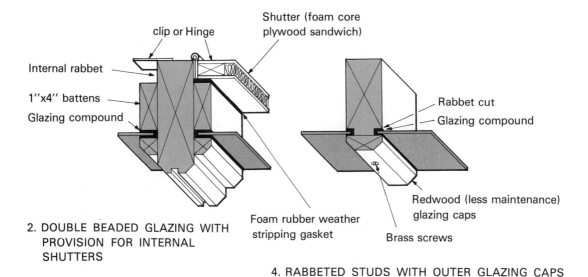

1. BEADED GLAZING WITH RABBETED STUDS

Rabbet cut

Glazing compound

Glazing beads
(this type construction
exposes joints to weather, detail
4, a more satisfactory method)

3. PUTTY GLAZING WITH STOP BEADS

Standard "lapped glass"
greenhouse glazing

1"x2" battens

Glazing fixed in secured
with glazing pins and
glazing compound

clip or Hinge

Shutter (foam core
plywood sandwich)

Internal rabbet

1"x4" battens

Glazing compound

2. DOUBLE BEADED GLAZING WITH PROVISION FOR INTERNAL SHUTTERS

Foam rubber weather
stripping gasket

Rabbet cut

Glazing compound

Redwood (less maintenance)
glazing caps

Brass screws

4. RABBETED STUDS WITH OUTER GLAZING CAPS

Figure 4.13. Various ways of building glazing bars for a timber-framed green-house.

5. All kinds of mastics and jointing compounds are available these days. If you are a first-class designer and craftsman, you might be able to do without them, but they are useful for protecting the odd bad detail.

Figure 4.12 shows some simple ways of detailing the various "junctions" found in any greenhouse structure, and Figure 4.13 shows various ways of constructing glazing bars for a timber-framed greenhouse. These details are more suitable for sunspaces attached to the home where a higher degree of finish is required, even though the construction is well within the capabilities of an amateur carpenter.

Freestanding greenhouses designed solely for plants need not be detailed so carefully. A lot of money and effort can be saved by using glazing materials such as fiberglass and polyethylene, which are easier to work with and can be fixed more easily to a simple framework made out of dimensional lumber.

References and Sources

Basic Construction Techniques for Houses & Small Buildings, Simply Explained, prepared originally by the Bureau of Naval Personnel. Dover Publications, New York. 1972. Paperback $5. Nearly 600 pages of information on all aspects of conventional construction, from logging operations to internal finishing.

Wood-Frame House Construction by L.O. Anderson. U.S. Department of Agriculture, Forest Service. Agricultural Handbook No. 73, revised 1970. The original standard text on simple frame construction techniques. Well illustrated, with all the basic information.

The National Greenhouse Company Catalog of Greenhouse Parts, Supplies and Accessories. National Greenhouse Company, Pana, Illinois 62577. The only greenhouse company that still sells (by mail order) redwood timber sections for conventional, well-designed timber greenhouses.

The Owner-Built Home and *The Owner-Built Homestead: A How-To-Do-It Book* by Ken and Barbara Kern. Charles Scribner's Sons, New York. 1975 and 1977. Both: hardcover $12.95 and paperback $6.95.

Build Your Own Greenhouse: How To Construct, Equip and Maintain It by Charles D. Neal. Chilton Book Co., Radnor, Pennsylvania. Hardcover $9.95. Very good on construction, plumbing and electrical work.

Your Homemade Greenhouse and How To Build It by Jack Kramer. Walker and Co., New York. $7.95. Easy-to-understand plans and details of several different types of greenhouses from window box to one-and-a-half story home extension.

5

Glazing Materials

For the first 2,000 years of greenhouses, glass was the only material available that could transmit and trap solar heat. But recently, a wide array of new transparent materials has flooded the market, confusing the would-be greenhouse owner with lists of advantages—which he may not want—and providing no basis for a sound comparative decision.

Strangely, though, no one has yet produced a material that combines all the most important qualities of glass: that it is resistant to all forms of decay, is scratchproof, highly transparent to the forms of solar radiation necessary for plant life, nonflammable, beautiful, and relatively cheap.

It is significant that every one of the new alternatives to glass is derived in some way from hydrocarbons, the main source of which is, of course, oil. Perhaps if we were not so deeply involved in oil-based chemistry, we would have long ago devoted more time to studying silicon, one of the most abundant materials on the surface of the earth and the basic material used in the manufacture of glass.

Having admitted openly their own preferences, the authors will now proceed to present a simple comparative analysis of various greenhouse glazing materials. Table 5.1 gives the basic facts and figures we are concerned with. And the following section offers further details about the materials themselves.

Table 5.1
Characteristics of Various Greenhouse Glazing Materials

MATERIAL	Glass		Fiberglass (flat)		Fiberglass (Corrugated)	Polyethylene		Polyvinyl Cloride	Polyester	Polyvinyl Flouride	Acrylic	Polycarbonate
TRADE NAMES	SSB (single strength grade B)	DSB (double strength grade B)	Filon, Lascolite, Resolite, Kaluwall, etc.	Most firms produce more than one grade	As for flat sheet	Visqueen Milrol Monsanto 602	Loretex Tu-Tuf	Filclair (reinforced)	Mylar	Tedlar	Plexiglass	Lexan
THICKNESS	1/16th inch	1/8th inch	4-8 oz per sq. ft. 20-40 mil.		As for flat sheet	Generally 2-8 mil.	3, 4, & 8 mil.	4-12 mil.	1-8 mil.	3 mil	1/10, 1/8 & 1/4 inch	1/16, 1/8, 3/16, 1/4 inch
AVAILABLE SIZES	Usually cut to the even inch (18, 20, & 24 inches are most common dimensions) Comes in boxes of 50 & 100 ft²		25" or 50" wide rolls up to 1200 ft long		26 & 52 inches wide, lengths from 6 to 30 feet	2 ft to 40 ft wide rolls up to 1000 ft long max width of unfolded roll—14 ft.		Generally 3 and 4 ft. wide 25-100 foot long	Rolls 48" wide 10-50 foot long	Rolls 26 and 50" wide 50 and 100 foot long	Generally 18 × 24 inches 36 × 48 inches other sizes available	Many sheet sizes available
LIGHT/HEAT TRANSMISSION — TO VISIBLE LIGHT	90%		95-85% (thicker sheets admit less light)		90-95%	85-90%		85%	90%	95%	91%	88%
TO TOTAL SOLAR RADIATION AT 90°	93%		90-75%			90-95%		90-95%	88%	93%	90% (1/8 inch)	86% (1/16 inch)
TO AVERAGE DAILY SOLAR RADIATION*	88% (DSB)		83% to 72% (25 mil) (40 mil)		78% (40 mil)	89% (4 mil)			87% (5 mil)	91% (3 mil)	~ 88%	85% (1/16 inch)
LONG WAVE TO THERMAL RADIATION*	3% (DSB)		12% (25 mil) to 6% (40 mil)		6% (40 mil)	85%			32% (5 mil)	43% (3 mil)	6%	6% (1/16 inch)
U VALUE†	1.13		0.7-0.95		0.7-0.95	1.60		1.30	1.05	1.16	1.09	1.10
EXPECTED LIFETIME	Unlimited except for breakage		3-4 years	20 years+ Manufacturers will provide figures on guaranteed lifetime	As for flat sheet	3-6 months (standard) 1-2 years (with U.V. inhibitors)	2-3 years (with U.V. inhibitors)	1-2 years (standard) 4-5 years (with U.V. inhibitors)	4-8 years	5-10 years	Unlimited but can be scratched & collects dirt	Unlimited, as for plexiglass
COST FACTOR (=APPROX ¢/ft² 1978 PRICES)	45	55	20-30	40-50	25-55	1-5	6-12	3-25	18-75	17	100-250	250-300
METHODS OF FIXING	Putty or glazing compounds, or dry glazing with gaskets and metal or wooden beads.		Nails or screws with rubber/plastic washers		Overlap corrugations & use special fixings	Staple to wooden framework together with a layer of vinyl batten tape, or trap between metal angles or timber battens.					As glass, can also be drilled & screwed	As acrylic
METHODS OF CUTTING	Wheel-type glass cutter required		Fine-tooth saw or shears			Knife or scissors					As glass can also be sawed with fine tooth saw	As acrylic
NOTES	Use only internally, or in small panes		Can be resurfaced with clear acrylic resin when "fuzziness" on surface begins to reduce transparency		Special foam draft strips available for eaves etc.	For external use, make sure film contains U.V. inhibitors			Good weatherability	Good weatherability & high solar transmission	Can be heat-formed and curved to shape	Very high impact resistance

†"U value" measures rate of heat transmission through the material, in vertical glazing conditions with a wind speed of 15 m.p.h. The higher the U value the faster the rate of heat loss through the material. Units are Btus/ft²hr.°F.
*Values taken from "Solar, Long Wave, and Photosynthetic Energy Transmission of Greenhouse Cover Materials."

Glass

Standard ⅛-inch-thick greenhouse glass transmits about 90 percent of all solar radiation. Solar radiation can be divided approximately into three different kinds of radiation with diferent wavelengths (Figure 5.2): (a) *ultraviolet radiation,* which gives us a sun tan; (b) *visible light,* which is useful because it allows us to see; and (c) *infrared radiation,* which constitutes most of the sun's heat, and together with visible light is useful for plant growth.

Glass transmits about 80 percent of the ultraviolet radiation, 90 percent of the visible light, and about 80 percent of the infrared radiation. This radiation is absorbed by plants in a greenhouse which manage to convert a minute fraction of it (usually less than 1 percent) into photosynthetic plant growth. The rest of the solar radiation is absorbed by plants and used in their process of transpiration (when the plant releases moisture to the surrounding atmosphere) or it is released in the form of heat, either to the surrounding air or by re-radiation to colder surfaces. Heat re-radiated from plants, however, occurs at a longer wavelength than solar radiation.

Solar radiation lies between wavelengths of 350 and 2,200 nanometers (nm), while the "thermal" radiation from the plants—or any object at around 95°F.—lies between 3,400 and 50,000 nm. At lower temperatures the thermal radiation reaches longer wave lengths. Glass will not transmit radiation at these wavelengths, thus it has the effect of "trapping" solar radiation. This is what is commonly known as the *greenhouse effect.*

This greenhouse effect does have its drawbacks, though. A greenhouse loses a great deal of heat, especially at night, by convection and by conduction. Convection losses take place when warm air escapes through leaks in the building; conduction occurs through the glass itself (glass has a relatively

Figure 5.2. Radiant energy transmittance of double-strength (1/8 inch) sheet glass. It transmits about 80 percent of ultraviolet radiation, 90 pecent of visible light, and about 80 percent of infrared.

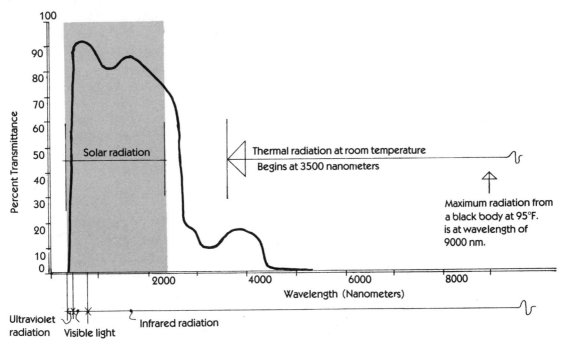

high thermal conductivity, or U value), which is heated from the inside by warmer air and by thermal radiation from plants and warmer surfaces. So the material needed by the ideal greenhouse would have high solar radiation transmittance, low thermal radiation transmittance, and low thermal conductivity. Anyone discovering such a material, providing it is relatively inexpensive, will completely revolutionize building technology!

SINGLE OR
DOUBLE GLAZING?

One way to decrease thermal conductivity, and thus reduce the building's heat loss, is to double glaze. But these gains take place at the expense of a slight loss in solar radiation transmittance. Every extra layer of glass reduces solar transmittance by 8 to 10 percent, but each additional air space cuts down on thermal conductivity, and thus cuts the building's heat loss.

Single glazing has a U value of around 1.13 Btu's per square foot per hour per degree Fahrenheit. For double glazing with a ¾-inch airspace, the U value is 0.65, and for triple glazing it is 0.36. It is significant that while double glazing can reduce heat loss by around 46 percent when compared to a single-glazed structure, adding a third layer results in an additional saving of only 16 percent, and is therefore not especially worthwhile. An air space of around 1½ inches is' optimal, though spaces between ¾ inch and 4 inches are considered effective. In wider air spaces, convection currents tend to form, increasing the heat loss between the two layers of glazing. With less than ¾ inch, the effectiveness of the air space is rapidly lost.

Several companies are working to develop an infrared reflective coating that can be applied to the surface of the glazing. This would have the effect of reflecting back a lot more of the thermal radiation from surfaces inside the greenhouse, which would otherwise be absorbed by the glass and conducted to the outside. Infrared reflective coatings on both inside surfaces of double glazing could reduce the overall U value to around 0.22 Btu's per square foot per hour.

One problem with any single-glazed greenhouse is the buildup of condensation on the inside surface of the glazing. The higher the temperature of the air, the more water vapor it can contain. Whenever the temperature of humid air (air containing a lot of water vapor) is lowered, as it is when in contact with the colder walls of the greenhouse, the water condenses into droplets which collect on the inside surface of the glazing. Condensation has the disadvantage of reducing the amount of light admitted to the greenhouse. Another disadvantage is that drips of water from the glass can damage plants below. On cold nights, however, the condensation layer can be an advantage since it causes a substantial reduction in heat loss by thermal radiation to the night sky. (This is especially true with plastic film greenhouses which transmit a high proportion of thermal radiation.)

Double glazing reduces condensation because it helps to keep the internal surface of the glazing warmer. Alternatively, spray-on coatings are also available to prevent the condensation layer from causing a reduction in light transmittance during the daytime. The coating becomes almost opaque when dry (as in summer, when there is often too much heat and little likelihood of condensation) and more transparent when wet (in winter, when the low temperature of the glazing is likely to cause condensation). When condensation does occur, it does not form into tiny droplets causing a reduction in light transmittance, but into a smooth wet layer on the surface of the glazing that is completely transparent. When relative humidity is low, and yet more light is desired, the film coating can be sprayed quickly with water to turn it transparent. These coatings are available for both glass and plastic greenhouses, and are well used in the greenhouse business. (They are manufactured by Solar Sunstill Inc., Setauket, New York 11733.)

WORKING WITH GLASS

When designing a greenhouse, use standard-size panes of glass. Greenhouse glass comes in widths of even inches, most often 20 or 24 inches, and the panes usually are square. But it will be necessary, no matter how well you plan the construction, to cut the odd-sized pane of glass. It is a difficult material to work with, but provided necessary care is taken, glass cutting is well within the scope of even the inexperienced amateur builder.

New glass is easy to cut. Old glass, because its molecular structure changes over time, is more likely to shatter. To cut a piece of glass, mark accurately with a felt-tip pen where you want to cut. Place a straight edge—preferably metal—along the line and with a single-wheel or diamond-point glass cutter (available at any hardware store), score along the line. Use a firm, even pressure from one edge of the glass to the other in one smooth stroke. Avoid having to repeat the scoring because it is unlikely your two lines will coincide precisely, and a rough or crazed cut will not break cleanly. Place the glass over the straight edge, or a straight piece of timber, with the scored line just over the edge of the timber. With one hand on each side of the line, press down firmly and the glass should break cleanly down the line.

When cutting off a narrow edge of glass, where it is impossible to put even pressure on the side to be broken off, use the "teeth" provided on the side of the cutter (or a pair of pliers) to "nibble" away at the edge. It may require several attempts before you get the knack of glass cutting, but it's something that can be done easily with a bit of experience.

Breakage will be a major problem only in areas where heavy hail storms occur regularly—in which case greenhouse glass should be protected with wire mesh. For those worried about glass breaking and injuring someone, tempered glass is less likely to cause dangerous cuts because it shatters into tiny pieces rather than large shards. Tempered glass also offers much more resistance to hail, wind and snow, but it is about 50 percent more expensive than standard window glass, and is not available in thicknesses of less than ¼ inch. Wired glass is less expensive and also offers assurance against injury if broken. It is often used in skylights where there is a danger of glass falling on someone. Wired glass also offers superior fire resistance in case there is any question of meeting municipal fire regulations.

GLAZING COMPOUNDS

Many commercial glazing compounds are on the market now, all seeking to replace the older but still useful material, putty. Putty is an oil-based compound that is soft to work with, but sets hard within a few days on the exterior. Inside, putty remains softer and resilient for a long time.

Glazing with putty is not difficult. It should be kneaded like playdough to make it more pliable, and pressed into the grooves where the glass is to fit. With an even layer of putty all around the opening, press the glass into place so that only a small layer (at most 1/16 inch) remains between the glass and frame. Pressing the glass into position should squeeze the excess putty through the gap between the glass and frame, both inside and outside the glass. Next, anchor the glass in place using glazing pins and a small pin hammer (there is such a device as a special glazing hammer). Drive the pins into the frame parallel to the glass and tight against it. If you are using a metal frame, you will require some commercial glazing clips that should come with the frame. These usually snap into position. Scrape off any excess putty on the outside of the glass, using a putty knife (in this case, it is worth getting the right tool, but you can make do with an old kitchen knife). Make as neat a joint as you can between putty and frame, especially at the bottom of the glass where the putty must allow water running down the glass to run over the edge of the frame and not collect in the groove.

Because putty is oil-based, unpainted or unprimed wood will absorb all the oil from the putty too fast and cause it to crack and allow water to seep in. Wooden structures, therefore, should always be primed or sealed before glazing with putty. For metal structures, use metal casement putty or a suitable commercial compound.

GLASS JOINTS

Standard practice in greenhouse glazing is to use overlapping glass joints. This is mostly for reasons of economy, though it also reduces the surface area of the frame and therefore admits more light. While the overlapping method is fairly easy, it tends to collect dirt and look unsightly; and it makes ventilation (and therefore temperature) more difficult to control because the overlap allows cold air to infiltrate the greenhouse.

If the greenhouse is to be part of the home, it is probably more suitable to use conventional horizontal glazing bars and make a series of windows, or use longer pieces of glass. On a sloping roof it is difficult to use horizontal supports because they inevitably prevent the roof from shedding rainwater properly, since the horizontal support is bound to have some kind of ledge that will collect water. One way to avoid this problem would be to use *silicone jointing compound* between abutting pieces of glass. This is a strong, translucent material. It is available in a tube dispenser, and a neat joint can be made fairly easily between two pieces of glass —a joint that is in fact much stronger than the glass itself. It is also useful for mending large pieces of broken glass. Unlike many recent mastics and jointing compounds, this material does represent a significant technological breakthrough, and it is worth considering how it can help your design if you intend to build a glass building.

Plastic Films

POLYETHYLENE

Polyethylene film (otherwise known as *poly* or *P.E.*) is the cheap-and-easy, low-cost, short-cut answer to enclosing and greenhouse. It is especially suitable for temporary structures, repairs to existing buildings, and as a stop-gap in situations where it may not be possible to glaze a structure immediately with more permanent material.

Do not expect polyethylene to last more than a few months, and in really hot, dry summers, any kind of "poly" may not last even that long. The thicker the film, the more resistant it is to wind and snow loads, and to breakdown by ultraviolet radiation, which is the prime cause of decay in polyethylene films. Ultraviolet inhibitors are now added to many films to slow this process, but at the most they will only double their brief lifetimes.

Yet many commercial growers prefer polyethylene. It is easy to put up and replace, and the cost of hail damage is not great. It can be removed easily during summer to allow plants to grow outside, if the climate permits this, and thus saves cost in watering and ventilating. On one hand, the thinner films admit slightly more sunlight than glass in wavelengths suitable for plant growth, but on the other hand they transmit about 80 percent of thermal radiation, which greatly increases heat losses to a cold night sky.

Anyone who has witnessed the polyethylene dump sites associated with many commercial plant nurseries will realize the horrendous problem presented by the disposal of this material after its usefulness has ended. It is also worth remembering that all those piles of useless polyethylene—like all the plastic alternatives to glass—represent another bit of the world's diminishing oil supply.

OTHER PLASTIC FILMS

Other types of plastic films are available that have better weathering characteristics than polyethylene, and are less transparent to long-wave thermal radiation. *Tedlar* has a particularly high light transmission, which makes it useful for double or triple glazing where light transmission can easily be cut significantly. *Vinyl film* is tougher than polyethylene and generally comes in thicker films that provide a strong, tear-resistant glazing. *Mylar* and *Tedlar*, both made by Dupont, have much better weathering characteristics than either polyethylene or vinyl, and they have much better resistance to ultraviolet degradation.

Both polyethylene and vinyl films are obtainable with a woven core. These stand up better to high winds and snow loads, and are useful in severe climates.

FIXING PLASTIC FILMS

Plastic films are easy to fix to a wooden frame, using a simple staple gun. A layer of canvas or polypropylene tape, or thin wooden strips, should be placed over the film wherever it is stapled, to reinforce the joint and prevent the staples from pulling through. Use as few folds as possible (i.e., buy wide rolls of film) because ultraviolet deterioration occurs first at the folds. A framework that supports plastic film should have a smooth outer surface, free from sharp edges or joints so the film can be draped over the whole structure without any danger of being pierced. For this reason, arched-frame or quonset-type greenhouses make the most suitable shapes for a polyethylene skin.

Several patented methods of fastening plastic films to a metal frame are now available, such as the *Ziplock* system. This involves trapping the layer of plastic film between two aluminum sections so it is evenly supported along the length of the metal struts.

Polyethylene and vinyl both can be heat-sealed at joints to provide a continous skin. this is done with a small gadget you can purchase that traps the two layers and heats them to exactly the right temperature so they fuse. Heat-sealing thick vinyl sheets should be done with commercial equipment usually available at plastics fabricators. Two layers of thick vinyl film, heat-sealed around the edges and inflated through a valve inserted in one side, produce a structurally rigid double-glazed "pillow" that has good thermal

Figure 5.3. Quonset-type greenhouses such as this one are suitable shapes for stretching a plastic skin over. This one has an entryway wide enough so a tractor can enter it for mechanized cultivation.

insulation qualities and can be used to rigidify lightweight timber structures. Some research suggests that the increase in insulation is offset by the fact that the double skin prevents the formation of condensation inside the greenhouse at night, and this condensation reduces heat losses by re-radiation.

Of all double-glazing systems, the most cost-effective for reducing heating needs, and the easiest to erect, consists of an internal layer of polyethylene inside an external layer of glass. The polyethylene can be stapled to the inside of timber glazing bars easily and, since glass cuts down a lot of the ultraviolet radiation, the polyethylene has a longer lifetime. Most authorities suggest that this type of double glazing will reduce winter heating costs by at least 20 percent, with a minimum of capital cost.

Fiberglass

Fiberglass is a term used loosely for all forms of glass-reinforced plastic (GRP) and fiber-reinforced plastic (FRP). It is generally translucent—it admits light, but one cannot actually see through it—and it appears to let in less light than fully transparent materials. Actually, it transmits at least as much useful solar radiation as glass, and often more. It also diffuses light more, which most plants enjoy.

Fiberglass comes in corrugated and flat sheets. The corrugated design has greater rigidity in the direction of the corrugations, and it is generally wide enough (26 inches) to allow for an overlap of one corrugation (2 inches) when the sheets are fixed to joists or studs at two-foot centers.

Flat sheets come in rolls, usually four feet wide. But without corrugation, the fiberglass requires fairly frequent supports, both parallel and perpendicular to the length of the roll. When used on a vertical wall, horizontal supports are needed only at the edges of the sheets, at ground and eaves level. When flat fiberglass is used on a sloping roof, however, support should be by means of joists at two-foot centers, with purlins (spanning between the joists) at three- or four-foot centers to keep the material from sagging.

Fiberglass is an easy material to work with. It can be cut with a fine-tooth saw or sheet-metal cutters; and it can be drilled, screwed, and nailed fairly easily. You must use protective rubber washers with nails or screws, and these are available wherever you buy the material.

Fiberglass comes in different grades, based on the quality and durability of both the fiber or glass cloth, which acts as reinforcement, and the resin, which provides the rigidity.

With an outer layer of a hard-weathering resin, such as *Tedlar* or PVF (polyvinyl fluoride), the fiberglass will last for twenty years or more. Other lower-quality resin finishes weather away more quickly, exposing the fibers below and causing a fuzzy texture. This texture considerably reduces light transmittance and weakens the material structurally. When the first signs of "fuzz" appear, you should refinish the fiberglass by rubbing it down with a medium grade of steel wool, and paint it with a coat of resin, available from any fiberglass retailer. Take care in selecting an appropriate time to do this. Hot weather will tend to break down the initial bond between the resin and the old surface, and rain will impair the newly made surface. Check the quality before buying any fiberglass. A reputable manufacturer should provide information on how long it will last under average conditions before it needs refinishing.

You can also make your own fiberglass sheets if you wish to start with the basic materials—fiber cloth and resin. These can be molded into fairly intricate and curved shapes if your design requires it. A good fiberlass roller (a series of small metal wheels on one axle) is needed to insure a good bond between resin and cloth, and force out any air that gets caught in between. Working with fiberglass is a useful extension of one's do-it-yourself skills, because the material has many useful applications.

Clear Rigid Plastics

Clear, rigid plastics such as *Lexan* and *Plexiglass* look much like glass. They have similar optical properties, with a solar radiation transmission of around 85 percent or more. They can be sawed with a fine-tooth saw, and heated and bent into curved shapes. They can be drilled and screwed into place, and jointed easily using a transparent solvent cement. Their major advantages over glass are superior strength and the ability to be bent into shapes. Their big disadvantage is their high cost. They also tend to scratch easily, and the surface is then virtually irreparable.

When installing sheets of these rigid plastics, leave the protective paper covering on until the sheet is in place, and then remove it immediately. When exposed to sunlight, the protective covering tends to stick to the plastic and becomes difficult to remove without damaging the surface. For this reason, the sheets should be stored out of the sunlight and in a cool place before use.

A rigid cellular double glazing made in both acrylic and polycarbonate is sold under the name *Acrylite*. This is very strong and can be used with lightweight structural members at spans of as much as 45 inches on center. In the acrylic form, the sheet has a high solar transmission (86 percent) and a U value as good as sealed double-glazing units (0.55) at a lower cost. The polycarbonate form is more expensive and manufactured mainly for its higher impact resistance.

Advances are continually being made in the science of glazing materials, both glass and plastics. New materials generally tend to take a long time before they are commercially available on a large scale and at a reasonable cost for the domestic greenhouse builder.

Weathering characteristics cannot, of course, be fully tested until a lifetime's field use is completed. There are already many claims against the premium-grade fiberglass manufacturers whose materials, guaranteed for twenty years, have been known to break down within five.

You cannot go wrong with standard window glass. Though it may cost more in both time and money initially, it remains the most useful of all the glazing materials.

Manufacturers and References

MANUFACTURERS

Glazing and double glazing (Thermopane) units:

Pittsburgh Plate Glass, One Gateway Center, Pittsburgh, Pennsylvania
Libbey-Owens-Ford Glass, Toledo, Ohio
American-Saint Gobain, Kingsport, Tennessee

Fiberglass:

Filon Corporation, 12333 South Van Ness Ave., Hawthorne, California 90250
Kalwall Corporation, 88 Pine St., Manchester, New Hampshire 03103
Lasco Industrial, 8015 Dixon Drive, Florence, Kentucky 41042

Lascolite Corporation, 3255 East Mira Loma Ave., Anaheim, California 92806
Resolite and Barelite, available from E.C. Geiger, Nursery Supplies, Box 285, Route 63, Harleysville, Pennsylvania 19438

Acrylic and Polycarbonate:

Rohm and Haas (acrylic), Independence Mall, Philadelphia, Pennsylvania 19105
Lexan (polycarbonate), General Electric, One Plastics Avenue, Pittsfield, Massachusetts 01201
Cyro Industries (acrylic), Wayne, New Jersey 07470

Plastic films:

Filiclair (reinforced PVC), 11 Glen Cameron Road, Thornhill, Ontario, Canada

Lorentex (woven polyethylene), American Bleached Goods Inc., 1460 Broadway, New York, New York 10036

Milrol (polyethylene), Canadian Industries Ltd., Box 10, Montreal, Quebec, Canada H3C 2R3

Mylar (polyester), Dupont de Nemours Inc., Wilmington, Delaware 19898

Tedlar (polyvinylfluoride), Dupont de Nemours Inc., Wilmington, Delaware 19898

Tu Tuf (reinforced polyethylene), Sto-Cote Products Inc., 2139 North Wayne Ave., Chicago, Illinois 60614

Vinyl, B.F. Goodrich Chemical Co., 3135 Euclid Ave., Cleveland, Ohio 44115

Insulated glazing:

Sunwall, Kalwall Corporation, 1111 Candia Road, Manchester, New Hampshire 03103. Fiberglass panels bonded to an aluminum grid core, made to a number of standard specifications. Panels are normally 2¾ inches thick, 4 or 5 feet wide, and 3 to 16 feet long. Clear spans of 8 feet 6 inches are possible for sheltered roofs. Standard solar transmission and Uvalues are shown.

Wasco-O'Keefe Skylights, Wasco Products Inc., Box 351, Sanford, Maine 04073. Manufacturers of double-skinned acrylic glazings for purpose-built skylights.

Suntek Corporation, Corte Madera, California 94925. This firm has a long history in the development of new materials for solar heating. It makes "transparent insulation," which is a system of glazing using multiple layers of highly transparent polymer film. Four layers of the film lining a standard glazed opening produces a U value of 0.2 (2½ times as good as double glazing) and an overall transparency of 76 percent. The polymer film retails at 35 cents per square foot.

Sunwall is available in multi-layered versions with increasing insulating values, decreasing solar transmission. In the chart below, the suffix to Sunwall denotes the number of air spaces, i.e. Sunwall III has three airspaces, four faces.

Sunwall	*Standard Solar* Transmission	"U"
I	77%	.41
II	70%	.35
III	65%	.28
IV	N/A	—
V	N/A	—

*Estimated @ 0° incident angle. Grid not included.

REFERENCES

"Solar, Long Wave, and Photosynthetic Energy Transmission of Greenhouse Cover Materials" by Bond, Gobey and Zornig, in *The Proceedings of a Conference on Solar Energy for Heating Greenhouses and Greenhouse-Residential Combinations,* March, 1977, Cleveland, Ohio. Available from: Department of Agricultural Engineering, Ohio Agricultural Research and Development Corporation, Wooster, Ohio, 44691. Paperback $5. A complete study of nine different glazing materials and their combinations in the form of double glazing.

"Greenhouse Coverings" by R.A. Aldrich and "Environmental Equipment and Traditional Energy Considerations for Heating Systems" by J.N. Walker and G.A. Duncan. Both published in the *Proceedings of the Tennessee Valley Greenhouse Vegetable Workshop.* March, 1975. Papers published by the National Fertilizer Development Center, Tennessee Valley Authority, Muscle Shoals, Alabama 35660. Useful information on the use of new glazing materials in the commercial greenhouse field.

6

Auxiliary Greenhouse Equipment

The business of selling greenhouses is flourishing. Like many hardware industries, it tends to produce gadgets that aren't really necessary and sells them to the public as if they were absolutely vital. If you buy a greenhouse these days, the manufacturer will try his best to double the amount you spend on the shell by offering you packaged heaters, coolers, humidifiers, and watering systems, all automatically controlled so you can go away and leave the plants to grow by themselves. It is worth analyzing the cost of a proposed greenhouse in detail and remembering that the equipment costs will considerably increase your initial outlay and running costs.

Such gadgetry is of course more necessary in a greenhouse structure that is designed without any thought of responding to the climate. Conventional greenhouses are designed with the expectation that the owner will only pay a visit occasionally to make sure all his automated garden aids are working well for him.

If you design and build your own greenhouse on the principles of solar energy capture and thermal storage outlined in Section IV, and you are prepared to perform a lot of the simple tasks of climate control manually, you can cut down considerably on your outlay and running costs. A glass-to-ground greenhouse is likely to experience wide environmental fluctuations that do not occur to the same extent in a greenhouse which has a lower rate of heat loss and a higher thermal capacity. The former requires regular attention, which can often only be provided by automated controls on heaters and ventilators. The latter, being a better balanced system, can cope on its own, unattended, for longer periods, though it may require brief attention once or twice a day.

The best solution is generally not one of the two extremes, but a combination of both approaches. Greenhouses that rely on solar heat for eleven months of the year may require an additional boost of artificial heat to protect the plants during the twelfth month. Certain automated controls, such as thermostatically operated ventilators and small unit heaters, can be useful if you cannot provide the required attention every day.

The wide variety of environmental control equipment should be studied carefully before you make any purchase. Decide whether you really need it, whether it is a suitable size for your greenhouse, and how long it will actually last in a greenhouse climate, which is ideal for encouraging corrosion. Visit as many garden centers as you can and check on options available. Also write for the literature of the big reputable mail-order firms that stock a wide range of equipment for both commercial and home greenhouse owners. A list of these firms accompanies this chapter.

Heating Equipment

The heating system in your greenhouse must have an adequate capacity to provide a continuous supply of heat equal to that which the greenhouse is losing to the outside air in the worst winter conditions. Simple procedures for calculating heat loss are outlined in Chapter 10. Most greenhouse companies will give their own rules of thumb for sizing the heating system you will require. If you design and build your own structure, it is a fairly simple procedure to estimate the size of heater you may require with as much accuracy as the companies selling packaged units.

Major Greenhouse Equipment & Supplies Companies

E.C. Geiger
Box 285
Harleysville, Pa.
Phone: (215) 256-6511

Lord and Burnham
Division of Burnham Corp.
Irvington, N.Y. 10533

Texas Greenhouse Co. Inc.
2717 St. Louis Avenue
Fort Worth, Texas 76110
Phone: (817) 926-5447

Everlite Aluminum Greenhouses Inc.
14615 Lorain Avenue
Cleveland, Ohio 44111
Phone: (216) 251-5572

Pacific Coast Greenhouse Mfg. Co.
430 Hurlingham Avenue
Redwood City, Calif. 94063
Phone: (415) 366-7672

National Greenhouse Company
Pana, Ill. 62557
Phone: (217) 562-3919

J.A. Nearing Co. Inc. (Janco)
10788 Tucker St.
Beltsville, Md. 20705
Phone: (301) 937-3300

EXISTING HEAT SOURCES

If your greenhouse is attached to the house, you may be able to heat it from the same boiler, furnace or stove that heats your house. Heating the greenhouse could be as simple a process as opening a few doors or vents through into the house, possibly with the assistance of a fan to achieve proper air circulation. Alternatively, you could run a separate system off your furnace if it has enough extra capacity and is suitably located. With a hot-air furnace in the basement it is a relatively simple operation to run an extra duct to a lean-to greenhouse on the south side of the building. A separate damper control and thermostat would be needed to control the greenhouse temperature. Seek the advice of a heating contractor before you undertake any work on the system. If your furnace does not have the extra capacity, you could perhaps achieve it by increasing the insulation of your house so you are not making as great a demand on the system as before. Remember, too, that the addition of a lean-to greenhouse will cut down slightly on the amount of heat the house itself requires.

Waste heat from household appliances can also be used to heat a lean-to greenhouse. The warm, humid air from a clothes dryer in the basement or utility room is normally vented to the outside air. This generally amounts to a lot of useful heat with a high moisture content that many plants like. Beware of using the exhaust from a gas-fired clothes dryer, however, since it may contain gases resulting from incomplete combustion which are harmful to plants, and will cause yellowing and scorching of the leaves. Freezers and refrigerators are also sources of "waste" heat. A 15-cubic-foot freezer provides at least 100 kw. of energy (340,000 Btu's) per month which is pumped out of the food you put in the freezer. This is a useful amount of heat for a small greenhouse-cum-utility room. If you have a chest-type freezer with a well-sealed lid, you should not have any problems with

the leakage of cold air causing cool spots in the greenhouse. An upright freezer, however, would leak a lot of cold air every time you open it (consequently it is much less efficient to run).

GREENHOUSE HEATERS

If it is impossible to heat your greenhouse from your house, then it will be necessary to install a separate heater. The questions then to be asked include the type of fuel, the initial costs and running costs of the system, and what degree of automation you require.

The choice of fuel is a major determinant. In terms of initial cost, an electric heater is cheaper to install—though you do require a separate fused circuit for it—but the running costs are probably more expensive than burning your own fuel. Utility costs vary considerably throughout the country. Electricity is theoretically clean and efficient, but it is worth remembering the considerable pollution caused by burning fuel to make electricity, though the power station may not be close enough for you to observe the effects yourself. Remember, too, that every time you increase your electricity usage, you increase our dependence on high-grade energy and ultimately provide nuclear energy enthusiasts with more reasons for advocating a plutonium economy. Electricity may *appear* to be 100 percent efficient, but it is worth considering its overall efficiency in terms of spent fuel at the generating station. Few of these run at more than 35 percent efficiency, so if you are concerned about saving energy and you use electricity for heating, you may be cutting down your own fuel bill but increasing society's.

Electric heaters should only be used in situations where a small amount of back-up heat is required in the middle of winter, or when you provide heat direct to the roots of the plant using soil-warming cables where there is no real alternative to using electricity.

Electric fan heaters (Figure 6.1) have the advantages that they are easy to install, do not require venting, and can be moved around easily. The fan can be used in summer without the heater to create better air movement and ventilation. Appliances are usually rated at between 1 and 5 kw. (providing between 3,000 and 17,000 Btu's per hour). The effectiveness of the fan should be considered in relation to the size of the building. Manufacturers will generally provide data on how far a fan will throw air. Air in a greenhouse should be moved around slowly in winter. Plants in the way of a powerful blast of hot dry air will suffer a great deal. It may therefore be worth purchasing two smaller units rather than one large one.

Any electricity installation will have to comply with local building codes, and they may require the work to be done by a qualified electrician whether or not you are capable of doing it yourself. Remember that extra safeguards against short-circuiting have to be taken in greenhouse installation where moist air can easily cause shorts to occur. Make sure the system is properly protected by a fuse or circuit breaker of the appropriate size. Check beforehand whether the heater will require a 110- or 220-volt supply, and make sure everything is properly grounded.

Figure 6.1. An electric fan heater.

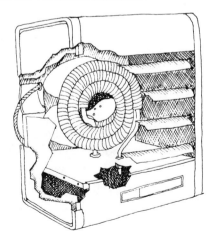

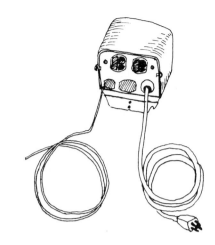

Figure 6.2. Soil-warming cables.

Soil-warming cables are the most effective way of heating hot beds, frames and propagating cases. The electric element usually heats up to about 70° F. It is buried four to six inches in the soil, usually in a layer of sand. To protect the cables against sharp trowels and spades, a layer of half-inch chicken wire or hardware cloth should be placed on top of the cables. Manufacturers usually suggest a coverage of about 10 to 15 watts per square foot, and the cables usually have a capacity of between 3 and 7 watts per foot length of cable. Cheap soil-warming cables, suitable for about 36 square feet of greenhouse soil bed, can be purchased for as little as $30, complete with thermostat and 120-volt plug (Figure 6.2). More heavy-duty, longer-lasting heating cables with a protective lead covering and more sensitive temperature controls can cost around $70 for the same power output, and are guaranteed to last many years.

Propagating mats (Figure 6.3) are similar to soil-warming cables though they look more like electric blankets. The heating cables are embedded in a tough plastic mat that can be placed underneath seed flats or plant pots. The temperature can be controlled with a simple thermostat. A temporary plastic shroud placed over the seed flats will insure a warm, humid environment in part of your greenhouse that is ideal for germination and propagation.

Figure 6.3. A propagating mat.

Electricity is ideal for small localized heat supply, but if your greenhouse requires a fairly continuous supply of heat of more than about 5 kw. (17,000 Btu's) then you would be better off with a gas- or oil-burning unit.

Gas heaters are cleaner and easier to install. It is possible to run gas heaters on propane or natural gas without flues. Certain manufacturers advocate this on the principle that the output from the heater, carbon dioxide, is actually used by the plants during photosynthesis. Yet any decrease in the supply of combustion air, or any draft near the heater, could easily cause it to function badly, resulting in incomplete combustion that produces fumes noxious to plants. If you do install a gas heater, be sure it is the type installed in the outside wall and vents all its combustion gas to the outside, or has a well-constructed sealed flue. The heat is then directed inside by means of an electric fan. Sizes range from 15 to 30,000 Btu's (Figure 6.4) for domestic greenhouses, though larger units working on a similar principle are available for commercial installations. To get an even distribution of heat, these units generally have a distribution duct attached that is made of clear plastic perforated with holes at regular intervals through which warm air can escape. The plastic tube is generally suspended from the structure of the greenhouse. One advantage of fan-assisted gas heaters is that they can be used for ventilation in summer.

Certain types of *gas- or kerosene-burning domestic heaters* available through hardware stores can be adapted to greenhouse heating. This kind of heater should preferably be located outside the greenhouse itself, or, if it is inside, should be well vented with a metal or masonry flue pipe, and provided with a supply of combustion air direct from the outside. This kind of heater often comes with an *electric blower* attached, to distribute the heat more efficiently, and sometimes with a *thermostatic control*. The thermostat will most likely be suitable for residential use (i.e. 60 to 80°F.). Lord and Burnham suggests that you buy this kind of heater locally, without the thermostat and purchase one of its greenhouse thermostats by mail order to replace it.

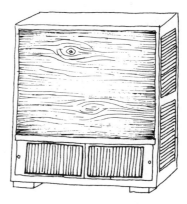

Figure 6.4. A gas-fired heater.

Oil-fired heaters are manufactured specifically for greenhouse heating, though they are generally of a large capacity, around 100,000 Btu's, and require a complete forced air, hot water, or steam distribution system similar to domestic heating (Figure 6.5). This obviously involves a large capital outlay, and is suitable only if you have a large greenhouse for growing tropical plants. Steam heating systems have the additional advantage that the steam can be used to sterilize your greenhouse soil.

All thermostatic controls, particularly the cheaper ones, should be checked against a good thermometer every now and then. Keep the thermostat well shaded and the sensor

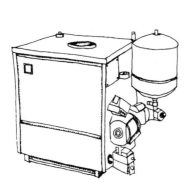
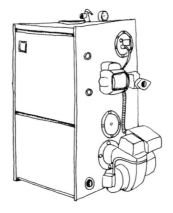

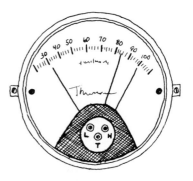

Figure 6.5. Oil-fired heaters.

terminals clean and free from dust, cobwebs and moisture.

Thermometers themselves are most useful greenhouse aids. It is worth placing them in different parts of your greenhouse to assess the way it performs and responds both to solar heat gain and to your artificial heating system. Use maximum-minimum thermometers to check on the temperature extremes your plants undergo. *Soil thermometers* (Figure 6.6) are also available from major suppliers. These have a metal prong attached to the thermometer dial that reads the temperature of the soil four or five inches down. By keeping a watchful eye on your greenhouse during the first winter, you will soon find out where the coldest spots are and may have to redirect your heating system to improve

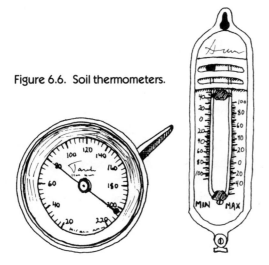

Figure 6.6. Soil thermometers.

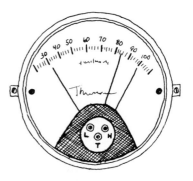

Figure 6.7. A temperature alarm.

those areas, or make sure you do not put the most sensitive plants there.

Temperature alarms (Figure 6.7) costing about $30 may be useful in telling you when your greenhouse needs attention. These gadgets set off an electric alarm bell when the temperature rises above or falls below predetermined settings. You may resent being dragged out of bed to switch on an extra heater, but if it means saving your winter vegetable crop from frost, it may be worthwhile.

Shading

Besides selling you an artificially controlled winter environment, a greenhouse salesman will try to sell you a whole range of equipment that will keep your greenhouse artificially cool in summer. Obviously the kind of greenhouse available on the commercial market will tend to overheat in summer because the intense midday sun is allowed direct access all day through the glass roof. If you have designed your greenhouse for maximum winter heat gain, then it will not overheat as readily in summer since the overhead sun will be excluded at least partially by a solid roof. The simplest way to prevent overheating is to exclude the sun in the first place, and this can be done by judicious planting so that summer foliage outside the greenhouse cuts out the overhead sun, or by using projecting rafters to form overhanging eaves in summer by draping them with bamboo mats or reeds (Figure 6.8).

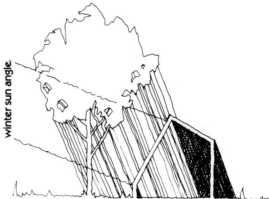
Deciduous trees in front of greenhouse provide shading in summer yet admit winter sunshine.

WHITEWASH

If you cannot rely on natural shading, it may be necessary to use some kind of external shade to cover your greenhouse glass in summer. The traditional method is to paint the glass itself with whitewash. If you paint the outside of the glass it will mean less disruption inside and the coat of whitewash should last through the summer rains and can be washed off with soap and water in the fall. Whitewash has been superseded these days by special shading compounds which can be purchased either in powder or liquid form. These are more effective though more expensive than whitewash, which contains lime that can cause deterioration in putty and paint. Commercial shading compounds can be diluted to the required strength and applied by roller (it is often useful to tie the roller to the end of a broom handle to extend your reach) or by spray gun. Ordinary latex housepaint diluted about 1:10 with water can also be used. All liquid shading compounds should be applied when the glass is cool, or else bubbles and blisters can occur. Compounds are also available for plastic films and fiberglass where whitewash or latex paint would be unsuitable.

Bamboo mats or timber slats can be laid across projecting rafters to provide partial shade when required. Solid roofs automatically exclude summer sun.

Vines & creepers can be trained up external trellises to provide natural shading in summer.

Figure 6.8. Three techniques for providing natural shading of a greenhouse. All are based on the sun's low rays in winter, high ones in summer.

BLINDS

If you do not require permanent shading during the summer, then a semitransparent fabric or slatted blind can be used when necessary and removed or rolled up during cloudy weather. The cheapest kind of external shading fabric is plastic shade cloth (Figure 6.9).

Figure 6.9. Plastic shade cloth.

There are various types of material on the market offering between 15 and 65 percent reduction in light transmission. The best materials are *woven polyester* and *polypropylene,* costing between 10 and 15 cents per square foot. These will last about four or five seasons before deteriorating in ultraviolet light. *Saranshade* (PVC) is heavier than polypropylene and not as strong. It is also more likely to shrink. Plastic shadecloth can be stapled or laced onto the outside of the building, or it can be fixed onto rollers at the ridge of the greenhouse and raised or lowered as necessary by means of pull cords.

A more traditional and durable shade is the *external roller blind* of wooden slats or bamboo, strung together and suspended from the ridge (Figure 6.10). This too can be pulled down and retracted easily from below. Most manufacturers will provide some kind of

Figure 6.10. Slatted roll-up shades.

blind to suit the size of their greenhouses as optional extras. Some companies make roller blinds of slatted aluminum that are lighter and more hard wearing than wood or bamboo, and also reflect the light very well. You pay for the extra quality.

Blinds are most effective and easiest to install on the outside of a greenhouse. They intercept the solar radiation before it has a chance to get through the glazing, and they do not get in the way of the plants. But if they only need to shade a few plants, commercial growers often use cheesecloth supported on stakes or suspended inside the greenhouse to form a shroud over the plants and protect them from intense direct sunlight.

Ventilation

ROOF VENTS

One of the easiest ways to reduce the temperature in the greenhouse in summer is to exhaust the air that has been warmed by the sun. To do this effectively requires ridge vents at the top as well as intake vents at the bottom to admit cooler outside air. There are various ways of controlling the opening and closing of these vents automatically. Roof vents can operate on a thermostatically controlled motor that opens and closes the vent by means of a gear and chain drive (Figure 6.11). The size of the motor depends on the weight of the windows you need to open. A simpler and cheaper kind of vent operator is available that works entirely under its own power. It works by expansion and contraction of a measured amount of liquid in a cylindrical tube with a piston at one end. As the tube heats, the liquid expands and forces the piston out. The piston is attached to the ventilator and causes it to open. When the liquid contracts, the weight of the vent forces the piston back down and the vent closes. The *Thermofor* automatic ventilator control unit (Figure 6.12) can be used on vertical and sloping vents and can operate heavy frames. The

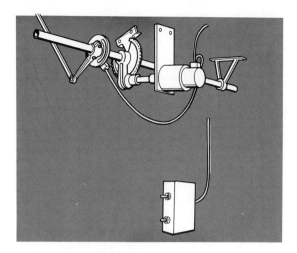

Figure 6.11. Motorized vent control.

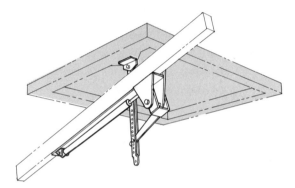

Figure 6.12. Non-motorized vent control.

Figure 6.13. Jalousie windows.

temperature at which it opens and closes the vent can be adjusted to any setting between 65°F. and 105°F. The vent can weigh up to 50 pounds.

LOUVERED WINDOWS

If large areas of ventilation are required, these are most easily controlled by using louvered or "jalousie" windows (Figure 6.13) that offer the maximum amount of free air space for the size of the window, are easily opened and closed, and do not project more than a few inches inside or outside the greenhouse, whereas other types of windows can obstruct both people and plants. A range of jalousie windows can be opened and closed by means of a thermostatically controlled electric motor for untended operation. Jalousies

do, however, provide a source of permanent ventilation even when shut. It is difficult to provide a tight seal where the glass panes overlap, though more expensive ones provide a better seal and allow less infiltration when shut. Louvered windows are useful in summer when large areas of ventilation are required. In winter, to reduce the heat loss by infiltration, they can be permanently closed by an internal storm window.

If you intend to use your greenhouse throughout the summer, on one hand, it is worth providing screens over all vents to prevent flying insects from entering and laying their eggs in your hospitable environment. On the other hand, make sure you fulfill the functions of useful insects which pollinate the flowers of vegetables such as squash and cucumbers. In fact, you might well introduce some beneficial insects like ladybugs to counteract the possibility of an attack of aphids.

FANS

One of the cheapest ventilation systems is a simple *wall-mounted fan* (Figure 6.14). Roof vents tend to be expensive items in any green-

AUXILIARY GREENHOUSE EQUIPMENT 87

Figure 6.14. Wall-mounted exhaust fan.

house and if you are building them yourself they need to be particularly well made to fit properly. One fan can take the place of several roof vents. A simple 12-inch-diameter fan with a small motor and a manually operated shutter can be purchased for about $60 and installed easily. This kind of fan, with one speed only, moves about 650 cubic feet of air in one minute. For domestic greenhouses, most manufacturers agree that a ventilation rate of between 2 and 3 cubic feet per minute per square foot of floor area is adequate for providing summer ventilation. A 650 c.f.m. fan would therefore be suitable for a greenhouse approximately 250 square feet in area (or about 2,000 cubic feet in volume). For greenhouses that are shaded during the summer, a much smaller fan would be adequate since the temperature rise would not be so great.

Figure 6.15. A circulating fan.

The difficulty with fans is that they tend to provide too much ventilation too quickly in winter when a slow ventilation rate is required. Opening vents makes it easier to adjust the ventilation rate, and a combination of these and a single extract fan may be the answer. An extract fan should always be provided with shutters that close when the fan is not in use. It is best to provide intake vents to insure a free flow of air through the greenhouse. In small greenhouses the extract fan should be placed high on one gable end, and the intake vent low at the other end. In tightly sealed plastic covered greenhouses it is necessary to open the intake vent every time the fan is in operation to prevent a reduction in interior air pressure. Or an open door may take the place of the intake vent. In greenhouses longer than about 25 feet it would be worth installing fans high at each end and intake vents low in the center of the sides.

A certain amount of air movement is good for plants, though hot or cold drafts can damage them. Stagnant air among leaves encourages insects and diseases and causes patches of excessively cool or warm air which can harm the leaves. A gentle, even flow of air is therefore desirable. Some greenhouse owners go to the trouble of installing a small air-circulating fan to keep the air moving when the vents are closed and there is no fan-assisted heating or cooling system (Figure 6.15). Plastic greenhouses suffer more from stagnant air than do glass greenhouses, which inevitably are less tightly sealed.

Evaporative Cooling

Commercial greenhouses, particularly in Southern states, generally operate throughout the summer using *evaporative coolers* (Figure 6.16) to reduce internal temperatures. Hot, dry air blown across wet fibrous pads causes water in the pads to evaporate. As the water evaporates it takes in heat from the air—heat which is used to change the state of the water from a liquid to a vapor. It takes only 1 Btu to raise the temperature of a pound of water through 1 degree Fahrenheit, but it takes 1,060 Btu's to change the same amount of water into vapor. So an evaporative cooler changes hot dry air to cooler, more humid air. The efficiency of the system depends, of course, on how dry the external air is, and the volume of air you are trying to keep cool. If the external climate is not too humid, and you size the cooler according to manufacturer's specifications, you should be able to achieve a reduction in temperature of between 15 and 20°F., relative to the outside temperature.

Evaporative coolers suitable for larger domestic greenhouses consist of a series of aspen pads (Figure 6.17), a water recirculating system to insure that they are sufficiently saturated, and a fan to blow outside air over them. The fan is generally sized to change the air in the greenhouse once every two minutes, and thermostatic controls are used to turn on the fan when the greenhouse temperature reaches a predetermined level. A complete system will cost about $300 and though the energy costs involved may not be too great (the fan will have a rating of between ¼ and ½ h.p.), the amount of water used on hot days may be as much as ten gallons per hour. In areas of water shortage

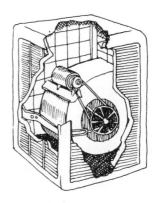

Figure 6.16. An evaporative cooler.

this kind of use should be avoided if possible by other methods of cooling such as ventilation and shading.

A primitive kind of evaporative cooling can be arranged simply by placing a tray of water, or better still a layer of wet sponge, next to the air intake vents.

Remember that evaporative coolers produce humidity as well as lower the temperature. This humidity can be beneficial to plants during the day and reduces the necessity of watering, but if the temperature were to fall considerably at night you might be faced with condensation problems and isolated pockets of still, damp, cool air that could be harmful. The humid air must be exhausted from the greenhouse before the temperature falls too far.

Figure 6.17. Evaporative cooling pads.

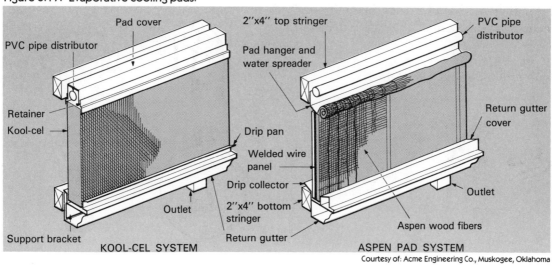

Pad cover
2"x4" top stringer
PVC pipe distributor
PVC pipe distributor
Pad hanger and water spreader
Retainer
Kool-cel
Drip pan
Return gutter cover
Welded wire panel
Drip collector
2"x4" bottom stringer
Outlet
Outlet
Aspen wood fibers
Support bracket
Return gutter
KOOL-CEL SYSTEM
ASPEN PAD SYSTEM

Humidity

More damage is caused in greenhouses by too much humidity (particularly at low temperatures) than by too little. Too little humidity will only be a problem in hot, dry summer conditions when the greenhouse is being well ventilated so that moisture is being removed too quickly from the plants' environment. The easiest way to keep relative humidity high in summer is by frequent hosing down of benches, floors, and walkways, or by placing wet pads near the air intake vents. As long as water is evaporating from surfaces around the plants there will be enough humidity in the air.

You can buy artificial humidifiers that operate automatically. These may be the *aerosol* type (Figure 6.18), where water is mechanically atomized and discharged into the air, the tiny particles being evaporated to make it more humid. The other type of humidifier is similar to an evaporative cooler in that it consists of a fan that blows air through wet aspen pads, or across a fine spray of water. This type can be connected to a *humidistat* (like a thermostat but it measures humidity, not temperature) so it operates only when the relative humidity falls below a certain level (Figure 6.19).

Another method of raising humidity and reducing the amount of watering is to install

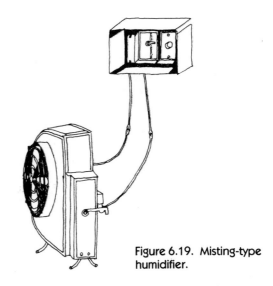

Figure 6.19. Misting-type humidifier.

a *mist propagation system*. Misting systems are particularly useful for seedlings and tropical plants. They are generally made up of a series of fine spray nozzles connected to a hose pipe. The supply can be turned on automatically by means of a time clock or a humidistat connected to a solenoid valve. You can buy various components from greenhouse equipment distributors and make up a system to suit your own needs for around $50 (Figure 6.20).

For most greenhouse plants, the humidity level should be maintained at between 50 and 70 percent. It is possible to keep a check

Figure 6.20. Components of an automatic watering system.

Figure 6.18. An aerosol humidifier.

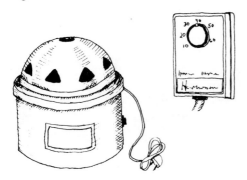

on this using a wet and dry bulb thermometer, or a hygrometer. These devices are
only really necessary if you intend to grow
fairly exotic plants that require unusual or
precise conditions.

Figure 6.21. An automatic pot-plant watering sytem.

Watering Systems

Watering the plants themselves will increase
humidity fairly rapidly, particularly if a fine-
spray hose or watering can is used. Avoid
leaving large droplets of water on the leaves
since these can cause scorching on the leaves.
If you wish simply to feed water to the plants
themselves it is better to use a standard noz-
zle and feed water directly into the soil. If
water is scarce, this is the most efficient system because none of the water is used to increase the humidity other than by transpiration of the plants themselves.

For automatic watering of potplants, systems are available that consist of a number of
narrow plastic tubes about 5 feet long connected to a larger diameter length of hose
(Figure 6.21). Each plastic tube is weighted
to anchor the tube in a particular plant pot. A
continuous stream of water is then supplied
direct to the soil in each pot when the hose is
turned on. For larger plants or seed flats, two
or more water outlet tubes can be grouped
together to provide the right amount of
water.

Nearly all plants benefit from good drainage conditions. The roots of a plant must not
stand in continually damp and stagnant soil.
Pot plants will benefit from being placed on
shelves or benches covered with gravel that
retains moisture which humidifies the air
around the plant and keeps the base of the
plant pot damp. Corrugated asbestos or sheet
metal can be used for benches, and the corrugations filled with gravel or vermiculite to
level off the surface. Rainwater gutters filled
with gravel make suitable shelves for small
pot plants.

Do not neglect the use of rainwater. Where

water is scarce, it is worth collecting rainwater from all nearby roofs and putting it to
the best possible use. Rainwater is generally
soft and is preferred by some species of plants.
Diverting gutters and drainpipes into a rainwater barrel inside or just outside your greenhouse can provide a useful source of water for
soaking newly planted cuttings and washing
pots, as well as watering the plants themselves. In some areas it could eliminate the
need for installing permanent plumbing or
using a long length of hose pipe.

Watering plants with very cold water can
give plants a sudden shock that might cause
a setback. In winter particularly, you will
save energy and encourage your plants by
using warm water.

Hydroponics

The ultimate in the high-technology approach to greenhouse gardening is the use of
hydroponic or soilless cultivation techniques.
Hydroponic gardening implies using water
as the medium for transferring nutrients to
the plants. The actual growing medium is an

inert material such as gravel, which serves merely to provide a bed for the plant roots. Hydroponics is not as recent a concept as many people think. The floating gardens of the Aztecs in what is now Mexico City, and the hanging gardens of Babylon are early examples of the hydroponic principle. The scientific basis for hydroponics—that the nutrients and water in the soil rather than the soil itself are essential to plant growth—has been understood for more than a century. During World War II, hydroponic production facilities were built by U.S. military forces in the south Atlantic and Pacific islands to produce vegetables for the troops. Some are still in use. With the onset of the "green revolution" in food production during the late 1960s a lot of interest was generated in hydroponics. Large-scale successful commercial operations are now located in many parts of the world, particularly in areas where water must be used wisely.

WHAT IS HYDROPONICS?

Hydroponic installations are essentially a form of chemical gardening using highly controlled techniques in the application of water and nutrients plus careful control of the plant climate. Many of its proponents would claim that hydroponics requires less labor and involvement on the part of the gardener, but this is not necessarily true unless he uses sophisticated automatic controls which could be applied equally to conventional greenhouse gardening. With unautomated systems you are likely to be involved in more work because you must provide plant food regularly and monitor the plants' intake as well as controlling the climate. Many other claims made for hydroponic gardening should also be examined closely. You will be able to grow more plants in a smaller area, but only if you supply the extra plant food and intensive care. You will be able to produce crops the year around if you can afford to create, year around, a suitable artificial climate. You will produce bigger crops, but only if you

use the right chemical fertilizer at the right time. Chemical fertilizers can never match organic manures in the variety of nutrients they provide; it is this variety that many people believe gives organically grown vegetables a superior taste and food value. It is also contradictory to believe in self-sufficiency with hydroponic units, since one is entirely dependent on chemical fertilizers, many of which originate on the opposite side of the world and require vast amounts of energy to produce.

Still, in certain circumstances, particularly in urban areas where space is at a premium, and in areas where water is scarce, hydroponics may be the best short-term answer to domestic food production. Small backyards or rooftops converted into greenhouses would be suitable situations. If you are interested in hydroponics it will require considerable time and effort to set up and manage a production unit. The basic elements required are a tray filled with the growing medium, a supply of nutrient, water, and a method of supplying nutrient and water at regular intervals.

A BASIC SYSTEM

At the most basic level, the tray can be a simple wooden box, six to nine inches deep, with a plastic liner. Drainage holes with plugs are required at the bottom to insure that excess nutrient solution can seep away and the system can be flushed with water before each planting. The growing medium can be pea gravel, granite chips, crushed bricks, vermiculite or perlite. Its purpose is merely to provide a support structure for the roots, to allow air around the roots and to retain nutrient solution on the surface of each particle when it is wetted. The liquid nutrient, at the simplest level, is supplied with a watering can at regular intervals.

At this level one is bound to encounter problems that arise due to the delicate balances in the hydroponic system. The moisture level, the amount of nutrient needed and the nature of the fertilizer used all require careful consideration. The simpler an ecosystem, the more susceptible it is to disease and infestation. You may need to experiment before you achieve success, and you must do a good deal of reading beforehand to avoid disasters.

AUTOMATIC SYSTEMS

At a more sophisticated level, automatic feeding systems and complete domestic-scale hydroponic kits are available that provide a better guarantee of success and less involvement by the gardener. The best systems use a tank of nutrient solution beneath the growing bed (Figure 6.22). Nutrient is pumped into the growing medium at predetermined intervals, the pump being activated by a time clock three or four times a day, or by a moisture sensor in the growing bed. Nutrient solution floods the growing medium, then drains back down into the tank. The plants

soak up the water and nutrients. As the bed dries out, it draws in air around the roots of the plants, necessary to prevent stagnation. At the next feeding, stale air is forced out and again replaced with nutrient solution. This system of "sub-irrigation" is used in most commercial installations. Complete small-scale systems are available through Water Works Gardenhouses, P.O. Box 905, El Cerrito, California 94530. This firm sells redwood and fiberglass greenhouses (8 x 12 feet to 8 x 24 feet) with all necessary environmental controls, together with planting trays, nutrient containers, and pumping systems. Other manufacturers of hydroponic systems and equipment are Eco-Enterprises, 2821 N.E. 55th St., Seattle, Washington 98105, and Burwell Geoponics Corp., Box 125 Rancho, Sante Fe, California 92067.

If you are considering hydroponic gardening, read as much as possible about it so you know exactly what you are getting involved in. The above-mentioned companies will pro-

Figure 6.22. A simplified diagram of a sub-irrigation hydroponic system.

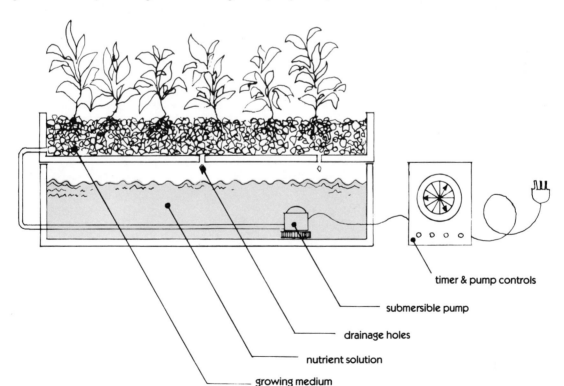

timer & pump controls

submersible pump

drainage holes

nutrient solution

growing medium

vide information on products available. Other good reference books are *Hydroponic Gardening* by Raymond Bridwell, *The Beginner's Guide to Hydroponics* by James Sholto Douglas, and *Home Hydroponics* by Lem Jones.

Artificial Lighting

Once you have artificially provided the right climate, nutrients, water supply and growing medium, the only other thing plants will need is light. Needless to say, this too can be provided artificially if you wish. Fluorescent lights are available that have been specially developed for growing plants. Traditional fluorescent lights, "Warmlite" and "Coollite" bulbs, produce only part of the spectrum required for efficient plant growth and are deficient in the red waveband of the spectrum. They require the addition of incandescent lights, which are an excellent source of the red light vital for stimulating growth and inducing blossoms. Fluorescents are now available that provide a wide spectrum of light from ultraviolet to far red, simulating fairly accurately outdoor lighting conditions.

Gro-lux wide spectrum, Naturescent, and *Agrolite* are trade names to look for.

Fluorescents provide less light and less heat than incandescents and therefore consume much less energy. If you have avoided the use of fluorescent lights because of the color of the light they emit you should consider using "Naturescent" fittings, which, in color, resemble natural daylight. Because fluorescent lights give off less heat, they can be placed close to plants without damaging them. Reflectors placed above the tubes will increase the level of illumination on plants below.

Artificial lighting is useful in certain circumstances where a high degree of control is required over the amount of light a plant receives, as when forcing plants into blossom, or encouraging germination. It may also be useful in urban areas where there is often not enough natural light available to grow many kinds of plants. For those restricted to their houses, it is the only way they will find satisfaction in gardening

For further information on different types of bulbs and fixtures, and details of various installations, write to Hoplite Co. Inc., 566 Franklin Ave., Nutley, New Jersey 07110. A good textbook on the subject is *The Indoor Light Gardening Book* by George A. Elbert.

III

Horticulture and Dynamics

The healthy greenhouse, in which green plants and colorful flowers thrive in conditions of good temperature and humidity, is the goal of all indoor gardeners.

7

Soils

Good soil is the basis of good gardening and, as all gardeners know, it is hard to come by. Leafmold, well-rotted manure, well-made compost and good topsoil are like money in the bank. They form the organic matter—the humus—in the soil and largely determine its quality. Ideally, a good soil should contain a wide range of relatively inert particles (coarse sand, silt and fine clay) held together by a high proportion of organic matter. The organic matter breaks down to provide nutrients; it acts like a sponge, absorbing water and nutrients; and above all it provides good soil structure, both binding together the inert particles and allowing sufficient space for air and water movement in the soil.

Good soil depends upon soil structure because nutrients can always be added later. A sandy soil is wasteful because the nutrients tend to leach out, and it needs to be watered more often. But plants will grow well in it if properly looked after, and it can easily be improved by the addition of more organic matter. A clay soil is difficult to work with and plants rarely grow well in it (though it is potentially more fertile than a sandy soil because it holds on to nutrients better). Clay tends to become waterlogged and to compact, forming an impervious crust. It can, with difficulty, be improved by the addition of sand and organic matter.

As organic matter is broken down by the

microorganisms in the soil, it provides most of the nutrients needed by growing plants. After several months, unless more nutrients are added, the soil will tend to run out of nitrogen and potassium. Out in the garden, decaying leaves, dead insects and the work of earthworms, insects, bacteria and fungi insure a continuous supply of nutrients, but in the greenhouse or with any potted plants the nutrients which the plant has used must be replaced by the gardener. Either fertilizer or fresh organic matter (compost or manure tea) must be added to keep the plant growing well.

Soil Testing

Soil tests should be done periodically to check the amounts of basic nutrients available. An organic gardener who is adding a fairly well-balanced range of nutrients to his soil should not need to test his soil more than once every few years. The usual recommendation is once a year, but a novice or anyone using concentrated chemical fertilizers in an intensive growing system might want to test the soil two or three times a year. In a small greenhouse for potted plants, soil testing may only be worth the trouble if the plants are not growing well.

The simplest way to do a soil test is to take a sample of dry soil (preferably several samples from different parts of the greenhouse mixed together) and send it to your state agricultural extension service. This office will do a soil test for a small charge, or sometimes for free, and tell you what basic nutrients your soil lacks. Alternatively, you can buy one of the many soil-testing kits on the market and do it yourself, although these kits generally only test a limited range of nutrients. Do-it-yourself kits are most useful for testing the pH level (described later in the chapter).

Plant Nutrition

The most important plant nutrients are nitrogen, potassium (potash) and phosphorus, though plants need small amounts of many other elements. As important as replacing those elements that have been used by the plant is maintaining: (1) the *soil structure,* which allows both air and water to get to the roots, (2) the *acidity* of the soil, which promotes the chemical exchange whereby the roots absorb nutrients, and (3) the *microbial life* of the soil, which decomposes matter into forms the plant can use.

Nitrogen is the most obviously influential element in plant nutrition. It encourages rapid growth, especially of leaves. Too much nitrogen produces a lush, rather weak, plant, and delays flowers and fruits. Too little nitrogen produces a stunted plant with yellow leaves.

Nitrogen exists in fairly large quantities in most soils (and in the air), but only becomes available to the plant when broken down into nitrates by bacterial activity. Pasteurizing the soil increases the amount of nitrates produced because it kills off all the competitors of nitrate-producing bacteria. In fact, pasteurization (or the addition of a lot of nitrogen-rich organic matter) encourages such a burst of bacterial activity that the bacteria can be temporarily overwhelmed by their own acid byproducts.

Pure nitrate fertilizers can be added directly, but such a sudden concentrated dose of food can upset the balance achieved by the plant, the soil and the bacteria. An excess of chemical fertilizer also leads to the formation of harmful salts in the soil that can burn the roots of the plant. The gradual breakdown of organic forms of nitrogen by the bacteria in the soil is a much slower, more long-lasting and more satisfactory solution.

Two good sources of organic nitrogen are blood meal and hoof-and-horn meal. Manure, cottonseed meal, seaweed, fishmeal, and bonemeal all contain somewhat less nitrogen but are better all-round fertilizers. The best way to add these organic fertilizers to your plants is via the compost heap, but they can also be sprinkled on the soil and gently scratched into the surface.

Phosphorus is needed throughout a plant's life, but only in small quantities. It encourages a good root system, sturdy growth and early ripening of flowers and fruit. It also helps to carry other nutrients through the plant's system. Like nitrogen, it becomes available as a result of bacterial activity, but only indirectly. It is dissolved by the weak acid solution the bacteria produce as a byproduct. Bonemeal (preferably steamed) is the main source of phosphorus, but pulverized rock phosphate is another concentrated source.

Potassium (commonly called *potash*) is required in large amounts by most plants, especially for well-colored, healthy fruit and flowers. It strengthens the plant, though an excess causes hard, woody, stunted growth. Too little potassium results in soft, lush growth—much like an excess of nitrogen. In fact, the amounts of potassium and nitrogen needed are closely interrelated. To be on the safe side you should add them together so they can modify each other's effects. Wood ash, greensand and granite dust are good sources of potassium (as are banana skins and corn cobs if well chopped up and composted). Potassium is very alkaline and can be used instead of calcium (lime) to "sweeten" an acid soil.

Trace Minerals. Sulphur, iron, magnesium, boron, manganese, zinc, copper, and molybdenum are all needed in small quantities by the growing plant. Decomposing organic materials are good sources of these trace elements. Using leafmold or compost in your greenhouse soil will make a deficiency of trace elements unlikely.

Acidity. Strictly speaking, the acidity of the soil is not a nutrient, but it seriously affects both the plant's ability to take up nutrients and the quantities of various nutrients available in the soil. A plant takes up nutrients by exchanging ions with the soil particles. This exchange takes place more readily in a slightly acid solution. Many minerals are also dissolved by a slightly acid solution and only in the dissolved form are they available to the plant.

Microorganisms play a dual role in soil acidity. They are themselves most active at digesting organic matter, breaking it down into a form which the plant can use, in slightly acid conditions. And they excrete acid compounds as a byproduct of their digestion. If the soil becomes either too acid or too alkaline, the bacteria will die off. But when the balance is redressed they will soon regenerate.

Soil acidity is defined in terms of the *pH level,* which measures the amount of exchangeable calcium in the soil. The more calcium there is, the less acid the soil is. Thus the higher the pH level, the more alkaline the soil. A pH of 7 is perfectly balanced, neither acid nor alkaline. Most plants and most soil bacteria prefer a slightly acid soil, somewhere between pH 5 and pH 6.5. Calcium and other alkaline minerals are easily leached out by excessive rain or overwatering, so in moist, cool climates like New England or the Northwest Coast, garden soil tends to be relatively acid. In hot, dry climates the soil usually is more alkaline.

Adding calcium in the form of ground limestone is the most common way of reducing soil acidity. Calcium is in itself a plant nutrient, helping to build strong cell walls, but its main function is in reducing soil acidity. Wood ashes can also reduce acidity, but they do it by adding potassium instead of calcium.

To increase soil acidity, add pine needles, peatmoss or compost rich in fresh organic matter (grass clippings, weeds, oak or beech leaves). Pasteurizing the soil will also increase its acidity. If necessary you can even sprinkle diluted vinegar on the soil to increase the acidity quickly.

Microorganisms. The fungi and bacteria growing in the soil are as important as its chemical analysis, for they render many of the elements available to the plant. They are not usually tested by an ordinary soil test, but any well-aerated soil with a good supply of humus, a reasonable pH level and no excessive salts will soon develop the necessary microorganisms.

Many different bacteria are involved in the breaking down of organic matter. Some of the most important ones decompose it into nitrites and then nitrates, in which form the plant absorbs most of the nitrogen it needs. Certain bacteria that live in conjunction with the roots of leguminous plants (beans, peas, vetches, clovers) are able to capture nitrogen from the air and convert it into usable forms. These "nitrogen-fixing" bacteria can be purchased, and it is a good idea to inoculate legume seeds with them if no legumes have been grown in the soil recently.

Greenhouse Soils

Greenhouse soil needs to be lighter and better aerated than garden soil because otherwise it would tend to become waterlogged and compacted from the frequent heavy waterings it receives. Greenhouse soil also needs to be richer than garden soil because there are more plants growing in a smaller and much shallower area. The roots of a greenhouse plant cannot reach down two or three feet to find the food supplies the plant needs. Thus a higher proportion of organic matter is needed in potting soil than is generally found in a garden.

Most greenhouse soils are made up of one part sphagnum peatmoss (a relatively inert, slow-to-decompose form of organic matter), two parts of good topsoil, leafmold, or compost (or better yet, one part topsoil and one part compost) and one part coarse sand, vermiculite or other inert gritty material. Bonemeal, lime and dried or well-rotted manure are the most common additions, but a soil test should be done to determine exactly what is needed.

A few plants, like African violets, cacti and the more acid-loving plants, require slight variations of the above mix, but in general most plants will thrive in it. Soil for planting seeds often contains a lower proportion of topsoil so it will drain more quickly and not cause the seeds to rot; less topsoil also means the flats are lighter and easier to handle.

Greenhouses provide excellent conditions not only for growing plants but also for encouraging insects and diseases. Because there are few natural predators inside the greenhouse, and no frosty nights or hard-driving rain, pests multiply rapidly. Unless fresh soil is used every year, disease organisms will build up. If fresh soil *is* used, it is likely to bring weed seeds in with it, and often undesirable insects as well. Well-made compost should be relatively disease- and insect-free, but if you use garden soil you run the risk of importing both pests and diseases. To save work, it might be worth running the risk for a year to see what problems develop. If all goes well, you can skip pasteurization for good, eliminating a laborious step in soil preparation. Well-made compost, sand, vermiculite, perlite and other inert materials should not need pasteurizing because they are naturally sterile.

Pasteurization. The simplest way to insure clean, healthy soil is to pasteurize it (often mistakenly called *sterilizing* the soil). You do not want to kill off *all* the life in the soil, only the harmful organisms. Fortunately, the important and beneficial nitrate-producing bacteria can survive the heat of pasteurization, but almost all weed seeds,

PASTEURIZING SOIL

Heating the soil to 180°F. for thirty minutes is the best and most common form of pasteurization. If you suspect the presence of eelworm cysts or virus diseases (see Chapter 9), then you will have to heat the soil to 200°F. to destroy them, but this will also destroy many beneficial bacteria.

To pasteurize a small amount, place three or four inches of moist soil in a baking pan. Cover it with tinfoil and heat slowly in the oven until a thermometer inserted through the foil reads 180°F. Then turn off the oven and leave for thirty minutes before removing the pan and taking off the cover. Alternatively, you can cook the soil in a pressure cooker for twenty minutes at five pounds' pressure. Or you can pour boiling water on a shallow layer of soil and immediately cover it to retain the heat for thirty minutes. The problem is making sure that all the soil is evenly heated, since even a small number of harmful organisms can quickly reinfest the soil.

For larger amounts of soil it might be worthwhile to set up a steam pasteurizer. A large sheet of perforated metal is set on top of a pan of water of equal size. Up to ten inches of soil can be placed on the perforated sheet. This is covered with tinfoil, heavy plastic, wet burlap bags or any other convenient heat- and moisture-retaining material. The water must be kept boiling for several hours, until the top of the soil reaches 180°F. Then the heat is turned off and the soil left for thirty minutes before removing the cover. Electric soil pasteurizers exist, but are more expensive than their usefulness warrants.

Many chemicals are available for pasteurizing soil, but none of them is as effective as well-applied heat treatment. And since all the chemicals work by creating a toxic gas, none of them is very good for you or for your plants, although the toxic effect does wear off in a few weeks. For the amateur gardener, heat treatment is the best form of pasteurization.

disease organisms and insects are killed off by it. Pasteurization is particularly important when starting seeds and cuttings because they are at a vulnerable stage.

Soil-less composts. If soil is not readily available, soil-less composts are a perfectly adequate substitute. Because they are lighter in weight and easier to pasteurize than ordinary soil-based media, they are useful for seedflats, for large pots that need to be moved occasionally, for rooftop gardens and for city gardeners.

Soil-less composts usually consist of peat mixed with sand, vermiculite, perlite or even polystyrene. The peat can be pasteurized by pouring boiling water over it while stirring, and the other materials are naturally sterile. The peat acts to retain water, and the sand or other gritty materials to aerate the compost.

Soil-less composts should be kept evenly moist. Too much water will cause the peat to become waterlogged. Too little will make it resist rewetting. Unlike soil-based composts, it should be given a little water frequently instead of a good dousing occasionally. Also unlike soil-based composts, it should not be pressed down into the pot at all or the peat may compact too much.

Plants in soil-less composts require more careful attention than those growing in ordinary soil. There are no reserves of food, so if you forget to add a particular nutrient when it is needed, the plant essentially starves. Harmful salts—byproducts of the breakdown of fertilizer—build up when conditions are not just right. Both the pH level and the amount of oxygen available to the bacteria in the soil-less compost must be carefully regulated to minimize the danger of high salt levels. Very few bacteria are originally present in a soil-less compost, which makes a nitrate fertilizer necessary to start with. But thanks to the omnipresence of bacterial spores, they soon build up in response to the presence of nitrogen-containing fertilizers.

Soil-less composts are ideal for propagation. Both seeds and cuttings thrive in a sterile, well-aerated medium. But as soon as they have developed a substantial root system, they need food and must be transplanted into soil or else carefully fertilized.

Growing plants in soil-less composts allows for a more careful and deliberate control and eliminates the need for pasteurizing the soil, but it requires more careful testing and adjusting of nutrients unless the recommended chemical fertilizers are used in strict accordance with the instructions as to rates and frequency of application.

Bags of soil-less compost are available commercially. But if you want to experiment, you can make your own mix with two or three parts (by volume) of medium-grade sphagnum peatmoss to one part of fairly coarse sharp sand. For seeds and cuttings, use one part peat to one part sand. Lime (half ordinary ground limestone and half dolomitic limestone) should be added to bring the pH level up to 5.5. Generally, about six ounces of lime and four ounces of all-purpose fertilizer, containing both nitrates and organic nitrogen compounds, are added to each bushel of the peat-and-sand-mixture. But careful testing and adjusting of nutrients even at this stage will pay off.

Hydroponics

A more extreme form of soil-less compost is hydroponics. The plants are grown without any form of compost. The plant roots are supported by an inert material, like sand or gravel, which is periodically moistened with a nutrient solution. Sometimes the plants are simply suspended in the nutrient solution, which is kept in constant movement (to aerate it so the roots get enough oxygen). The solution should be tested every few days and completely replaced every few weeks. If any disease develops, it quickly spreads to all the plants, so sterile conditions must be maintained. Hydroponics is often used by commercial growers, but it is an expensive, high-technology operation not really suited to the home greenhouse.

Ring culture. A modified form of hydroponics, called *ring culture,* is often used for growing tomatoes. Large plants with extensive root systems like tomatoes, cucumbers, or melons ordinarily are grown directly in the ground the greenhouse stands on (this is called *border culture*). But after a few years the build-up of pests and diseases in the soil is likely to be great, especially if the same crop is grown each year. It is almost impossible to pasteurize more than the top ten inches of soil, so several alternative growing methods have been developed. They are all based on the principle of containing the nutrients in a small area while allowing the roots to absorb water from quite a large sterile area below. These methods are also suitable for greenhouses that do not rest directly on the earth but have some sort of impervious floor. The plants could, of course, be grown in large pots, but these would be clumsy and space-consuming, and they would require the pasteurization of a large amount of soil for each plant.

In ring culture, plants are grown in a relatively small amount (about a gallon bucketful) of pasteurized soil. The soil is placed in a bottomless pot or plastic bag open at both ends (about ten inches across and eight inches deep). This "ring" is then placed on a six inch layer of gravel, vermiculite or other inert material. Alternatively, the soil can be placed in a pile on a straw bale or mound of peat. If straw is used, it will provide some nourishment and a bit of extra warmth as it decomposes, but be sure the straw was never sprayed with weed killer, or your plants may suffer.

The gravel is kept half covered with water. If you use straw or peat, it is kept thoroughly moist at all times. The plant gets a strong start in the soil and gradually extends its roots down into the inert material below to absorb water. Nutrients are added to the soil as necessary (usually after flowers have appeared). A plastic sheet below the inert material will prevent contamination from the soil in the border and will retain the water where it is needed. As with any soil-less compost, both nutrient levels and salt levels should be checked frequently (tomatoes, for example, are particularly sensitive to excess salts).

Plant rotation. If ring culture seems like too much trouble for your larger plants, then try a three- or four-year rotation of unrelated plants in the border of the greenhouse. For example, you could grow eggplants (or tomatoes or peppers, but not more than one of these solanaceous plants) one year, chrysanthemums the next, then melons and finally okra. If you are careful to buy or raise disease-free plants, then you should have no trouble. But once a disease does set in, it is difficult to eradicate, so do burn any diseased plants, keep the greenhouse clean and watch for pests. The soil in the border will have to be amply replenished with good compost and well-rotted manure if it is to continue producing healthy plants. Bonemeal, wood ashes and some form of nitrogen should either be incorporated in the compost or worked into the soil directly. Ideally, the soil should be enriched after each crop is harvested before planting the next, but renewing all the soil once a year is a satisfactory compromise.

Soil replacement. If you are determined to grow the same crop every year in the border, then you will need to replace the top twelve to eighteen inches of soil every few years. Some people get away without doing this, but they are inviting disaster. Nothing is more depressing than a greenhouse full of dying plants.

Staging

Except for the largest plants, growing on raised benches called *staging* is more sensible than growing them directly in the soil of the border. Each plant is more readily visible, enabling you to nip potential problems in the bud. Air circulation is better, and the air temperature should be slightly warmer on raised benches. But above all, you are not forever bending over, and the reduction in backache should be reason enough to build good sturdy staging. Benches for staging must be solidly built to carry the weight of many pots or several inches of earth. They should be no more than three or three and a half feet wide so that plants at the back can be reached easily. A central bench, accessible from both sides, can of course be twice that wide. A comfortable height for a kitchen table should be about right for the benches. Sides four to eight inches high will prevent pots being knocked off and will retain soil or gravel, but if you use your greenhouse mainly for the propagation of seeds and cuttings in flats, then sides are not really necessary.

The surface of the staging can be either *slatted* or *solid*. If slatted, like a park bench, then water drips straight through so pots are less likely to pass diseases to one another or to become waterlogged. Air circulation is better with slats, and a certain amount of light will filter through them, allowing ferns and other shade-loving plants to grow underneath.

Solid staging can be filled with soil and the plants grown directly in that without the use of pots. But the sides need to be extra high (12 inches to 20 inches), and the whole structure must be reinforced to bear the enormous weight of soil. A 1-inch to 3-inch layer of gravel or other free-draining material is placed in the bottom with 8 inches to 16 inches of soil (depending on the size of plants to be grown) on top. If the plants have similar requirements their day-to-day management is easier this way because the moisture level and temperature of such a large amount of soil will fluctuate less rapidly than when divided into pots. But moving a plant is difficult since all the roots soon become entangled. And you may find one or two plants trying to take over the whole bench.

Pots can also be used on solid staging. They are usually placed on a layer of gravel, sand, or peatmoss so they drain well. The layer of inert material is kept permanently damp so it adds extra humidity to the air. A certain amount of the moisture will be drawn up into the pot by capillary action when the pot is dry, making your arrival with a watering can at exactly the right moment less crucial. Frequently, extensive roots will grow down out of the bottom of the pot, especially if you use peat. As long as you do not move it, the plant will thrive with these extra roots (this is probably the original form of ring culture), but it will resent being moved more than a plant whose roots are all contained within the pot. Alpine plants are almost always buried up to the brim of the pot with gravel to retain moisture while allowing them to drain freely.

When using solid staging, you should leave a space between wall and bench to encourage air circulation. A few plants can be grown underneath solid staging along the sunny side, but in general the space under the bench will be too dark for anything except storage, or possibly for ferns.

Extra shelves are often added above the staging to provide more space, but they tend to cut out a substantial amount of light from plants below. They should be not more than one pot's width and should be made of glass or wire mesh to minimize light reduction. Hanging baskets can also be used to gain more growing space in a greenhouse, but beware of putting them where you might hit your head on them.

Bibliography

Let It Rot by Stu Campbell. Garden Way Publishing, Charlotte, Vermont. 1975. Paperback $3.95. A breezily written guide to composting. Includes lots of sources for different nutrients and several methods of composting to produce good soil.

The Organic Gardener by Catharine Osgood Foster. Alfred A. Knopf, New York. 1972. Hardcover $8.95, paperback $2.95. A good introduction to the basic cycles which enrich or impoverish the soil.

Describes the basic plant nutrients—where they come from and what they do for the plant—as well as the function of humus. Good on composting and companion planting.

Organic Gardening by Lawrence D. Hills. Penguin Books. 1977. Paperback $2.95. Good chapters on composting, organic fertilizers and "green manures" (crops grown specifically to enrich the soil).

Growing Conditions

Most plants are eager to grow and will survive all but the most adverse conditions. But to produce beautiful, healthy plants, each species dictates certain general conditions. Some of course are more flexible than others. Some are willing to tolerate poor conditions and resume growing with renewed vigor when things improve, while some will be permanently damaged or even killed by prolonged adversity. In particular, many vegetables that survive a drought or a long, dark cold spell will become tough or bitter. Ideally, everything should grow as quickly and strongly as possible for best flavor and for most handsome appearance. (Herbs are an exception—slow, stunted growth concentrates their flavor.)

Healthy plants in a greenhouse can provide beauty and pleasure indoors and out. Plants in bloom can be brought into the house to be admired; a few weeks of dim light and dry air in the dining room won't hurt them. Hundreds of annuals can easily be started in the greenhouse to bloom outdoors from June to frost. And remember that healthy vegetables in the greenhouse can be as beautiful as any foliage plant.

Growing your own vegetables is a considerable contribution to saving fossil fuel energy. Fresh vegetables bought in a store are fairly sound ecologically, but any processed vegetables are among the most energy-intensive food we eat. Growing your own flowers and vegetables can also make a big saving in cash. An inexpensive packet of

Figure 8.1. The authors' own temporary coldframe for raising seedlings. It is shown with the plastic lid open and folded back.

seed can produce as many lettuces as a family of four could eat in a year. And a packet of celery seed could produce enough celery for a village. A pot of bulbs about to flower costs more than several dozen bulbs ordered in advance. And one bouquet would pay for all the flower seed you could use.

Unless you are lucky, you will have to reach some sort of compromise between the requirements of different plants you want to grow and the conditions you can afford to maintain in the greenhouse. It is sensible to grow only those things that you are fond of, that are compatible with each other, and that do not make inordinate demands on your money or time. Local conditions—cloudy days, subzero winter weather, scorching summers—will have a strong influence on your choice of plants. But remember that different areas of the greenhouse can provide fairly different microclimates. Grow the heat-lovers at the apex, the light-lovers which can withstand cold nights at the front, the cold-sensitive light-lovers in the middle or against the back wall, and the shade-lovers down below.

Experiment with different types of plants

and different regimes. You may find certain plants do better with less water or extra light or a greater drop in night temperature. Beg cuttings and young plants from your friends and see what grows well for you. You will almost certainly be able to pay them back with something they have had no success with.

The tables of growing conditions that follow are only a general guide; modify them as you go along. Every greenhouse has its own peculiarities of orientation, shading, ventilation, or soil composition. Only you can know what will grow well where and under what conditions in your greenhouse.

Houseplants

Houseplants are grown for the beauty of either their flowers or their foliage. Those that are usually grown from bulbs or as annuals are included in separate sections.

Most ornamental plants will grow well in a mixture of two parts loam to one part peat to one part sand. Seeds and cuttings can be propagated in either one part loam to one part peat to one part sand (or vermiculite) or a soil-less compost of one part peat to one part sand. Special soil mixes preferred by certain plants are noted under the individual entry. The proportions given are always for volume rather than weight.

"Good indirect light" ideally means a northern exposure with no direct sun, but partial shade cast by other plants or a place at the back of a greenhouse with a solid roof will do almost as well.

"Partial shade" ideally means shade for a few hours at midday and direct sun the rest of the time, but good indirect light all day will usually do instead. Generally, foliage plants prefer, or at least accept, indirect light. Most flowering plants need lots of sunshine (african violets, begonias and impatiens are the major exceptions to this rule). They will continue to grow with less light but will get long and spindly, and will soon stop flowering.

Houseplants

Name	Propagation by Seed	Vegetative Propagation	Growing Conditions	Comments
African Violet *Gesneriaceae* *Saintpaulia* *Ionantha*	Sow seed on surface of peat-sand mix (70°F) in good light. Sprouts in about 3 weeks. Blooms in 6-10 months.	*Take leaf cuttings, inserting stalk in peat sand, or just sand or water (70°F.) Pot up when rooted, in about 3 weeks. Blooms in about 1 year. Divide mature plants in early spring.	60-70°F. (min 55°F.) Good indirect light 1 loam/1 peat/1 sand	Likes high humidity, warmth and shade from direct light. Likes warm nights. Water from below to prevent splash marks on leaves and possible rotting. Keep moist but not sodden, and use tepid water. A light, free-draining, humusy soil is essential. Culture of other gesneriads (achimenes, episcia, gloxinia, streptocarpus etc) is similar.
Asparagus Fern *Liliaceae* *Asparagus* *Plumosus,* or *Sprengeri*	Sow seed in April or May (60-70°F). Soaking for 48 hours helps germination which may take up to 2 months.	Divide plants in spring.	50-65°F. (min 45°F.) Good indirect light.	Keep moist and shade from direct sun.
Azalea *Ericaceae* *Rhododendrum* *Indicum,* and other varieties	Sow seed in early spring on moist peat, sprinkling sand over top (55-60°F). Keep shaded and moist.	*Take cutting in spring or summer, inserting in 1 peat/2 sand (60°F). Layer by making small slit in young stem and burying 2" deep. Sever after 2 years.	50°F. in fall, up to 70°F. when blooming (min 35°F.). Full sun in winter, partial shade in summer. 1 loam/1 leafmold 1 peat/1 sand	Likes acid soil, moisture, semi-shade and cool conditions. Prefers to be somewhat potbound. Spray daily when buds form and keep atmosphere humid.
Begonia fibrous-rooted *Begoniaceae* *Begonia* *Semperflorens* and others	Sow seed in early spring (60-70°F) on surface of soil in good light. Sprouts in 2-3 weeks. Blooms in 4-6 months.	*Take cuttings any time. Root in peat-sand or water (60-70°F.). Flowers in 2 months.	60-70°F. (min 50°F.) Good indirect light.	Very easy to grow. Prefers warmth, humidity and indirect light, but very tolerant. Water well. Pinch back for bushy plants.
Begonia (rhizomatous) *Begoniaceae* *Begonia Rex,* and others	Sow seed in early spring on surface. of soil (65-70°F.).	Divide plants in April. *Take leaf cuttings in spring. Nick underside of main veins and place flat on peat-sand mix (65-70°F.). Will root from each wound. When 2 or 3 leaves each, separate little plants and pot.	60-70°F. (min 55°F.) Good indirect light.	Easy to grow. Culture as for fibrous-rooted begonias.

*Preferred method of propagation

(Continued next page.)

Houseplants, cont'd

Name	Propagation by Seed	Vegetative Propagation	Growing Conditions	Comments
Begonia (tuberous) *Begoniaceae* *Begonia tuber-hybrida,* and others	Sow seed on surface of soil in February (65-70°F.). Blooms in 4-5 months.	Divide tubers in March, one shoot per section. Take stem cuttings in early summer in peat-sand mix (65°F.). Pinch back and remove buds until November, then treat as ordinary tubers.	60-65°F. (45°F. in winter). 50-55°F. for Lorraine and Hiemalis varieties when flowering. Good indirect light	When leaves die back naturally, overwinter tubers at 45°F. giving little watering. In early spring increase heat to 60°F. and increase watering to start growth. Keep atmosphere moist and avoid drafts. Stake large flowers.
Cactus (except epiphytes, *see* Christmas Cactus) *Cactaceae*	Sow seed on surface of soil (70°F.). Sprouts in about 1 month. Transplant when ½" (may take a year). Some bloom in 3 years, some much longer.	Divide varieties which produce offshoots in early spring. Take cuttings in late spring or early summer. Cut at joint or 4" from tip. Dry for 24 hours then pot in sand or peat-sand mix.	55-70°F. (min 40°F.) Full sun 1 sand/1 loam with extra lime.	Likes well-drained soil and lots of light. Do not overpot, 3½" is about right for most. Keep dry in winter, gradually increase watering in spring until in mid-summer water whenever dry. Needs very little plant food.
Christmas Cactus *Cactaceae* *Schlumbergera*		Take cuttings at joints in spring or summer. Dry for 2 days then pot in sand or peat-sand mix. Keep covered to maintain humidity until rooted.	60-70°F., night 55°F. (min 50°F.) Partial sun in summer. Full sun in winter 1 loam/1 peat/1 leafmold/1 sand *or* 2 peat/2 leafmold/1 loam.	Keep moist and maintain humid atmosphere when in bud and flower. Decrease water after flowering, but do not allow to dry out completely. Can place out of doors in semi-shade in summer. A cold period at the end of summer will encourage bud formation. Culture of other epiphytic cacti is similar.
Carnations & Pinks *Caryophyllaceae* *Dianthus*	Sow carnation seed in winter (65°F. until it sprouts, then 50°F.). Sow pinks seed in spring (65-70°F.). Blooms in 4 months.	*Take 3" cuttings of perpetual carnations in winter (though will root anytime). Insert in sand (65°F. reducing to 50°F. when begin to grow). Take cuttings of pinks in summer. Pot in 1 peat/1 loam/1 sand mix. Keep in partial shade Cuttings bloom in 4-8 months. Layer sideshoots of pinks, border and annual carnations in mid-summer. Sever after 6 weeks, transplant 1 month later.	60°F., night 50°F. (summer 5°higher) (min 45°F. for perpetual carnations, others are frosthardy). Full sun.	Pinch young plants at least once (except for border and annual carnations) to ensure many flowers and bushy plants. Remove all but one bud on each stem if you want large flowers. Support stems with canes or string. Ventilate freely.

*Preferred method of propagation

Continued

Name	Propagation by Seed	Vegetative Propagation	Growing Conditions	Comments
Chrysanthemum *Compositae* *Chrysanthemum*	Sow seed shallowly (55-60°F.). Sprouts in about 2 weeks.	Divide perennial species in early spring. *Take 2-4" cuttings and pot shallowly in sand or peat-sand mix (55-60°F). Roots in 1-3 weeks. Blooms in 6 months.	50-60°F. (min 45°F.) Full sun. Buds only formed if continuous darkness for 10 hours daily.	Plant shallowly and support large plants with canes. Give good ventilation. Water thoroughly, but allow to dry out between waterings. Pinch out the growing tip for more flowers and bushier plant. Or, on standard mums, remove all but one main bud to produce a single enormous flower. Do not grow too close together or few flowers will appear. Time of flowering (2 months from beginning of 10-hour nights) can be accurately controlled by lengthening dark period in summer or giving extra light in fall. Outdoor plants are often lifted in fall to bloom indoors after frost.
Coleus *Labiatae* *Coleus* *Blumei*	Sow seeds in late winter on surface of soil in good light. (70-75°F.). Sprouts in 2-3 weeks.	*Take cuttings in late summer or early spring (60-65°F).	55-65°F., not over 60°F. in winter. Medium to good indirect light.	Pinch back for bushiness and remove any flowers which form. Keep moist in summer, fairly dry in winter. Best to start new plants from cuttings or seed each year.
Ferns many genera and species	Reproduce by spores which produce prothalli which in turn produce little ferns.	Some species can be divided.	Tropical species, 65-70°F. Temperate species, 55-65°F. Medium indirect light, partial shade. 3 peat/1 loam/1 sand	Maintain humid atmosphere. Use humusy soil and do not overpot. Use rainwater if possible. Many ferns are sensitive to pollution in either air or water.
Fuchsia *Onagraceae* *Fuchsia*	Sow seeds in spring (60°F.).	Take 3-4" cuttings in peat-sand mix (60°F.).	50-60°F. (min 35°F.) (max 70°F.). Good light, full sun in winter, some shade in summer.	Pot lightly. Keep moist, but water less in winter. Too much heat will cause buds to drop so give partial shade in hot weather. Cut back in fall or late winter.
Geranium *Geraniaceae* *Pelargonium* *Domesticum* "regal pelargonium" *Hortorum* - zonal or "ordinary geranium" *Peltatum* - "ivyleaf geranium"	Sow seeds in early spring (60-65°F.). Flowers in 5-9 months.	*Take 3-4" cuttings in late summer or early spring, in sand or peat sand mix (60-65°F.). Flowers in 6-8 months (3-4 months if taken in spring).	Summer 50-60°F., winter 45-50°F. (min 40°F.). Full sun.	Water thoroughly, but allow to dry out between waterings. Keep fairly dry in winter. Shade only if necessary to prevent over-heating in summer. Will stop flowering if too hot. Does well out of doors in summer. Cut back in fall before taking in. Pinch tips of young plants.

*Preferred method of propagation

Houseplants, cont'd

Name	Propagation by Seed	Vegetative Propagation	Growing Conditions	Comments
Gloxinia, *see under* Bulbs				
Impatience ("Busy Lizzie") *Balsaminaceae Impatiens Sultani*	Sow seed in spring or summer on surface of soil in good light (65-75°F.). Sprouts in 2-3 weeks. Blooms in 3-4 months.	*Take 3" cuttings any time. Root in water or peat-sand mix (60°F). Flowers in 1-2 months.	55-65°F. (min 45°F., 55°F. to flower). Good indirect light.	Keep moist, but water less if below 55°F. Pinch back young plants. Prune old plants hard in early spring.
Ivy *Araliaceae Hedera, Helix,* and others		Take 3-4" cuttings in summer. Root in water or peat-sand mix.	45-60°F. Good indirect light. Winter sun all right.	Keep only just moist, especially in winter. Do not overpot. Prune in spring.
Jasmine *Oleaceae Jasminuss Officinale,* and others	Sow seeds in fall.	Take 3-4" cuttings at a node, in late summer. Root in peat-sand mix (4050°F). May take several months to root. Layer shoots in early fall, sever a year later.	50-60°F. (min 40°F.) Full sun.	Keep moist, especially in summer. Ventilate well. Train up wires or canes. Thin after flowering. Can be set outdoors in summer.
Orchid *Orchidaceae*	Propagation by seed is a difficult, highly specialized business.	Mature plants can be divided. Each piece of rhizome should have at least 1, preferably 2 or 3, pseudobulbs attached.	Temperature depends on species. Full sun in winter. Partial shade or good indirect light in summer. Terrestrial orchids - 1 coarse peat/1 loam/1 sand/1 sphagnum moss. Epiphytic orchids - 2 osmunda fiber/1 sphagnum moss, *or* 1 coarse peat/1 perlite/1 sphagum moss.	Avoid stagnant air. Most species like a lot of heat if there is sufficient humidity (70% up to 100% for tropical species), but avoid waterlogging soil though should be moist especially in summer. Plunging pots in water once or twice a week is helpful. Do not over-fertilize. Many orchids have a dormant period in fall or winter when they require very little water. Grow epiphytic orchids on a piece of bark, a wooden basket or a special perforated pot for sufficient aeration.
Palm *Palmae Howea (or Kentia),* and others	Sow seed in February (80°F.). May take months to sprout.		50-60°F. Partial shade in summer, full sun in winter.	Water well in summer, keep fairly dry in winter. Keep atmosphere moist in spring and summer.
Philodendron *Araceae Philodendron*	Some species can be propagated by seed sown in April (75°F.).	*Take 4-6" cuttings in October. Root in peat, sand or water (70°F) Some species can be divided.	55-65°F. (min 50°F.) Good indirect light. Add extra peat to soil.	Keep soil and atmosphere moist, especially in summer.

*Preferred method of propagation

Name	Propagation by Seed	Vegetative Propagation	Growing Conditions	Comments
Poinsettia *Euphorbia* *Pulcherrima*		Take 6-7" cuttings in spring, dip in powdered charcoal and root in peat-sand mix (60-65°F). Water young plants freely.	Winter 55-60°F. rest of year 60-75°F. Full sun in winter, partial shade in summer.	Keep just moist in winter, gradually dry off after flowering and cut back. Keep humid atmosphere when growing. Can be put out of doors in summer. Needs long nights to flower. Provide 2 hours extra darkness from October on to produce flowers by Christmas.
Primula *Primulaceae*	*Sow seed (as fresh as possible) very shallowly in spring (60-70°F.). Maintain humidity and shade lightly. Sprouts in 2-4 weeks. Flowers the next spring.	Some species can be divided after flowering.	Tender varieties 50-55°F (min 45°F). Polyanthus (*Primula vulagaris elatior*) is frost hardy, prefers 45-50°F. Partial shade. Add extra peat to soil.	Keep moist and cool and ventilate well. Likes humusy soil. Avoid wetting leaves or crown. Best grown from seed each year.

Snapdragon, *see* Bedding Plants

Name	Propagation by Seed	Vegetative Propagation	Growing Conditions	Comments
Spider Plant *Liliaceae* *Chlorophytum* *Elatum* *"Variegatum"*		Set small plants on surface of soil in separate pots. Sever when well rooted. Divide large plants in spring.	50-60°F. (min 45°F.). Full sun or partial shade.	Keep moist in spring and summer, somewhat drier in fall and winter. Avoid drafts.
Wandering Jew *Commelinaceae* *Tradescantia,* and *Zebrina* *Purpusii*		Take 3" cuttings in summer. Root in peat-sand mix or just water (60-65°F).	50-60°F. (min 45°F). Partial shade or indirect light.	Hard to keep for more than a few years, but easy to propagate. Pinch young plants to promote bushiness. Remove any non-variegated shoots. Water freely in summer, less in winter.
Wax Plant *Asclepiadaceae* *Hoya Carnosa*		Take 3-4" cuttings of mature stems in summer. Root in peat-sand mix (60-65°F). Layer shoots in spring	Winter 55-65°F (min 45°F.), rest of year 60-70°F. Full sun in winter partial shade in summer.	Pinch back young plants, but do not prune older ones. Keep moist in summer, cooler and drier in fall and winter.

*Preferred method of propagation

Bedding Plants, or Annuals

In general, these plants are started in flats in the greenhouse to be planted out of doors in summer, but most of them can also be sown in late summer or fall to bloom indoors in winter or spring if sufficient light and heat can be given. If winter-flowering or indoor varieties are available, use them for forcing indoors in winter.

Sow the seed of annuals thinly and shallowly. If it needs light to germinate, just press the seed into the surface of the soil. Cover the seed box with plastic or glass to retain humidity until the seeds have sprouted, then remove the cover and allow air to circulate. Most seeds will germinate faster given more heat, especially bottom heat. Transplant or thin as soon as the leaves touch. Gradually harden off those which are to be planted outside. Annuals are usually planted out two or three weeks after the last possible date of frost in your area.

Annuals

Name	Growing Temp.	Sowing Conditions	Time to Germinate	Date to Sow for Blooming Season
Ageratum *Compositae*	45-60°F.	65-75°F. in light	1-3 weeks	August for spring February-March for summer
Alyssum *Cruciferae*	45-60°F. tps	65-75°F. in light	1-3 weeks	August for winter March for summer
Aster *Compositae*	60-70°F.	65-75°F.	1-3 weeks	August for winter December for spring February for summer
Begonia, *see under* Houseplants				
Calendula *Compositae*	40-55°F.	65-75°F. in dark	1-3 weeks	January for spring March for summer August for winter
Candytuft *Cruciferae* *Iberis*	45-60°F.	60-65°F	1-2 weeks	December-February for summer Fall for spring
Carnation **Chrysanthemum** } *see under* Houseplants **Coleus**				
Cosmos *Compositae*	55-65°F.	60-70°F. (max 70°F.)	2 weeks	March for summer October for spring
Dusty Miller *Compositae* *Artemisia* *Stelleriana*	50-70°F.	60-70°F. in dark	2 weeks	February-March for May-June
Geranium, *see under* Houseplants				
Heliotrope *Boraginaceae*	45-65°F.	60-65°F.	3-4 weeks	February for summer July for winter. Cuttings bloom in 4-6 months
Impatience, *see under* Houseplants				

Annuals, cont'd

Name	Growing Temp.	Sowing Conditions	Time to Germinate	Date to Sow for Blooming Season
Lobelia *Campanulaceae*	50-60°F tps	60-75°F.	1-3 weeks	February for summer September for winter December for spring
Marigold *Compositae* *Tagetes*	50-65°F. (min 45°F.)	65-70°F.	1-2 weeks	February for spring April for summer August-September for winter
Nasturtium *Tropaeolaceae*	45-60°F.	55-65°F. (hard to transplant, use peat pots)	2 weeks	August-September for winter February for summer
Pansy *Violaceae*	45-60°F.	60-70°F. (in dark)	1-3 weeks	December for spring March for summer July for winter
Petunia *Solanaceae*	45-60°F. tps	60-70°F. (on surface)	1-2 weeks	November for spring March for summer
Phlox *Polemoniaceae*	50-60°F.	55-65°F. (in dark)	1-3 weeks	March for summer September for spring
Pinks & Sweet William *Caryophyllaceae* *Dianthus*	50-60°F.	65-75°F.	1-2 weeks	March for summer
Portulaca ("moss rose") *Portulaceae*	50-70°F.	65-70°F. (in dark)	2 weeks	March for summer
Primula, *see under* Houseplants				
Salpiglossis *Solanaceae*	55-65°F. (min 50°F.) tps	65-70°F. (in dark, on surface)		February for summer September for winter December for May
Salvia *Labiatae*	55-60°F	70-80°F.	1-2 weeks	March for summer
Scabious *Dipsacaceae*	50-60°F.	65-75°F.	1-3 weeks	March for summer
Snapdragon *Scrophulariaceae* *Antirrhinum* *Majus*	45-65°F. tps	70-75°F. (in light)	1-3 weeks	Sow anytime for flowers in 3-4 months (up to 6 months in winter)
Stock *Cruciferae* *Matthiola*	50-55°F. (min 45°F., max 65°F.)	70-75°F.	1-2 weeks	January for summer August for winter
Sweet Pea *Leguminosae* *Lathyrus* *Odoratus*	45-55°F.	55-60°F. (in dark)	2-3 weeks (soak seed)	January for spring June for fall August for winter
Sweet William, *see* Pinks				
Tobacco Plant *Solanaceae* *Nicotiana*	45-60°F. tps	65-70°F. (in light)	1-2 weeks	March for summer August for spring
Zinnia *Compositae*	60-75°F.	65-75°F.	1 week	April for summer August for winter

tps—tolerates partial shade

Bulbs

In general, plants grown from bulbs will not come true from seeds. It is fun to experiment, but you are unlikely to improve on the parent variety.

Hardy bulbs (like crocus, hyacinth, narcissus, tulip) need a cold, dark rooting period. They can be forced to flower at any time of the year if the cold period can be given. Some people put pots of bulbs in the refrigerator in August or September to be sure of flowers by Christmas. For later blooming they are better left outside under a pile of leaves or straw once the weather turns chilly. You can buy specially preconditioned bulbs which are ready to be forced into extra early bloom.

Any good free-draining greenhouse soil is suitable for growing bulbs. Equal parts of peat, sand and loam (or compost) is a good mixture. Many bulbs can be grown successfully in bulb fiber, peatmoss with some charcoal, or even plain gravel, but they will use up all their stored energy and are unlikely to survive to bloom another year out of doors.

Bulbs and Corms

Name	Planting Time	Planting Depth	Growing Conditions	Propagation	Comments
Amaryllis *Amaryllidaceae Hippeastrum*	September-October for February (treated bulbs for January)	Half bulb depth	60-70°F. (min 55°F.) Full sun	Sow seed in March (60-65°F) takes 2-8 years to bloom, usually poor quality.	Dry out and rest for 3 months after leaves yellow. Water sparingly to restart growth in fall. Water more after bud appears.
Anemone *Ranunculaceae Anemone*	September-October for January-March	2 inches	50°F. (60°F. when in flower) Full sun	Sow seed in late summer, takes several years to bloom.	Needs good drainage. Water sparingly until growing well. Reduce water in winter.
Begonia, tuberous, *see under* Houseplants					
Crocus *Iridaceae Crocus*	September-October for December-January (6-8 weeks in dark plus 2-4 in light).	Just cover bulb	40°F. in darkness until well rooted. Then 50°F. in full sun.	Offsets will bloom the following year. Sow seed in summer, takes 2-4 years to bloom.	"Winter-flowering" varieties will be ready first. Chionodoxa, snowdrops and scillas can be grown like crocuses.
Cyclamen *Primulaceae Cyclamen*	August for winter	Leave tip of bulb showing	Day 60-70°F. night 50°F. Full sun 2 loam/1 peat/1 sand	Sow seed in Aug or Sept (60°F). Takes up to 2 months to sprout, 15-18 months to bloom. Can take leaf cuttings with bit of corm attached.	Keep moist but provide good drainage and avoid wetting corm. Dry off and rest after blooming. In August repot and begin watering to restart growth.
Daffodil, *see* Narcissus					

(Continued next page.)

Bulbs and Corms, cont'd

Name	Planting Time	Planting Depth	Growing Conditions	Propagation	Comments
Freesia *Iridaceae* *Freesia*	August-November for December-April	1 inch	Day 65°F., night 50°F. (min 40°F.). Full sun	Offsets will bloom the following year. Sow seed in spring (60°F.). Do not transplant. Takes 9-12 months to bloom.	Water sparingly until buds appear. After blooming, grow on for 2 months, then dry off, lift and store corms until ready to replant. Support leaves and flowers with canes.
Gloxinia *Gesneriaceae* *Sinningia* *Speciosa*	January-March for summer	Crown level with surface	Day 70°F., Night 65°F. (min 60°F., max 70°F.) Partial shade.	Divide tubers in March. Root stem cuttings with sliver of tuber attached in water or peat-sand. Sow seed in fall or winter (70°F), takes 1-2 years to bloom.	Needs humid warm atmosphere, but avoid wetting leaves. Gradually dry off when leaves yellow, then store at 50-60°F. in darkness.
Hyacinth *Liliaceae* *Hyacinthus*	Prepared bulbs-September-November for December-February. Unprepared bulbs October for March-April (both bloom 3-5 weeks after being brought into light).	Leave tip of bulb showing.	35-45°F in darkness until well rooted and buds showing. Then 55°F. for 10 days in semi-shade. Then 65-70°F. in full sun till blooms, then 60°F.		Specially prepared bulbs should be used for very early flowers. Can be grown in sand, sand and peat, bulb fiber, pebbles or just water. Large flowers will need staking. Bulbs can be planted outdoors (6" deep) after flowering. Grape hyacinths are more difficult to grow.
Iris *Iridaceae*	November-January for February-April	Leave tip of bulb showing.	40-50°F. until buds color, then 60-65°F. Full sun.	Divide tubers after leaves die back. Offsets will bloom in 1-3 years.	Buy specially treated bulbs for forcing. Not so easy to grow as hyacinths and narcissi.
Lily of the Valley *Liliaceae* *Convallaria* *Majalis*	October-November for February-March	Leave tip of bulb showing.	40-50°F. until January then 60-70°F. Partial shade.		Buy specially prepared pips for forcing. Keep moist.
Narcissus *Amaryllidaceae* *Narcissus*	September-November for December-March. (Tazettas 5-8 weeks after planting; others 6-10 weeks in dark plus 3-4 weeks in light).	Just cover bulb.	40°F. in darkness (except for Tazettas which can be placed in cold sunny place immediately) until well rooted, then 50-55°F., in full sun.	Offsets will bloom in 1-2 years. Sow seed in summer, when ripe, takes 3-7 years to bloom, usually poor quality.	Buy specially prepared bulbs for very early flowers. Tazetta narcissi (with several flowers on one stalk, e.g. "Paperwhite" or "Soleil d'Or") will bloom sooner than others.

(Continued on p. 118)

Bulbs and Corms, cont'd

Name	Planting Time	Planting Depth	Growing Conditions	Propagation	Comments
Narcissus, cont'd					Plant in sand, gravel, bulb fiber or soil. Keep some in dark longer for succession of blooms. Flowers may need staking if too hot, last longer if cool. After blooming, hardy varieties potted in soil can be grown on, gradually drying off as leaves yellow, then planted outside (6" deep).
Orchid, *see under* Houseplants					
Tulip *Liliaceae* *Tulipa*	September-October for January-February (8-12 weeks in dark plus 3-5 weeks in light).	Just cover bulb. Put flat side of bulb toward outside of pot.	35-45°F. in darkness until well rooted, then 50-60°F. in full sun.	Some produce offsets which will bloom in 2-3 years. Sow seed in summer to bloom in 5-7 years, usually poor quality.	Single and double earlies will bloom soonest and are easiest to force.

Figure 8.2. Commercial plastic cloches, shown next to ancient English stone barns, are used to protect entire rows of tender plants from cold weather.

Vegetables

Virtually all vegetables require good light for optimum growth. But those that are grown for their leaves or roots rather than for their fruit will usually grow moderately well, though more slowly, when partially in the shade. Winter vegetables should be well advanced by mid-autumn. They will stay in good condition but won't make much more growth in the depths of winter.

Most vegetables are grown in the standard soil mix of two parts loam to one part peat and one part sand. The depth of soil needed depends on the final size of the plant and whether most of its growth takes place above ground or below ground (carrots will obviously need deeper soil than lettuce, even though they take up less room above ground). Generally, ten to sixteen inches is sufficient, with a two- to four-inch layer of gravel or other free-draining material below.

Most vegetable seed will germinate at 50-60°F., though it will sprout sooner with more heat. A few plants absolutely require more heat to germinate and this is noted in the individual entry.

Vegetables

Name	Planting Seeds	Growing Conditions	Time from Seed to Harvest (in ideal conditions)	Comments
°**Beans** *Leguminosae*	2" deep 5" apart	50-70°F. 10" apart full sun	bush 2-3 months pole 3-4 months soya 4-5 months	Bush beans take less space and crop sooner, but produce less and have less flavor.
†**Beets** *Chenopodiaceae* *Beta vulgaris* *Crassa*	½" deep 1" apart	40-70°F. 2" then 4" tps	2 months (greens in 1-1½ months)	Quite hardy. Greens are good to eat. Efficient user of space if pull every other plant for greens when 4-5" high. Likes lime.
*****Cabbage family** (broccolli Brussels sprouts cabbage cauliflower collards kale kohlrabi, etc.) *Cruciferae* *Brassica*	½" deep ½" apart 60°F.	40-65°F. 18" x 18" (Brussels & cauliflowers 24"×24") tps	broccoli 3 months Brussels 6-7 months cauliflower 4-5 cabbage 3-5 months kale 5 months	Quite hardy, but worth starting plants indoors February or March. If hardened off, can plant outdoors quite early, before last frost. Probably not worth growing inside because they take a lot of space for a long time. If you have enough room, they are reliable producers, but should be fed well with manure or fish emulsion.

See also Chinese Cabbage & Turnips

---

*Commonly started indoors in flats in early spring to be planted out in the garden after the last frost.

°Difficult to transplant, but often worth starting indoors to extend the growing season. Use peat pots (2 seeds per pot, removing the weaker seedling) to reduce transplanting shock.

†Good winter crop in a cool greenhouse (min. 35°F., average 40-45°F.).

tps—tolerates partial shade (almost all vegetables prefer full sun, especially in winter, but these will grow in some shade).

Vegetables, cont'd

Name	Planting Seeds	Growing Conditions	Time from Seed to Harvest (in ideal conditions)	Comments
†**Carrots** Umbelliferae Daucus Carota	¼" deep thinly	45-65°F. 1½" (3" for large carrots) tps	2-4 months	Quite hardy. Slow to germinate, often sown with radishes to mark rows and reduce thinning. Keep cool and moist. Likes deep sandy soil. Can't transplant. Use stump-rooted varieties.
†**Chinese Cabbage** Cruciferae Brassica Cernua	½" deep 1" apart 60°F.	35-60°F. 18" x 18" tps	2½-3 months	Difficult, but worthwhile. Needs rich moist soil and coolness. Sow in fall for winter crop. Can't transplant.
***Celery & Celeriac** Umbelliferae Apium Graveolens	½" deep thinly 60°F.	35-60°F. 12"×12" tps	celery 6-7 months celeriac 45 months	Needs rich moist soil and cool conditions. Not easy or quick to grow.
†**Chard** ("swiss chard" or "seakale beet") Chenopodiaceae Beta vulgaris	1" deep thinly	8" x 8" tps	2 months	Easy to grow. Pick outside leaves continuously. "Rhubarb chard" is a beautiful deep red, slightly smaller and sweeter.
Chicory, see Endive or Escarole				
†**Cress** Cruciferae Lepidium Sativum	¼" deep thinly (in dark)	50-60°F. likes shade	10 days-3 weeks	Very easy and quick to grow. Does not need much sun but likes rich, very moist soil.
°**Cucumbers** Cucurbitaceae Cucumis Sativus	½" deep 2" apart 70-80°F.	65-85°F. (min. 50°F.) 36" x 36" full sun	2 months (sow 5 weeks before planting date).	Needs rich soil, warmth, humidity and some shade in the height of summer if grown inside. Pick frequently. May need to be hand pollinated. Can be grown up trellis to take less room.
°**Eggplant** Solanaceae Melongena Ovigerum	¼" deep 2" apart 70-80°F.	65-75°F. 24" x 24" full sun	3-4 months (sow 8 weeks before p'anting date)	Needs lots of warmth, light and rich soil. May have to be potted on before being planted outside.

---

*Commonly started indoors in flats in early spring to be planted out in the garden after the last frost.

°Difficult to transplant, but often worth starting indoors to extend the growing season. Use peat pots (2 seeds per pot, removing the weaker seedling) to reduce transplanting shock.

†Good winter crop in a cool greenhouse (min. 35°F., average 40-45°F.).

tps—tolerates partial shade (almost all vegetables prefer full sun, especially in winter, but these will grow in some shade).

Name	Planting Seeds	Growing Conditions	Time from Seed to Harvest (in ideal conditions)	Comments
†**Endive** (chicons, Belgian or French endive) *Compositae Cichorium Intybus*	½" deep thinly Outside in June	45-60°F. (60°F. max) In dark when forcing.	7 months (3-5 weeks of forcing)	Sow outdoors, in fall cut off leaves to about 2", dig up and store in damp, dark, cold place. To force, plant roots vertically, close together, in damp sand or soil. Cover with 6" of dry sand or just invert a box over the top. Keep in dark until ready when 5-6" long. If broken rather than cut, more will grow. Start a new crop of roots every few weeks.
†**Escarole** (chicory or curly endive) *Compositae Cichorium Endivia*	¼" deep thinly	40-65°F. 9" x 9" tps	3 months	Quite hardy, a good winter crop. Bitter, but the heart can be blanched for 2-3 weeks when plant is almost full grown to reduce bitterness. Just tie the outside leaves together or cover with a box.
†***Lettuce** *Compositae Lactuca Sativa*	¼" deep thinly	45-60°F. (max 70°F.) 4" x 4," then 8" x 8." tps	2 months (up to 4 months in midwinter).	Good winter crop (especially looseleaf varieties like Bibb and Buttercrunch). Needs moisture, light soil and good ventilation. Harvest every other plant when leaves touch, or pick outside leaves continuously.

Melons, *see under* Fruit

Name	Planting Seeds	Growing Conditions	Time from Seed to Harvest (in ideal conditions)	Comments
†**Mushrooms** *Agaricaceae Psalliota Campestris*	Sow fine spawn thinly & shallowly. Or plant 1" lumps 1½-2" deep, 10" apart.	50-60°F. in dark	2-3 months	Keep moist and dark. Grow in composted manure (horse manure is best). Should be able to harvest for several months.
°**Okra** *Malvaceae Hibiscus Esculentus*	1" deep 2" apart 65-75°F.	60-80°F. 18" apart full sun	3½-4½ months	Very tall, heat-loving plant with pretty flowers. Pick pods when 2" long.

*Commonly started indoors in flats in early spring to be planted out in the garden after the last frost.

°Difficult to transplant, but often worth starting indoors to extend the growing season. Use peat pots (2 seeds per pot, removing the weaker seedling) to reduce transplanting shock.

†Good winter crop in a cool greenhouse (min. 35°F., average 40-45°F.).

tps—tolerates partial shade (almost all vegetables prefer full sun, especially in winter, but these will grow in some shade).

Vegetables, cont'd

Name	Planting Seeds	Growing Conditions	Time from Seed to Harvest (in ideal conditions)	Comments
Onion family (leek, onion, scallion, shallot, etc.) *Alliaceae Allium*	½" deep thinly	40-70°F. 2-5" apart (scallions & leeks tps)	From seed—4 months From cloves, sets or plants—3 months Leeks—5 months	Quite hardy, but not usually worth growing indoors because they store well. Bulbs grow slowly in winter, so scallions, leeks and chives will do better than onions or garlic.
Chives & Garlic, *see under* Herbs				
†**Peas** *Leguminosae Pisum Sativum*	2" deep 1" apart	40-60°F. 2" apart tps	2 months	Quite hardy, needs cool, damp conditions. Not much yield for space taken, but delicious. "Snow peas" ("mange-tout" or "edible pod" peas) produce a larger crop if kept carefully picked.
*****Peppers** *Solanaceae Capsicum Annuum*	¼" deep 1" apart 70°F.	55-80°F. 12" apart full sun	3½-4 months	Needs a long season and quite a lot of warmth and sun, but not difficult to grow. Needs hand pollination indoors.
†**Radishes** *Cruciferae Raphanus Sativus*	¼" deep thinly	55-65°F. 1" apart tps	3-5 weeks	Easiest and quickest of all crops to grow. Will grow in shade of other crops. Good between rows of larger, slower plants.
†**Spinach** *Chenopodiaceae Spinacia Oleracea*	½" deep ½" apart	40-50°F. 3" then 6" tps	2 months	Quite hardy, will withstand moderate freezing, Dislikes heat. Good winter crop. Can harvest whole or pick outside leaves continuously.
°**Squash** *Cucurbitaceae*	½" deep 3" apart	60-75°F. (min 55°F.) 36-48" full sun	Summer squash 2 months; winter squash 3-5 months	Needs rich soil, lots of water, sun and heat. Takes a lot of space, but bears prolifically. Use bush varieties. Pick summer squash when young for more and better yield. Needs hand pollination indoors.

*Commonly started indoors in flats in early spring to be planted out in the garden after the last frost.

°Difficult to transplant, but often worth starting indoors to extend the growing season. Use peat pots (2 seeds per pot, removing the weaker seedling) to reduce transplanting shock.

†Good winter crop in a cool greenhouse (min. 35°F., average 40-45°F.).

tps—tolerates partial shade (almost all vegetables prefer full sun, especially in winter, but these will grow in some shade).

Name	Planting Seeds	Growing Conditions	Time from Seed to Harvest (in ideal conditions)	Comments
*°**Tomatoes** *Solanaceae* *Lycopersicon* *Esculentum*	¼" deep 1" apart 75°F.	60-80°F. (max 90°F., min 55°F.) 24" apart full sun	2-4 months	Needs rich soil, lots of water, sun and a fair amount of heat. Hand pollinate indoors. Stake or tie to strings. Remove suckers. Does well all fall if transplanted indoors from the garden. Summer-sown tomatoes should produce in the fall and again in the spring. Cherry tomatoes produce over a longer period and are likely to be healthier. Most areas in U.S. have insufficient light in winter to set fruit.
†**Turnips** *Cruciferae* *Brassica* *Rapa*	¼" deep ½" apart	45-60°F. 2" then 4" tps	2 months (greens in 1 month)	Needs cool conditions. Pull every other one for greens when the leaves touch.

*Commonly started indoors in flats in early spring to be planted out in the garden after the last frost.

°Difficult to transplant, but often worth starting indoors to extend the growing season. Use peat pots (2 seeds per pot, removing the weaker seedling) to reduce transplanting shock.

†Good winter crop in a cool greenhouse (min. 35°F., average 40-45°F.).

tps—tolerates partial shade (almost all vegetables prefer full sun, especially in winter, but these will grow in some shade).

Herbs

All herbs, except possibly mint, prefer as much sun as they can get. They have more flavor if given a lot of sunlight and a relatively slow rate of growth. Be careful not to plant in too rich a soil or to overfertilize. Many herbs will make large, handsome shrubs lasting several years, if given greenhouse protection in winter.

Generally, herb seed is slow to germinate, and often the plants do not make enough growth for a significant harvest until the second year. It is interesting how many apparently unrelated herbs are in the genus *Labiatae,* which is basically the mint family.

Herbs

Name	Propagation	Growing On	Comments
Basil *Labiatae* *Ocimum* *Basilicum*	Sow seed thinly ¼" deep, 55-60°F.	8" apart min 45°F. Full sun	Very vulnerable to cold.
Bay Leaves *Lauraceae* *Laurus* *Nobilis*	Can take cuttings, but usually bought as a small tree.	Full sun Min 45°F.	Can be put outdoors in summer, brought in for winter.
†Chives *Alliaceae* *Allium* *Schoenoprasum*	Sow seed thinly ¼" deep. Divide mature clumps.	8" apart tps min 35°F.	Two years from seed. Keep cut back and remove all flowers.
†Comfrey *Boraginaceae* *Symphytum*	Plant roots 6" deep.	36" apart tps	Large vigorous plant, keep cutting.
Dill *Umbelliferae* *Peucedanum* *Graveolens*	Sow seed thinly ¼" deep, every few weeks.	8" apart full sun	Cannot transplant. Both leaves & seeds good. Takes 2 months.
Garlic *Alliaceae* *Allium* *Sativum*	Plant cloves 1-2" deep	6" apart full sun	Pull & dry when leaves die. Takes 5 months.
***Marjoram** *Labiatae* *Origanum* *Majorana*	Sow seed thinly ¼" deep. Take cuttings or divide.	6" apart full sun	Grows slowly, milder than oregano. Likes lime.
†Mint *Labiatae* *Mentha*	Plant section of root 1-2" deep.	8" apart likes shade	Keep moist, grows rampantly.
†Oregano *Labiatae* *Origanum* *Vulgare*	Sow seed thinly ¼" deep. Divide or take cuttings.	6" apart full sun	Grows slowly, is perennial. Likes lime.
Parsley *Umbelliferae* *Carum* *Petroselinum*	Sow seed thinly ½" deep. Soaking speeds germination.	4" apart tps	Very nutritious. "Flat leaf" or "Italian" better flavored. Can be wintered over, but start seed annually.
†Rosemary *Labiatae* *Rosmarinus*	Sow seed thinly ¼" deep. Take cuttings in late spring.	8" apart (36" when full grown) full sun	Slow growing, but if frostfree will grow up to 4' in several years.
†Sage *Labiatae* *Salvia* *Officinalis*	Sow seed thinly ¼" deep. Take cuttings in spring.	6-12" apart full sun	Will last 2 or 3 years.

†Fairly hardy perennials, often grown outdoors, will overwinter quite far north if given some protection. But also often brought inside or grown inside to insure active growth and harvesting in winter.

Name	Propagation	Growing On	Comments
†**Savory (winter)** *Labiatae* *Satureja* *Montana*	Sow seed thinly on surface in August (in light). Take cuttings in spring.	12" apart full sun	Perennial, stronger flavor than summer.
†**Savory (summer)** *Labiatae* *Satureja* *Hortensis*	Sow seed thinly ¼" deep.	6" apart full sun 45-55°F.	A more subtle-flavored annual.
†**Sorrel** *Polygonaceae* *Rumex*	Sow seed thinly ¼" deep. Divide mature plants.	9" apart tps	Two years from seed.
†**Tarragon** *Compositae* *Artemisia* *Dracunculus*	Transplant runners in early spring. Take cuttings in fall. Sow seeds of Russian tarragon.	12" apart full sun	Best to start new plants every few years. Russian is bigger, less flavor.
†**Thyme** *Labiatae* *Thymus* *Vulgaris*	Sow seed thinly ¼" deep. Divide or take cuttings.	6" apart full sun	Likes lime. Lemon thyme very fragrant.

†Fairly hardy perennials, often grown outdoors, will overwinter quite far north if given some protection. But also often brought inside or grown inside to insure active growth and harvesting in winter.

Fruit

Use dwarf varieties indoors. It is generally better to buy fruit trees as young trees rather than starting them from seed (do not use seed you have saved because it is unlikely to produce edible fruits). All fruits need a lot of sunlight to ripen properly.

Fruit

Name	Propagation	Growing On	Comments
Citrus fruits (Grapefruit, Lemon, Orange, Tangerine) *Rutaceae citrus*	Sow seeds in March (60°F., ½" deep). Take cuttings in summer (60-65°F., peat-sand mix).	Days 60°F. (65-70°F. for fruit). Nights 45°F. (min 40°F.) Full sun	Likes acid soil. Water sparingly in winter and repot if necessary. Needs only frost protection, not much heat unless you want fruit in winter. May be pruned in early spring. Move outdoors in partial shade for summer. Needs hand pollinating indoors.
Figs *Moraceae* *Ficus* *Carica*	Layer (sever in 12 months). Take 4-6" cuttings in peat-sand mix (may take months to root).	50-65°F. (min 40°F.). Full sun	Takes a lot of space. Move outdoors in summer. Keep frost free in fall and winter (will often lose leaves). Can be given longer season by moving into warmth in late winter to restart growth early.

Fruit, cont'd

Name	Propagation	Growing On	Comments
Figs, cont'd			Keep fairly potbound. Likes humidity when hot. Will often produce two crops a year.
Grapes *Vitaceae* *Vitis* *Vinifera*	Take 2" cuttings in February, bury except for eye (55-60°F.). Or take 12" cuttings in fall.	50-65°F. (min. 40°F., max 80°F.) Full sun	Prune hard in autumn and train up a trellis. Allow each plant to produce only after 2 years and then only a few bunches until well established. Ventilate well.
Melons *Cucurbitaceae* *Cucumis* *Melo*	Sow seed on side ¼" deep, 2" apart, or 2 per pot thinning to 1 (75°F.).	60-80°F. (min 60°F. except cantalopes 55°F.). Full sun.	Takes a lot of space. Can be trained up trellis if fruits are supported (can then be 24" apart instead of 48" apart). Hard to transplant. Needs hand pollinating indoors. Limit to 6 fruits per plant. Keep humid atmosphere.
Peaches & Nectarines *Rosaceae* *Prunus* *Persica*	Sow stones 1" deep in fall (45-50°F).	45-55°F. until fruit sets, then 55-70°F. (Min 35°F., max 80°F.) Full sun.	Comments as for figs (except do not keep potbound).
Strawberries *Rosaceae* *Fragaria*	Plant rooted runners. Sow seed for alpine varieties.	50-70°F. Full sun 9-12" apart	Likes rich, well-drained soil, plenty of water. Pick off all blossoms the first year. Next year allow one runner to develop from each plant to make replacement. Needs hand pollinating indoors.

Companion Planting Guide

It has been known for centuries that some plants grow better when certain other plants are growing nearby. Science has gradually unearthed reasons why some combinations of plants are successful, but many other combinations that can be observed to be beneficial have as yet received no explanation.

In general, herbs and other aromatic plants like tomatoes, marigolds and onions are helpful in warding off insects. Usually, the more powerful the smell of the plant, the more effect it has. Certain colors, like the orange of nasturtium and marigold flowers, are thought to repel some harmful flying insects.

Sometimes, one plant's physical structure benefits that of another. Melons or cucumbers will provide dense shade for the roots of corn, while the corn provides a windbreak and some shade for the vines below. Many plants produce root exudates that discourage burrowing insects, or that cause chemical changes in the soil and benefit other plants. On the other hand, some plants produce root exudates that are hostile to other plants. Sunflowers, for example, tend to inhibit the growth of nearby plants. And some plants seem to lower the resistance to disease of others grown nearby. Potatoes—which you are unlikely to grow in a greenhouse in any

Companion Plants

Legend: ⧄ Good Companions ⊠ Bad Companions

	Beans, bush	Beans, pole	Beets	Brassicas	Carrots	Celery	Corn	Cucumbers	Eggplant	Lettuce	Melons	Onions	Peas	Peppers	Radishes	Spinach	Squash	Strawberries	Tomatoes
Tomatoes	⧄			⊠	⧄	⧄	⊠					⧄							
Strawberries	⧄			⊠						⧄									
Squash							⧄								⧄				
Spinach				⧄					⧄								⧄		
Sage			⧄	⧄			⊠												
Radishes	⧄	⧄								⧄			⧄						
Pigweed																			
Peppers																			
Peas	⧄	⧄			⧄		⧄					⊠			⧄				
Parsley					⧄														⧄
Onions	⊠	⊠	⧄		⧄					⧄			⊠					⧄	
Nasturtiums																	⧄		
Melons							⧄												
Marigolds	⧄	⧄																	
Lettuce	⧄	⧄			⧄			⧄							⧄			⧄	
Eggplant	⧄	⧄											⧄						
Cucumbers	⧄	⧄		⧄			⧄			⧄			⧄						
Corn	⧄	⧄						⧄			⧄		⧄				⧄	⊠	
Celery				⧄						⧄		⧄						⊠	
Carrots	⧄	⧄						⧄		⧄		⧄	⧄						⧄
Brassicas	⧄		⧄			⧄						⧄						⊠	
Beets	⧄	⧄								⧄		⧄							
Beans, pole					⧄		⧄	⧄				⊠			⧄				
Beans, bush		⧄	⧄	⧄	⧄	⧄	⧄	⧄				⊠	⧄		⧄				⧄
Basil																			⧄

SPECIAL COMPANIONS

Plant	Special companions
Beans, bush	savory, tansy
Beans, pole	savory, tansy
Brassicas	all strong herbs
Carrots	sage, no dill
Corn	no strong herbs
Onions	savory
Peas	turnips
Radishes	no hyssop
Spinach	cauliflower
Tomatoes	mint, no fennel

case—are vulnerable in this respect because their resistance is lowered by many other plants.

Some plants are used as "trap" crops so that when grown near more valuable plants, they will attract harmful insects away. But as a general rule, plants that attract the same harmful insects should not be grown close together or they will invite a proliferation of the pest.

Even fairly large animals can be discouraged by companion planting. Rabbits dislike onions, so garlic and chives are usually grown with the leafy greens rabbits like so well. Rue, a hardy blue-green herb, is said to repel cats, and pot marigolds keep dogs away.

Some of the plants that are commonly believed to benefit each other are in the accompanying chart. Those that do well when grown together are shown by a slash (/). Those that should *not* be grown near each other are marked by an asterisk (*).

Some valuable references on companion planting and natural insect repellents are *Companion Planting for Successful Gardening* by Louise Riotte, *The Bug Book* by Helen and John Philbrick (both Garden Way Publishing) and *The Organic Gardener* by Catharine O. Foster (Knopf).

Growing Conditions Bibliography

Companion Planting for Successful Gardening by Louise Riotte. Garden Way Publishing, Charlotte, Vermont. 1975. Hardcover $8.95, paperback $4.95. Hundreds of different plants which help or hinder each other, together with their effects on animals and insects you may want to lure in or keep out. Very interesting.

Encyclopedia of Organic Gardening J.I. Rodale, editor. Rodale Books, Emmaus, Pennsylvania. 1972. The A to Z reference of gardening terms.

Fern Growers Manual by Barbara J. Hoshizaki. Alfred A. Knopf, New York. 1975. $15.95. A beautifully illustrated and comprehensive guide to growing all sorts of ferns. Includes a section on the fine art of propagating ferns and one on the various ills they are heir to.

The Great American Tomato Book by Robert Hendrickson. Doubleday. 1977. $8.95. Probably more than you ever wanted to know about tomatoes, but makes fascinating reading.

Greenhouse Gardening as a Hobby by James Underwood Crockett. Doubleday. 1961. $7.95. A bit old-fashioned. Most of the book is devoted to good descriptions of various plants and their culture.

Greenhouse: Place of Magic by Charles H. Potter. E.P. Dutton & Co., New York. 1976. $3.95. Lots of information on different varieties of flowers, but

nothing on growing vegetables. Recommends chemical fertilizers and pesticides.

Home Orchid Growing by Rebecca T. Northen. Van Nos Reinhold. 1970. $22.50. The most complete and authoritative guide to growing your own orchids.

How To Grow Vegetables and Fruits by the Organic Method by J.I. Rodale and Staff of *Organic Gardening and Farming* Magazine. Rodale Books. 1961. $13.95. A bit dated, but still a reliable standby for organic gardeners. Primarily deals with fruits and vegetables outdoors, but includes a chapter on greenhouses and lots of relevant information under individual plant names.

Making Things Grow (Indoors) by Thalassa Cruso. Knopf. 1976. $4.95. The best all-round book on houseplants. Useful, though not written specifically for greenhouses. No information on growing fruits and vegetables, but excellent on enjoying and caring for potted plants.

Organic Gardening by Lawrence D. Hills. Penguin Books. 1977. Paperback $2.95. An excellent short guide to gardening organically. Written for the outdoor vegetable gardener in England, but it nonetheless has lots of sound ideas for use indoors in the United States.

Reader's Digest Encyclopaedia of Garden Plants and Flowers, published by Reader's Digest Association Ltd., London. 1971. The most thorough and authoritative collection of information on how to grow and propagate every conceivable garden plant, including many grown under glass, as well as all sorts of fruits and vegetables. Detailed descriptions and hundreds of color photographs allow you to identify plants you may have seen elsewhere. Oriented primarily toward growing things in the mild English climate, so needs adapting for local conditions in the United States, but invaluable as a source of information.

Success With Small Food Gardens by Louise Riotte. Garden Way Publishing. 1977. Paperback $5.95. A good short book on growing fruits and vegetables in a small space (essential in a greenhouse). Not written specifically for greenhouses, but has lots of relevant ideas. Good section on edible flowers.

Winter Flowers in Greenhouse & Sun-Heated Pit by Kathryn S. Taylor and Edith W. Gregg. Scribner's. 1976. $4.95. A wonderfully thorough discussion of general principles and individual plants for solar greenhouses in New England. Deals only with flowers.

Your Kitchen Garden by George Seddon and Helena Radecka. Mitchell Beazley Publishers Ltd. and Edenlite, London. 1975. A wonderful book, half devoted to careful, thorough descriptions of how to grow hundreds of varieties of vegetables and fruits, and half devoted to unusual recipes for cooking the food you have grown. Immaculately illustrated. Oriented primarily toward the outdoor gardener in England, but lots of information on cloches and some on greenhouses.

6

Pests and Diseases

From time to time, every greenhouse gardener finds a plant overrun by insects or infected with some serious disease. Greenhouses provide good growing conditions for pests as well as for plants. But a well-run greenhouse is much less susceptible to calamities. Healthy, fast-growing plants are less attractive to insects and can resist many diseases.

Good ventilation and good sanitation are probably the two key factors in reducing the incidence of pests and diseases in the greenhouse. Fungus diseases especially, but also many pests, are encouraged by stagnant, moist air conditions. Open the vents for half an hour in the afternoon even on cold days to dry out the air before the night chill sets in. A circulating fan is helpful in winter to keep the air moving when the vents are closed.

Keep the greenhouse clean and tidy. Dead leaves, bits of litter, even old cloths left lying about form breeding places for pests, and they can harbor the spores that will reinfect even the most carefully pasteurized soil. Weeds allowed to grow under the benches can hide pests you have eliminated in the rest of the greenhouse.

Once a year empty the greenhouse and scrub it from top to bottom. Fumigate it if you have had a bad infestation. Washing the glass periodically (inside and out) will improve light transmission and decrease chances of condensation dripping on plants.

Checking each plant individually and

thoroughly at frequent intervals will almost always reveal any problem at a stage where it can easily be dealt with. Once an infestation is allowed to run rampant, it is much more difficult to control, requiring strong chemicals or even the destruction of some of your favorite plants. If you can catch it when it is just beginning, almost any problem can be cured, and it can be prevented from spreading to other plants. For this reason it is important to check any new plant carefully before allowing it in your greenhouse. Some people keep new plants separate for a week or two to be sure they don't develop any problems they might pass on to their neighbors.

An isolation ward is a good idea for any plants that look unhealthy. By keeping them separate from other plants until you have

A NOTE TO THE READER

In this treatment of greenhouse pests and diseases, it will be clear to the reader that the authors' bias is toward the "organic" approach and against the "chemical." Both of these terms are inadequate if taken literally, but they describe the two camps in which gardeners generally find themselves. This discussion is aimed primarily at problems the home greenhouse keeper encounters on a relatively small scale, and is not oriented to the more specialized and large-scale problems found in commercial greenhouse management.

Those who disagree with these "organic" methods and prefer the "chemical" or poison approach are referred to their agricultural extension service for specific advice. These state-federal agencies try to keep up to date with the many periodic changes in government regulations pertaining to the use of pesticides and herbicides. The regulations are subject to such frequent modification, as new dangers come to light, that it is probably not wise in any case to include this sort of advice in permanent book form.

identified and dealt with the cause of their distress, you are sure to keep the problem within reasonable bounds. Badly infested plants should be destroyed. Even if you can cure the problems they have, they are likely to be so weakened that they will be susceptible to other problems for some time.

Wash your hands (and any tool you have used) after inspecting any sick plant before moving to the rest of your plants, to prevent the problem from spreading. Do not work with plants when they are wet because diseases are transferred more easily then. Don't smoke in or near a greenhouse, and if you have handled tobacco, wash your hands in skim milk before touching any tomato, pepper, petunia or other related plant (to avoid spreading tobacco mosaic virus).

Besides the damage they do in their own right, sucking insects like aphids and white fly frequently carry disease from one plant to another, so controlling the insect population is another way of preventing the spread of disease.

Using pasteurized soil for seeds and cuttings will help eliminate almost all the diseases which young plants are prone to get. Once they are growing sturdily, potting up in pasteurized soil is not necessary, but it is still a wise precaution, especially if you have had any serious diseases in your greenhouse in the last year. Pasteurized soil also eliminates the problem of weeding for some time until new weed seeds gradually drift in.

The same crop should never be grown for more than a year or two in the soil of the border unless you are able to pasteurize it in some way, because the pests and diseases that attack that plant are bound to increase year by year.

Scrub pots after use and before storing. Only use clean pots for repotting. Some people sterilize their clay pots with boiling water, and plastic pots with well-diluted bleach. Old clay pots covered with a hard white encrustation (due to hard water or excess fertilizer salts) should be scraped clean if possible. Otherwise the crust will prevent air and water from passing through the clay, and roots are more likely to be torn when repotting.

Always set newly potted plants in water halfway up the sides of the pot until the soil glistens with moisture. Leave clay pots in a few hours longer to be sure the pot is thoroughly wet and will not draw moisture from the soil. When bringing in plants that have spent the summer out of doors, soak them overnight to drown any insects in the soil.

The following tables list the most common symptoms that trouble plants in greenhouses, and give some of the possible causes. Only those causes that affect many varieties of plants are included, because each plant has some diseases or pests that are specific to it, but which are not likely to occur unless you grow masses of that one plant. Commercial growers who have whole greenhouses devoted to a single crop are subject to all sorts of problems that hardly ever arise in the mixed culture of a domestic greenhouse. If you want to concentrate on just one crop, or are especially interested in the health and well-being of one particular kind of plant, then it is probably worth investing in a specialist's guide to growing that plant.

Those symptoms that are common to almost all plants affected by a particular insect or disease are listed first. But the same insect or disease sometimes produces different symptoms in a particular variety of plant, and a list of these distinctive symptoms follows, divided into vegetables, flowers and fruits.

Each possible cause of a symptom is followed by a (P) or a (D) to indicate whether a description of that problem is to be found in the Pests section or the Diseases section. Some symptoms are due neither to a pest or a disease, but rather to the wrong growing conditions, such as too little sun, or more likely an imbalance in the soil fertility (discussed in Chapter 7).

In the Pests section and the Diseases section, each problem is described and some simple, natural remedies are given. For severe outbreaks, it may be necessary to use stronger measures. There are several natural insecticides such as pyrethrum, rotenone, nicotine extracts and diatomaceous earth, which are described in the Natural Insecticides section. Only revert to the really powerful chemical poisons in desperation. They are dangerous to you as well as to the beneficial insects, fungi, and bacteria in the greenhouse. Beware of using poisonous chemical on a plant you intend to eat.

The Bug Book by Helen and John Philbrick (Garden Way Publishing, 1974. Paperback $3.95) is a great help in identifying and combatting insect pests. Several organic insecticides can be found in *Gardening Without Poisons* by Beatrice Trum Hunter (Houghton Mifflin, 1972. $6.95).

Symptoms Common to Many Plants

Symptom	Possible Causes
seedlings collapse	damping off disease (D) fungus gnat larvae (P)
seedlings cut off at base	woodlice (P) cutworms (P) millipedes (P) leatherjackets (P)
rot at base of stem, plant wilts and dies	stem rot or root rot (D)

Symptom	Possible Causes
plant pale and spindly	not enough sun
stunted growth	aphids (root) (P) spider mites (P) symphilids (P) white fly (P) mosaic viruses (D)
bluish leaves	symphilids (P) phosphorus deficiency excess potash

Symptoms Common to Many Plants, cont'd

Symptom	*Possible Causes*
yellowing leaves and/or wilting in strong sun (probably the most common symptoms of distress in a plant, generally associated with some damage to the root system)	soil too dry soil consistently too wet cold soil and warm air nitrogen deficiency stem or root rot (D) viruses (D) borers (P) eelworms (P) symphilids (P) millipedes (P) leatherjackets (P) wireworms (P) only if heavily infested, in which case the pest should be fairly visible aphids (especially root aphids) (P) scale insects (P) spider mites (P) thrips (P) white fly (P) wilt (D)
yellowing leaves, but veins remain green	excess alkalinity iron deficiency if affects young leaves magnesium deficiency if affects older leaves
discolored leaves	viruses (D)
mottled leaves (usually light and dark green) sometimes distorted	mosaic virus (D) manganese deficiency (often due to excess acidity)
yellow patches on leaves	downy mildew (D) mosaic virus (D) aphids (P) leaf hoppers (P) scale insects (P) white fly (P)
brown patches on leaves	powdery mildew (D)
small brown spots on leaves	capsid bugs (P)
brown spots under leaves	thrips (P)
brown patches on stem	gray mold (D) stem rot (D) eelworms (stem) (P)

Symptom	*Possible Causes*
yellow or brown spore masses on leaves	rust (D)
brown or orange patches between leaf veins	magnesium deficiency eelworms (P)
watery spots on leaves or buds	eelworms (P)
stippled leaves	spider mites (P) thrips (P) white fly (P) leafhoppers (P)
edges of leaves scorched	potash deficiency
growing tips pale and spindly	aphids (P) cuckoo spit (P)
top of plant withers	borers (P)
distorted leaves & buds	capsid bugs (P) eelworms (P) spider mites (P) thrips (P)
leaves curl	temperature fluctuates too much leafrollers (P) sometimes aphids (P)
malformed flowers	aphids (P) capsid bugs (P) cyclamen mites (P) cuckoo spit (P) eelworms (P) midge larvae (P) thrips (P)
buds or flowers drop, or fail to set fruit	not enough sun temperature fluctuates too much air too dry soil too dry too many drafts excess nitrogen thrips (P)
brown spots or patches on flowers	aphids (P) cyclamen mites (P) thrips (P)

Symptom	Possible Causes	Symptom	Possible Causes
raggedly chewed leaves or flowers	caterpillars (P) cockroaches (P) crickets (P) earwigs (P) slugs or snails (P)	white powder on leaves	powdery mildew (D)
		fruit and/or flowers rot, may show gray fuzz	gray mold (D)
stem gnawed	cutworms (P) leatherjackets (P) millipedes (P) slugs or snails (P) springtails (P) symphilids (P) woodlice (P)	thin white mold on soil white wooly covering on roots and soil	funguses (D) aphids (root) (P)
		sticky, wooly, white bumps	scale insects (P) (mealy bugs)
only lower leaves chewed	cutworms (P) symphilids (P) woodlice (P)	brown or whitish waxy bumps on stem or leaves	scale insects (P)
small holes in leaves	flea beetles (P) springtails (P) earwigs (P) capsid bugs (P)	white froth in leaf axils or on stem	cuckoo spit (P)
		pale webbing in leaf axils or growing tips	spider mites (P)
galls on leaves, deformed buds and flowers	midge larvae (P)	webs with caterpillars visible inside	leaf webbers (P)
galls on roots	eelworms (P)	clouds of tiny white insects fly up when leaf disturbed	white fly (P)
sticky honeydew on leaves (often covered with a sooty mold)	aphids (P) scale insects (P) white fly (P)	black specks on leaves, fruit and leaves scarred	thrips (P)
black mold on leaves	funguses (D)		

Symptoms in Vegetable Plants

Symptom	Possible Causes	Symptom	Possible Causes
Lettuce		**Squash, Melons & Cucumbers, cont'd**	
edge of leaf scorched	too dry excess fertilizer	watery spots at leaf nodes	gray mold (D)
watery spots on leaf	gray mold (D)	slimy, bad-smelling spots on fruits, split fruits	gummosis (D)
Peas			
roots then stem black	wilt (fusarium) (D)		
Squash, Melons & Cucumbers		**Tomatoes**	
part of vine wilts	borer (P)	seedlings purplish	mosaic virus (D)
pale spots turn brown, leaf edges watery	stem rot (D)	plants purplish, wilt easily, fibrous roots	eelworms (potato cyst) (P)

Symptoms in Vegetable Plants, cont'd

Symptom	Possible Causes
Tomatoes, cont'd	
pale lower leaves, wilts easily, fibrous roots	eelworms (root knot) (P)
mottled leaves, bushy plant, small seedless fruits	aspermey (D)
leaves eaten except for veins	caterpillars (P)
pitted leaves	leafminers (P)
infested seed leaves	leafminers (P)
brown patches on stem	excess manganese

Symptom	Possible Causes
bronzing of fruit	too hot
	boron deficiency
	mosaic virus (D)
green shoulders on fruit	excess sunlight
	potash deficiency
light-colored patches on fruit which remain hard	irregular feeding
	irregular watering
fruits split	irregular watering
	temperature fluctuates too much

Symptoms in Flowering Plants

Symptom	Possible Causes
African Violets	
yellow spots on leaves	too much sun
	water splashes
Azaleas	
flowers and young leaves streaked white	thrips (P)
Begonias	
yellow patches with brown spots between veins of leaf	mosaic virus (D)
Carnations	
small white spots on leaves	spider mites (P)
Chrysanthemums	
yellow-green spots above brownish warts below	rust (D)
flowers small, distorted	aspermey (D)
flowers raggedly chewed	earwigs (P)
holes in leaves & buds	caterpillar (angleshade moth) (P)
tiny white spots on leaves, then silver lines	leafminers (P)
⅛" cone-shaped galls on leaves and stems	midge larvae (P)

Symptom	Possible Causes
Chrysanthemums, cont'd	
yellowing of lower leaves, few flowers	overcrowding
Cyclamen	
weak, yellowed plant	root rot (see stem rot) (D)
buds rot, outer leaves curl up	cyclamen mite (P)
Gardenias	
yellow leaves	too cold
Geraniums	
watery spots on leaves	stem rot (D)
rings of brown spore masses under leaves, yellow patches above	rust (D)
purple spots on leaves	too cold
red leaves	too sudden an increase in sun
Roses	
yellow or purple spots on leaves, gray fur below	downy mildew (D)
stunted growth, small galls on roots	eelworms (dagger) (P)

Symptoms in Fruit Trees

Symptom	Possible Causes
red or yellow leaves, twig or leaf distortion	aphids (P)
yellow spotted leaves, turning brown	spider mites (P)

Symptom	Possible Causes
young shoots wilt and die, fruits rot	gray mold (D)
white grubs in fruit	midge larvae (P)

Symptoms in Strawberry Plants

Symptom	Possible Causes
red spots on distorted leaves	mosaic virus (D)
discoloration, distortion, and stunting of leaves	viruses (D)
younger leaves stunted and wrinkled, older leaves silvery brown	cyclamen mites (P)

Symptom	Possible Causes
young leaves crinkled, midribs swollen below	eelworms (stem) (P)
young leaves distorted with rough gray-brown spots	eelworms (leaf and bud) (P)

Pests

Aphids (also called blackfly, greenfly and plant lice). Very small creatures, usually pale green, but sometimes red, black, yellow or brown. They are normally wingless, soft-bodied creatures slowly crawling up the plant, but when overcrowded some types develop wings and can fly to a new host. They suck the sap out of young leaves, usually congregating around the growing points of the plant. The first sign of attack may be the sticky "honeydew" they excrete, or it may be just the pale sickly appearance of the leaves. Close inspection will usually reveal dozens of aphids on young shoots. Some species of aphids feed on the roots of the plant, producing a white wooly fur on the roots and nearby soil.

Washing a plant with soft soap and water twice, about a week apart, will usually overcome an aphid invasion. Spraying with a garlic and red pepper solution is also effective, and the same solution can be poured on the soil to control root aphids. Nasturtiums and chives growing nearby are supposed to discourage aphids. Since aphids are often brought to a plant by ants, tansy, mint and other ant-discouraging plants planted around the greenhouse should help to control the aphid population. Ladybugs and their larvae (which look like spotted crocodiles) are the aphids' biggest predators and should be encouraged.

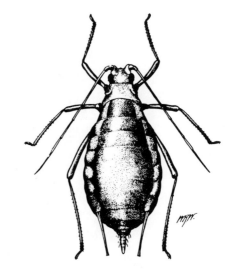

Figure 9.1. A sketch of a wingless female pea aphid.

Figure 9.2. An infestation of pea aphids convening on pea leaves.

Figure 9.3. Bean aphids vying for right-of-way on the stem of a nasturtium.

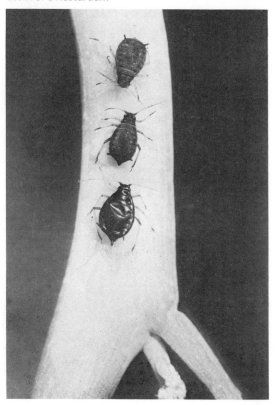

Bishop bugs. See *Capsid bugs.*

Borers. Usually found only in the garden, these moth larvae devour the stem of the plant from within. The first sign of trouble is usually the sudden collapse of the plant above the point of attack. The damaged stem will have to be cut off, except in squash, melons and cucumbers. In cucurbits (the squash family), the stem can be split open, the borer removed and the wound buried in the earth. The vine will then usually heal itself. Nasturtiums and garlic will discourage the moth, and planting either very early or very late will avoid the time at which the female moth is laying her eggs.

Figure 9.4. A squash borer and the damage it has inflicted on a squash plant.

All photos in this chapter are courtesy of the U.S. Department of Agriculture

Capsid bugs (including tarnished plant bugs or bishop bugs). Bugs which suck the sap from many kinds of plants, usually producing tiny holes surrounded by brown spots. Both leaves and flowers are likely to become stunted and distorted. The young nymphs are green and wingless. The adults are green or brownish with two wings, and are about one-quarter inch long. They are usually troublesome in late summer, spending most of the year in weeds. *Organic Gardening Under Glass* suggests spraying with a red pepper solution.

Caterpillars. The larvae of any moth or butterfly, often greatly attracted to the succulent plants growing in a greenhouse. They are usually voracious eaters, chewing great holes in the leaves. They often pupate in the greenhouse, emerging to lay more eggs and produce more caterpillars. Screening the doors and ventilators to prevent the first moth getting in, and hand-picking any caterpillars or egg clusters you find are the best methods of control. Many caterpillars are susceptible to a disease caused by a bacteria called *Bacillus thuringiensis*. See Natural Insecticide section. See also *Borers, Cutworms, Leafminers, Leaftiers, Leafwebbers.*

Click beetles. See *Wireworms.*

Crane fly larvae. See *Leatherjackets.*

Cockroaches. Not uncommon in heated greenhouses, they are rapacious feeders. One to one and a half inches long and dark brown, cockroaches can move startlingly fast when disturbed. They can be trapped by burying bottles level with the soil and putting a small amount of beer or any sweet syrup in each. Removing possible hiding places near the source of heat will hinder their breeding cycle.

Crickets. One-half to one inch long, these chirruping, long-distance jumping insects are usually more charming than harmful.

But more than one or two in a greenhouse can cause quite a lot of damage by gnawing stems, leaves or flowers of almost any plant.

Cuckoo spit. Actually the protective, white foam covering the young of the froghopper. The adults are a quarter inch long, yellow or brown and able to jump long distances, as their name implies. The young are yellowish green, but are usually hidden in a frothy mass of cuckoo spit. It is the young which do the most damage, so removing any patches of foam you see will control the problem. A hard spray of water (or better, tobacco solution) will get rid of those that are hard to reach.

Cutworms. A menace in the garden, but less common in the greenhouse, these fat, brown caterpillars, one to two inches long, are the larvae of certain moths. They live underground and feed on young plant stems during the night, often cutting completely through them at ground level. A few species crawl up the stem and feed on the leaves. They can all be defeated by a paper collar or tin can placed around the seedling and half buried in the earth. *The Bug Book* suggests a

Figure 9.5. A southern armyworm chews its way through the leaf of a bean plant. This species of climbing cutworm produces four or more generations a year and feeds on buds, leaves and fruits of vegetable crops, as well as those in orchards and vineyards.

Figure 9.6. The variegated cutworm: A the moth, B the extended larva and C the curled cutworm.

Figure 9.7. A granulate cutworm larva.

sliver of wood inserted next to the stem to prevent stem-eating cutworms from encircling the stem and gnawing through it. During the day cutworms sleep, curled up, near the surface of the soil and can usually be found and killed by a little digging near damaged plants. Oak leaves are said to discourage them.

Cyclamen mites (also called strawberry mites). Minute, colorless mites which feed on very young leaves. Leaves and buds are small, distorted and spotted with brown. Cyclamen mites affect african violets, begonias,

cyclamen, fuschias, geraniums, strawberries and other plants. They are difficult to control. *Organic Gardening Under Glass* suggests immersing the whole plant in 110°F. water for two minutes. *Gardening Without Poisons* suggests fumigating the greenhouse with smoldering oak leaves.

Earwigs. Dark brown shiny insects about ¾ inch long with a pair of curved pincers for a tail. They feed on leaves, flowers and fruits during the night. In the daytime they hide in dark dry places, usually under bits of rubbish. They can easily be caught in an earwig trap—a bit of dry moss put in the bottom of a flower pot or other container that is turned upside down on a stake. It will attract earwigs as a safe refuge after a night's feeding. They can then be knocked out of the pot during the day and killed. Large flowers like dahlias provide a natural earwig refuge, and if shaken vigorously can be used as earwig traps.

Figure 9.8. The earwig.

Eelworms (also called nematodes). Many, many varieties of this microscopic worm exist. Several of them are a serious menace to growing plants both in the greenhouse and in the garden. Other nematodes are innocuous or even beneficial, feeding on harmful insects in the soil. A soil rich in humus will encourage the beneficial nematodes and discourage the harmful ones. Most of the nematodes that damage plants live in the soil and attack plant roots, causing them to form small cysts, but some feed on leaves and buds. One of the worst species is the *potato-cyst eelworm,* attacking all solanaceous plants (tomatoes, peppers, eggplants, potatoes, etc). Eelworms are difficult to control, requiring pasteurization to 200°F. to be sure of eradicating them. Marigolds are said to repel many varieties, especially if grown as a crop and turned under in fall. *Organic Gardening Under Glass* suggests that mustard and asparagus will also discourage certain nematodes. Many plants have varieties that are resistant to nematode attack.

Flea beetles. Minute black insects that jump away when disturbed. They are not such a pest in the greenhouse as they are in the garden. They eat tiny round holes in the leaves of seedlings and young plants, but a fast-growing plant will not be seriously harmed by them since they will leave it alone as soon as its tissues begin to mature. Nettle tea (see Natural Insecticides section) will drive them away when sprinkled on the plants, but this is necessary only if you have a real epidemic.

Froghoppers. See *Cuckoo Spit.*

Fungus gnat larvae. Tiny black gnats which lay eggs on the soil. The larvae (a quarter inch long, pale with black heads) burrow down and feed on root hairs or occasionally foliage. The plant stops growing, may wilt and eventually die. The larvae can be drowned by immersing the pot in water to soil level for six hours. Adult gnats can be discouraged from laying their eggs by spraying the plant with tobacco solution.

Gall midges. See *Midge Larvae.*

Leafhoppers. Pale jumping insects one-eighth inch long that suck the sap from leaves, producing pale blotches and weakening the plant. They are especially fond of chickweed, which should be removed from the neighborhood of the greenhouse if leafhoppers are a problem. Spray the underside of the leaves of infested plants with tobacco solution every two weeks.

Leafminers. The larvae of any of several flies or moths which burrow inside the leaf itself. Their tunnelling trails are visible from outside the leaf as light-colored wiggling lines. Affected leaves should be picked and burned.

Figure 9.9. Two phases of the leafminer: its maggots are seen in a photograph taken after removing the membranous surface of a leaf; its larval cases are shown, with one larva emerging from a case.

Leaftiers (also called leafrollers). The caterpillars of various moths, which twist a leaf about themselves for protection. If the leaves are fairly stiff they may simply glue two adjacent leaves together with the fine white webbing they exude. Usually you will find a small caterpillar inside each twist or leaf sandwich. Even if they are empty, however, pick off any stuck-together leaves and burn because there may be eggs in his hiding place. Nearby leaves often show ragged holes where the caterpillar has fed.

Leafwebbers. The caterpillars of any of several moths that live together in a tent of fine webbing, which they spin to protect themselves while they feed on the leaves inside the web. Branches bearing large webs should be cut off and burned. Small webs can be picked off, taking care to get rid of all the caterpillars. Leafwebbing caterpillars rarely get to be a serious problem in a greenhouse because, though they are voracious feeders, their webs make them very visible.

Leatherjackets (larvae of crane flies). Thick, dark, worm-like creatures, one to one and a half inches long, with a tough skin. The adults are large delicate flies with gauzy wings and long, dangling legs. The larvae live just below the surface of the soil, feeding on roots and stems. They like damp soil and dense vegetation, so clearing out weeds, cultivating the soil surface and letting the soil dry out between waterings should all help to eliminate them.

Mealy bugs. See *Scale insects.*

Midge larvae (gall midges). Little white maggots which develop into small flies. The larvae feed on leaves and flowers, causing them to distort. They gather in warty growths, (galls) on leaves, and any such growths should be burned immediately.

Millipedes. Many-legged insects with segmented bodies one-third to one inch long. They may be cream, brown or black. Distinguished from centipedes (which are usually beneficial) by having two pairs of legs on each body segment instead of one. Also millipedes are less active, often merely curling up rather than running away when disturbed. At night they feed on the roots and stems of seedlings and occasionally eat the

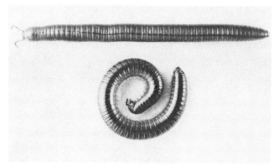

Figure 9.10. A millipede, the Julius impressus, shown extended and curled up.

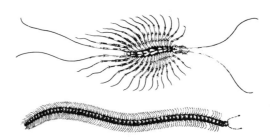

Figure 9.11. A centipede at the top, and below it a millipede. The names derive from the Latin prefixes for one hundred and one thousand. In both cases, the numbers are an exaggeration, but the general idea is that the millipede has a lot more legs than the centipede.

seeds themselves. During the day they curl up in decaying humus or rich soil. Scratch around near any affected plant and kill any millipedes you find. Using pasteurized soil for seed sowing usually eliminates the problem since millipedes are only fond of very

---

IS IT GOOD OR BAD?

In general, if in doubt about an insect, leave it alone; you will do far more harm killing one predator than you will do good by killing one pest. There is, however, an old rule that is about 70 percent right: "The easier you can catch it, the better that you should kill it." The grain of truth in this rule is that predators generally need to move fast to catch their prey, while insects that eat plants can be quite sedentary.

---

young plants (or those which have been previously damaged by some other pest). Drenching the soil with tobacco solution helps, especially if more tobacco solution is sprayed on those which come to the surface.

Mites. See *Cyclamen mites* and *Spider mites*.

Nematodes. See *Eelworms*.

Pillbugs. See *Woodlice*.

Plant bugs. See *Capsid bugs*.

Scale insects (including mealy bugs). Small insects which move very slowly if at all. They look like brown or white waxy bumps on stems or underneath leaves. Mealy bugs are closely related, but can move slowly over the plant. They are white and rather furry or waxy looking. All scale insects excrete a sticky "honeydew" which encourages mold. They suck the sap of the host plant, causing the leaves to turn yellow and wilt. Washing the plant, and if possible scrubbing it, with soapy water or tobacco solution a few times will get rid of most of the pests. If there are only a few, touching each with a dab of rubbing alcohol, turpentine or kerosene will kill them.

Slaters. See *Woodlice*.

Slugs and snails. Closely related slimy creatures, one with a shell and one without. They can quickly chew enormous ragged holes in leaves or fruit, or destroy large numbers of seedlings overnight. They usually spend the day in dark, damp hiding places, coming out to feed mainly at night. Their soft bodies leave behind a shining trail of mucus as they move. Any rough or dehydrating surface is irritating to their tender bodies, and they will try to avoid it. Cinders, lime, or ashes will discourage them, and salt will kill them outright, dissolving them into slimy puddles. They can easily be trapped with saucerfuls of honey or beer, which stimulate

Figure 9.12. The common garden slug.

them to a fatal overindulgence. Looking under empty flower pots or seed flats will often disclose a few slugs, which can be quickly dispatched with the shake of a salt cellar. Their eggs look like clusters of small transparent balls, a pale version of caviar. These should be destroyed whenever found.

Sowbugs. See *Woodlice*.

Spider mites (or red spider mites). Tiny, almost invisible pests that are often red, but sometimes yellow-green or tan. The first signs of trouble are usually the small pale cobwebs in leaf axils and on growing points. Mites suck the plant's sap, causing a fine pale speckling on the leaves, which eventually becomes mottled yellow with a papery texture. A hard spray of water (especially on the underside of the leaves) will dislodge many mites and should be repeated frequently. Dipping affected plants in buttermilk is supposed to drive away spider mites. *Ced-o-flora* (a nonpoisonous insect deterrent) is effective against mites. Maintaining a cool, humid

Figure 9.13. An adult female of the two-spotted spider mite.

atmosphere will go a long way toward preventing an attack. Spider mites are resistant to chemical insecticides and in fact often benefit from them because their predators are killed off. For severe infestations, a supply of predatory mites known as *Phytoseiulus persimilis* can be purchased (see section on beneficial insects).

Springtails. Tiny white insects which jump violently when disturbed. They do not usually do much harm, but occasionally they feed on root hairs or young seedlings. Young leaves will show tiny holes in the surface of the foliage. When a pot plant is heavily watered, the springtails float to the surface of the soil, where they can easily be seen. They thrive in damp soil on decaying plant matter, so keeping a tidy greenhouse and avoiding overwatering should prevent an excessive number of them.

Strawberry mites. See *Cyclamen mites.*

Symphilids. Soft white centipede-like creatures, about a quarter inch long, which live in the soil and feed on young roots. If a plant is weak, wilts easily and has bluish leaves, turn it out of its pot and look for symphilids in the soil. They quickly burrow back into the soil when exposed, so look carefully. Dunking the root ball in a bucket of water should bring any symphilids to the surface. If you find them, kill them, cut off any damaged roots and repot in pasteurized soil.

Thrips. Very tiny, fast-moving insects which attack both leaves and flowers causing small pale scars. They also leave behind a deposit of black specks. The most troublesome variety is usually the onion thrip, which sucks the sap of members of the onion family and for some reason also fancies carnations, chrysanthemums and several other flowers. Spraying with soapy water, tobacco solution or garlic and red pepper should help to control all thrips. Reducing the heat and increasing the humidity will also help.

HEAT AND COLD

Extremes of temperature will get rid of most pests that thrive in the controlled environment of a greenhouse. In midsummer, removing all the plants on a sunny day and shutting the vents can push the temperature up above 100°F. If you have a greenhouse heater or any portable heater you can put on as well, so much the better. In midwinter, if the greenhouse can be emptied or if only very hardy plants are growing in it, you can kill many insects by freezing them out. Simply leave the doors and vents wide open during a cold spell. The temperature should quickly drop to the freezing levels outside, but it is a good idea to leave the greenhouse open for several days to be sure the soil has frozen through.

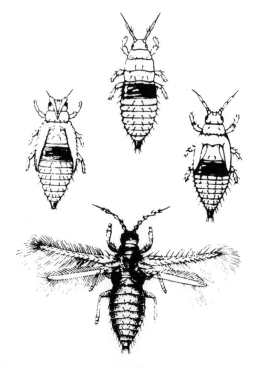

Figure 9.14. Four phases of the red-banded thrip: From the top clockwise, the full-grown larva, prepupa, adult female, and pupa.

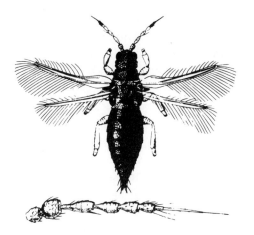

Figure 9.15. A much-enlarged sketch of the female greenhouse thrip, with an ever more-enlarged view of its antenna. The true size of the thrips is about that of the dots over the i's on these pages.

Tortrix moths. See *Leaftiers*.

White fly. A tiny, mothlike sap-sucking insect usually found on the underside of leaves, but which rises in clouds when disturbed. Infested plants are weakened, the leaves becoming mottled with yellow and often covered with a sticky honeydew. It is commonly found in greenhouses and is dif-

ficult to control. Spraying with soapy water, tobacco solution or *Ced-o-flora* helps. Repeat once a week, paying special attention to the undersides of leaves, until no more white flies are visible, and even then keep a sharp eye out for reinfestation. Rhubarb, peruvian ground cherry and nasturtiums planted in the greenhouse are said to repel white flies. There is a special wasp called *Encarsia formosa* which is parasitic on white flies and very effective at getting rid of them.

Wireworms (larvae of click beetles). Look like hard, shiny yellow worms, about one inch long, but have three pairs of legs and powerful jaws. The adults are dark brown beetles, about a half inch long, which when they fall on their backs can right themselves with a loud snap. The larvae feed on roots and bulbs of many plants. They are most common in soil that has not previously been cultivated, so be sure to pasteurize soil from pastureland or waste patches of ground.

Woodlice (also called sowbugs, slaters and pill bugs). Gray-brown creatures about one-half inch long which roll up in a ball when disturbed. They are fond of damp, decaying matter and are usually found out of doors under rocks or old pieces of wood, emerging at night to feed. It is unnerving to discover them in the greenhouse under old pots or seed

Figure 9.16. Nymphs and adults of the greenhouse whitefly.

Figure 9.17 A sketch and photograph of the pillbug, also known as the sowbug and the woodlouse. When disturbed, it often rolls into a perfect circle, hence the name "pillbug."

boxes, but they do not often do much harm, although they occasionally attack seedlings. If you suffer from an infestation of these queer creatures (with their hard segmented shells and many legs, they are most closely related to lobsters!) you can get rid of many of them by using an earwig trap with the addition of a piece of fruit or vegetable in the bottom of the pot to act as bait.

Diseases

Aspermey. A virus disease of tomatoes that also affects chrysanthemums. The plant becomes bushy and somewhat stunted. The leaves become mottled and distorted. Tomato fruits are small, often seedless. Chrysanthemum flowers are small, distorted and show color changes. Aphids spread this virus, so be sure to deal with them. Destroy infected plants and take cuttings only from healthy stock.

Botrytis. See *Gray mold.*

Damping off disease. Any of a variety of fungus diseases that cause seedlings to collapse suddenly and completely, stem and/or roots having rotted. Plants cannot be revived, but good ventilation and drier soil and air conditions will prevent the fungus from spreading. Use pasteurized soil to prevent initial infection, avoid overcrowding and re-

---

MANURE TEA

Manure tea is a wonderful fertilizer and restorative for hard-pressed plants. Soak dried manure (or rich compost) in warm water, using about one pint of manure to one gallon of water. After twenty-four hours, strain it and either water the plant with it or use as a foliage spray. Nettle tea has much the same effect.

---

move any sickly seedlings quickly. *Gardening Without Poisons* suggests spraying with camomile tea. Maintain optimum growing conditions because fast-growing seedlings are much less liable to infection.

Downy mildew. A white fungus growing in patches on the undersides of leaves. The part of the leaf above the mildew often turns yellow. Destroy infected leaves. Increase ventilation, and perhaps heat, to reduce humidity. Avoid splashing the leaves when watering.

Funguses. There are hundreds of varieties of fungus diseases that attack plants, causing molds, mildews or rotting spots on leaves, flowers, fruits, roots or soil. Fungus diseases are common in greenhouses. Their presence indicates overwatering or too high a level of humidity in the air. The plant will usually revive if the infected part is cut off and humidity is reduced. Fungus growths on the soil should be scraped off and watering reduced. A black mold on the leaves is usually caused by a fungus that grows on the "honeydew" secreted by aphids and scale insects; the treatment is simply to get rid of the insects and wash off the sooty covering on the leaves. Camomile flowers, chives, equisetum ("horsetail"), and horseradish leaves are all said to help prevent mildew. Pour boiling water on a handful of one and steep for fifteen minutes. When cool, strain and use as a spray. Wilts and funguses that cause the plant to rot (see *gray mold, gummosis, stem rot* and *wilt*) are a much more serious menace than the unsightly molds and mildews that frequently occur in greenhouses. Generally, pasteurizing the soil, removing any dead or infected leaves and maintaining good ventilation will greatly reduce the likelihood of fungus infections.

Gray mold (also called botrytis). A fungus disease encouraged by high humidity. Fruit, flowers, leaves and stems may all show rotting spots, usually covered with a gray fur. Reduce humidity, increase ventilation and

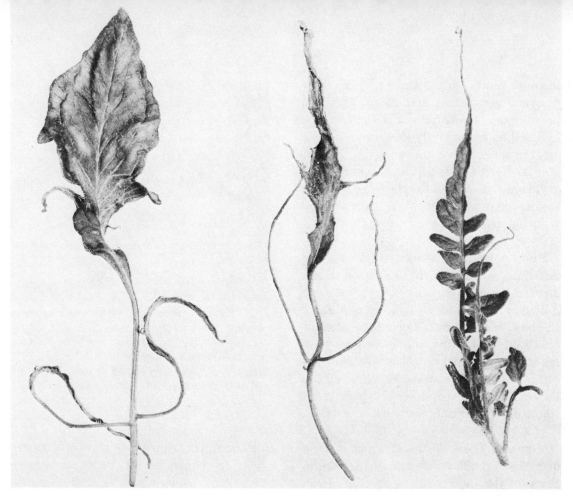

Figure 9.18. Cucumber mosaic virus on tomato leaves. It is nicknamed the "shoe-string" virus for good reason.

remove infected parts of the plant. Wash your hands after handling infected plants because the disease spreads easily.

Gummosis. A fungus disease affecting cucumbers, melons and squash. Gray, oozing spots develop on young fruits, which eventually split open, exposing a green fungus inside. Destroy any infected fruits. Reduce humidity by increasing heat and ventilation. If gummosis is a persistent problem in your greenhouse, you can grow resistant varieties.

Mosaic viruses. There are several varieties of mosaic, some specific to certain plants, others more widespread. One of the commonest forms is tobacco mosaic virus, which is often spread by people who handle tobacco. Tomatoes, peppers and other solanaceous plants are particularly susceptible to tobacco mosaic, but orchids, cacti and other plants can get it also. A cucumber mosaic

virus affects all members of the squash family and several flowering plants as well. Most mosaic viruses cause yellow patches on leaves, giving a mottled appearance overall. They sometimes stunt and distort leaf growth as well. Skim milk is quite good at inhibiting mosaic viruses. Dipping your hands in skim milk after smoking will prevent the spread of tobacco mosaic virus. Spraying a plant with skim milk helps to protect it against all mosaic virus diseases.

Powdery mildew. A fungus that covers leaves and young shoots with a sort of grey or white powder. Brown patches on leaves with a gray powder beneath are another sign of powdery mildew. Prevention is the same as for downy mildew.

Root rot. See *Stem rot.*

Rust. Any of several fungus diseases affecting mint, carnations, asters, snapdragons, geraniums, and roses. Yellow or brown spore masses form on the leaves. Mint leaves become severely distorted. Destroy any infected leaves or severely infected plants. Keep plants and atmosphere fairly dry, being careful not to splash the leaves or stems when watering. Make sure there is sufficient potassium available in the soil.

Stem rot (including root rot). One of several fungus diseases that cause either the stem or the roots (usually both) to rot. Dark brown or black patches can often be found at the base of the stem. The plant becomes increasingly unhealthy, the lower leaves yellowing, and the whole plant wilting easily until it finally collapses. Remove any infected plants immediately. Use pasteurized soil to prevent initial infection.

Viruses. There are many kinds of virus diseases that affect different kinds of plants. Some of the most virulent are the mosaic

Figure 9.20. An orchid afflicted by a virus similar to common tobacco mosaic virus. This virus attacks cattleya orchids, the mainstay of the orchid business, by causing the color of the lavendar flowers to break into darkly pigmented streaks and spots, making them unsaleable.

viruses (see *Mosaic viruses*). Once a virus infects a plant, the whole plant will be diseased and cannot usually be saved. Most viruses are first indicated by mottled or discolored leaves. Insects, tools or even your own hands can spread a virus disease, so destroy infected plants, wash your hands and tools after handling any plant you suspect, and control insect populations. Aphids and other sucking insects are common carriers of viruses.

Figure 9.19. The gladious stem at right has been infected with cucumber mosaic virus, spread by aphids, causing a symptom called flower breakage, as seen in the spike. The spike at left is normal, for comparison.

Figure 9.21. A tomato plant with symptoms of bacterial wilt. All branches have wilted at about the same time because of bacterial infection in the stem.

Wilt. Verticillium wilt and fusarium wilt are the two most common types of this fungus disease. Leaves gradually become yellow, and wilt—usually old leaves first and gradually progressing up the plant. Pasteurizing the soil and keeping a clean greenhouse go a long way toward controlling this fungus. Resistant varieties of most plants can be obtained.

Beneficial Insects

Aphid lions. See *Lacewings.*

Braconid wasps. Small wasps which lay their eggs in caterpillars. The larvae make tiny white cocoons which stick out all over the caterpillar like fat spines. The caterpillar gradually is eaten alive by the wasp larvae, which then hatch out and go on to lay their eggs in other caterpillars.

Damsel flies. See *Dragonflies.*

Dragonflies. Like their smaller relatives the damsel flies, dragonflies are skilled hunters. They catch other insects in midair or swoop them from the surface of the water. They are especially fond of mosquitos.

Encarsia formosa. A tiny parasitic wasp that can decimate the white fly population in a few months. It lays its eggs in the white fly larvae, turning them black. They are so effective that sometimes they starve themselves out by eradicating all the white flies. Probably more worthwhile in a large greenhouse. It is worth keeping one badly infested plant elsewhere to be sure the wasps will have enough white flies to reproduce in, especially during the winter when white flies breed more slowly.

Fireflies. Besides being the delight of summer evenings, fireflies eat slugs and snails for you, and their larvae eat cutworms. So if your children catch any of these dull, black elongated beetles with their phosphorescent green taillights, ask them to release their fireflies in your greenhouse. They may not stay long, but they might eat a few pests on their way out.

Hover flies (syrphid flies). Their larvae look like small green slugs and eat enormous quantities of aphids. It might be worth planting convolvulus tricolor (a small relative of the morning glory) near the greenhouse to feed the adult hover flies so they will lay their eggs among your aphids.

Ichneumon flies. Really a long slender delicate wasp (up to two inches long). It looks like it might sting but it does not; it uses what looks like its stinger to lay eggs in many kinds of caterpillars. The larva eats the caterpillar from within.

Lacewing flies. These flies look like gauzy, pale green flies with golden eyes. Their larvae, nicknamed *aphid lions*, are small ferocious-looking creatures which eat aphids and many other small insects with gusto. Available from: Rincon-Vitova Insectaries, Box 95, Oak View, California 93022; or Vitova Insectary, Box 475, Rialto, California 92376; or Insect Pest Advisory Service, 762 South First St., Kerman, California 93630.

Ladybugs. The prime predator of small soft-bodied insects, especially aphids. Their cheerful red shells with black spots are a common and welcome feature of most gardens and many greenhouses. Less well known, but almost equally voracious, are their larvae—like small black crocodiles with yellow or orange spots down their backs. Ladybug eggs are bright yellow and come in clusters, usually on the underside of the leaves. Ladybugs should be protected and encouraged in every way. They are available from: Bio-Control Co., 10180 Ladybird Ave.,

Auburn, California 95603; Greenberg Control Co., Route 4, Box 1891, Oroville, California 95603; Insect Pest Advisory Service, 762 South First St., Kerman, California 93630; Lakeland Nursery, Hanover, Pennsylvania 17331; H.A. Mantyla, Route 2, Box 2407, Auburn, California 95603; Montgomery Ward, 618 West Chicago Ave., Chicago, Illinois 60610; G.C. Quick, 367 East Virginia Ave., Phoenix, Arizona 85000; Robert Robbins, 424 North Courtland, East Stroudsburg, Pennsylvania 18301; L.E. Schnoor, Box 114, Rough & Ready, California 95975; or World Garden Products, 2 First St., East Norwalk, Connecticut 06855.

Phytoseiulus persimilis. A tiny mite that is a predator on the red spider mite. Both nymphs and adults eat spider mite eggs. The predatory mite reproduces rapidly and keeps the greenhouse spider mite population well under control. Available from Rincon-Vitova Insectaries, Box 95, Oak View, California 93022.

Praying mantises (walking stick insect). A large awkward-looking insect, two to five inches long, surprisingly able to blend into surroundings and look like a twig. Has a long stiff body, long legs and big green eyes. Eats many varieties of insects. The egg cases can be bought in winter. They should be attached to the stem of a large plant or to an out-of-the-way part of the greenhouse and left alone. In spring they will hatch out and begin foraging. Available from: Ted P. Bank, 608

AND TOADS, TOO

Toads, frogs, newts, salamanders, chameleons, and snakes if you can find them, will all do a magnificent job of eating a variety of insects in a greenhouse. It is a good idea to leave out saucers of water for them and perhaps provide extra food in winter when the insect populations are low.

Eleventh St., Pitcairn, Pennsylvania 15140; Burnes, 109 Kohler St., Bloomfield, New Jersey 07003; Bio-Control Co., 10180 Ladybird Ave., Auburn, California 95603; H.P. Comeaux, Route 2, Box 259, Lafayette, Louisiana 70501; Eastern Biological Control Co., Route 4, Box 482, Jackson, New Jersey 08527; Gothard Inc., Box 370, Canutillo, Texas 79835; Lakeland Nurseries Sales, Insect Control Division, Hanover, Pennsylvania 17331; Little Gem Farm, Box 9024, Huntington, West Virginia 25704; Mantis Unlimited, Glenhardie Farm, 625 Richards Road, Wayne, Pennsylvania 19087; Mincemoyer, 104 Hackensack St., Wood Ridge, New Jersey 07075; L.R. Murray, Aguila, Arizona 85320; Robert Robbins, 424 N. Courtland St., East Stroudsburg, Pennsylvania 18301; or Sidney A. Schwartz, The Mantis Man Inc., East Northport, New York 11731. Several commercial seed houses also offer praying mantis cases.

Spiders. Very useful in catching endless small flying insects. Unless you can't bear the untidy look, their webs should be left alone.

Syrphid flies. See *Hover flies.*

Tachnid flies. Look like large house flies but move more quickly. They lay their eggs in many species of caterpillar, in Japanese beetles, earwigs and grasshoppers, so are decidedly helpful.

Trichogramma wasps. Minute wasps, 1/50 of an inch long, which are parasitic on the eggs of most varieties of caterpillars. The larvae of trichogramma wasps can be bought, but they are probably more useful out of doors unless you are subject to severe attacks of caterpillars. One packet contains up to 4,000 wasp larvae and should be able to control an area of several acres. Ideally, wasps should be released at the time the moths are laying eggs. Available from: Rincon-Vitova Insectaries, Box 95, Oak View, California 93022; or Gothard Inc., Box 370, Canutillo,

Texas 79835, or Insect Pest Advisory Service, 762 South First St., Kerman, California 93630.

Natural Insecticides

Ammonia. Household ammonia is a good fumigant to get rid of wood lice and earwigs in a greenhouse. Simply shut all the vents, sprinkle ammonia liberally over the floor and leave the greenhouse shut up tight overnight.

Bacillus Thuringiensis (*Thuricide* or *Biotrol*). A bacterial disease that affects several varieties of caterpillars. It is long-lasting, effective, and harmful only to caterpillars, but is probably more useful in the garden than in the greenhouse.

It is available from many of the major seed companies, including Farmer Seed and Nursery Co., Faribault, Minnesota 55021, and Joseph Harris Co., Moreton Farm, Rochester, New York 14624, as well as the following: Eastern States Farmers Exchange Inc., 26 Central St., West Springfield, Massachusetts 01089; Grain Processing Corp., Muscatine, Iowa 52761; International Minerals and Chemical Corp., Crop Aids Department, 5401 Old Orchard Road, Skokie, Illinois 60076; Hubbard-Hall Chemical Co., Box 233, Portland, Connecticut 05480; Pennsalt Chemical Corp., Philadelphia, Pennsylvania 19100; and Thompson-Hayward Chemical Co., Box 2383, Kansas City, Missouri 66110.

Ced-o-Flora. A natural insect repellent made of pine oils and other plant essences. Very effective against aphids and mealy bugs. Available from most garden shops.

Derris. The roots of a South American plant which is the main ingredient in rotenone. Good against chewing and sucking insects but harmful to fish, nesting birds and some beneficial insects, including bees and lady bug larvae. Effective for about forty-eight hours. Available from garden shops.

Diatomaceous earth (*Tripoli*). The fine silica remains of the skeletons of millions of prehistoric one-celled creatures. Kills on contact, probably by dehydration after the silica pierces the insect's body. Very effective and harmless to other creatures, including earthworms. Can be sprinkled on, or diluted with water and sprayed on. Available from: Desert Herb Tea Co., 736 Darling St., Ogden, Utah 84400; Perma-Guard Division, Bower Industries Inc., 1701 East Elwood St., Box 21024, Phoenix, Arizona 85036.

Garlic and red pepper. The organic gardener's standby. Many combinations are possible, but a typical recipe would be:

3 cloves of garlic or 1 tablespoon
  garlic powder
1 large onion
1 tablespoon ground cayenne, or two whole
  hot red peppers, or 1 tablespoon tabasco sauce
½ ounce soft soap or 1 tablespoon liquid
  detergent (see *Soft Soap*)
1 quart water

Blend, strain and use immediately, or store in a glass or plastic container in the refrigerator. Mustard, or mint or horseradish leaves are sometimes added. Deters most insects.

Hot water. Potted plants can be dipped in hot (140-150°F.) water for five minutes to kill aphids, scale and most other pests, but it may damage the plant as well. It is best to try this only when the plant is relatively dormant.

Nettle tea. An old biodynamic recipe, useful both as a fertilizer and as insect repellent. Fill a bucket with stinging nettles and cover with water (preferably rain water). Cover it and leave in the sun to ferment. In about a week the nettles will have rotted to a slimy mass and the brew will smell terrible. Dilute it one to five and spray on plants or drench the soil around them. Excellent against aphids and flea beetles, also good stimulant for sickly plants.

Nicotine. See *Tobacco*.

Pyrethrum. The dried flowers of a plant closely related to chrysanthemums. Good against many insects including thrips and whitefly, but harmful to fish, bees and lady bugs. Harmless to warm-blooded animals except that some people are allergic to it. It is best to grind up the flowers yourself. This can be dusted directly over the plant, or a spray can be made by steeping one teaspoon of ground flowers in one quart of hot water for three hours. Strain, add a half ounce of soft soap, and spray. Loses its potency twelve hours after the flowers are ground up. Pyrethrum may be grown outdoors near the greenhouse.

Seeds are available from George W. Parks Seed Co., Greenwood, South Carolina 29646. The dried flowers are often available in garden shops, if not, write to the Pyrethrum Information Center, 744 Broad St., Newark, New Jersey 07102, for the name and address of a source near you.

Quassia. The ground-up wood of a South American tree with an intensely bitter taste. Makes a good spray against aphids, thrips, slugs and small caterpillars. Soak two ounces of quassia in one gallon of water for three days. Then simmer slowly for three hours. Strain and mix with two ounces of soft soap. Available from: Desert Herb Tea Co., 736 Darling St., Ogden, Utah 84400; Indiana Botanic Gardens, Box 5, Hammond, Indiana 46320; Meer Corporation, 318 West 46 St., New York, New York 10036; George W. Parks Seed Co., Greenwood, South Carolina 29646; or Charles Siegel & Son, 5535 North Lynch Ave., Chicago, Illinois 60630.

Red pepper. *See Garlic and red pepper.*

Rotenone. See *Derris*.

Rubbing alcohol. Effective against mealy bugs and almost all other insects. Individual pests can be executed with a Q-tip dipped in pure rubbing alcohol (or turpentine or kerosene), but be careful not to get any on the plant. In a heavy infestation, the plant can be sprayed with a mixture of one tablespoon rubbing alcohol in one pint of water. A teaspoon of camphor dissolved in the alcohol will make it even more effective.

Salt. Effective dry sprinkled on slugs, and it can also be used in a weak solution (one teaspoon salt to one quart water) sprayed on brassicas against cabbage worms or on other plants to combat spider mites. Be careful not to get too much salt on the soil because it reduces fertility.

Soft soap. Fels Naptha, ordinary hand soap (chopped up or leftover slivers), green soap, or Ivory Flakes left in enough water to cover for a few days will form a jelly-like solution that can be added to other aromatic ingredients to form a spray that adheres better and will penetrate the protective coating of many insects. If you are in a hurry, you can boil up the soap and it will liquefy faster. Liquid detergent could be used instead, but many people think it may be harmful to plants. Diluted with water (two ounces per gallon), soft soap can be used by itself as a spray. Or small potted plants can be dipped in the suds; cover the soil and turn the pot upside down, swishing the plant through the suds, rinse well afterwards. Good against aphids and cabbage worms, moderately effective against scale and mealy bugs.

Tobacco. Every form of tobacco is an effective insecticide. It is also highly toxic to most other creatures including humans, so use with care. Do not breathe it in or get it on your skin or in your eyes, and be sure to wash your hands after using. Fortunately, its toxicity dissipates gradually and is pretty much gone in two or three days. It is especially useful against caterpillars and it does no harm to ladybugs. Nicotine is the active ingredient in tobacco and can be bought in concentrated form. Nicotine sulphate (*Blackleaf 40*) is less powerful but longer lasting.

You can extract the nicotine yourself by steeping tobacco dust, tobacco stems, chopped up plug tobacco or even cigarette butts in boiling water. Leave them twenty-four hours, then strain and dilute with four parts of water to one part tobacco extract. This can be used as is or a quarter ounce soft soap per quart can be added for a more penetrating spray. Tobacco dust can also be shaken directly over the plants. Nicotine fumigation is effective at getting into all the nooks and crannies of a greenhouse where pests lurk unseen waiting to reinfest a plant after you have cleaned it up.

Nicotine fumigants are available from: California Spray Chemical Corp., Richmond, California 94800, or Fuller System, 226 Washington St., Woburn, Massachusetts 01801. Nicotine sulphate is available from most garden supply stores. Tobacco dust is available from: Odlin Organics, 743 Dennison Drive, Southbridge, Massachusetts 01550; or Quaker Lane Products, Box 100, Pittstown, New Jersey 08867. Tobacco stem meal is available from: Brookside Nurseries, Darien, Connecticut 06820.

Water. A good hard jet of plain water will remove a proportion of the insects on a plant, will remove dust and dirt that have accumulated on its leaves and seems to have a stimulating overall effect. Hosing the undersides of leaves is especially important since insects congregate there, so cover the soil and turn the plant upside down to get a better aim. Rain water is better than tap water both for watering and for making sprays. Some plants resent the residues from hard water; others resent water-softening chemicals.

Bibliography

The Bug Book, by Helen and John Philbrick. Garden Way Publishing, Charlotte, Vermont. 1974. Paperback, $3.95. Probably the best book on organic controls of insect pests. Helpful on identification. Includes many bio-dynamic recipes as well as untested but traditional remedies from old gardening books.

Companion Planting for Successful Gardening, by Louise Riotte. Garden Way Publishing, Charlotte, Vermont. 1975. Paperback, $4.95. Very good on plants that ward off insect pests.

The Complete Book of Greenhouse Gardening by Ian G. Walls. Quadrangle Press, New York, 1975. $14.95. Has an extensive section on identifying both pests and diseases according to the damage appearing on particular varieties of plants. Advocates chemical controls.

The Encyclopedia of Organic Gardening, by J.I. Rodale. Rodale Press, Emmaus, Pennsylvania. 1959. $14.95.

The Gardener's Bug Book, by Cynthia Westcott. Doubleday. 1973. $12.95. A massive reference work on identifying and combating all insect pests.

Gardening Without Poisons, by Beatrice Trum Hunter. Houghton Mifflin. 1972. Paperback, $2.95. A thorough investigation into natural ways of dealing with pests and diseases, emphasizing prevention rather than cure. No help with identification, and includes many remedies without much attempt at evaluating their relative merits.

Organic Gardening Under Glass, by George and Katy Abraham. Rodale Press. 1975. $8.95. Good chapter on insect controls.

Pests of Ornamental Plants, by Peterson Becker. Ministry of Agriculture, Fisheries and Food Bulletin 97, Her Majesty's Stationery Office, London. 1974 (third edition). Paperback $3.95. A fantastically thorough survey of the life cycle of every pest affecting ornamental plants in England (which includes virtually all the pests you would find in vegetable gardens, orchards or greenhouses, even in the United States). Detailed but clearly written. Photographs of the pests, and of the damage they do, help enormously in identifying the problems. Advocates chemical controls.

IV

Solar Energy Conservation

Drawn by a single electric motor that turns rods running the length of this 50,000-square-foot greenhouse in Guilford, Connecticut, a thermal insulating blanket opens or closes over indoor beds of roses. Ways to conserve the sun's heat and to prevent its escape are being devised for greenhouses in the age of energy-consciousness.

10

Insulation

Heating a greenhouse in the northern United States can be an expensive proposition. The heating bill for one winter might be as much as the total cost of all materials used in building the greenhouse. A conventional single-glazed greenhouse in southern New England, heated to 60°F. on winter nights probably consumes around 65 watts (200 Btu's) of energy every hour for every square foot of ground it covers. At 7 cents per kilowatt, this works out at an average of about 45 cents per hour for every one hundred square feet of greenhouse space, which would give a winter heating bill of about $600.

This cost can be reduced dramatically, if not eliminated completely, simply by paying careful attention to the design and construction of the greenhouse so that, first, the rate at which it loses heat can be kept to a minimum, and second, it makes the best possible use of that free and infinitely available energy source, the sun.

Understanding energy conservation requires a basic understanding of the three ways in which heat moves. *Radiation* is the passage of heat directly from one surface to another. *Convection* is the passage of heat through a fluid, such as water or air. And *conduction* is the passage of heat through a solid body (Figure 10.1).

Radiation. The "greenhouse effect" depends on the way glass (and other transparent material) transmits radiation of different

157

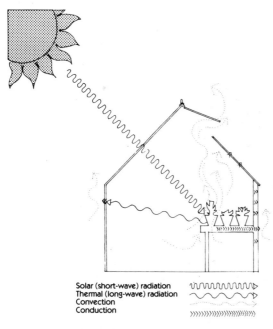

Solar (short-wave) radiation
Thermal (long-wave) radiation
Convection
Conduction

Figure 10.1. Three ways in which heat moves: Radiation is the passage of heat directly from one surface to another. Convection is the passage of heat through a medium such as air or water. Conduction is the movement of heat through a solid body.

wave lengths. Short-wave solar radiation passes through the transparent cover of the greenhouse and is absorbed by the earth, the plants and whatever else it strikes. The plants become warm and reradiate heat in the longer wavebands of thermal (or "infrared") radiation. Most transparent material, particularly glass, will not transmit much infrared radiation, and thus the greenhouse can be said to be a radiant heat trap.

Radiation depends heavily on a temperature difference between the two bodies. We radiate a little heat all the time to everything that is cooler than we are. But the amount of radiation only becomes significant when the temperature difference is fairly great (e.g., the sun's temperature compared to the earth's, or a stove's temperature compared to yours, or your temperature compared to an uncurtained window on a winter night). The amount of radiation increases exponentially—that is, it increases as the fourth power of the difference in temperature.

In many ways, radiation is the most com-plex and difficult to understand of the methods of heat transfer. The concept of heat passing from one surface to another without affecting the air in between is hard to grasp, but that is exactly what happens when we warm ourselves in the sun or in front of an open fire.

Convection. Air is not warmed by radiation, it only becomes warm through contact with warmer surfaces. When the plants and earth in your greenhouse absorb solar heat and become warm, the air immediately next to them also warms up. The warmer the air the less dense it becomes. Warm air is therefore lighter than cold air and tends to rise in relation to it. This causes "convection currents" that mix the air and insure that heat is distributed fairly rapidly. The movement of heat in any fluid (air, water, oil) works in the same way and is known as convection.

You can feel the effects of convection by walking up an enclosed stairway—it is always warmer at the top. The updraft through a chimney is also evidence of convection because all the precious warm air from the living room rushes up and out to the atmosphere. In a greenhouse, some air movement is necessary for healthy plant growth, but excessive ventilation, or leaving the door open longer than necessary, can waste a lot of heat quickly.

Greenhouses trap convective heat by preventing air movement to the outside. Polyethylene greenhouses, which transmit a high proportion of infrared radiation, work primarily because they are convective heat traps.

When plants in a greenhouse absorb heat, much of that energy goes into "transpiration." This process uses energy to change water in the plant's tissues into vapor which then increases the humidity of the surrounding air. The warmer the surrounding air, the more the plants will transpire since, like human perspiration, it is a way of cooling themselves. It requires at least a thousand times more heat to turn one drop of water into water vapor than it does to raise the temperature of the water 1°F. So the amount of energy involved in this process is considerable if you have a greenhouse full of plants. This energy can be lost easily when you ventilate humid air from the greenhouse, or when water condenses out of the humid air against the cold surface of the glazing, passing the heat to the glass and then outside.

Conduction. The third form of heat loss is the easiest to understand and the most important in trying to reduce heat loss from a greenhouse. If you hold a metal spoon over a flame it will soon burn your fingers; if you hold a wooden spoon over the same heat source it will begin to char before it gets too hot to hold. The reason for this is the difference in their rates of heat conduction. Metal is a good heat conductor; wood is not. Unfortunately for the greenhouse, glass and all the transparent plastic substitutes are relatively good conductors of heat. For obvious reasons they are also very thin. So when the transparent covering of the greenhouse is warmed by contact with the warm air on the inside, it conducts the heat rapidly to the cool air on the outside.

Reducing Heat Losses

Conserving energy in greenhouses involves reducing the rate of heat loss by radiation, convection and conduction to reduce the rate at which heat has to be pumped into the greenhouse to maintain a reasonable temperature for plants.

By radiation. The rate of heat loss by radiation from a greenhouse depends mainly on the type of covering material used. Glass and fiberglass are virtually opaque to infrared radiation; polyethylene is fairly transparent to infrared. Therefore glass and fiberglass will trap more radiant energy inside.

Heat loss by radiation is most significant at night. A clear night sky will absorb almost as much heat from the earth as the earth has

received during the day. The effective temperature of the night sky is about −48°F., so any surface exposed to the night sky will lose heat rapidly by radiation. An uncovered skylight loses heat much more quickly than an uncovered window because it faces the night sky more directly.

Although glass and fiberglass do not transmit radiant heat directly, at night they do become very cold; they absorb radiant heat from the people or plants below, conduct it to the outside and reradiate it to the night sky. It is only by decreasing the rate of heat loss by conduction through the transparent covering that the overall radiant heat loss can be reduced (double-glazing, shutters and curtains all reduce the heat lost by conduction through the glass). In calculating the total heat losses of a greenhouse, radiant heat loss is usually included with losses by conduction.

By convection. Heat loss by convection can be considerable if the greenhouse is continuously ventilated. Even when all vents are closed and all fans are shut off, there is still likely to be some heat loss by "infiltration" (warm air leaking out through the structure and cold air leaking in). The rate of infiltration or ventilation is normally expressed in *airchanges per hour*.

A well-sealed greenhouse covered with plastic film could have an infiltration rate as low as one half airchange per hour. In a greenhouse glazed with unsealed, lapped panes of glass and with poorly fitting doors and vents, it would be difficult to reduce the rate to below three or four airchanges per hour (or even more if there were a strong wind blowing). This means that once every fifteen minutes or so, the warm air in the greenhouse is being replaced with cold air from outside which has to be heated to the required temperature. If the outside air temperature is 10°F. and inside it is 50°F. then each hour a volume of air equal to four times the volume of the greenhouse must be heated through 40°F. to maintain a stable temperature in the greenhouse.

Even though the amount of heat required

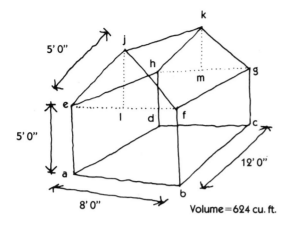

5' 0"

5' 0"

8' 0"

12' 0"

Volume = 624 cu. ft.

Greenhouse Volume

volume = surface area of end wall × length
$$= (abfe + \triangle\ efg) \times bc.$$
$$= (40 + 12) \times 12$$
$$= 52 \times 12$$
$$= 624 \text{ cubic feet.}$$

Greenhouse Surface Area

area of sidewalls	bcgf	= 12'×5'	= 60 sq. ft.
	adhe	= 12'×5'	= 60 sq. ft.
area of endwalls	abfe	= 8'×5'	= 40 sq. ft.
	dcgh	= 8'×5'	= 40 sq. ft.
$\triangle\ efj = 1/2\,ef \times jl$		= 3'×4'	= 12 sq. ft.
$\triangle\ hgk = 1/2\,mg \times mk$		= 3'×4'	= 12 sq. ft.
area of roof	fgkj	= 5'×12'	= 60 sq. ft.
	ehkj	= 5'×12'	= 60 sq. ft.
total surface area			= 344 sq. ft.

Heat Loss by Convection/Infiltration

N. number of airchanges per hour = 4.
V. volume of greenhouse = 624 cu. ft.
A. heat capacity of air. = 0.02 Btu's/cu. ft./°F.
T. temperature difference = 40°F.
   inside to outside
H.L. = N × V × A × T
     = 4 × 624 × 0.02 × 40
     = 1997 Btus/hr

Figure 10.2. How to calculate a greenhouse's heat loss involves knowing its total surface area, volume, air-changes each hour, heat capacity of the air, and the inside-outside temperature difference.

to raise one cubic foot of air through one degree Fahrenheit is tiny, (about 0.02 Btu's), the heat loss by infiltration every hour in an 8×12-foot lapped-glass greenhouse with a volume of 624 cubic feet (the example shown in Figure 10.2) would be 1,997 Btu's. This is what the greenhouse heater would have to supply just to keep up with the rate of infiltration.

By taking care with the construction of the greenhouse this rate can be reduced considerably (even in a glazed greenhouse with doors and vents). It is essential to keep the rate of infiltration to a minimum in winter. Only the amount of ventilation necessary to the health of the plants should be carried out in winter.

Ventilation. Electric fans, providing they can be sealed with backflaps when not in use, are an efficient way of ventilating a greenhouse, but remember that a fan capable of coping with the ventilation rates necessary summer will probably be able to change the air in the greenhouse once every few minutes. This is much faster than is necessary or desirable for winter ventilation. Unless you have a variable-speed fan, use it sparingly in winter, and remember that some ventilation is going on all the time through air leaks in the building.

A large quantity of warm air escapes every time you open the door of your greenhouse. If you can do so, incorporate an air lock or entrance room in the design so that you lose less warm air every time you enter. The air lock can serve as a potting shed, a storage area, or location for the kind of heater that needs to be outside the greenhouse. Attaching an unheated greenhouse to a hothouse will serve the same sort of function since the heat lost when you open the door to the hothouse will not be as great as if you had entered from outside (besides which, plants in the cold greenhouse will no doubt appreciate an occasional gust of warm air). Greenhouses that can be entered directly from inside the house avoid the problem of heat loss through an outside door, and of course they minimize heat loss through the attached wall.

Because so much heat is lost by conduction

in a poorly insulated building, the proportion of heat lost by convection is relatively low. But if the heat lost by conduction is reduced by adding insulation, then infiltration losses become more significant, and more effort should be made to reduce them.

It is easier and more effective to take steps to reduce infiltration when you are building your greenhouse rather than later. Use well-seasoned wood that won't shrink or move to open up cracks. Use caulking compound between all timber joints. A good-quality silicone sealing compound will be capable of taking up movement between the joints, while poorer ones will disintegrate or dry up within a few years. Make sure that opening windows, ventilators and doors are as tight-fitting as you can make them. It might be worth buying factory-made door and window frames if you don't trust your carpentry skill. Weatherstrip all openings with suitable materials. Rubber-gasket weatherstripping, available from most hardware stores, is suitable for hinged doors and windows. Thin strips of foam rubber or felt can be used to fill in larger gaps. They should be glued in place in the rabbets of the frames rather than on the doors and windows, where they tend to peel off faster. Taking care when you build can save a lot of effort with caulking guns, tape or weatherstripping later on. A well-built structure will "leak" air at a very slow rate and the tightness will reduce maintenance costs over the lifetime of the building.

By conduction. In such a thin-skinned building as a greenhouse it is the heat loss by conduction that is most significant, and it is worth looking closely at ways this can be minimized.

The rate of heat loss by conduction is dependent on three factors. First is the *surface area* of the building. Obviously the larger the building, the greater the glass area and the more heat the glass will lose by conduction and reradiation. Second is the *difference in temperature* between inside and out; the greater the difference in temperature, the faster the rate of heat loss. Third is the U

value, or *thermal transmittance*, of the walls and transparent covering of the greenhouse. Typical U values for various types of construction are given in Figure 10.3.

The U value is a measure of the amount of heat that is conducted through one square foot of a window, wall or roof in one hour, assuming a difference in temperature between one side and the other of one degree Fahrenheit. The U value of a wall is not directly proportional to its thickness. Doubling its thickness will not double its U value. Additional factors such as the texture of each surface of the wall and the rate of air movement across it affect the rate of heat loss and hence the U value. The heat loss is much greater (and the U value higher) when there is air flowing freely over the surface, and consequently U values vary considerably according to the degree of exposure to prevailing winds.

The U value also takes into account any cavities or air spaces within the structure of the wall. Two sheets of plywood, or two sheets of glass, with a closed cavity between have a much higher U value than if the two sheets were adjacent, partly because of the addition of two more surface-to-air resistances at the faces of the cavity, and partly because of the dead air space between. The rate of heat conduction through air is extremely low, which makes air a good insulating material providing air currents (which would transmit the heat by convection) are not allowed to form.

The best insulating materials, like polyurethane foam, polystyrene foam and glass fiber, contain isolated pockets of air that prevent convection currents from forming. These materials are more effective the tighter the air pockets they form; thus a rigid-foam plastic slab that has a closed-cell construction is more effective than a looser insulation like glass wool or vermiculite. Rigid closed cell foams also have the advantages that they do not absorb water, they are seldom attacked by vermin, and they do not compress easily. Polyurethane and some precompressed types of polystyrene foam can be buried underground to provide underfloor in-

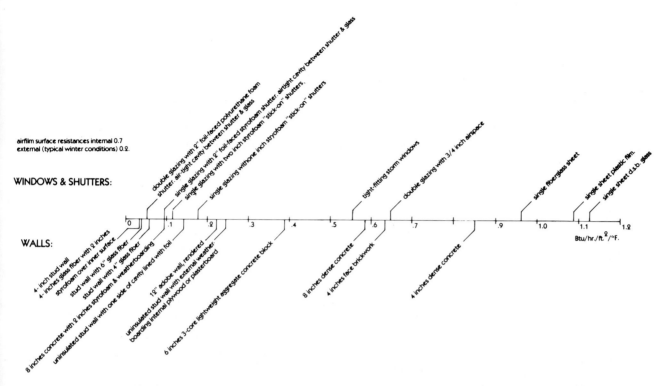

Figure 10.3. U values, measuring thermal transmittance, are shown for various types of construction. From left to right, best to worst.

sulation without deteriorating. They can also be used in walls and ceilings, but since rockwool and glass fiber batts are generally cheaper, they are more often used.

Urethane foam also comes in liquid form, which can be applied through a spray gun into a formwork or onto the outside of a building. This is a skilled operation and requires hiring or buying expensive mechanical equipment that often tends to go wrong. Unless you know someone who is experienced with spray-on foams, you should stay away from them.

Most foam plastics, like plastic sheeting, will deteriorate in the sun. If the foam is to be left exposed on the outside of a building, it should be painted with several coats of "intumescent" paint that prevents deterioration caused by ultraviolet radiation. Remember also that most foam plastics, particularly polyurethane foam, are a fire hazard. Even with flame-spread retardants they give off noxious gases. Urethane foam should never

be used unprotected and exposed inside a building. *Icocyanurate* foam (*Technifoam*), which has good insulating qualities and is less flammable than other foam plastics, is now becoming more widely used. Unfortunately, it is still relatively expensive. Plastic foams are likely to increase in price faster than conventional insulation because they are oil-based, but it makes far more sense ecologically to use a gallon of oil to provide twenty years of insulation than it does to use it to provide one night's heating.

Insulation values of various materials (called *R values*) are given in Figure 10.4. Unlike U values, R values measure the rate of insulation, that is, the rate of *resistance* to heat transmission rather than the rate of heat transmission, so the higher the R value the better the insulation. R values do not take into account surface resistances, so they are proportional to the thickness of the material.

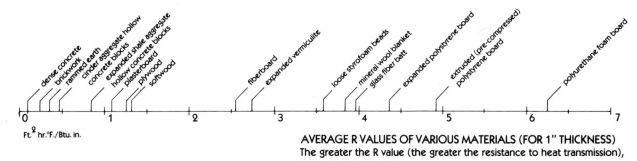

AVERAGE R VALUES OF VARIOUS MATERIALS (FOR 1" THICKNESS)
The greater the R value (the greater the resistance to heat transmission), the better the insulation.
The R values are for one inch thickness of material, thus 2 inches of expanded vermiculite would have the same insulation value, almost, as one inch of polyurethane foam.

Figure 10.4. R values, measuring thermal resistance, are shown for various kinds of materials. From left to right, worst to best.

The R value is used as a measure of the relative insulation value of a wall more often than the U value. Thus one will refer to R11 stud walls (with 3½ inches of mineral wool batt) or R19 walls (with 5½ inches of mineral value, being the rate of heat transmission rather than of resistance to transmission. Thus a typical value of R11 would have a U value of 1/11 or 0.9 in average conditions of exposure.

It is possible to calculate the rate of heat loss by conduction at any time if we know: (a) the surface area of the greenhouse, (b) the average U value of the greenhouse, and (c) the difference in temperature between inside and out. Multiplying these three factors together gives the rate at which heat is lost from the building. Applying this formula for the severest winter conditions (that is, imagining the maximum possible temperature difference between inside and out) tells us what the greatest heat loss by conduction will be.

If we take as an example the simple even-span greenhouse shown in Figure 10.2, we can do a sample calculation. The surface area of the greenhouse is 344 square feet. The U value for single glazing (which most of the building consists of) is 1.1. Assuming that the mean minimum winter temperature is 10°F. and that we wish to maintain an internal temperature of 50°F., the temperature difference is 40°F. Multiplying these together

gives a heat loss by conduction of 15,136 Btu's per hour (Figure 10.5A). This calculation assumes that the heat loss downwards is negligible, which is generally true if there is perimeter insulation around the base. It also assumes an average U value for all four walls and the roof, though actually these will vary depending on orientation and wind condi-

Figure 10.5. Examples of reducing heat losses by making more and more walls of the greenhouse either solid or shuttered. The different configurations of 10.5A through G, and the resulting Btu's per hour needed to heat each one, are discussed in the accompanying text.

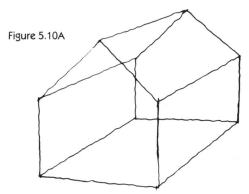

Figure 5.10A

Single Glazing

Ag   area of single glazing   = 344 sq. ft.
Ug   U value   = 1.1 Btu/hr/sq ft/°F
T   temperature difference   = 50°-10°
                                   40°F

H.L.   = Ag×Ug×T
       = 344×1.1×40
       = 15136 Btus/hr.

tions. And it assumes that the structure holding the glass is of negligible surface area compared to the glass.

The heat loss by conduction (15,136 Btu's) when added to the convective heat loss calculated previously (1,997 Btu's) gives us a total heat loss of 17,133 Btu's per hour. This approximate figure can be used to calculate the size of heating unit needed to maintain the temperature in the greenhouse during the severest winter conditions. Allowances must be made for the inefficiency of the heating unit. Oil burners are approximately 60 percent efficient, gas burners average 70 percent. Electrical heating is almost 100 percent efficient (though if one considers fossil fuel consumption at the generating station the overall efficiency is only about 30 percent). So the typical, inefficient greenhouse shown in Figure 10.5A would require an oil burner with a capacity of around 25,000 Btu's per hour to cope with the severest winter conditions.

Reducing the heat loss by conduction can be done in any of three ways. We could reduce the size of the greenhouse, we could reduce the internal temperature, or we could reduce the average U value. The first alternative is only a last-ditch solution. The second is a reasonable possibility. If the internal temperature is allowed to drop 10°, to 40°F. (remember that this is an average temperature—certain areas near the glass would then be almost at freezing point), the heating bill will be cut by a fourth. The third variable, the average U value, is where most energy conservation can take place.

If we double-glaze the whole greenhouse with an internal layer of plastic film (Figure 10.5B), the average U value will be reduced to about 0.6, thus reducing the conductive heat loss by 40 percent, to 8,256 Btu's per hour. Alternatively, the glass area could be reduced. For instance, if the greenhouse were on an east-west axis, the north wall could be made of insulated studwork instead of glass

Figure 10.5B

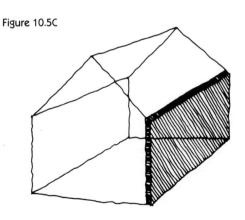

Double Glazing

Ag	area of double glazing	= 344 sq. ft.
Ug	U-value	= 0.6 Btu/hr/sq ft/°F
T	temperature difference	= 40°F.
H.L.	= Ag×Ug×T	
	= 344×0.6×40	
	= 8256 Btus/hr.	

Figure 10.5C

Solid North Wall

Ag	area of single glazing	= 284 sq. ft.
Ug	U-value	= 1.1 Btu/hr/sq ft./°F
Aw	area of insulated wall	= 60 sq. ft.
Uw	U-value	= 0.06 Btu/hr/sq. ft./°F
T	temperature difference	= 40° F.
H.L.	= (Ag×Ug+Aw×Uw) x T.	
	= (284×1.1+60×0.06) × 40	
	= (312.4+3.6) × 40	
	= 316×40	
	= 12640 Btus/hr.	

Figure 10.5D

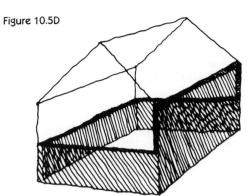

Base Walls/Single Glazing

Ag	area of single glazing	=	214 sq. ft.
Ug	U-value	=	1.1 Btu/hr./sq. ft./°F.
Aw	area of insulated wall	=	130 sq. ft.
Uw	U-value	=	0.06 Btu/hr./sq. ft./°F.
T	temperature difference	=	40°F.

$$
\begin{aligned}
H.L. &= (A_g \times U_g + A_w \times U_w) \times T \\
&= (214 \times 1.1 + 130 \times 0.06) \times 40 \\
&= (235.4 + 7.8) \times 40 \\
&= 243.2 \times 40 \\
&= 9728 \text{ Btus/hr.}
\end{aligned}
$$

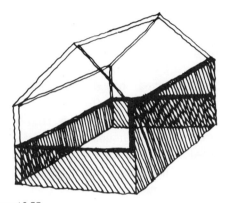

Figure 10.5E

Base Walls/Double Glazing

Ag	area of double glazing	=	214 sq ft
Ug	U-value	=	0.6 Btu/hr/sq ft/°F
Aw	area of insulated wall	=	130 sq ft
Uw	U-value	=	0.06 Btu/hr/sq ft/°F
T	temperature difference	=	40°F

$$
\begin{aligned}
H.L. &= (A_g \times U_g + A_w \times U_w) \times T \\
&= (214 \times 0.6 + 130 \times 0.06) \times 40 \\
&= (128.4 + 7.8) \times 40 \\
&= 136.2 \times 40 \\
&= 5448 \text{ Btus/hr.}
\end{aligned}
$$

Figure 10.5F

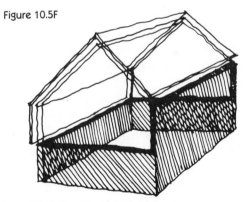

(Figure 10.5C), which would reduce the heat loss for the whole structure to about 12,640 Btu's per hour, even with single glazing. If, in addition, the south, east and west walls were solid below 2 feet 6 inches (about bench height), then the ratio of glass to wall would be about 2:1, and the heat loss would drop to 9,728 Btu's/hour, saving about 30 percent on the heating bill, even with single glazing (Figure 10.5D). (Significantly, by doing this the amount of direct sunlight admitted to plants on staging is hardly reduced at all, and the loss of indirect light is only slight. Of course, plants growing directly in the ground would be adversely affected by a solid perimeter wall.) Combining the effects of reducing the glazed area by one third and of double-glazing the remaining two-thirds with plastic film, would reduce the total conductive heat loss to 5,448 Btu's per hour, representing a saving of about 65 percent (Figure 10.5E).

Base Walls/Double Glazing/Shutters

Ag	area of double glazing	×	64 sq. ft.
Ug	U-value	=	0.6 Btu/hr./sq. ft./°F.
Aw	area of insulated wall	=	130 sq. ft.
Uw	U-value	=	0.06 Btu/hr./sq. ft./°F.
As	area of shuttered glazing	=	150 sq ft.
Us	U-value	=	0.2 Btu/hr./sq. ft./°F.
T	temperature difference	=	40°F.

$$
\begin{aligned}
H.L. &= (A_g \times U_g + A_w \times U_w + A_s \times U_s) \times T \\
&= (64 \times 0.6 + 130 \times 0.06 + 150 \times 0.2) \times 40 \\
&= (38.4 + 7.8 + 30) \times 40 \\
&= 76.2 \times 40 \\
&= 3048 \text{ Btus/hr.}
\end{aligned}
$$

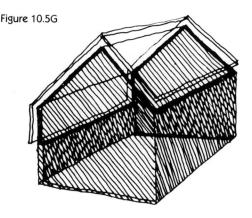

Figure 10.5G

Base & End Walls/Shutters

As area of shuttered glazing = 150 sq ft.
Us U-value = 0.2 Btu/hr/sq ft/°F
Aw area of insulated wall = 194 sq ft
Uw U-value = 0.06 Btu/hr/sq ft/°F
T temperature difference = 40°F

$$
\begin{aligned}
H.L. &= (As \times Us + Aw \times Uw) \times T \\
&= (150 \times 0.2 + 194 \times 0.06) \times 40 \\
&= (30 + 11.6) \times 40 \\
&= 41.6 \times 40 \\
&= 1665 \text{ Btus/hr}
\end{aligned}
$$

Further reductions in heat loss can be achieved by adding some kind of insulating shutters to cover the south-facing glazed areas, which are responsible for the largest part of the remaining heat loss. Slabs of polystyrene foam or sacks of leaves placed over the glass at night (Figure 10.5F) would reduce the heat loss to 3,048 Btu's per hour, or about 20 percent of the original estimate of 15,136 Btu's per hour. The one remaining source of heat loss would then be the end walls, which would be difficult to provide shutters for. Even if double-glazed, they would still lose heat two or three times as quickly as the shuttered areas. One way to achieve further reductions in heat loss would be to solidify the end walls completely (Figure 10.5G). This would result in a loss of direct sunlight during early morning and late afternoon, as well as a reduction in the level of indirect lighting throughout the day, especially near the ends of the greenhouse. It would, however, reduce the conductive heat loss to 1,665 Btu's per hour if the rest of the glass were shuttered.

Assuming we also reduce *convective* heat losses to a minimum, say two airchanges per hour, which would lose 998 Btu's per hour, then the total heat requirement during the severest conditions would be 2,663 Btu's per hour. This heat load could be met by a small set of soil-warming cables rather than a large oil-fired burner. More important, it could easily be supplied by solar heat stored in the building during the day and released at night to cope with the increased heat loss.

The savings in conductive heat loss are largely achieved by double-glazing the greenhouse with plastic film. This is primarily because all the glazed area, that is, virtually all the greenhouse in the first example, is affected. Obviously, as more of the greenhouse becomes either solid or shuttered, double-glazing becomes less significant by comparison, though if one wants to reduce heat losses to an absolute minimum, then it is very necessary. In some areas with low levels of illumination and only moderate winter temperatures, the extra layer of glazing might not be worthwhile, particularly if a shutter system were installed to reduce heat loss at night.

Sealed double-glazing units are somewhat more effective than an inner layer of plastic film, but they are not worth the enormous extra cost except for aesthetic reasons, where the greenhouse is part of the home. Various insulated double-glazing systems made from fiberglass and acrylic are now available at less than the cost of double-glazed glass. Details of these are given in Chapter 5, on glazing materials.

Reducing the glazed area is the next most important factor in reducing the heat loss by conduction. But depending on what plants you wish to grow, and the amount of sunlight your area receives in winter, the reduction in glazed area may interfere with plant growth, particularly if the end walls are made solid. Obviously in a longer greenhouse the level of illumination at the center would be less affected by solid end walls.

Insulating Shutters

Perhaps the most significant feature of this brief study of energy conservation in greenhouses is the value of insulating shutters. If the area to be shuttered can be reduced to manageable proportions, the insulating effect is dramatic. The reduction in heat loss by double glazing (approximately 40 percent) is only minimal compared to that achieved by an effective shutter system consisting of two inches of polystyrene foam or the equivalent placed in front of the glass with an airspace in between (reducing the heat loss by almost 90 percent). Polystyrene foam is relatively cheap, and if it is possible to devise a convenient way of storing the shutters, then the problem of heating a lean-to, or partially solid-walled, greenhouse is enormously simplified. Unfortunately, it is rarely practical to try to cover a glass-to-ground even-span greenhouse with shutters. The awkward shapes required and the difficulties of storing so many shutters conveniently make double-glazing a more attractive alternative if the greenhouse has no solid walls.

To achieve minimal heat loss from a greenhouse and enable it to be totally solar heated, some kind of insulating shutter system is required in most parts of the country. This is often difficult to incorporate and should be carefully considered before starting to build.

The simplest form of insulating shutter is a sheet of expanded polystyrene foam ("beadboard") that is fixed in place on the inside of the glass during the night and removed during the day. The foam sheet can be kept in place with magnetic clips (obtainable from Zomeworks, which developed the idea), or with "velcro" cloth fastenings (obtainable at most fabric stores). The foam should be attached to the frame of the greenhouse rather than to the glass to leave a gap of one half to one inch between glass and shutter. This dead air space, if sealed all around, adds considerably to the insulation value of the shutter. The foam should be covered with light-colored reflective cloth, or painted on the outside to reflect light, prevent deterioration and stop heat from building up in the space between the glass and the shutter to such an extent that the foam begins to melt or to produce noxious gases, which can occur when temperatures exceed 150°F. This has been known to happen when internal shutters were not removed on a sunny day.

One inch of beadboard can reduce the U-value of glass from 1.13 to about 0.18. With two inches of beadboard, the U value becomes 0.11. If the beadboard is covered on the side facing the glass with a reflective foil such as ordinary tin foil, a foil-faced vapor barrier, or an aluminized plastic film ("mirror paper"), then the U value is reduced to about 0.09. This is because the reflective foil absorbs and emits radiation poorly, so the radiant heat transfer across the cavity between the glass and the shutter is reduced considerably. If two inches of closed-cell polyurethane foam is used instead of polystyrene, then the U value is further reduced to about 0.067. These U values of course depend on conditions of air movement both inside and outside the greenhouse. They also assume a tight, dead air space between shutter and glazing. Shutter systems and thermal curtains are less effective if this space leaks air.

Storage problems. The difficulty with "stick-on" shutters is storing and handling them. Large slabs of one-inch-thick foam are fragile and awkward to move around. The foam can easily be covered with canvas or some decorative material that will strengthen it and protect the edges, but putting the shutters in place without damaging the plants is more difficult. If at all possible, some system for sliding the shutters into place and storing them when not in use should be devised beforehand.

Various ways of storing shutters are shown in Figure 10.6. The first three are internal shutters, the others are exposed to the weather and therefore require more design consideration.

Rigid foam slabs are generally impervious to water, but do degenerate when exposed to sunlight (some of the harmful ultraviolet rays are screened out by glass, so internal shutters are less affected by the sun). Foam shutters can also be damaged easily by wind since they are lightweight and yet have a

Figure 10.6. Various ways of arranging and storing insulating shutters. Three of them are internal, three external.

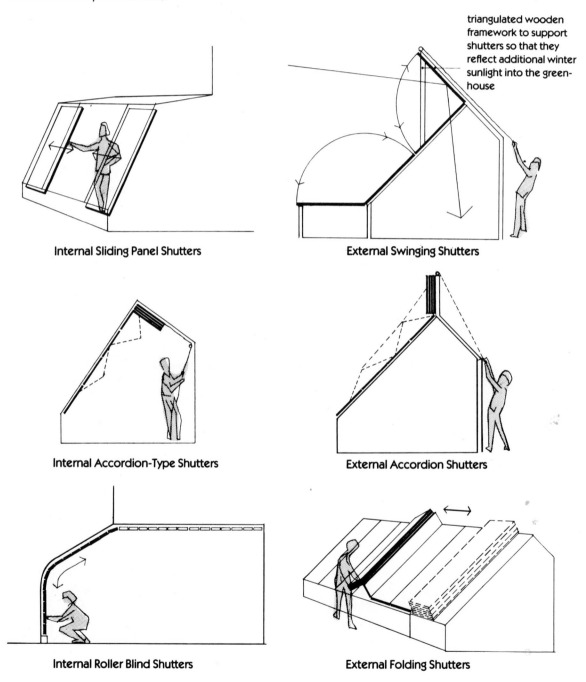

triangulated wooden framework to support shutters so that they reflect additional winter sunlight into the green-house

Internal Sliding Panel Shutters

External Swinging Shutters

Internal Accordion-Type Shutters

External Accordion Shutters

Internal Roller Blind Shutters

External Folding Shutters

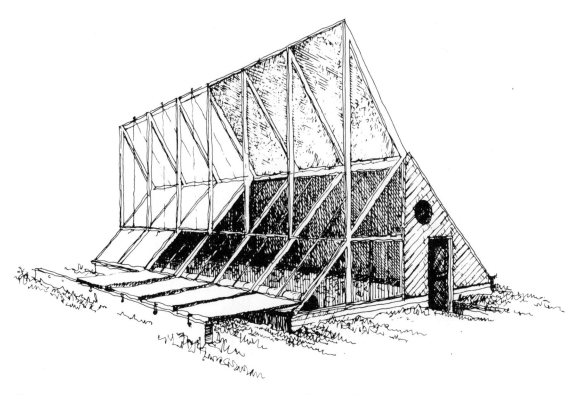

Figure 10. 7. A wide-span A-frame solar greenhouse with reflecting shutters, rigged to an external pulley system. This kind of shutter must be braced strongly to withstand high winds.

large surface area. External shutters of rigid foam should therefore be covered with canvas or other opaque material that will offer protection from the sun as well as reinforcing the edges; and they should be firmly secured at all times.

Snow loading is also a potential problem. Snow collecting on top of an external shutter must be removed manually, while on a conventional greenhouse the snow would soon melt from heat below. Snow falling during the day when the shutters are open will need to be cleared off in order to close the shutters properly.

Pulley systems for shutters are the easiest to operate but they are difficult to construct. You automatically halve the weight of the shutters with a simple pulley and you can rig up a system to halve that again, so raising and lowering a large series of shutters can be made easy work. Foam shutters are, however, very light in any case. The external

pulley system (Figure 10.7) allows the insides of the shutters to act as light reflectors in the daytime. They can be painted white or even covered with reflective foil, which would increase the level of illumination on plants below. The angle of the shutters could be altered to suit the monthly variations in the altitude of the sun.

Sliding shutters are the easiest to construct. You should use plastic or rigid nylon guides in the tracks and fixed to the shutters themselves to make them slide easily. The major disadvantage of sliding shutters is that they require an amount of wall space alongside the window equal to the area of the glass itself (unless two or three tracks are used so that sections of the shutter can slide across each other and be stored in half or a third of the glass area). Sliding shutters are more suitable for vertical or near-vertical glazing, and are well suited to windows in houses, where there is usually plenty of wall space alongside.

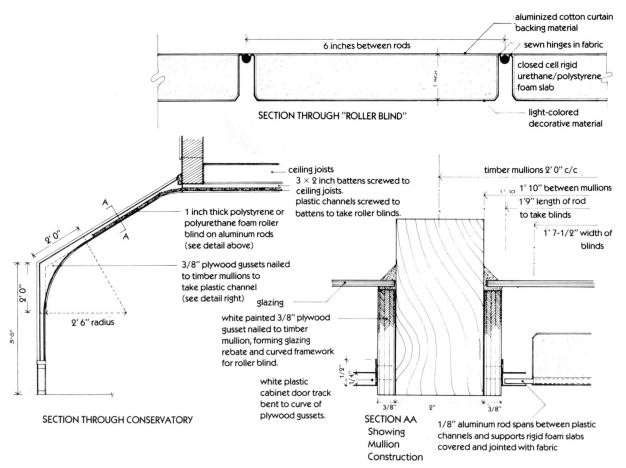

SECTION THROUGH "ROLLER BLIND"

aluminized cotton curtain backing material

sewn hinges in fabric

closed cell rigid urethane/polystyrene foam slab

light-colored decorative material

6 inches between rods

timber mullions 2' 0" c/c

1' 10" between mullions

1'9" length of rod to take blinds

1' 7-1/2" width of blinds

ceiling joists
3 × 2 inch battens screwed to ceiling joists. plastic channels screwed to battens to take roller blinds.

1 inch thick polystyrene or polyurethane foam roller blind on aluminum rods (see detail above)

3/8" plywood gussets nailed to timber mullions to take plastic channel (see detail right)

glazing

white painted 3/8" plywood gusset nailed to timber mullion, forming glazing rebate and curved framework for roller blind.

white plastic cabinet door track bent to curve of plywood gussets.

2' 0"
2' 0"
5'0"
2' 6" radius

SECTION THROUGH CONSERVATORY

SECTION AA Showing Mullion Construction

1/8" aluminum rod spans between plastic channels and supports rigid foam slabs covered and jointed with fabric

Figure 10. 8. Construction details for a rigid foam roller-blind shutter system, especially suitable for curved-glass greenhouses.

The roller-blind system in Figure 10.8 allows you to store shutters up against the ceiling of a room to which the greenhouse is attached. These would be particularly suitable for use with lean-to greenhouses, which are curved at the eaves. Curved-glass greenhouses are available commercially or you can use fiberglass on a curved framework made of plywood. The illustration shows plywood gussets attached to the mullions to hold channels for the roller blind to slide in. The roller blind itself is made of strips of rigid foam strung together with fabric hinges. At each joint is a metal rod which supports the blind by slotting into the channels on the mullions. The disadvantage of this kind of blind is that its insulation value is reduced at each hinge and it is difficult to get a tight seal at the edges, but it does provide an easy way of shuttering a curved structure.

An automated version of a polystyrene shutter has been devised and is marketed by Zomeworks Corporation. Polystyrene beads are blown in between two layers of glazing, about three inches apart. A pair of vacuum motors controls the flow of beads in and out of the double-glazed window (Figure 10.9). When not in use, the beads are stored in converted oil drums, connected by flexible hoses to the top and bottom of the cavity between the sheets of glass (one connection only is required if the length of the panel is less than five feet).

The main disadvantage of this *Beadwall* system is that it requires two fairly large vacuum motors to provide the suction between the window and bead-storage container. Besides the expense, this also means that the whole system, including the glazing, must be able to withstand pressures up to 500 pounds per square inch. Consequently, a high quality of construction is required to make sure that the double-glazed units are properly sealed. If glass is used, it must be at least ¼" thick, preferably tempered; if fiberglass is used it must be well fixed on the framework. The cost of the system is reduced considerably if fiberglass glazing is used. The Beadwall system is expensive to install and also takes up a considerable volume in storage containers but it does work efficiently and easily. Its main virtue is ease of operation; the insulation can be blown into place at the flick of a switch. The visual effect of the beads being blown in or out of the glazed units is very exciting. For Beadwall license and plans, write to Zomeworks, P.O. Box 712, Albuquerque, New Mexico 87103.

At the other end of the scale from the highly automated Beadwall system is the use of bags of dried leaves thrown over the outside of the glass. This simple and cheap form of insulation was used by Kathryn Taylor and Edith Gregg who discuss it in their excellent book, *Winter Flowers in Greenhouse and Sun-heated Pit*. The leaves are stuffed into burlap or canvas bags which are then sewn together in strips and thrown over the greenhouse at night. An old rake is a useful tool for hauling the leaf shutters on and off. During the day they are stored at the back of the pit. According to the authors, beech leaves are better than maple or elm leaves, which disintegrate faster. A tarpaulin over the top of the bags keeps the rain off and provides another layer of air for insulation.

Curtains, Blankets and Shades

Because of the volume taken up by insulating shutters, much work has been done recently in developing insulating roller shades and curtains that are made out of thin material and therefore do not take up as much space as rigid shutters. Shades or curtains can reduce heat loss by convection and radiation, but to do so they must fit tightly against the framework of the greenhouse to enclose a completely dead airspace or series of air spaces between the curtain and the glazing.

Thermal blankets. Experiments have been carried out at Pennsylvania State University to test various different kinds of "thermal blankets," primarily for use in the commercial greenhouse business. The different kinds of materials tested included close-weave porous plastic materials such as *Folyon XA-2425* and *Tyvek*. Both these materials have a reflective surface on one side. The porous materials were selected to allow the migration of some water vapor and therefore avoid condensation, which could cause water to drip down onto the plants below. Other materials tested included 4-mil black polyethylene and clear polyethylene. These acted primarily as a barrier to convective heat loss.

The initial test results showed that the Folyon and Tyvek reduced the heat loss by more than 55 percent, and in glass-covered greenhouses gave a nighttime U value of approximately 0.38. A black polyethylene cover, however, provided a 46 percent saving in heat and gave a U value of 0.46, which proved the value of simply creating an "attic" space above the plants and reducing the volume of greenhouse air to be heated. It is es-

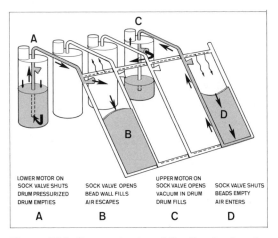

LOWER MOTOR ON SOCK VALVE SHUTS DRUM PRESSURIZED DRUM EMPTIES	SOCK VALVE OPENS BEAD WALL FILLS AIR ESCAPES	UPPER MOTOR ON SOCK VALVE OPENS VACUUM IN DRUM DRUM FILLS	SOCK VALVE SHUTS BEADS EMPTY AIR ENTERS
A	B	C	D

Figure 10.9. The mechanics of the Beadwall system, showing the barrels used for storage of the beads when they are not serving their insulating purpose.

Figure 10.10. Photos show how a huge thermal blanket, made of Folyon, is drawn by an electric motor to cover the Pinchbeck rose greenhouse in Guilford, Connecticut. The motor turns rods that run the full length of the structure; cables suspend the curtain, which fits into channels at each side.

timated that non-porous reflective materials would produce even greater reductions in heat loss.

One successful commercial application of a "thermal blanket" (or "heat sheet" as it is called in the trade), is in the Pinchbeck greenhouse at Guilford, Connecticut (Figure 10.10). Here, a Folyon blanket is used to cover almost 50,000 square feet of a rose-growing glasshouse. The blanket is rolled in and out using a single electric motor which turns rods running the full length of the greenhouse to open or close the curtains at the flick of a switch. The blanket is suspended from cables running above the plant canopy, and fits snugly into a channel section at each side of the greenhouse.

For a large domestic greenhouse it would be possible to arrange a similar motorized system, but over short lengths of glazing it is relatively easy to devise a blind that can be closed manually. The essential points to remember are: (1) to avoid storage problems the material should be as thin as possible and be able to be compacted easily, (2) to reduce convective heat loss there should be a tight fit between the "heat sheet" and the framing, particularly at the bottom of the glazing where cold air will leak out into the greenhouse fast.

For this reason it is often better to provide storage space under the sloping south glazing so that the bottom edge of the fabric can be permanently sealed to the glazing sill. Thin steel or nylon wires will provide a suitable track for the material, which needs to be attached at intervals of about 18 inches using nylon hook eyes. The thermal blanket can be raised to the ridge of the glazing using pulleys or rotating rods similar to the gear used to raise and lower awnings. Allow enough space for the fabric to be raised and lowered without touching the plants.

Roller shades. For use against vertical glazing there are a number of roller shades available that have good insulating qualities. These shades generally try to get the benefit of producing one or more dead air spaces between the shade and the window or within the shade itself. One of the essential characteristics, therefore, of any insulating shade is that it forms a tight seal against the window jambs (sides), head and sill.

The Insulating Shade Company manufactures an ingenious multi-layered shade which fits onto a standard wooden spring roller and when rolled up is hardly bulkier than a standard roller shade. When pulled down, the various layers open up to form a series of dead air spaces (Figure 10.11). An unusual plastic spacer is used to separate the layers of shade material which are made of aluminized plastic film to prevent radiant heat loss. A five-layer shade, in conjunction with double glazing, has an R value of 15, which according to the manufacturer will save enough heat through nighttime use to pay for itself in three to five years.

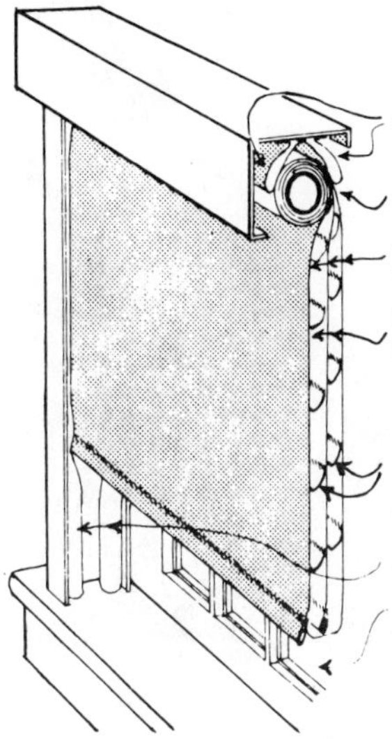

Ordinary drapes. If you decide to use ordinary drapes to conserve heat, it is worth using a half-inch Dacron backing to provide a quilted curtain between the inside material and the lining. This means that the curtain will not bunch up easily at the side of the window, and you will have to draw it back against the adjoining wall to provide a day-time wall hanging. But this has the advan-

cover with double head seals
compact roll design
3 or 5 layers expand to form dead air spaces
reflective surfaces to develop high resistance to heat transfer
spacers collapse when rolled up yet expand when pulled down
cover with double jamb seals
thermally effective summer through winter at windows and sliding doors

Figure 10.11. An ingenious insulated shade, which expands by means of collapsible spacers when it is drawn down. It is made by the Insulating Shade Company of Guilford, Connecticut.

tage of freeing up the window space entirely, thus admitting more light during the day which would otherwise be intercepted by the drapes.

The great advantage of insulating shutters, shades or curtains, is that they can provide much higher resistance to heat transmission at night when heat loss is generally much higher. It is possible to achieve high R values with multi-layer glazings, but these have the disadvantage of reducing solar heat transmission during the day. Movable insulation for windows, which was common in the eighteenth century, is due for a revival.

References and Sources

MANUFACTURERS OF THERMAL
INSULATING MATERIALS

Zomeworks Corporation, Box 712, Albuquerque, New Mexico 87103.

Beadwall

Plans and a license to build a Beadwall (444 square feet, $15) are available from Zomeworks.

Components such as tanks, blowers, sock valves and beads are also available for licensees.

Nightwall Clips

Magnetic clips for beadboard panels are sold at around 30 cents each by Zomeworks. Clips are required every 18" around the perimeter of the beadboard shutter. Zomeworks also sells beadboard, though this is generally available locally.

Figure 10.12. Skylid insulated louvers, which are activated automatically by a freon device.

Skylid

Skylids are freon-activated insulated louvers which are placed beneath skylights, or on the inside of sloping glass walls or vertical glazing. These large louvers (standard size 6'10" long x 2'10" wide) open automatically during sunny weather and close during very cloudy periods or at night. They are constructed of an aluminum skin curved over wooden ribs which enclose fiberglass insulation, and are activated by a couple of canisters of freon attached to each side of the louver. The freon migrates from one side of the louver to the other according to whichever side is warmer, and thus tips the balance of the louver, opening it or closing it automatically. There is also a manual override control (Figure 10.12).

The Insulating Shade

The Insulating Shade Company, 17 Water Street, Guilford, Connecticut. A multi-layer roller shade with jamb seals which rolls up like a standard roller shade, and when pulled down expands to form a series of dead air spaces. Independently tested R values up to 15, with a five-layer shade. Cost approximately $2.75 per square foot for the shade, and 50 cents per linear foot for the jamb seal strips.

Thermo Shade

Solar Energy Construction Co., Box 718, Valley Forge, Pennsylvania 19481. A plastic roller blind consisting of a series of horizontal semi-circular sections joined by flexible plastic connections. Rolls up into a valance box above the window and runs down between sealed jambs at the sides. Can be used on tilted glazing.

Window Quilt

Appropriate Technology Corporation, Box 975, Brattleboro, Vermont 05301. A quilted roller blind on dacron enclosing a reflective foil membrane. A lining material is quilted to each side. Forms a thick roll at the top of the window when closed. R value of 5.5.

MANUFACTURERS OF ALUMINIZED PLASTIC FILMS FOR REFLECTIVE HEAT CURTAINS

Duracote Corporation, 350 North Diamond Street, P.O. Box 512, Ravenna, Ohio 44266. Manufacturers of *Folyon,* reflective foil- polyester film. And *Al-Blac,* an opaque vinyl cloth.

Dupont de Nemours and Co. Inc. Textile Division, Wilmington, Delaware 19898. Manufacturers of *Tyvek,* a vacuum metalized plastic cloth.

MANUFACTURERS OF EQUIPMENT FOR OPERATING THERMAL CURTAINS

Simtrac Inc. 8243 North Christiana Ave., Skokie, Illinois 60076.

Rollout Insulation Systems Inc., P.O. Box 31, East Aurora, New York 14052.

SOURCES

"Window Design Strategies to Conserve Energy" by S. Robert Hastings and Richard Crenshaw, National Bureau of Standards, Center for Building Technology. June, 1977. $3.75 from the Government Printing Office, Washington, D.C. 20234. A survey of design ideas and insulating shades for windows.

"Thermal Balance at Heat-Reflecting, Multi-Element Windows" by J.G.F. Littler. Working Paper No. 25, Autarkic House Research Group, Cambridge University School of Architecture, Cambridge, England. A study of the U values that can be achieved with double layers of glass or plastic with heat-reflecting coatings on the inside of the glazing, including evacuated or Krypton-filled double-glazing units.

"Beadwalls: A Technical Note" by David Harrison. *Solar Energy,* vol. 17, pp. 317-19. Technical information including performance evaluation and costing of Beadwalls by the inventor.

11

Light and Heat

A vital greenhouse design decision involves the tradeoff between light and heat. Optimizing the amounts of light available and the amount of solar heat collected, while insulating any wall and roof areas that are not contributing significantly to either, is the key to an efficient solar greenhouse.

The major difference between a solar greenhouse and a conventional one lies in the attempt to capture heat rather than light. Obviously, a solar greenhouse tries to lose as little light as possible, but some sacrifice will be necessary to save heat. A conventional greenhouse makes no attempt to save heat, relying on an artificial heat source.

Solar energy is available to plants from direct sunlight and from diffuse sky radiation. The average light intensity, a combination of both direct and diffuse light, is often critical in determining what plants can be grown and what form the greenhouse should take. The average amount of light reaching the earth's surface varies from zero at the beginning and end of each day to as much as 10,000 to 15,000 footcandles (the standard unit of light intensity) at noon on a clear summer day, depending on latitude and altitude. On cloudy, overcast days there is no direct radiation and the average illumination intensity is often less than 1,000 footcandles. The minimum intensity for most forms of plant growth is around 1,500 footcandles, while 2,500 footcandles produces healthy, reasonably rapid growth in most plants. At intensities above 3,000 footcandles the rate of increase in plant growth slows considerably, so at noon much light is in fact wasted.

Total illumination throughout the day is actually more important than the intensity at any given time: 10,000 footcandle hours per day is considered the minimum necessary for healthy plant growth. Bear in mind, however, that greenhouses rarely transmit more than about 70 percent of available radiation (due to transmission losses in the glazing and shadows cast by the structure). So the average illumination required would be more like 15,000 footcandle hours. This can be provided either by a moderate amount of direct sunlight or a large amount of diffuse radiation.

Direct Sunlight

The amount of light and heat available from direct sunlight is about ten times that available from an overcast sky, so it makes sense to design the building to receive maximum direct sunlight in areas where there is a significant amount of sunshine in winter. The correlation between footcandles and solar radiation (measured in Langleys or in terms of heat radiation in Btu's per square foot) is a difficult one to measure, and few figures are available regarding levels of illumination around the country. But the chart showing available direct solar radiation (Figure 11.1) gives a reasonable idea of the relative amount of illumination. From this it is apparent that there are almost twice as many hours of direct sunshine available in the United States Southwest as in the Northeast. Greenhouses designed exclusively to receive direct sun in winter (that is, with glazing only on those areas directly facing the winter sun) would therefore be more successful in the Southwest. In the Northeast, particularly in inland areas, diffuse light is an important part of the total daily illumination, so more glazing facing the sky is needed.

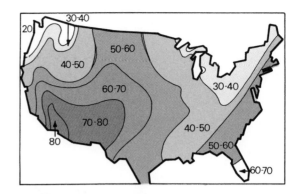

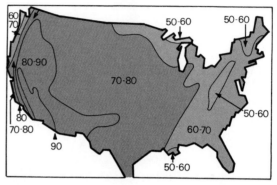

Figure 11.1. Graphs show the percent of possible sunshine that falls on the continental United States during a normal winter (above) and summer (below). The charts are based on those in The Climate Atlas of the United States by Stephen Visher (Harvard University Press, 1966).

To capture the maximum amount of direct sunlight, glazed surfaces must be as near as possible perpendicular to the sun's rays. Thus, it is necessary to become aware of the sun's movement pattern at the latitude where you live. The sun's position at any time can be described in terms of its altitude and azimuth. The altitude is the angle, in a vertical plane, between the sun and the horizon. The azimuth is the angle, in a horizontal plane, between the sun and due north. Seasonal extremes in azimuth and altitude are shown in the sunpath diagrams (Figure 11.2). Detailed measurements of these angles enable one to calculate the sun's position at any time and also the number of hours of sunshine potentially available at any time of the year. It is then possible to estimate how much sun any site will receive on a sunny day at a particular time of the year and when the

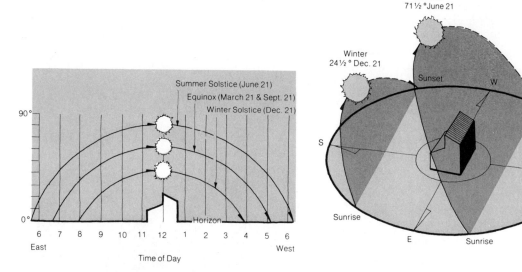

Figure 11.2. More of the sun is seen in June than in December because the sun is higher in the sky, and it's there for a much longer period of time. The sun's position in the sky relative to the horizon is called its altitude, and figures are expressed in degrees, rather than in distance. For those interested in precise scientific diagrams of the sun's path at different times of year, and at different latitudes of the earth's surface, the book <u>Architectural Graphic Standards</u> by Ramsey and Sleeper (John Wiley & Sons, New York, 1970) is recommended.

Figure 11.3. The study of optimum glazing angles for solar-oriented greenhouses has a long history. All these examples were collected by J.C. Loudon for his book <u>Remarks on the Construction of Hothouses</u>, published in London in 1817. It is noteworthy that all the greenhouses are south-facing, with solid north walls. Loudon's comparative analysis of the effects on light of increasing the size of glazing bars was drawn in 1815.

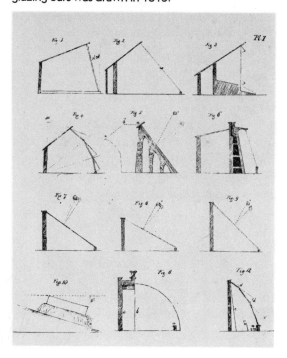

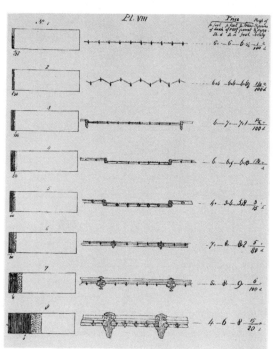

site will be shaded by nearby trees or buildings. From tables in the Appendix it is also possible to calculate the angle at which the glazing would be perpendicular to the winter sun. But this can be approximated by making the angle between the glazing and the horizontal about equal to the angle of latitude plus 15 degrees.

If capturing direct winter sunlight is the only aim of the greenhouse, then this angle would be ideal. But computer studies at the Brace Research Institute, at the beginning of its extensive solar greenhouse program, indicated that the angle was not so critical as some solar energy enthusiasts had predicted. In optimizing the angle of the south-facing glazing for a greenhouse in Quebec (latitude 47° north) for spring, winter and fall, a range of values between 40 and 70 degrees to the horizontal was found to be adequate. For winter collection alone, the higher figure would obviously be more suitable. In the end, for constructional reasons, a glazing angle of 35 degrees was adopted, since this enabled the longest frame members to be kept within the maximum length of standard readily available timber. The few degrees off optimum did not significantly affect the trans-

mission of radiant energy into the greenhouse in winter, although it did result in the transmission of more solar energy than was desired in summer.

Steeply sloping south glazing is optimum

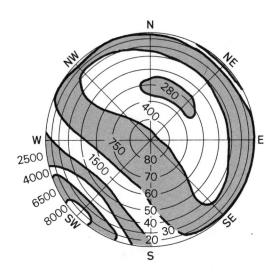

Figure 11.5. Diagrams show the distribution of the light intensity of the sky on clear and cloudy days. Above is a typical clear day (2:30 p.m., Oct. 2, Latitude 51 degrees north) where the sun is at altitude 20 degrees, azimuth S 45 degrees W. Below is a typical overcast day (10 a.m., Oct. 10, Latitude 51 degrees north) where the sun—invisible—is at altitude 20 degrees, azimuth S 22 degrees E. Concentric circles indicate degrees of elevation above the horizon (numerals running north-south). Other numerals indicate measurement of sky illumination in footcandles of the areas bounded by thick lines.

Figure 11.4. The graph shows the reduction in light transmission for various glazing materials at increasing angles of incidence.

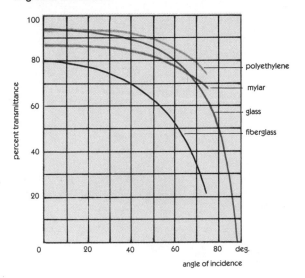

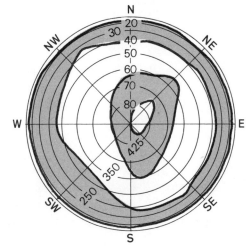

Adapted from Science and the Glasshouse by W.F. Lawrence.

only where heat collection is a major priority, or in areas where the percentage of direct sunshine in winter is high. If one considers the wellbeing of plants in cloudy areas, then diffuse light is often the critical factor. Most glazing materials will admit a high percentage of direct sunlight over a wide range of angles of incidence (Figure 11.4) so that the losses from reflection are often overemphasized. Shallower slopes to the south-facing glazing provide more indirect solar radiation, as well as more plant growing area, and are often to be preferred.

On a cloudless day, roughly 80 percent of the diffuse sky radiation comes from that half of the sky toward the sun. This clear-day diffuse radiation contributes considerably to the overall level of illumination. It is also significant that a cloudless sky tends to be brighter near the horizon than it is overhead (Figure 11.5). Thus an area of near-vertical south-facing glazing will receive diffuse light from the brightest part of a cloudless sky as well as receiving the maximum amount of direct winter sun.

Diffuse Sunlight

On overcast days, the illumination pattern of the sky is different. The uniformly overcast sky is normally 2½ to 3 times as bright overhead as it is near the horizon. About five-sixths of the overall illumination available comes from that portion of the sky above an altitude of 30 degrees from the horizon. This emphasizes the importance of overhead glazing in areas without a dependable supply of direct sunlight. It is also significant, however, that there is considerably more light in the southern half of the sky than in the north even in uniformly overcast conditions, so that if exposure is to be limited, it is the northern half of the sky that is least valuable.

Reflected Light

A good deal of the light available to plants comes from ground reflection, particularly close to the plant itself. The average amount of ground reflection on a clear day is generally assumed to be around 20 percent of the direct sunlight, though in sandy areas with light soils it can be more, and in areas with considerable ground cover or dark soils it is likely to be less. A fresh covering of snow can increase the percentage to more than half of the direct sunlight available. In areas with long-lasting winter snowfalls and clear skies, it therefore makes sense to orient the greenhouse glazing to take advantage of this reflected light. This means that a steeper slope to the south-facing glazing is justified, and for sunspaces attached to the house, vertical glazing may be more suitable, since it also has considerable advantages when considering insulated shutters and shades.

Reflective panels. The use of reflective panels to increase the intensity of light on greenhouse plants can overcome certain deficiencies in natural lighting, and is the subject of much research. Materials commonly used to reflect light can be divided into specular and diffuse reflectors. Specular reflectors such as bright aluminum foil or mirror surfaces provide direct beam reflection. Diffuse reflectors such as flat white paint scatter the incident radiation fairly uniformly. White paint is better for use inside the greenhouse because plants actually prefer a high level of diffuse illumination, and specular reflectors can cause "hot spots" of concentrated sunlight that can scorch the leaves. For concentrating direct sunlight into a greenhouse, or onto a heat sink such as a water wall, then a specular reflector is more useful because it is possible to achieve a directional beam. Remember, however, that the directional beam will move with the sun, so its usefulness at certain times of day or year will be limited.

The reflectivity of materials increases slightly as the angle of incidence increases between reflector and incoming light. Thus it is more difficult to bounce light back when incoming light is perpendicular to the reflective surface, and easier when the light strikes the reflective surface at a shallow angle. The reflected beam has the same angle with the reflective surface as the incoming beam. The reflectivity of different surfaces is given in Figure 11.6.

Research done by William Lawrence at the John Innes Research Institute in England showed that in the cloudy winter conditions that prevail there, lettuce plants in front of a white painted north wall of a greenhouse did not grow as well as those in front of a glazed

Figure 11.6. The reflectivity of different materials.

Snow	90%
Bright aluminum foil	88%
Gloss white paint	80%
White paper	75%
Flat white paint	70%
Buff brickwork	60%
Aluminum paint	55%
Red brickwork	45%
Concrete	40%
Red paint	24%
Brown quarry tiles	20%
Gloss black paint	9%
Flat black paint	2%

north wall. Further experiments with young tomato plants and a specular reflector showed that the increase in illumination on the plants during periods of direct sunlight produced a significant increase in plant growth, with young tomato plants requiring a much higher level of illumination than the lettuces.

Drawings adapted from R.W. Langhans et al., Cornell Univerity.

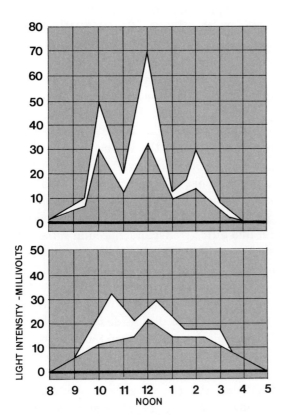
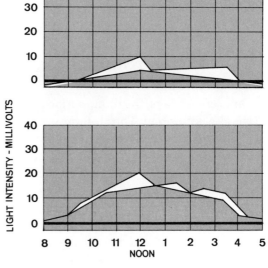

Figure 11.7. Graphs show measurements of light intensity under different conditions. At left, it's a bright sunny January day, and the top measurements are light intensity with half of the north greenhouse roof covered with reflective insulation; the bottom is a conventional fully glazed greenhouse. At right, it's a cloudy January day, and again the top chart shows light intensity with half of the north roof covered with reflective insulation, and the bottom the conventional glazed greenhouse. On a cloudy day, the fully glazed unit gets a bit more light. On a sunny day, the reflective covering yields more light.

Similar research work in Canada at the Brace Research Institute, and in the United States at Cornell University's Department of Agricultural Engineering, has proved the value of reflective insulation on the north walls of greenhouses. The researchers at Cornell concluded that, in general, reflective insulation reflected enough light in winter to at least partially make up for the losses in diffuse sky radiation. This tendency diminishes, however, as the sun reaches higher angles in the sky, and by March there was a loss of illumination, even on bright sunny days. Figure 11.7 compares the light levels in two test greenhouses. Note that on a cloudy day the light intensities are higher in the full-

Figure 11.8. Foil-faced parabolic reflectors, right, cover the north wall of the Ecotope greenhouse in Seattle, Washington. The reflected heat is focused on an aquaculture tank that also serves as a heat sink.

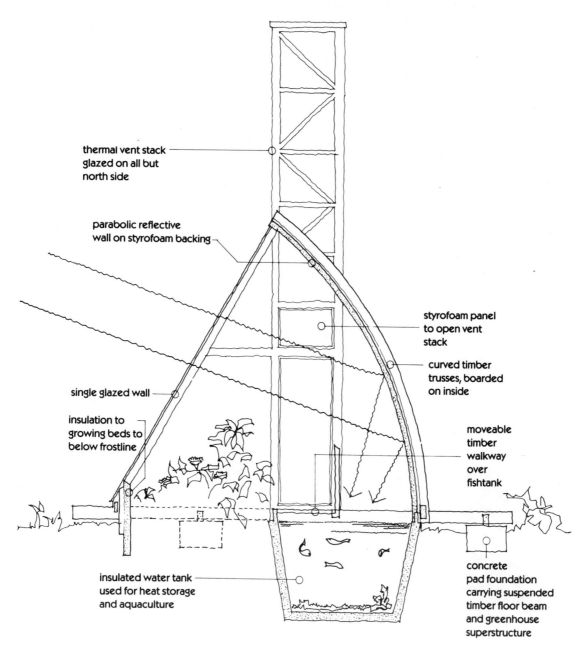

thermal vent stack glazed on all but north side

parabolic reflective wall on styrofoam backing

single glazed wall

insulation to growing beds to below frostline

insulated water tank used for heat storage and aquaculture

styrofoam panel to open vent stack

curved timber trusses, boarded on inside

moveable timber walkway over fishtank

concrete pad foundation carrying suspended timber floor beam and greenhouse superstructure glazed greenhouse; on a sunny day they are higher in the greenhouse with reflective insulation.

Parabolic reflectors forming the north wall of a greenhouse are a feature of one of the designs produced by the Ecotope group in Washington state (Figure 11.8). The primary heat sink of the greenhouse is a large buried water tank used for aquaculture. The parabolic reflector is designed to provide a fairly diffuse focus on the tank during winter months. In summer, very little direct sunlight hits the reflector so the concentration of light is minimized. Using specular reflective materials inside a greenhouse requires that the greenhouse glazing be transparent and not translucent. Translucent glazing such as fiberglass diffuses light so that there is no longer a direct beam that can be refocused by a reflective panel. The parabolic greenhouse built by Ecotope used standard glass with an

inner layer of clear vinyl film to preserve the qualities of direct sunlight.

Detailed research work on the increased illumination level with horizontal reflective panels has been carried on at Marlboro College in Vermont, in conjunction with Jeremy Coleman of T.E.A., Harrisville, New Hampshire. The calculated results for a simple horizontal reflective panel in front of a vertical greenhouse wall showed that an increase in direct illumination of 21 percent was possible in December, increasing to around 40 percent in October or March. These values were for a specific example only, though the calculation procedures could be used for different designs at different locations. The added benefit of these external reflective panels is that they can also be used as nighttime shutters when raised into position against the glass.

In the Cape Cod Ark (Figure 11.9), a cable and king-post truss is used to support the glazing. Here, a simple steel tie with a 2-by-2 wooden glazing bar supports fiberglass glazing over a span of more than 20 feet. Most of the resistance to bending is taken up in the steel tension rod, and the glazing bar is reduced to a size that is determined by the qualities of the fiberglass rather than by the structural capacities of the wood.

Similar steel and timber trusses were used in many nineteenth-century greenhouses (Figure 11.10).

If you use solid timber framing, you can compensate partially for any shading caused by the wood's thickness by painting it white, preferably in gloss paint to achieve maximum reflection. Home-made greenhouse builders should err on the side of safety, while bearing in mind that lightweight structures can increase transmission of light significantly.

Solar transmittance. In areas with little direct sunlight in winter, it is important to consider the solar transmission of the glazing material, or combination of materials, as well as the percentage of incidence radiation that is blocked out by the structure of the greenhouse. It is virtually accepted that

Figure 11.9. The Cape Cod Ark, built by a group known as the New Alchimists in Falmouth, Massachusetts, has a cable and kingpost truss to support its fiberglass glazing. This maximizes transmission of both light and heat because there is virtually no shading caused by structural supports.

Hilde Maingay photo.

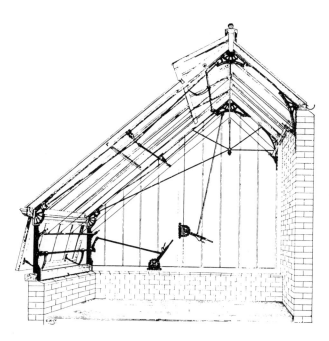

Figure 11.10. Steel- and timber-trussed rafters were used in 19th century greenhouses to minimize the shading effects of the structure itself. This sketch is adapted from a catalog of Messenger & Co. Ltd., which described itself as "horticultural builders, heating engineers and iron founders."

Shading. The thickness of structural members that support glazing should be given careful consideration where illumination levels are low. Older greenhouses were often built with thin sections of high-quality lumber (Figure 11.11) that was free from knots and had a greater resistance to bending than most dimensional lumber one might buy today. These old timber sections could be reduced almost to the size of the aluminum sections now in use, but they retained of course a superior resistance to heat transmission.

Figure 11.11. A view of the greenhouses in the Botanical Gardens in Cambridge, England, illustrates the use of thin timber structural supports that were common in the early 20th century.

double glazing of some kind is essential for solar greenhouse construction in most areas. Double glazing a south-facing window in a house generally produces a net heat gain, whereas single glazing provides a net heat loss. The extra layer of glazing, however, does cut light and heat transmission by around 10 or 15 percent for most glazing materials. When using two skins of glazing, therefore, in areas where light levels are critical, it is important to insure that they have a relatively high solar transmittance. Double glazing with two skins of eight-ounce fiberglass sheets will reduce the average daily transmission to around 50 percent incident radiation. This particularly high reduction is also due to the fact that the transmittance of fiberglass falls off faster than other glazing materials as the angle of incidence of incoming radiation increases. Only with highly transparent thin films such as Tedlar, or with glass, is it possible to achieve double glazing with average daily transmission of more than 80 percent.

References and Sources

Science and the Glasshouse by William F. Lawrence. Published by Oliver and Boyd. London. 1963 (revised edition). This is a series of useful studies that deal with optimizing the form of a greenhouse for maximum light penetration while also reducing heating costs. The work pertains to greenhouses in England, where for three or four months of the year, light levels are critically low for the growth of most plants. Useful documentation even though the work is now outdated.

The Proceedings of a Conference on Solar Energy for Heating Greenhouses and Greenhouse Residential Combinations. Sponsored by the Ohio Agricultural Research and Development Center and federal Energy Research and Development Agency. Cleveland, Ohio. March, 1977. These proceedings include a paper by R.W. Langhans and colleagues at the Department of Agricultural Engineering at Cornell University, Ithaca, New York, on the use of reflective insulation and simple solar-collection systems for commercial greenhouses. Also included is a paper on the solar, long-wave, and photosynthetic energy transmission of green-house cover materials, by Bond, Godbey and Zornig. This covers the energy-transmission properties of nine different greenhouse cover materials and all possible combinations of them in the form of double glazing. The information is detailed and complete.

The Proceedings of a Conference on Energy-Conserving Solar-Heated Greenhouses, held at Marlboro College in Vermont in November, 1977. These conference proceedings contain papers submitted by the Ecotope group of Seattle, Washington, on its parabolic aquaculture greenhouse, and on work by the energy research group at Marlboro College on the use of insulated reflective shutters.

The ASHRAE Handbook of Fundamentals. Published by the American Society of Heating, Refrigerating and Air-Conditioning Engineers, 345 East 47th St., New York, New York 10017. 1972. Chapter 9 of this standard reference is titled "Environmental Control for Animals and Plants" and contains a detailed discussion of light and its effects on plant growth.

12

Solar Heat Storage

The most common heat-storage materials used in solar greenhouses are water, earth, rocks and masonry. They all have different characteristics, advantages and disadvantages (Figure 12.1). Generally a combination of more than one storage material is used.

Earth Storage

The earth in a greenhouse provides a certain amount of heat storage, though this is not generally very significant because the canopy of plant growth prevents much direct radiation from striking the earth. Raised beds can be advantageous in this respect because the sun falling on the sides of the beds helps to heat them. The storage capacity of the earth is generally proportional to its water content. Dry soil has a heat capacity of 20 to 25 Btu's per cubic foot per degree F., whereas saturated soil has a capacity of around 55 to 60. Conductivity also increases with the moisture content. But the greater the moisture content of the soil, the greater the heat lost to the air through evaporation. So earth beds are not ideal as heat sinks. It is important, however, to prevent heat loss from ground-level earth beds by insulating the perimeter of the greenhouse down to the frost line. Heat lost downwards is then negli-

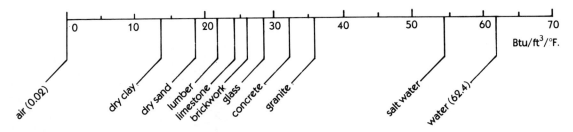

Figure 12.1. Heat capacities of various materials: the amount of heat (Btu's) required to raise the temperature of one cubic foot of each material through one degree Fahrenheit.

gible because any heat that sinks into the earth during the day is likely to rise back up at night.

Water Storage

The easiest way to increase the thermal mass of a greenhouse is to use water storage. A given volume of water will store more than twice as much heat over a given temperature difference as the same volume of masonry, and three times as much as dry earth (Figure 12.2). Heat is also transferred faster through water due to the formation of convection currents. With large volumes of water, temperature stratification can occur easily, resulting in overheating at the top of the tank and a negligible rise in temperature at the bottom. The top of the tank will then lose heat quickly to the surrounding air, and will not act as a very efficient solar collector. This problem can be overcome by insuring that the bottom of the tank receives most direct sunlight, the top being shaded by planting beds or by the greenhouse roof. In these circumstances, it might also be advisable to insulate the top of the tanks to provide better heat storage.

One of the most readily available containers for water storage is the standard 55-gallon steel oil drum. During recent years the secondhand value of these drums has increased considerably. The demand for a storage container that was both lightweight and durable has led to the production of fiberglass tubes for water storage. These tubes are made by the Kalwall Corporation and have been installed in many solar-heated buildings in the Northeast (Figure 12.3). They can be filled with dyed liquid, or painted flat black to absorb solar radiation. The standard diameters are twelve inches and eighteen inches and heights range from four to ten feet. They are supplied with the bottom end sealed, and a lid is provided for the top. They are relatively inexpensive, particularly if you are located in the New England area and do not have to pay considerable transportation costs.

Circular storage tanks use up more floor

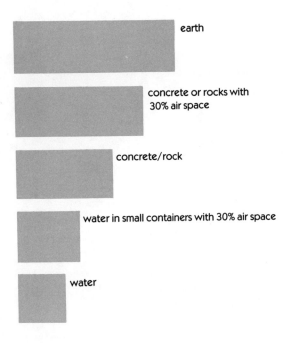

earth

concrete or rocks with 30% air space

concrete/rock

water in small containers with 30% air space

water

Figure 12.3. Fiberglass tubes for storing heat in water are light in weight and durable. These are made by the Kalwall Corporation (88 Pine St., Manchester, New Hampshire 03105).

area for a given storage volume than rectangular units which can be packed closer together. The cylindrical units also have an increased surface area (around the back of the tank) which loses heat rapidly by convection. Water "walls" with a high storage capacity for a given floor area can be created by stacking five-gallon rectangular tins or the squared-off plastic containers used for storing household cleaning fluids. When stacking bottles or cans, consider the increase in pressure on the bottom layer of containers with every extra layer placed above. A shelving system is generally required for stacking plastic bottles more than three layers high. David MacKinnon, who has experimented extensively with water-storage walls, devised a method of suspending plastic bottles from a vertical framework of chicken wire along the back of his greenhouse in Flagstaff, Arizona. MacKinnon used a Rit black dye in the water to help absorb solar radiation. By dividing the storage volume into a series of smaller containers, the stratification problem encountered with large volumes is greatly reduced because convection currents are limited to each individual bottle.

A recently developed water-wall system by One Design Inc. of Winchester, Virginia, consists of fiberglass reinforced polyester modules that can be stacked on top of one another to form a structural wall, or placed inside of one another to allow for easy packaging and therefore reduced transportation costs (Figure 12.4). This ingenious solution to the problem of producing a compact self-supporting module for a water wall is still undergoing development but should be available soon.

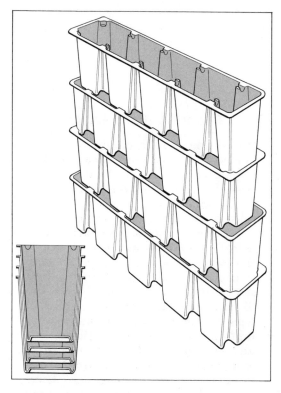

Figure 12.4. Water-wall modules, developed by One Design Inc. (Mountain Falls Route, Winchester, Virginia 22601) are stackable in two ways—to form a heat-storing wall, or for transportation.

Fish farming. Large water-storage tanks in greenhouses can be used for fish farming. Several experiments with small-scale intensive fish farming have been carried out at the New Alchemy Institute on Cape Cod for a number of years. In their more recent experiments, the New Alchemists have used five-foot diameter Kalwall storage tanks for growing tilapia and other edible fish. They also incorporate small ponds into their greenhouse designs to act as a source of irrigation water and as a natural habitat for frogs, turtles and other desirable aquatic and amphibious mammals which help regulate the insect populations in the greenhouse. Natural aquatic environments in warm greenhouses are ideal locations for the growth of algae. The algae darken the water and thus increase solar heat collection as well as using solar energy in their own photosynthetic processes. In addition, they oxygenate the water to provide a suitable environment for fish. Setting up complex biological systems such as those involved in greenhouse aquaculture requires considerable knowledge and experience, as well as a good deal of space.

In large greenhouses or sunspaces attached to the home, water storage can also be in the form of swimming pools. These require a dark surface on the sides and the bottom of the pool to absorb solar radiation, and insulation is necessary around the perimeter of the pool.

Rock Bed Storage

One of the problems with heat storage in a greenhouse is that the storage mass is often in competition with the plants for direct sunlight. In addition, the transfer of heat to the surface of the storage mass, and through the mass itself, is often not as rapid as the transfer of heat to the surrounding air. This results in the greenhouse overheating and requiring ventilation even on sunny winter days when the heat collected is very precious. One solution to both these problems is to circulate air through or around the storage so that the greenhouse air is cooled, and heat that would otherwise have been wasted is stored for use at night. This also means that the heat-storage mass does not necessarily have to be in direct sunlight, and more sunlit space is therefore available for plants. The disadvantage of this kind of system is that it often requires the assistance of a small fan to circulate air, though it may be possible to get a certain amount of heat flow by natural convection. Even with a fan, the additional energy required is minimal, compared with the amount of heat collected. Resultant air movement within the greenhouse is beneficial to the plants, particularly in conditions of high humidity.

Forced-air method. With a forced-air circulation system, the easiest type of storage material to use is rocks or pebbles. Smooth rocks and pebbles, when packed together, leave air spaces between them of around 30

CHEMICAL HEAT STORAGE

Heat storage in the crystallization of certain salt solutions has always looked promising. The change of state between crystals and solution requires an input of heat far greater than that required to raise the temperature of either the crystals or the solution. This means that more than 100 times as much heat can be stored in a given volume of salt solution as it changes into crystals than can be stored in a similar amount of water. Until now there have always been problems getting the change of state to work uniformly throughout the solution over and over again. The most interesting research on this subject at the moment is in the use of "solar ceiling tiles." These consist of two quarter-inch layers of salt solution enclosed in a one-inch-thick polyester-concrete tile. The lifetime of the salt solution going through continual changes of state from solid to liquid and back again can be greatly extended if the solution is in thin layers. The storage capacity of the solution as it changes state is equal to that of a 9-inch-thick slab going through a 30-degree temperature swing. For further information, see a paper, "New Building Materials and Components for Passive Heating of Buildings" by Timothy Johnson, in the Proceedings of the Passive Solar Heating and Cooling Conference, May, 1976, Albuquerque, New Mexico.

percent of their total volume. These spaces provide passage for the air to flow through. The solid-to-air ratio does not vary much with the size of the rocks, and successful rock-storage beds have been constructed with the aggregate normally used for concrete (half-inch to three-quarter-inch diameter), as well as with fist-sized rocks. Rock-storage beds with smaller pebbles have more surface area and therefore increased heat-transfer characteristics, though they also impede the air flow more, and may require more powerful fans.

Figure 12.5 shows a simple air-circulation rock-storage system that will operate at least partially by natural convection. During the day, hot air rises to the top of the greenhouse to be replaced by cooler air which is drawn in from the base of the rock-storage bed. The warmer air then loses its heat to the rock storage as it sinks through it. At night, the cool air next to the glazing sinks to the bottom of the greenhouse and is replaced by the warm air from the top of the storage container. As long as the temperature difference between the top and the bottom of the rocks is great enough, the resultant pressure difference will cause air to circulate. A rock-storage system such as this would probably operate quite well without fan assistance on all except the hottest days, when the rate of air circulation would not be able to cope with the heat the greenhouse collected. At such times a fan, located at the base of the storage bed, could assist in the distribution of heat throughout the rocks and avoid problems caused by overheating. At night the fan would distribute stored heat back into the greenhouse.

Underfloor heat storage. Rock-storage beds can also be situated underneath the greenhouse floor, where they take up less room. In this position, however, they certainly require fan-assisted collection, and often distribution, to effect adequate heat transfer from the greenhouse air to the rocks and back again at night. Figure 12.6 shows a simple fan-assisted underfloor rock bed. Air is sucked down from the ridge of the greenhouse either through a simple sheet metal duct, or (as in this example) through a false wall at the back of the greenhouse which also acts as a collector. Heat distribution at night is by radiation through the floor slab and by reverse circulation to the greenhouse via the

Figure 12.5. In a greenhouse with a bed of rocks for heat storage, daytime and nighttime convection patterns are shown.

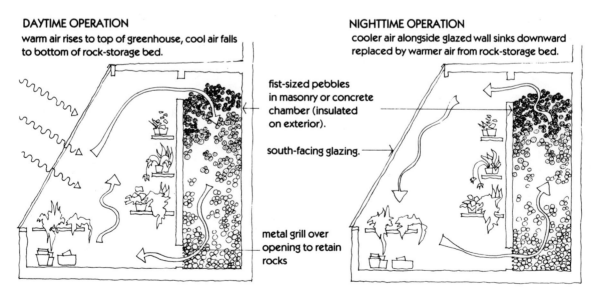

DAYTIME OPERATION
warm air rises to top of greenhouse, cool air falls to bottom of rock-storage bed.

NIGHTTIME OPERATION
cooler air alongside glazed wall sinks downward replaced by warmer air from rock-storage bed.

fist-sized pebbles in masonry or concrete chamber (insulated on exterior).

south-facing glazing.

metal grill over opening to retain rocks

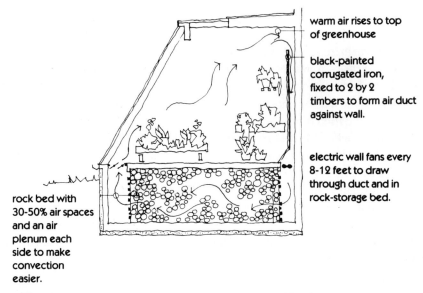

warm air rises to top of greenhouse

black-painted corrugated iron, fixed to 2 by 2 timbers to form air duct against wall.

electric wall fans every 8-12 feet to draw through duct and in rock-storage bed.

rock bed with 30-50% air spaces and an air plenum each side to make convection easier.

Figure 12.6. A fan-assisted underfloor rock-storage bed. Air from the ridge is drawn through a false wall into the rocks during the day. At night, the heat rises by radiation through the floor slab.

duct. Figure 12.7 shows an exceptional situation where the greenhouse is built into a south-facing slope, and a thermosiphoning air collector heats the rock bed which then releases its heat to the greenhouse at night through registers in the floor. A backdraft damper is required to avoid heat wastage through the collector at night.

One of the advantages of rock-storage beds in conjunction with solar heating of any kind is that the heat is not diluted throughout the bed as would occur with forced circulation through a water-storage system. A high temperature differential can easily be maintained between the end of the storage bed where the warmed air is drawn in, and the

Figure 12.7. A rock-storage bed with air-cooled solar collector. The collector heats the rocks, which then release the heat into the greenhouse at night.

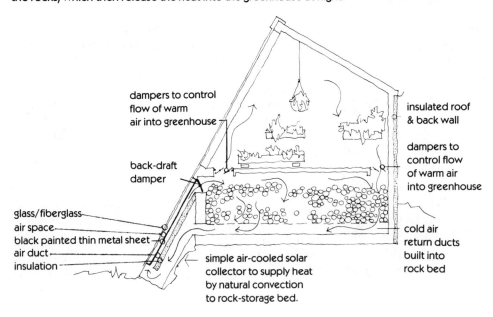

dampers to control flow of warm air into greenhouse

back-draft damper

glass/fiberglass
air space
black painted thin metal sheet
air duct
insulation

simple air-cooled solar collector to supply heat by natural convection to rock-storage bed.

insulated roof & back wall

dampers to control flow of warm air into greenhouse

cold air return ducts built into rock bed

other end where the cooler air leaves. In effect this means that it is easier to distribute the heat usefully because it is stored at a higher temperature. If one is considering building an attached greenhouse or sunspace and hoping to collect excess heat for the home, then rock-storage systems are especially suitable. Another advantage of rock-storage beds used in conjunction with solar heating is that they can easily be used to get rid of excess heat collected on hot summer days. By operating the fan at night and flushing cool air through the system, excess heat collected during the day can be released to the atmosphere.

Heat storage in back wall. In the O'Bryne greenhouse at Noti, Oregon (designed and built by architecture students from the University of Oregon under the direction of Ed Mazria and Stephen Baker) a vertical rock bed at the back of the greenhouse serves as a retaining wall and also as the primary heat storage. Air is drawn down from the ridge of the greenhouse to the base of the rock wall where the heat is concentrated. The air rises gradually through the rocks and releases heat as it rises (Figure 12.8). The rock wall is kept in place by a layer of wire mesh stretched between the post-and-beam construction which holds up the roof. The rocks are painted black and absorb energy by direct radiation as well as by fan-assisted convection. This greenhouse operates throughout the winter without any backup heat at temperatures which rarely go below 50 degrees F. The success of the greenhouse is primarily due to the efficient collection and storage system.

Heat storage under plants. At the Agricultural Engineering Department at Cornell University, the space under the plant benches has been used to form a container for rock storage. Bench units are constructed of plywood with steel straps and are filled with crushed limestone rocks to within 5 inches from the top of the bench. Hot air from the ridge of the greenhouse is forced along this 5-inch deep void and diffuses down through

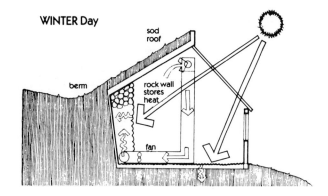

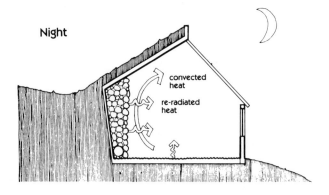

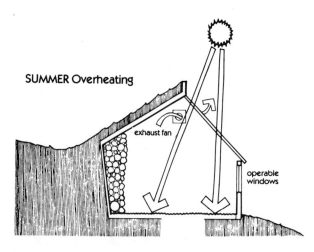

Figure 12.8. An efficient heat-collection and storage system designed at the University of Oregon. The rock storage is in the rear wall.

the rocks (Figure 12.9). Tests have shown that the hot air will distribute itself uniformly down through the rock at maximum flow rate. The air then exits through steel mesh slots at the bottom of the benches. A separate fan is used to suck air out of the storage units at night by reversing the flow of air. The collection duct is blocked off automatically

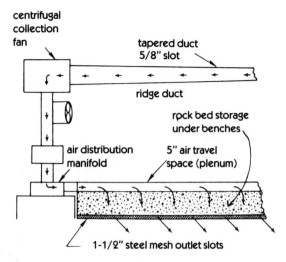

centrifugal collection fan

tapered duct 5/8" slot

ridge duct

rock bed storage under benches

air distribution manifold

5" air travel space (plenum)

1-1/2" steel mesh outlet slots

COLLECTION

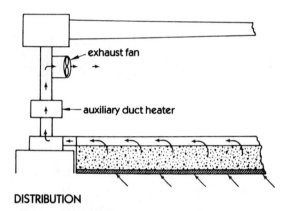

exhaust fan

auxiliary duct heater

DISTRIBUTION

Figure 12.9. Diagrams of collection and distribution modes through under-bench rock beds in experimental greenhouses at Cornell University.

during heat recovery by a motorized damper. It is estimated that the rock bed could reach temperatures of around 105°F. during collection without damaging the plants. At night, the heat storage is useful down to a temperature of around 55° F. (in a domestic solar greenhouse growing hardier plants, it could be useful to a lower temperature than this). Rock storage under planting beds takes up little useful space and is cheap to install since it requires no excavation or major structural work. The researchers at Cornell appear to have devised a system that is suitable for both commercial and domestic greenhouses.

Rock-storage beds in attached greenhouses can be located either in vertical stacks or in underfloor spaces. Vertical stacks use up useful living space and require strong constructional details because the weight of the rocks can be quite considerable. Cylindrical metal or concrete containers used normally for underground sewer construction can be used to contain the rocks. A storage box could also be constructed from masonry or reinforced concrete, or from studwork providing that horizontal steel ties were used at the corners or through the center of the box at regular intervals. The foundation or floorslab underneath the rock storage box needs to be thickened and reinforced. One advantage of vertical storage containers is that the hot air collects at a high level in the greenhouse and can easily be drawn down through the rock bed. It is also easier to store heat at high temperatures in a rock bed with a small cross section since the heat remains concentrated at the intake end without being diluted through the whole bed. Underfloor heat storage is, however, cheaper to install since the excavation is probably necessary anyway for the foundation and footings, and the rock bed can provide a suitable base for casting a reinforced slab to provide a finished floor.

Useful test work on underfloor rock-storage systems is being carried out at the Farallones Institute in northern California. Several small cabins (Figure 12.10) have been constructed using different methods of passive heat collection. The rock-storage beds that collect heat from three of the cabins were housed within the insulated concrete foundations of each house. Typically they were two feet deep with a six-inch-wide plenum on each side to provide an even distribution of the air through the bed (Figure 12.11). The principle was to charge the rock-storage bed using a small fan (1/6 h.p. for a rock bed thirteen by eleven by two feet deep) and then allow heat distribution to the cabin by radiation and convection from the slab as the heat load on the building increased at night. The main problem encountered with the initial rock-bed designs was horizontal stratification. The storage bed and slab were heated

Figure 12.10. Several small cabins at the Farallones Institute in Occidental, California, use different types of passive solar-heat collection.

only at the side where the hot air was blown in. This led to uneven heat distribution. A considerable proportion of the heat collected could not be used because when the temperature of the rocks fell to below 70 degrees, the slab became ineffective as a radiant heat source.

A further cabin was built using a vertically charged rock bed with a series of perforated plastic pipes laid through the rocks just underneath the slab, and another series at the bottom of the rock bed. Hot air was introduced through the top series of pipes and removed through the bottom. Heat distribution was much more even than in the previous designs, but there were still problems

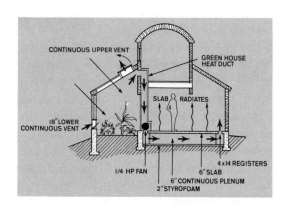

Figure 12.11. Diagram shows the general principle of the Farallones Institute underfloor rock storage and air-distribution system.

with releasing the heat from the rock bed at night. It was speculated that a number of registers in the slab could solve this problem because the heat could then be distributed by natural convection as well as radiation. The use of passive-heat transfer from storage to space at night increases the efficiency of a rock-bed system, which normally would require fan-assisted heat distribution as well as collection, resulting in a fairly continuous use of electrical energy.

Much more research needs to be done in the field of rock-storage systems to insure that they can operate effectively with a minimum of expensive duct work, damper controls and fans, which can be both noisy and costly. Small rock-storage areas such as the O'Bryne greenhouse are failsafe solutions to greenhouse heating. When considering rock-storage beds for sunspaces in the home, more engineering skills are needed to calculate pressure drops through the rock bed, to predict storage temperatures, and to solve problems of collection and distribution.

Masonry Walls

Because it generally makes sense to incorporate as much thermal mass in a solar-heated greenhouse as possible, it is logical to use dense concrete blocks or bricks or adobe to provide the structure for the opaque walls of the greenhouse. The amount of heat that can be stored in a wall exposed to direct sunlight is very little by comparison with the amount provided by either water walls or rock-storage beds. The heat penetrates the blocks relatively slowly, and any heat collected at the surface of the wall will tend to be released to the air rather than be conducted through the wall. A more efficient system of heat transfer to the inside of the wall could be made by using hollow concrete blocks and aligning the hollow spaces to form vertical ducts within the wall. Air blown through these ducts would then heat the inside of the wall.

Any masonry walls used for direct heat storage should be painted a dark, flat color (dark red, brown or blue are almost as good as black). Moveable insulation covering the outside of these walls at night should be installed to help store the heat.

For comfortable temperature conditions for plants as well as people, the radiant temperature of the surrounding surfaces are quite significant. Lower air temperatures are more tolerable when offset by higher-than-average radiant temperatures at surrounding wall surfaces.

Sizing Heat Storage

The size of the heat-storage mass needed by a greenhouse depends on the heat capacity of the storage system and its collection and distribution efficiency, as well as the amount of solar radiation available and the heat loss of the building. Computer simulations can be used to determine the optimum storage volume for a given building in a given location. Usually, however, the storage volume is calculated to provide an amount of heat necessary to cope with the heat loss of the building over a period of one to four days depending on the climate, and it is envisaged that auxillary heating would be used over longer cloudy spells. A reasonable initial estimate for the amount of heat storage required for a well-insulated, double-glazed greenhouse in a cold winter climate would be around 45 Btu's per degree Fahrenheit for every square foot of south-facing glazing. This means that for a greenhouse with 200 square feet of south-facing glazing, the storage should take in 9,000 Btu's for every degree Fahrenheit rise in temperature. This would indicate the need for approximately 9,000 pounds of water (150 cubic feet) or 45,000 pounds of rocks (approximately 360 cubic feet).

In many situations the storage volume will be determined by the space available and by architectural constraints rather than by detailed calculations. It is significant that there is little danger of increasing the overall useful thermal mass of a greenhouse too much. Plants do like a difference in temperature between day and night, but it is unlikely that the thermal mass of a greenhouse would completely dampen down the daily tempera-

ture fluctuations. One of the easiest ways to improve the efficiency of an existing greenhouse is, after double glazing it, to increase its thermal mass by adding water barrels or rock beds under the benches. The absorption of daytime heat for rerelease at night will soon cut down on heating bills.

References and Sources

The Solar Greenhouse Book, edited by James McCullagh. Rodale Press, Emmaus, Pennsylvania. 1978. Contains a useful chapter on heat storage by David MacKinnon, including descriptions on the water wall he designed for his Flagstaff, Arizona, greenhouse.

"Experimental Results of a Greenhouse Solar Collection and Module Gravel Storage System," by R.W. Langhans et al. of the Department of Agricultural Engineering, Cornell University, Ithaca, New York 14853. Published in the *Proceedings of a Conference on Solar Energy for Heating Greenhouses and Greenhouse Residential Combinations,* in Cleveland, Ohio, March, 1977.

Noti Solar Greenhouse Performance and Analysis, by E. Mazria et al. 1977. Available for $2 from the Center for Environmental Research, School of Architecture and Allied Arts, University of Oregon, Eugene, Oregon 97403.

A Comparison Study of Four Passive and Hybrid Space Heating Systems, by Peter Calthorpe, with Bruce Wilcox and Don Stauffer. 1978. Published by the Farallones Institute, 15290 Coleman Valley Road, Occidental, California 95465.

EQUIPMENT

Thermal Storage Containers

Kalwall storage tubes are manufactured in sizes shown (Figure 12.12) from premium-grade Kalwall Sunlite fiberglass. Send for prices and order form from Solar Components Division, Kalwall Corporation, 88 Pine St., Manchester, New Hampshire 03103.

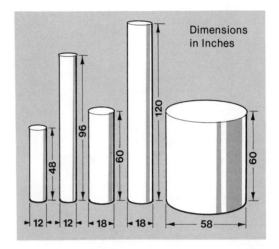

Figure 12.12. Sizes and shapes of available Kalwall storage containers.

Water-Wall Modules

Being developed (but not ready for sale at this printing) by One Design Inc., Mountain Falls Route, Winchester, Virginia 22601.

Electric Fans and Blowers

A full range of centrifugal (squirrel-cage) blowers and duct fans are available from the Solar Mail Order House, Kalwall Solar Components Division, Box 237, Manchester, New Hamphsire 03105. Phone (603) 668-8186.

Items include Airtroll booster fans for five-, six-, and eight-inch diameter ducts, providing 55, 75, and 150 cubic feet per minute air-flow rates, respectively. Also Dayton blowers delivering air at rates ranging from 265 to 1,800 cubic feet per minute.

V

Solar Designs and Adaptations

Extensive simulation tests preceded the construction of this prototype greenhouse-residence combination in Easley, South Carolina. The building uses a greenhouse to preheat the air, which then passes throught the roof-mounted solar collector above. The heat is then transferred to a rock-storage bed under the house. In conjunction with a heat pump, the house was calculated to provide more than 90 percent of the winter heat requirement and about 20 percent of the summer cooling load. It was designed by Harold F. Zornig, AIA, an architect with the Rural Housing Research Unit of the U.S. Department of Agriculture's Science and Education Administration.

13

Solar Greenhouses

Interest in energy conservation and home food production have come together in recent years in the construction of many solar greenhouses. Though designs differ widely, basic principles remain similar. They are all heavily insulated, oriented for optimum collection of solar heat in winter, and incorporate thermal storage so that excess heat normally available during the day can be held for use at night.

Different climatic conditions for which they are designed, and variations in the expectations of owners, have led to a number of different design solutions. In most locations, the only way to insure vegetable growth throughout the winter is to provide a backup source of light, or heat, or both. But if one is prepared to follow the dictates of climate to a certain extent, and not demand too much of one's greenhouse in the middle of winter, it is possible to provide a greatly extended plant growing season using only solar energy.

How Much Sunlight?

The amount of sunlight available in winter is, of course, the critical factor in determining performance and design of a solar greenhouse. Figure 13.1 gives the average daily number of hours of winter sunshine available across the continental United States. From this chart, it is obvious that Arizona and New

Mexico, with between seven and eight hours each day of sunshine, are ideal locations for solar greenhouses. Not surprisingly, this region has seen much of the formative work take place in this field.

At the other extreme, the Appalachians, the New England mountain regions, and parts of the Northwest, have very little direct sunshine, and the average amount of illumination makes it difficult to grow anything but leafy vegetables. Some solar greenhouse owners report that even these will remain fairly dormant for one or two months in the middle of winter. In these regions, light rather than heat is the limiting factor in plant growth; without the provision of artificial illumination, plants cannot be expected to do well. Often in these regions a solar greenhouse is designed more for spring "starts" and for continuing summer growth into the fall, and it is recognized that during winter the greenhouse will allow plants to survive, but not to grow.

Cloudy means mild. One advantage of cloudy winter climates is that the cloudy spells are generally associated with above-average outdoor temperatures. Clear skies allow the earth's heat to re-radiate into space, and therefore both earth and air temperatures tend to be colder even though there is more solar radiation available during the day.

The intermediate zone between these two extremes covers a vast area of the country which is subject to great climatic variations. The amount of sunshine available, as well as temperature and wind conditions, may produce awkward growing conditions at different times of the year. Local climates should be studied carefully before designing any greenhouse.

The use of the greenhouse at different times of the year is also important when considering its initial design. In climates with cool, short summers the greenhouse provides an ideal location for growing long-season crops such as cucumbers, peppers, tomatoes, squash, and even sweet corn. In this kind of

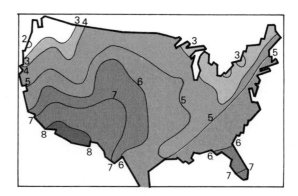

Figure 13.1. Average number of hours per day of winter sunshine in the continental United States.

location it may be important to you that the greenhouse performs as well in summer as in winter, so ventilation and shading may be crucial.

Figure 13.2 considers some of the strategies involved in designing solar greenhouses for different climates. The climatic categories are broad, and are only intended as a guideline to the design process. The examples following are selected as being interesting responses to the demands made by different climatic conditions and different planting programs.

The sun-heated pit. Because of their year-round viability, greenhouses have always been more popular in the north than in the south, where overheating in summer can be severe. A number of greenhouses built around Boston in the 1930s and '40s foreshadowed the present-day interest in solar heating. These are documented by Kathryn Taylor and Edith Gregg in *Winter Flowers in the Sun-Heated Greenhouse and Pit*.

The greenhouses were sunk into the ground to benefit from the insulating qualities of the earth, and to reduce their exposed surface area. They generally had a solid north wall and roof, and a glazed south wall tilted at around 45 degrees to the horizontal. They were designed to catch sufficient direct and diffuse light throughout the long New England winters to keep chrysanthemums and many other house plants flowering. They

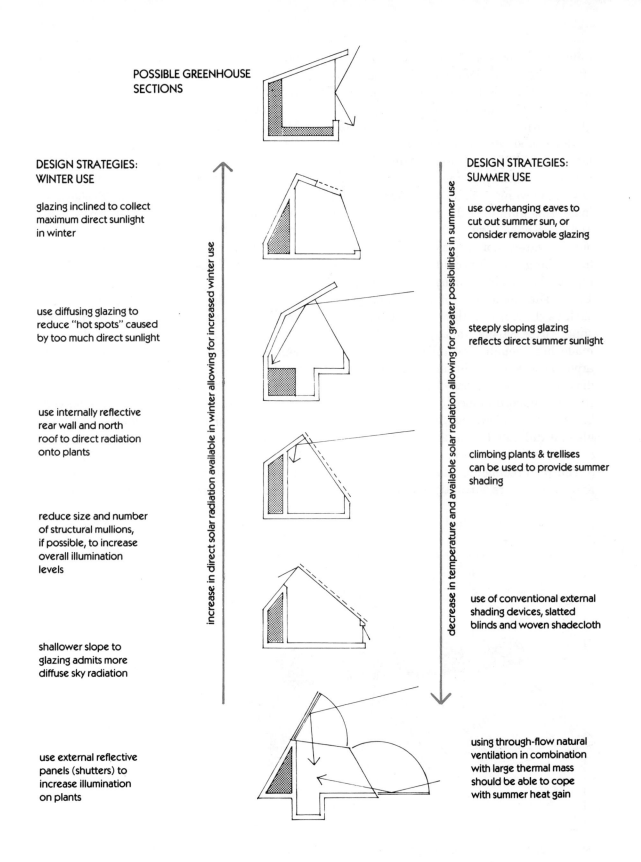

POSSIBLE GREENHOUSE
SECTIONS

**DESIGN STRATEGIES:
WINTER USE**

glazing inclined to collect
maximum direct sunlight
in winter

use diffusing glazing to
reduce "hot spots" caused
by too much direct sunlight

use internally reflective
rear wall and north
roof to direct radiation
onto plants

reduce size and number
of structural mullions,
if possible, to increase
overall illumination
levels

shallower slope to
glazing admits more
diffuse sky radiation

use external reflective
panels (shutters) to
increase illumination
on plants

increase in direct solar radiation available in winter allowing for increased winter use

**DESIGN STRATEGIES:
SUMMER USE**

use overhanging eaves to
cut out summer sun, or
consider removable glazing

steeply sloping glazing
reflects direct summer sunlight

climbing plants & trellises
can be used to provide summer
shading

use of conventional external
shading devices, slatted
blinds and woven shadecloth

using through-flow natural
ventilation in combination
with large thermal mass
should be able to cope
with summer heat gain

decrease in temperature and available solar radiation allowing for greater possibilities in summer use

Figure 13.2. Different design strategies consider both summer and winter uses.

relied totally on solar heat, and a good deal of effort went into insulation. The solid walls were insulated with four inches of fiberglass; the south walls, in later models, were double glazed with an inner skin of plastic film, and were covered with insulation at night. Burlap bags full of leaves were swung onto the north side of the greenhouse roof during the day, and swung back at night to provide an insulating quilt over the glazing. A superior and more expensive kind of quilt was made out of waterproof canvas pads filled with loose fiberglass. This could be rolled up to the top of the glazing during the day (Figure 13.3). The advantage of insulating quilts such as these is that they can be made to fit snugly over the glass and, provided they are made big enough, are unlikely to leak air around the edges as shutters might do. Their disadvantage is that they leak, however well they are made, and once the insulation inside becomes wet, it is virtually useless. They can also be difficult to manage when frozen or covered with snow or ice.

The pit greenhouses discussed by Taylor and Gregg were virtually self-heated, and derived benefit from the relatively stable temperature of the earth as well as from the heat of the sun.

Jim DeKorne's greenhouse in El Rito, New Mexico, is a development of that same idea. Partially sunk into the ground, with earth berms to the north, it provides a controlled environment throughout the winter with an average temperature around 20°F. above the external air temperature. DeKorne's many interesting experiments in hydroponic cultivation and organic gardening are described in his book *The Survival Greenhouse.*

Water-table factors. Building underground or, ideally, into a south-facing hillside, provides many advantages. It is essential, however, to research ground water conditions before attempting to do this. A high water table would necessitate making a completely watertight concrete tank for your greenhouse, or lining the whole structure of the pit with asphalt to prevent seepage. Remember, too, that water tables can change from time to time, and if you neglect to make your pit greenhouse waterproof it may sud-

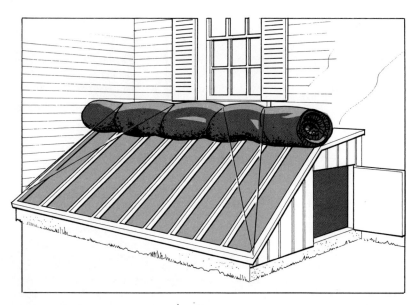

Figure 13.3. Burlap bags filled with leaves, or canvas stuffed with loose fiberglass, serve as night insulating shades in this drawing adapted from the book <u>Winter Flowers in Greenhouse and Sun-Heated Pit</u> by Kathryn S. Taylor and Edith W. Gregg (Scribner's, 1969).

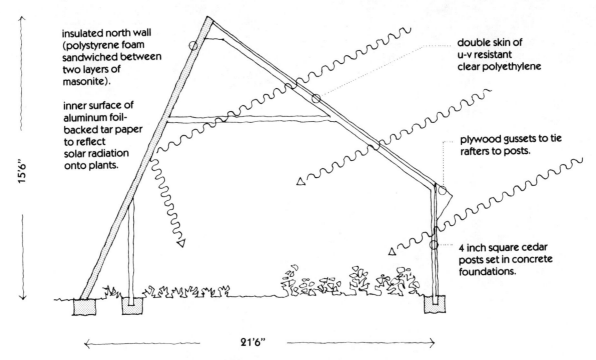

insulated north wall (polystyrene foam sandwiched between two layers of masonite).

inner surface of aluminum foil-backed tar paper to reflect solar radiation onto plants.

double skin of u-v resistant clear polyethylene

plywood gussets to tie rafters to posts.

4 inch square cedar posts set in concrete foundations.

15'6"

21'6"

Figure 13.4. A cross-section of the experimental greenhouse designed at the Brace Research Institute, Laval University, Quebec, in 1973, shows how a highly reflective surface on the insulated north wall increases light levels on plants on the north side during sunny midwinter days.

denly become sodden. To get maximum benefit from the earth's heat you need to excavate below the frost line and insulate the outside of the retaining walls above that level.

Energy-Saving Pioneers

Pioneering work in the field of energy conservation in commercial greenhouses was begun at the Brace Research Institute in Quebec in 1973. The aim was to produce a greenhouse that, when compared with a standard commercial vaulted structure, showed a significant saving in heating costs without significant loss of light. The Brace design was one of the first to incorporate a highly reflective surface on the insulated north wall (Figure 13.4). This resulted in increased light levels on the planting beds on the north side of the greenhouse during sunny days in midwinter. When compared to

a conventional greenhouse, the Brace design in no way interfered with apparent plant growth, and yet savings of between 35 and 40 percent in heating costs were realized. This saving was primarily due to insulating the north wall, which also served as a windbreak against prevailing cold winds. Later versions of the Brace design incorporated heat storage materials at the rear of the greenhouse to reduce daily temperature swings.

A patient attitude. The solar greenhouse built by Helen and Scott Nearing at their house on the coast of Maine is designed for year-round use. It provides good exposure not only to the direct sun in winter but also to a large area of the sky. The north and east walls are made of stone, and are eighteen inches thick. These provide a barrier to prevailing winds while cutting down only minimally on diffuse light. The Nearings believe in growing what they can. With the aid of their hand-crafted solar greenhouse they can

Figure 13.5. The sun-heated greenhouse of Helen and Scott Nearing on the coast of Maine utilizes heat trapped by the 18-inch-thick stone walls, which also divert prevailing winds. The photo appears in their book Building and Using Our Sun-Heated Greenhouse.

enjoy added benefits from their garden all year long. Part of their secret is a patient attitude toward the climate, and their plants. Part is due to more than forty-five years of homesteading experience. They describe their greenhouse, and how they use it, in their book *Building and Using Our Sun-Heated Greenhouse.*

Experimental fish farming. The Ecotope group in Seattle, Washington, is primarily interested in fostering energy conservation and using renewable sources of energy. Members concentrate on designing low-energy buildings, and increasing public awareness of the simpler uses of solar energy. Into this category comes the development of solar greenhouses for a climate characterized by mostly cloudy conditions all winter. One of their more important projects has been the construction and testing of solar greenhouses for growing fish as well as vegetables.

They use a parabolic reflector (Figure 13.6) to direct sunlight down onto a large fish pond sunk into the ground on the north side of the greenhouse (see also Figure 11.8 in the chapter Light and Heat). The rear wall of the greenhouse consists of prefabricated curved studs, boarded on the inside and lined with three inches of expanded polystyrene. This forms the backing for a layer of aluminized mylar, with a Teflon surface to minimize degradation. At winter solstice, the parabolic reflector focuses light down onto the front of the tank at a point about four feet away from the north wall. As the sun's elevation increases, the reflection becomes increasingly diffuse and closer to the rear wall. In summer, the reflector becomes almost insignificant as the angle of the incoming sun moves further away from the axis of the parabola, and in midsummer, the ridge of the roof actually shades the reflector so it does not contribute any increase in heat.

During the first winter's operation it became obvious that, though the water tank was absorbing heat fast, it was also losing it too fast at night. To overcome this, steps were taken to decrease the heat loss of the building by better draft stripping, and a vinyl cover was added to reduce heat loss from the pond, the cover being removed on sunny days so it did not reduce the solar heat input.

The greenhouse is expected to provide a natural environment for growing algae and tilapia fish for about ten months of the year. During the two remaining months, lack of sunlight causes too great a reduction in the growth of algae, with the result that the ecosystem which provides the fish with both food and oxygen would break down were it not for the provision of artificial aeration and filtration. These systems have been carefully detailed into the design of the parabolic greenhouse, and appear to function well. The

Figure 13.6. The exterior form of a parabolic reflector is evident in this photograph of one of the Ecotope greenhouses in Seattle, Washington. The reflector directs sunlight down onto a sunken fish pond.

Ecotope group has already produced detailed preliminary reports on its aquaculture experiments, and plans to issue further reports of extensive tests.

A solar chimney. The group has also designed and built simpler greenhouses in the area around Seattle, and has co-ordinated workshops in which simple passive solar collectors such as water heaters and green-

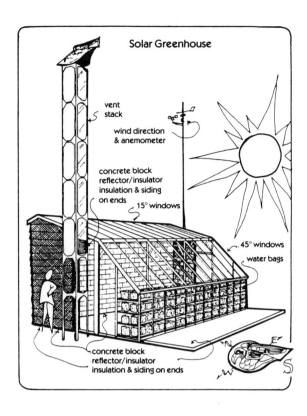

Solar Greenhouse

vent stack

wind direction & anemometer

concrete block reflector/insulator insulation & siding on ends

15° windows

45° windows

water bags

concrete block reflector/insulator insulation & siding on ends

Figure 13.7. and 13.8. Illustrated in a sketch and photo is the solar chimney of the Ecotope group. Only the south side of the twelve-foot stack is glazed, with the rest sheathed solidly. It is designed to provide ventilation of 900 cubic feet per minute on a summer day—the equivalent of a sizeable greenhouse fan— without using any electrical power.

houses have been built. One of the features used in these greenhouse designs is a solar chimney for ventilating excess heat. The chimney consists of a two-foot-square shaft rising twelve feet from the top of the greenhouse. The south side is glazed; the other three sides are sheathed in exterior grade plywood, painted black on the inside. The air in the chimney heats up and causes an up-draft, which increases with the rate of solar heat input. At the base of the chimney (at the top of the greenhouse) is a styrofoam panel trap door operated by a heat motor (a thermostatic vent control which operates solely on heat). The chimney is expected to provide a ventilation rate of 900 cubic feet per minute, equivalent to a sizeable greenhouse fan, on a hot summer's day, and requires no artificial energy to operate it.

Vertical rock storage. The O'Bryne greenhouse in Noti, Oregon, is another solar greenhouse designed for the cloudy northwest. It was built by students at the nearby school of architecture in Eugene, under the direction of their professor, Ed Mazria, and

Steven Baker. Made entirely out of recycled materials and using simple construction techniques, it cost only $900 in materials, plus a good deal of donated labor. It is built into the side of a south-facing hillside. The retaining wall is loose rock held up by a vertical layer of galvanized chicken wire strung between laterally braced fir pole columns that hold up the roof structure. The 28,000 pounds of rocks in the wall also provide heat storage for the greenhouse. They receive solar heat both by direct radiation and by convective heat transfer from the air. Hot air rises to the ridge of the greenhouse and is sucked down by a fan into a perforated duct running through the base of the rock wall. As this air gradually rises through the rocks, it releases its heat before reentering the greenhouse.

Under extreme winter conditions, back-up heat will be provided by a wood-burning stove located in an attached sauna. The sauna has not yet been installed, and the greenhouse survived its first winter without falling below 47°F., though outdoor temperatures reached a low of 16°F. Summer overheating is avoided by the roof configuration which cuts out direct solar heat on the mass wall during summer months. The wall itself dampens down temperature extremes, absorbing unwanted heat in summer as well as storing useful heat in winter.

The Noti greenhouse is not insulated to the high degree often found in solar greenhouses in colder climates. The end walls contain three and a half inches of fiberglass, but there is no insulation in the north-facing roof other than the homosote decking and twelve inches of sod, which does not provide good thermal resistance when wet. Nor is the back of the rock wall insulated. In retrospect, the designers would perhaps have increased the insulation levels, and thereby further improved the thermal performance on the greenhouse in winter.

The 45-degree slope on the south-facing glazed roof exposes both the planting bed and the rock wall to a good deal of diffuse sky radiation as well as direct sunlight. This is not enough, unfortunately, to promote plant growth in December and January, given the cloudy conditions in Oregon. But by the beginning of February, the greenhouse was becoming useful for seed germination.

The main success of the Noti greenhouse seems to be its highly efficient solar-heat collection and storage. With a simple fan-assisted circulation system, a high percentage of the available solar radiation is stored in the

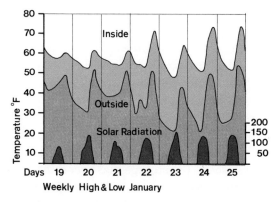

Figure 13.9. A chart of winter temperature differentials in the O'Bryne greenhouse in Noti, Oregon.

rock wall, which keeps the inside temperatures on average 15 degrees above the outside. The fan, which helps to store heat, also provides air movement necessary for healthy plant growth. Creating efficient heat transfer to and from storage is one of the essential attributes of a good solar greenhouse.

A greenhouse ecosystem. The New Alchemy Institute has its headquarters at Woods Hole on Cape Cod in eastern Massachusetts. It has been experimenting for several years with biological systems run on solar energy, growing plants intensively, and developing small-scale fish-farming techniques. Its philosophy is as important as its practical experiments in understanding and developing the relationships between man and the natural ecosystems he can cultivate. The group's most recent solar greenhouse at Woods Hole is a large aquaculture-horticulture building christened The Ark, which is entirely self-sufficient in heating energy during the cold and often sunless winter of coastal New England.

The building is about 90 feet long and 30 feet wide. It is well insulated, with six inches of fiberglass in the opaque side walls and roof, and a concrete retaining wall to the north that is insulated on the outside with two inches of styrofoam, and completely buried in an earth berm. The south-facing transparent wall is inclined at 45 degrees, and glazed with two layers of Kalwall "sunlite" fiberglass, bent into grooves in the glazing bars in such a way as to form a series of concave channels from the outside. This method of glazing provides rigidity to the fiberglass between widely spaced purlins, and allows both rainwater and condensation to drain off the timber glazing bars.

The potential heat-storage mass in the greenhouse is large. At the west end there are nine cylindrical fiberglass water tanks, each five feet in diameter and five feet high, which are used for rearing algae and fish. There is another large concrete water tank in the center of the greenhouse used for pre-heating irrigation water, and for fish-

Figure 13.10. The New Alchemy Institute's Ark on Prince Edward Island, Canada, is dominated by south-facing solar panels. A glass wall divides domestic and commercial greenhouses. The building, the group says, "symbolizes a search for alternative ways of living on earth—a response to the threat of dwindling resources, a new morality based on prudence."

breeding experiments. This brings the total volume of water storage to around 10,000 gallons. A rock storage bin behind the concrete tank contains about 2,000 cubic feet of loosely packed rocks. A fan, which generally operates from 9 am to 3 pm in winter months, circulates air from the top of the greenhouse through the rock bed to prevent overheating and reduce the need for ventilation. The fan comes on again at night to recirculate heat stored in the rocks. The total heat storage capacity exceeds 100,000 Btu's per degree Fahrenheit, or around 500 Btu's for every square foot of glazing. This vast amount of heat storage makes the whole system very stable. There is little change in the temperature of the water, which fluctuates between 45 and 50°F. in winter. The soil also remains at a fairly constant temperature of around 55°F. Daytime winter air temperatures are in the upper 50s, sinking to the lower 40s at night, but maintaining a level 20 or 30 degrees above the average outside temperature.

The system demonstrates the advantages of increasing the greenhouse storage mass.

The result is not an increase in average temperature, but simply a dampening of the daily temperature swing. Even in midwinter the internal temperatures, combined with a reasonable amount of light, through the 45 degree glazing, mean that all kinds of salad greens and lettuces can be grown as well as brassicas such as cabbage and kale.

A community "ark." The larger version of the New Alchemy Ark on Prince Edward Island in Canada (Figure 13.10) has been well publicized. It is a community-size development of the building at Woods Hole. The larger scale allows for a more complete and stable ecosystem to be developed, in what the New Alchemists have christened a "bioshelter." The building contains a 200-square-foot living area, and a 22,000-square-foot commercial greenhouse. There are more than 20,000 gallons of water as well as a large rock bed to provide heat storage for the building. At this scale, the storage mass operates on a seasonal as well as a diurnal basis by absorbing heat in summer for use in winter.

The glazing consists of Acrylite SDP

double glazing, which combines the advantages of low thermal transmittance with high light transmission and fairly good visual transparency. It also admits more ultraviolet light than fiberglass which, according to the New Alchemists, helps to regulate bacterial and fungal populations, and possibly reduces the incidence of plant diseases.

The Ark is intended as a demonstration building to try to prove that a system that uses natural energy and biological control mechanisms can compare favorably with conventional greenhouse practices dependent upon energy-intensive cultivation techniques. The initial success of the project has been overwhelming, despite critics who point out the construction costs of around $500,000. The local demand for fresh winter vegetables from the commercial greenhouse facility has far outstripped the potentially large supply.

Interest aroused by the structure and its educative value have already proved its worth. It will be some time before the principles being developed in the Ark begin to have wider applications in society, but that time, for the New Alchemists, is precious time in which to develop a third and fourth generation of experimental structures with emphasis on decreasing costs, and increasing the sophistication of the system while at the same time making it easy for a relatively uneducated person to maintain it.

There is an increasing awareness among solar-energy enthusiasts that photosynthesis is a primary and most useful means of harvesting solar energy. We must begin to consider hybrid systems of all kinds in an effort to maximize the benefits the sun brings us. The Ark experiments, together with descriptions of the many other research projects that the New Alchemists are involved in, are fully described in *The Book of the New Alchemists* and in their annual journals.

A season extender. The Farallones Institute in northern California is, like the New Alchemy Institute, devoted to continuing experiments in community self-sufficien-

cy. The construction of a solar-heated greenhouse was a natural extension of the Farallones' research work into organic gardening techniques and in the use of passive solar energy to heat buildings. The greenhouse is used primarily as a season extender rather than for growing winter vegetables. The 45-degree tilt to the south-facing glazing intercepts maximum direct radiation during late fall and early spring. Center-pivoted insulated ventilators are placed along the low wall at the front of the greenhouse, and also in the north-facing section of the roof to provide through-flow ventilation. Water storage drums line the back wall. A series of coldframes has been added to the front wall of the greenhouse for hardening off seedlings in spring (Figure 13.11).

The greenhouses illustrated so far have all been designed for climates with a relatively low percentage of direct sunlight in winter. It is therefore necessary to use a shallower pitched glazing than would normally be optimal for collecting direct radiation. In the southwest United States, with an abundance of sunshine during winter months, it makes

Figure 13.11. A solar-heated greenhouse of the Farallones Institute in northern California features a 45-degree bank of glazing, a rear wall lined with drums of water, and a series of low coldframes along the front wall.

sense to tilt the glazing more steeply toward the winter sun. This also minimizes problems of overheating in summer.

Luxurious sunshine. The recent growth of interest in solar greenhouses in New Mexico has been due largely to the work of Bill and Susan Yanda, who introduced and popularized the notion as a way of utilizing the luxurious supply of winter sunshine there. For several years, the Yandas have been running a "Solar Sustenance Project," with state funding, which has succeeded in bringing the benefits of solar energy to low-income families throughout New Mexico. The construction of ten demonstration units during the first phase of the project sparked so much interest that within a year another 50 solar greenhouses were built with private investment. The second phase of the project was to emphasize this "snowballing" effect by concentrating more on publicity and media coverage of another twelve solar greenhouses built by community groups. A good deal of initial organizational work was necessary to get each project going. Public meetings and lectures were held, from which a caucus of interested people was formed and a site for a demonstration unit was chosen. Then during an intensive two-day workshop, a greenhouse was constructed. Each one was extensively monitored and reports from owners were documented. The educational benefits of the project were enormous. Yanda estimates that a year later about 300 similar units had been built.

Simple design and construction techniques are an important part of the success of the project. Designed primarily for winter use in a climate with a high percentage of direct winter sun, the south-facing glazing is tilted at an angle of around 75 degrees to the horizontal. The glazing used is five-ounce "Lascolite" fiberglass sheets fitted to a simple studwork frame, with an inner layer of Monsanto 602, an ultraviolet-resistant polyethylene film fixed to the inside during winter. The roof slopes at an angle of 15 degrees to the horizontal. The front portion of the roof is glazed, using corrugated fiberglass

Figure 13.12. The principles embodied in the Yanda greenhouses have been incorporated into many free-standing greenhouses in the Southwest. These photos show a large solar greenhouse in El Rito, New Mexico, built by Peter Van Dresser and many enthusiastic helpers. In concept it is much like a typical Yanda lean-to unit, though it is built up against an existing south-facing stone retaining

wall, which provides a good deal of thermal mass. Van Dresser is a solar-energy pioneer whose long experience in the field has earned him much respect, both locally and now internationally. His continuing work in the field of passive solar energy has been documented in his book, Homegrown Sundwellings.

Jeff Kahane

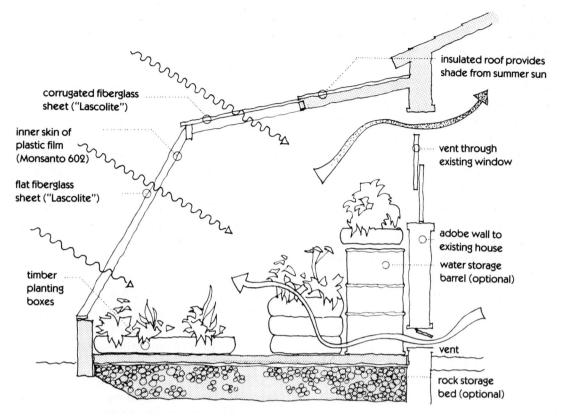

corrugated fiberglass
sheet ("Lascolite")

insulated roof provides
shade from summer sun

inner skin of
plastic film
(Monsanto 602)

vent through
existing window

flat fiberglass
sheet ("Lascolite")

adobe wall to
existing house

water storage
barrel (optional)

timber
planting
boxes

vent

rock storage
bed (optional)

Figure 13.13. A diagram of a typical "Solar Sustenance" greenhouse in New Mexico—one of at least 300 built to provide winter vegetables for low-income families. In this example there are three heat-storage media: a rock bed underneath, the adobe wall of the attached house, and 55-gallon water barrels.

(the corrugations give strength to support snow loads); the rear portion is opaque and insulated, to cut out unwanted sunlight in summer (Figure 13.13).

Heat storage is provided by rock floors, insulated underneath with a layer of pumice rock, by the earth beds in the greenhouse, and where possible, by the wall of the house. In New Mexico, adobe is the traditional building material, so a lean-to greenhouse is likely to have a north wall with a high thermal capacity. Additionally, a number of water-filled 55-gallon oil drums are generally placed along the rear wall in Yanda's greenhouses, to add thermal capacity.

The payoff in terms of both heat collected and food produced from the Solar Sustenance greenhouses has been tremendous. On average, the greenhouses provide 40 to 60 percent of each family's vegetables throughout the winter. One family reported saving $40

per month on vegetables (at 1976-77 food prices). In general, vegetables grown during winter are the common leafy greens such as lettuce, spinach, chard and broccoli, though the higher levels of illumination also allow for the growth of tomatoes, cucumbers and chili peppers even during winter months. The value of food produced is the primary economic justification for Yanda's solar greenhouses. Figures documenting the first phase of the project showed that more than 90 percent of the recovered income is in the value of food produced. The remaining 10 percent is in energy supplied to the house.

At a cost of about $2.50 per square foot (1977 prices) the economics of the Solar Sustenance greenhouses looks sound. The payback period in terms of food and heat produced is about one and a half years for an owner-built greenhouse, and nearly three years for a contracted one. No solar heating system or conventional greenhouse seems to be able to match these figures. In addition to money saved, there are other advantages such as having an extra living space attached to the home. The Yandas use part of their own greenhouse as a study, and part has a sandbox for their young daughter to play in. Other advantages, which are impossible to place a monetary value on, include having the satisfaction of building part of your own home, and providing a major portion of your winter food supply, knowing what went into producing it.

Further information on this project, including slides, charts and data collected, is available from Bill Yanda, Solar Sustenance Project director, Box 1077A, Santa Fe, New Mexico 87501. In addition to publishing two reports on the project, Yanda has also written a full-length book, *The Food and Heat Producing Solar Greenhouse: Design, Construction, Operation,* which covers all the details of these designs that are particularly adaptable to the American Southwest.

Construction Details

As demonstrated by the examples shown, the detailed design of solar greenhouses depends upon their location and intended use. The following pages provide some construction details for a free-standing solar greenhouse that could be adapted to suit many different locations.

The design shown (Figure 13.14) has a south-facing transparent wall inclined at 60 degrees to the horizontal, suitable for maximum direct solar gain in winter for most of the continental United States. For areas with a lower percentage of direct radiation it might be advisable to reduce the angle of glazing to around 45 degrees (Figure 13.15). This would result in a higher "knee-wall" at the front of the building that could be glazed to allow direct radiation, either to ground beds or to heat storage such as containers of

water with raised beds above. For simplicity of construction, as well as for achieving a good deal of internal reflection from the north roof, the angle of 90 degrees should be maintained between the solid north-facing roof and the south-facing glazing.

The design includes provision for opening vents in the roof which could be made transparent, if necessary, to increase the amount of diffuse radiation at times of year when the heat loss of the building was not too severe. During coldest months, skylights could be blocked off by styrofoam panels cut to size and wedged or tacked into the framework. The concept of skylight panels that can easily be blocked off with insulation allows for a certain amount of experimentation with the greenhouse to get the right balance between heat loss and illumination requirements, and allows the greenhouse to be adapted to severe or mild winters.

If you have an electrical supply available, it might be worth dispensing with roof vents altogether and installing a gable wall fan for ventilation. This would eliminate problems which might arise if bad workmanship caused the roof vent to leak—either rainwater or cold air. Simple axial-flow greenhouse fans can be bought from most greenhouse suppliers. Make sure they are provided with well-seated back flaps for when the fan is not in use. They can also be made to operate in conjunction with a series of louvers at the bottom of the opposite gable wall to let in fresh air, though the louvers provide another series of cracks that are difficult to seal when you don't require ventilation.

To get additional thermal storage into the greenhouse, and to avoid venting heat to the outside air, the rear portion of the adjacent storage and work area shown on the plans could be converted into a vertically charged rock-storage bin through which the greenhouse air could be circulated.

The end walls of the greenhouse are insulated studwork, and the north wall is constructed of eight-inch solid concrete blocks, insulated with two inches of styrofoam on the outside. The north-facing sloping roof is also

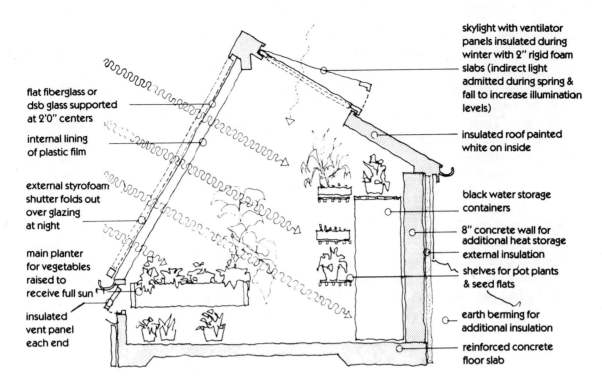

flat fiberglass or
dsb glass supported
at 2'0" centers

internal lining
of plastic film

external styrofoam
shutter folds out
over glazing
at night

main planter
for vegetables
raised to
receive full sun

insulated
vent panel
each end

skylight with ventilator
panels insulated during
winter with 2" rigid foam
slabs (indirect light
admitted during spring &
fall to increase illumination
levels)

insulated roof painted
white on inside

black water storage
containers

8" concrete wall for
additional heat storage

external insulation

shelves for pot plants
& seed flats

earth berming for
additional insulation

reinforced concrete
floor slab

Figure 13.14. A basic design for a solar greenhouse, adaptable to many regions of the United States, has a south-facing glazed wall inclined at 60 degrees.

Figure 13.15. Another basic design has glazing inclined at 45 degrees, which creates more "kneewall" at the front. The 45-degree slope would be for regions that get less direct solar radiation.

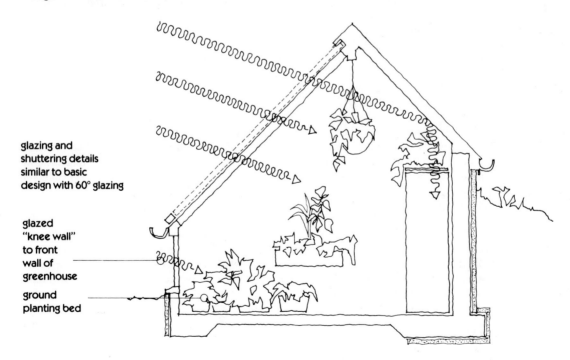

glazing and
shuttering details
similar to basic
design with 60° glazing

glazed
"knee wall"
to front
wall of
greenhouse

ground
planting bed

insulated and painted white inside to reflect light down onto the plants. The level of insulation depends on the severity of the climate. As a rough guide, in climates of up to 3,000 degree days, use at least 3½ inches of fiberglass batt in 2 x 4 stud walls. In climates with up to 6,000 degree days, use at least 5½ inches of fiberglass in 2 x 6 walls. In more severe climates it would be worth lining the outside of the stud walls with two inches of rigid foam prior to sheathing to provide additional insulation, and reduce heat loss through the studs.

The construction details shown in the accompanying design are intended only as a guide in helping you with your own solar greenhouse. It may be easier for you to use different construction techniques which you are more familiar with, or you may find it necessary to alter the details to accommodate recycled materials you might be able to come by cheaply. Some solar greenhouses have cost their owners a great deal; others have been constructed for next to nothing by scavenging extensively and discounting self-help labor costs. But a solar greenhouse needs to be built to last, and needs to be built well. Good, tight construction is essential if heat loss is to be reduced, and it is worth making the extra investment in time and energy. It will pay for itself over and over again for many years to come.

References and Sources

Proceedings of a Conference on Energy Conserving Solar-Heated Greenhouses, edited by John Hayes and Drew Gillett. Conference held at Marlboro College, Marlboro, Vermont 05344, in November, 1977. Proceedings are available from the college at $9 postpaid. This collection of papers is the most useful survey of current research in the field of solar greenhouses. The list of participants provides a series of nationwide contacts of those interested in the subject.

The Solar Greenhouse Book, edited by James McCullagh. Rodale Press, Emmaus, Pennsylvania 18049. 1978. $8.95. A lengthy and complete paperback covering the design, construction and operation of solar greenhouses, with much technical information and opinions from solar greenhouse owners. Contributors include David J. MacKinnon, James B. DeKorne, Leandre Poisson, John White and Conrad Heeschen.

The Food and Heat Producing Solar Greenhouse: Design, Construction, Operation, by Rick Fisher and Bill Yanda. John Muir Publications. 1976. $6.50 from the publishers, Box 613, Santa Fe, New Mexico 87501. A complete guide to the pioneering work in solar greenhouse design in New Mexico.

Building and Using Our Sun-Heated Greenhouse, by Helen and Scott Nearing. Garden Way Publishing, Charlotte, Vermont 05445. 1977. Paperback $6.95, hardcover $11.95. The Nearings discuss the year-round operation of their homemade solar greenhouse on the coast of Maine.

Winter Flowers in Greenhouse and Sun-Heated Pit, by Kathryn S. Taylor and Edith W. Gregg. Charles Scribner's Sons, New York. Revised edition, 1969. Paperback $4.95. First published in 1941, this book is still regarded as a definitive work on growing winter flowers in solar greenhouses.

The Book of the New Alchemists, edited by Nancy Jack Todd. Dutton. 1977. $6.95. Well-illustrated account of both the philosophy and the practical research work of the New Alchemy Institute, including articles on the "Arks" at Woods Hole and Prince Edward Island.

The Survival Greenhouse: An Ecosystem Approach to Home Food Production, by J.B. DeKorne. Published by the Walden Foundation, Box 5, El Rito, New Mexico 87530. 1975. Ideas on integrated food-production techniques and details of a solar-heated pit design.

Homegrown Sundwellings, by Peter Van Dresser. Published by the Lightning Tree Press, Box 1837, Santa Fe, New Mexico 87501. $5.95.

"The Development and Testing of an Environmentally Designed Greenhouse for Colder Regions," by T.A. Lawand et al. in *Solar Energy,* Vol, 17, pages 307-312. 1975. A description of the initial testing of the Brace Research Institute's solar greenhouse at Laval University, Quebec. For more information on activities of the institute, send a stamped, self-addressed envelope to Brace Research Institute, Macdonald College of McGill University, Ste. Anne de Bellevue, Quebec, Canada H9 X 3M1.

ORGANIZATIONS

(Send stamped, self-addressed envelopes when writing for information to these groups; they are all non-profit.)

The New Alchemy Institute Inc., Box 432, Woods Hole, Massachusetts 02543.

The Farallones Institute, 15290 Coleman Valley Road, Occidental, California 95465.

The Ecotope Group, 2332 East Madison, Seattle, Washington 98112.

The New Mexico Solar Energy Association, Box 2004, Sante Fe, New Mexico 87501. This is the largest and most active of the state solar-energy associations. Individual membership costs $10 a year, which includes a subscription to a monthly bulletin that is full of interesting articles about low-technology applications of solar energy.

SOLAR GREENHOUSE DESIGNS AND PREFABRICATED UNITS

The Vegetable Factory, 100 Court St., Copiague, Long Island, New York 11726 (see Figure 13.16).

The Solar Room, Box 1377, Taos, New Mexico 87571 (see Figure 13.17).

Figure 13.16. The interior of a Vegetable Factory greenhouse, one of the most popular and adaptable pre-fabricated commercial brands. These come in several components for lean-to or stand-alone uses, and can be expanded to suit the owner's needs and location. The units are "solar" to the extent that they are made of two layers in between, bonded to a rigid supporting aluminum frame. But the owner must provide his own solar heat-retaining apparatus if he wishes, or may install any kind of auxiliary heat. Only minimal foundations are said to be required. The firm's mailing address is 71 Vanderbilt Ave., New York, New York 10017, and it has a toll-free number for out-of-town calls: (800) 221-2550.

Figure 13.17. Two adaptations of the prefabricated lean-to greenhouse and solar-collector unit made by the Solar Room Company of Taos, New Mexico—one attached to a log home, the other to a Southwestern adobe house. Prices in 1978 ranged from $899 for a 12-foot model to $1,394 for a 39-foot-long model, not installed.

Figure 13.18. A prototype of the Provider greenhouse being developed for sale by a Los Angeles firm. Prices for a constructed greenhouse, on a foundation site built by the buyer, ranged in 1978 from $2,200 for a model eight by twelve feet, to $2,500 for a model twelve by sixteen feet.

Provider Greenhouses, Box 49708, Los Angeles, California 90049 (See Figure 13.18)

Solar Technology Corp., 2160 Clay St., Denver, Colorado 80211

PLANS

"The Garden Way Solar Room," designed by Robert Holdridge and Doug Taff. Plans available from Garden Way Publishing, Charlotte, Vermont 05445, for $9.95. (Also available are plans for making a coldframe at $1.95, a solar hot-water heater at $3.95, and a window greenhouse at $2.95.)

14

Coldframes and Window Greenhouses

Coldframes are simply small, ground-level greenhouses. They provide shelter for plants, not humans. Like cold greenhouses, coldframes rely solely on the sun for warmth. The transparent cover transmits heat and light while the low walls provide a small amount of insulation.

A coldframe is most useful for "hardening off" seedlings and cuttings that have been grown in the controlled and gentle environment of a heated greenhouse or propagating case and need to be introduced gradually to the outdoors. Sudden changes of temperature, high winds or heavy rain, can all be fatal to young seedlings. The protection of a coldframe allows you to shelter young plants when necessary, and you open the covers for a little longer each day until the plant tissues have become mature enough to withstand the rigors of outdoor weather.

The Adaptable Coldframe

Coldframes are particularly useful in spring for giving an early start to plants that need a long growing season. In summer, a coldframe with some kind of shading (either a coat of shading compound over the glass, or a lath blind, or a leafy vine) provides a suitable place for keeping winter-flowering house-plants. In fall, the coldframe can be used to protect long-season fruits and vegetables from wintry weather. At night, the coldframe can be covered with an old blanket to prevent damage from early frosts.

A coldframe generally consists of a low-perimeter wall supporting a transparent cover. The cover slopes slightly to shed rainwater and to admit more sunlight. Traditional coldframes were covered with glass "sashes" (wooden frames to support the glazing material, in this case greenhouse glass in lapped sheets). The sashes can be either propped up at one end or slid back to allow for ventilation. Modern sashes are often covered with plastic films or fiberglass sheets. These have the advantages of being lightweight and less breakable, though plastic films have a short lifetime and fiberglass often requires refinishing (see Chapter 5).

The cover of the frame is usually sloped in one direction only and faces south to admit more direct sunlight. Even-span coldframes with sashes sloping away on either side from a central ridge have the advantage of better ventilation (both sides can be opened to allow air to pass straight through). But they are more difficult to construct and take up more room because access is required from both sides. Even-span coldframes should be positioned with the ridge running north-south for maximum sunlight.

Solar-energy benefits. Coldframes benefit from solar heat storage in the same way as greenhouses. If you can increase the thermal mass inside the house it will reduce the temperature rise during the day and keep the frame warmer at night. One of the major problems of coldframes is overheating, causing the plants to transpire too much and wilt. The smaller the frame the more rapid the rise in temperature. As discussed previously, the earth itself will provide some heat storage. A few black-painted water bottles placed on top of each other at the rear of the frame will greatly increase the thermal capacity. As with greenhouses, the problem will generally be the conflict for space between the plants and the heat sink.

In a coldframe used for seedlings and early starts, it is generally more important that the plants get full exposure to as much light as possible (which means they must be open to the sky). The heat-storage material, however, will benefit most from intercepting direct radiation and collecting heat directly from the air, so the north-facing wall is a suitable unobtrusive location for it.

The more heat storage you introduce into the frame, the more necessary insulation becomes to make the heat storage work for you. Make sure the insulation is water and rot resistant. Styrofoam sheet is generally most suitable and can be buried in the ground.

What size to make it? The size of the frame depends on how much you intend to use it and what transparent covering you decide to use.

Most coldframes are made in multiples of one of the two standard sizes for glass sashes: 3 feet by 6 feet or 3 feet by 4 feet. These sizes are roughly coordinated with the size of seed flats. Twenty 9-by-13-inch flats, or six 18-by-23-inch flats, can be housed in a 3-by-6-foot coldframe. The simplest homemade coldframes use second-hand windows or storm windows for a cover, in which case the size of these will dictate the size of the coldframe. If you use fiberglass sheets or plastic film, the sashes can be much larger and still be manageable because the glazing material weighs less.

The height of the coldframe will depend on what you want to grow in it. For most plants, one or two feet between the surface of the soil and the cover is sufficient. The higher the walls, the longer the shadow they cast. The south wall particularly should not be more than about one foot above ground. The smaller the volume of the frame, the easier it is to heat, so keep the headroom to the minimum needed by the plants.

Allow a slope of at least one inch per foot for the cover of the frame, to make sure the rainwater will drain off. When using old windows as covers, the main disadvantage is rainwater collecting in the rabbeted junction between the glass and the frame, where it tends to rot the wood. This is often unavoidable, though the deterioration can be minimized by chamfering off the rabbet at the bottom of each pane of glass, or filling it with putty. Make sure that the rabbet is well painted to provide a waterproof surface.

Permanent or mobile? Coldframes can be either permanent or mobile structures. For a permanent one, select a site that is exposed to full sunlight and yet protected from the wind. The space in front of the south wall of a greenhouse provides a good site. If the greenhouse has a masonry base wall, then this will provide a suitable north wall for the coldframe.

Permanent coldframes are best built on a brick or concrete block foundation wall. They benefit from being sunk into the ground slightly so that the earth shelters and insulates some of the outside wall. The whole site should be excavated, the topsoil removed for replacement in an enriched form when the frame is complete. Unless you are constructing the frame on unstable soil which is likely to cause uneven settling, there is no real reason to lay a concrete foundation. There is little weight in such a low wall, and bricks or blocks can take up a good deal of movement in the joints. A detailed design for a permanent coldframe accompanies this chapter.

The glass covers can be raised up at the front and held in place with a timber to enable varying degrees of ventilation. It should be possible to open the cover entirely and either secure it in a vertical position or swing it back to rest on the ground behind the frame. Coldframes can easily be destroyed by strong gusts of wind. Be wary of opening up a glass cover on a windy day. If the cover is resting on the timber under its own weight

and is not held firmly in place, a gust of wind could easily lift it up and drop it, smashing the glass.

A mobile coldframe is much like a permanent one, except of course that it has no masonry base and must be both lighter and stronger to be moved around easily. The base is usually made of timber or aluminum, and the cover of fiberglass sheet or plastic film. A design for a simple mobile coldframe will also be found in this chapter.

The mobility of this kind of coldframe is a great advantage, giving shelter to different crops when and as they need it, but it must be securely anchored down or it may blow off and ruin nearby plants, as well as those inside.

Cloches

Small, mobile coldframes for covering just a few plants are called "cloches." The term comes from the original type of cloche developed in France and shaped like a large glass bell (Figure 14.1A). It was designed to enclose and protect a single plant. More recent versions of the cloche are tunnel-shaped, covering several plants in a row.

These tunnel cloches usually take one of three forms: (1) a metal framework that secures four sheets of glass, (2) curved metal wires that support polyethylene film, or (3) molded fiberglass that is stiff enough to support itself (Figure 14.B and C). The ends of the tunnel can be blocked off for additional protection.

A cloche will protect young seedlings from a moderate frost and will allow hardy varieties of plants like lettuce, spinach, parsley and spring onions, which don't mind a light frost, to grow all winter long in a moderately cold climate. A cloche only moderates the temperature, so a severe frost (below 20°F.) will affect whatever is growing inside.

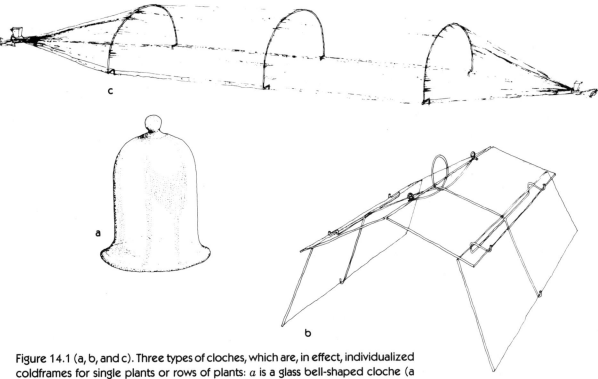

Figure 14.1 (a, b, and c). Three types of cloches, which are, in effect, individualized coldframes for single plants or rows of plants: *a* is a glass bell-shaped cloche (a cut-off plastic gallon jug would serve the same essential purpose); *b* is a barn-shaped cloche made of wire frame and glass or plastic sheets; and *c* is a polyethylene tunnel cloche supported by metal hoops, to cover a row of plants.

Hotbeds

A hotbed is simply a heated coldframe. The addition of heat makes the coldframe more useful and more dependable for a much longer part of the year. It is particularly suitable for starting heat-loving plants that require more than just protection from the frost. In very cold climates, a hotbed might be needed for growing melons even in mid-summer, and would certainly be needed in spring and fall to give the crop a long enough growing season in which to mature. Herbs, salad greens and spinach can be grown all winter long despite bitterly cold weather.

Manure hotbeds. To turn a coldfame into a natural hotbed, you can use the heat from a decomposing manure pile. A mobile cold-frame, which can be placed on top of the manure pile, will save the work of shoveling the manure into, and eventually out of, a permanent coldframe, but it is not really necessary.

The ingredients for a good manure hotbed are fresh farmyard manure mixed with about one-third its volume of straw or dried leaves. The ratio of manure to vegetable matter is important since pure manure will probably ferment too rapidly and give off too much heat. These ingredients should be watered and left for a few days to start decomposing. Turn the pile over after three or four days to incorporate more air. After another three or four days the manure should be ready.

If you are using a mobile coldframe, excavate an area at least twenty-four inches deep and six inches wider in each direction than the size of the coldframe. If you are using a permanent coldframe, just remove the soil to a depth of about two feet. The manure should be shoveled into the pit in successive layers about four inches deep, and each layer should be well trodden down. It is best to have at least two feet of manure, and it is better, though not crucial, for the top of the pile to be at or below ground level.

Put the mobile coldframe in place if you are using one. In any case, leave the cover of the coldframe open for a few days. Usually at this stage fumes and moisture will be given off which could be harmful to plants, and the cover should not be shut until these gases have dissipated and the temperature inside the pile has fallen to about 95° F.

A good layer of pasteurized loam about six inches deep should be placed on top of the manure when it is ready. Even if the hotbed will only be used for seed flats or pot plants, it is worth putting a layer of loam in to act as an insulator. Overheating is always a danger with manure hotbeds, and they are unpredictable. It is well worth having a gardening thermometer (preferably a maximum-minimum type) to record changes in temperature in the hotbed. The thermometer when buried in the top layer of manure should read between 80° and 90°F. for the healthy growth of most plants. During the day, the cover of the coldframe will usually have to be opened to prevent the sun from raising the temperature too much.

Manure hotbeds were used extensively until the advent of greenhouse steam-heating. In seventeenth-century England, horticultural experts grew pineapples and other exotic fruits on manure hotbeds. The problems, then as now, were to avoid burning the roots of the plant with excess heat, and to maintain the heat over a sufficiently long period of time.

A good hotbed will give off heat for about four to six weeks, and if you are lucky the temperature should remain fairly constant. Select the right time of year to start the bed. It is generally most useful toward the end of winter when extra heat is required to give plants an early start and avoid damage from late frosts. At this time the greenhouse is usually full to capacity with seedlings and any extra space under glass becomes invaluable. If you time the bed properly (i.e., if you can forecast the weather well) the heat from the manure should begin to run out about the time the spring sun is strong enough to provide all the heat the plants need.

Electrically heated hotbeds. For a steady temperature and a more reliable heat source, consider installing electric heating. It is possible to heat a small coldframe sufficiently to avoid frost damage by using an electric light bulb and covering the glass at night with a heavy blanket (the blanket is a worthwhile energy-saving measure whatever kind of heat you rely on). Light bulbs should only be regarded as temporary heating systems, however. They were never designed for heating; they heat the air in the frame instead of the soil, and they are quite likely to "short out" due to condensation, which can collect around the terminals before the bulb is switched on. Plants prefer warmth from below rather than above, and if you are installing electric power in your coldframe anyway, it is worthwhile buying heating cables that are designed for heating soil to the right temperature and keeping it there.

Soil-heating cables are fairly cheap to buy ($30-$50 worth of cable should heat an average coldframe). They are cheap to run and are easy to install. To avoid wasting both heat and effort, heating cables should only be used in a permanent coldframe with masonry base walls.

To prepare a coldframe for heating cables, place a two-inch layer of vermiculite at the bottom of the frame. This vermiculite prevents unwanted heat loss and allows water to drain through easily. From an energy-conserving point of view it is even more important to put insulation around the edges of the frame to prevent heat loss through the side walls. Styrofoam slabs, two inches thick, would be ideal for this purpose.

For convenience, the electric socket should be installed in one corner of the coldframe at the level of the top of the vermiculite. Starting from the plug, the heating cables are then spread out evenly over the surface of the vermiculite. Instructions are provided with each heating unit. Cover the cable with two inches of sand and then a protective layer of half-inch wire mesh to prevent yourself from digging into the system later.

Last, add four to six inches of fertile, well-pasteurized topsoil. As with any kind of cold-frame, heated or unheated, you should take care over the soil you put in it. It is best to screen the soil to break down any lumps, remove stones and introduce air. Add about one-sixth part sand and one-sixth part peat-moss to improve drainage and water retention. Also add any nutrients which your soil may be lacking (see Chapter 7).

The hotbed is now ready for use, and you will soon learn to make the most of it. A thermostat that comes with the heating cables can be set to any desired temperature to insure a steady supply of heat and prevent overheating except on the brightest of days, when the cover will have to be opened. An hour's ventilation on mild days will be much appreciated by the plants, to replenish their supplies of fresh air, and even on cold days a little ventilation should be given.

A permanently heated hotbed will provide a continuous supply of fresh green vegetables throughout the winter. Herbs such as parsley, rosemary, sage, thyme and marjoram can be wintered over and will provide you with a small fresh supply during cold months. Spring greens, spring onions, lettuce and spinach can easily be grown all winter long. In the spring, tender vegetables like melons, squash, and tomatoes can be given an early start and good growing conditions until all danger of frost is past. The thermostat will insure that the heating cables will be used less and less as the weather gets warmer.

In summer the hotbed will be less useful. Except in the coldest climates or for the most heat-loving plants, the heating cables should be switched off and the hotbed used as an ordinary coldframe. Overheating and lack of ventilation are the two great problems with coldframes in summer months. On most days the coldframe should be opened wide, and if possible some sort of shading should be provided.

Window-box Greenhouses

For those with limited garden space, a window-box greenhouse provides a useful enclosure for a wide variety of house plants or a few vegetables and herbs. A window-box greenhouse consists of a glass, fiberglass or plastic enclosure projecting out from the window. It is accessible through the window from the inside and exposed to much more light (from three sides and above) than plants placed on the window sill. The window should have sliding or sash-type opening sections, since casement or pivoted windows which open outward would get in the way of the plants. It should also face as due south as possible, though easterly or westerly orientations are suitable if they receive unobstructed sunlight. Window-box greenhouses are ideal for city apartments and houseplant fanatics, but remember that the plants, if arranged in tiers across the window, will filter out a lot of daylight from the room, and the secondary enclosure will limit the amount of ventilation you normally get from opening the window.

The smaller the greenhouse, the more rapid will be temperature fluctuations it undergoes, and the more difficult it is to control its environment. Window-box greenhouses in many climates would be unusable in summer due to overheating unless it were possible to provide ventilation at both top and bottom. Preferably the whole top of the structure should lift off to exhaust warm air, and the bottom should be louvered to admit fresh air and allow a natural breeze through the plants. In winter, adequate ventilation could be provided by opening the window to the room. If necessary, fresh air could be admitted through the bottom shelf even in

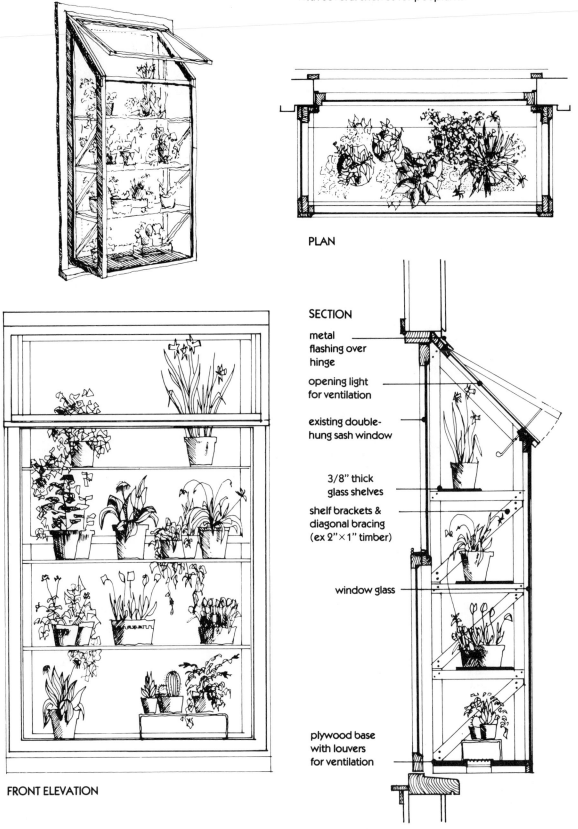

Figure 14.2. A window-box greenhouse, designed with several shelves for pot plants.

PLAN

SECTION

metal flashing over hinge

opening light for ventilation

existing double-hung sash window

3/8" thick glass shelves

shelf brackets & diagonal bracing (ex 2"×1" timber)

window glass

plywood base with louvers for ventilation

FRONT ELEVATION

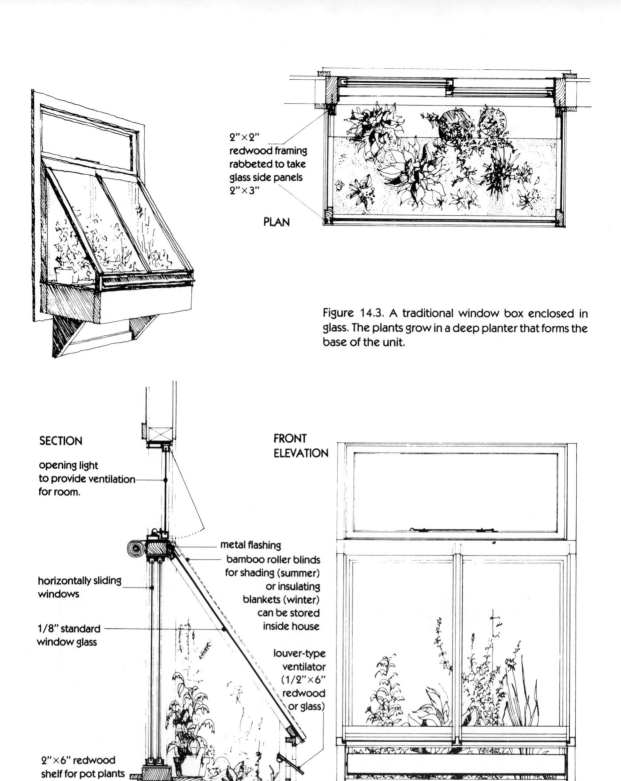

2"×2"
redwood framing
rabbeted to take
glass side panels
2"×3"

PLAN

Figure 14.3. A traditional window box enclosed in glass. The plants grow in a deep planter that forms the base of the unit.

SECTION

opening light
to provide ventilation
for room.

horizontally sliding
windows

1/8" standard
window glass

2"×6" redwood
shelf for pot plants

window box made of
2 inch thick redwood
boards, tongued and
grooved joints.

window box screwed
to studwork and
supported on 2"
thick redwood brackets

FRONT
ELEVATION

metal flashing
bamboo roller blinds
for shading (summer)
or insulating
blankets (winter)
can be stored
inside house

louver-type
ventilator
(1/2"×6"
redwood
or glass)

1/2" drainage
holes

Styrofoam
insulation around
sides of window box

winter. Since cold air does not tend to rise, any fresh air admitted from below will mix slowly with the warmer air in the enclosure and will not disturb the plants as much as if cooler air were to enter from the top.

On winter nights, the window-box greenhouse can be heated by opening the window into the room or by means of a small electric heater inside the enclosure itself. With a blanket for insulation on the outside, an electric light bulb left on overnight should produce enough heat to prevent frost.

Two basic types. Window-box greenhouses come in two basic varieties. Those designed for pot plants have several shelves, spaced about one and a half to two feet apart to allow sufficient headroom for the plants (Figure 14.2). Others are essentially traditional windowboxes enclosed in glass. The plants are grown directly in the soil of a deep planter that forms the base of the little greenhouse (Figure 14.3).

Either type must be capable of supporting a good deal of weight, so the framework of the greenhouse must be structurally rigid. It must be strong, yet should not obstruct too much light from the plants or from the room beyond.

Window-box greenhouses for potted plants can be bought as kits. They usually have a metal framework. Make sure you get the appropriate size for your window. If you wish to make one yourself, timber would be an easier, though bulkier, material to use for the framework. The shelves can be made of slatted wood, wire mesh, or three-eighth-inch glass with ground edges. Glass shelves are surprisingly strong and admit as much light as possible to plants below.

A planter-type window-box greenhouse can have a base made of timber or of reinforced concrete. The planter is going to be filled with earth and will be very heavy. It should be carefully braced against the adjacent wall with timber or metal struts.

If you use reinforced concrete for the planter, you will need to make timber forms of the appropriate size. The concrete will need to be poured in two stages. The bottom should be cast first, around a mesh of reinforcing rods. Set two or three pieces of tubing into the forms to provide drainage holes. Leave some of the reinforcing rods sticking up at the edges so that the sides of the planter can be cast around them. Once the base has set, arrange the formwork and reinforcement for the sides. Before pouring the concrete, wet the base of the planter to help achieve a good bond between the bottom and sides.

If you use timber for the base, it is worth paying the extra money for redwood or red cedar heartwood, which are rot-resistant. To prevent unsightly staining at the joints due to water seeping through, you should use tongue-and-groove joints if at all possible. These should be glued together with a waterproof glue to provide a well-sealed container. You do need to allow for drainage in the planter, but it is much better that this should take place through two or three holes drilled in the base rather than through cracks in the joints where water seeping through could damage the wood and force the joints apart.

Terrariums

The only kind of greenhouse normally used indoors is a terrarium. This is a sealed glass case which forms a complete miniature environment for plants. The most common form of terrarium today is a five-gallon jug, but the idea reached a height of popularity in the late nineteenth century when terrariums were to be found in the living rooms of most well-to-do households. They were then known as Wardian Cases (Figure 14.4) after a Mr. Ward who is credited with inventing them, and they often housed ferns or tropical plants that could not survive the toxic fumes given off by the gas lamps then in general use. They were elaborate pieces of furniture in themselves, made of wrought iron or carved wood

Figure 14.4. A Victorian-era "Wardian case" was a popular predecessor of what is known today as a terrarium.

indoors are greatly extended (the array of gadgetry for the indoor gardener, from misters to gro-lights, helps to extend the possibilities even further.)

For those who live with a well-cared-for array of houseplants that occasionally threaten to overrun the living room, a window-box greenhouse can alleviate the problem by providing extra (and more suitable) display space. For those in the privileged position of thinking about building a house, consider the place you want your plants to occupy, just as you would consider the place for the washing machine or your favorite piece of furniture. A home can gain a great deal from being designed to accommodate plants as well as people (Figure 14.6).

with a tightly sealed glass frame. They provided complete microclimates for the plants, with the water given off by transpiration condensing on the glass and dripping back onto the soil. In this way it was possible for a plant case to last for a year or more without being opened or receiving any attention.

A Wardian case consisted of a perforated metal tray above a metal drawer which caught any water that dripped through. The tray was covered with a layer of gravel, then a layer of peatmoss (or some other fibrous material to retain water) and finally a layer of rich humus. The ferns or pot plants were arranged in it to form a miniature woodland scene, as natural as possible. The glass cover was put on and the case placed in a room where it would receive the right amount of heat and light for the plants inside.

The craze for houseplants and floral decoration that arose toward the end of the last century is now recurring. City dwellers are bringing life back into their homes and apartments with the introduction of houseplants and, on a small scale, herbs and vegetables. With a plant case or an enclosed windowbox, the possibilities of raising plants

Figure 14.5. These window greenhouses were the fashion a century ago. This is adapted from "The Floral World and Garden Guide" of February, 1879.

Figure 14.6. Window-box greenhouses and plant conservatories can easily be integrated into the design of a new home to provide a functional and attractive feature, ideal for plants and plant lovers, and visually interesting from both inside and outside the house.

A Design for a Permanent Coldframe

This coldframe is built on a permanent base wall, but the whole top section (made of wood) can be taken off and moved to another part of the garden because it is itself a rigid structure simply resting on the masonry base wall. This design is suitable for use with old timber windows as covers, but the dimensions of the coldframe should be altered to suit (on each side, the framework should be ¾" smaller than the total size of the windows, except on the back side where the cover is flush with the frame).

Base wall. Having chosen a permanent location for the coldframe, set out the dimensions of the base wall and excavate about 9 inches of earth from the whole area. Save the topsoil for later use, but dispose of any subsoil. Tamp down the edges of the hole, which

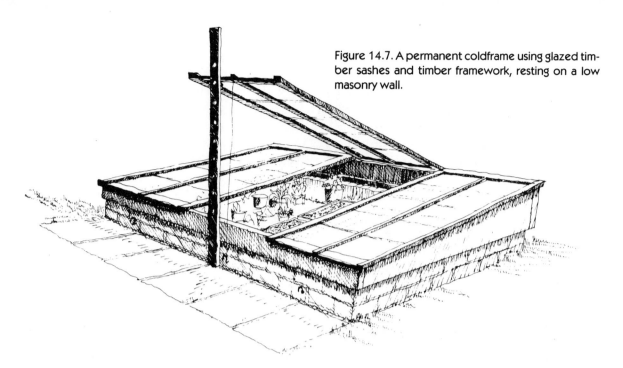

Figure 14.7. A permanent coldframe using glazed timber sashes and timber framework, resting on a low masonry wall.

Figure 14.8. Parts of a permanent coldframe, shown in an axonometric projection. Numbered components are explained in the accompanying text.

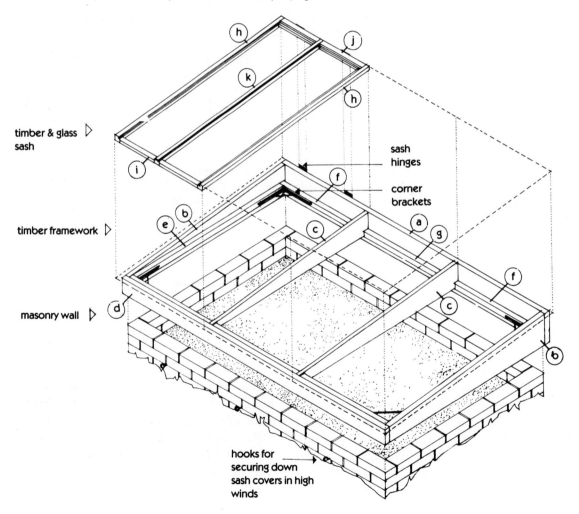

timber & glass ▷
sash

sash
hinges

corner
brackets

timber framework ▷

masonry wall ▷

hooks for
securing down
sash covers in high
winds

will form the base of the wall, and make sure it is firm and level.

Set out the bonding pattern for the bricks or blocks by laying one course of the wall without mortar. If you are using old windows as covers, adjust the size of the mortar joints or use a half brick if necessary to make up for any difference in length entailed by using the windows. When the bonding pattern is set, go back and lay the bricks or blocks in mortar (details given in Chapter 4). Work from the corners toward the center of the wall. Keep checking that the outside dimensions of the wall are correct and square, since the timber framework must fit snugly around the outside edge. When you are one course from the top, set a brass hook into the mortar joint at the front of the wall directly under the center of each sash. This will prove useful in securing the sashes on windy days.

Note that if you use blocks, you will need to lay only two courses of blocks, but they will be about three inches higher than the five courses of bricks shown in the drawings. You can simply accept a taller coldframe, or you can compensate for the increase by sinking the wall three inches lower in the ground.

Timber frame. The timber for the framework need not be planed, but should be of good quality, redwood or cedar if you can afford it. Cut to size all the pieces of wood shown in Figure 14.9. If you are using old windows as covers, you will need to adjust the lengths to suit. Coat each piece of wood with a good wood preservative (not creosote, which gives off fumes harmful to plants), taking special care over the end grain, which is the part most likely to rot.

To begin, screw the 2"×3" "ledge" sections (e, f and g) to their respective sides or ends (a, b or d) of the framework. Use 2¼" galvanized or brass screws spaced every eight inches or so.

Covers. If you have no suitable old windows to use as a cover, you can easily make the 3'2"×6' sashes shown in Figure 14.10

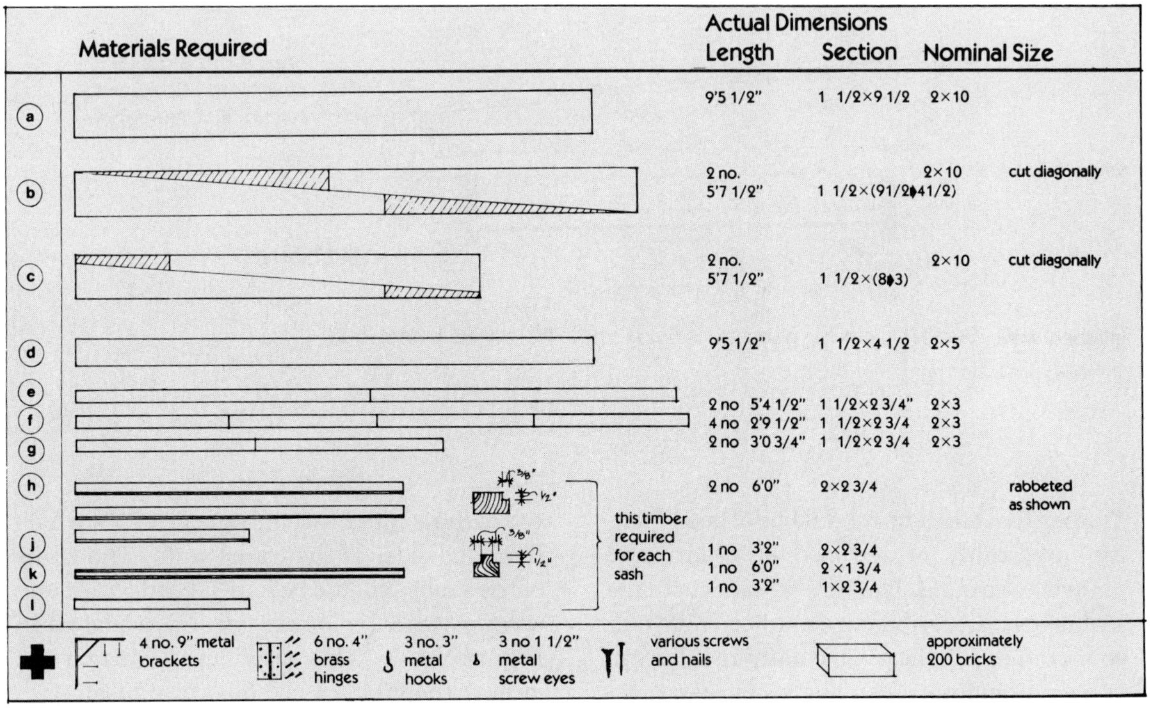

Figure 14.9. A list of all materials required for the permanent coldframe components, including hardware.

	Materials Required	Actual Dimensions Length	Section	Nominal Size
a		9'5 1/2"	1 1/2×9 1/2	2×10
b		2 no. 5'7 1/2"	1 1/2×(91/2◆41/2)	2×10 cut diagonally
c		2 no. 5'7 1/2"	1 1/2×(8◆3)	2×10 cut diagonally
d		9'5 1/2"	1 1/2×4 1/2	2×5
e		2 no 5'4 1/2"	1 1/2×2 3/4"	2×3
f		4 no 2'9 1/2"	1 1/2×2 3/4"	2×3
g		2 no 3'0 3/4"	1 1/2×2 3/4	2×3
h		2 no 6'0"	2×2 3/4	rabbeted as shown
j		1 no 3'2"	2×2 3/4	
k		1 no 6'0"	2×1 3/4	
l		1 no 3'2"	1×2 3/4	

this timber required for each sash

✚ | 4 no. 9" metal brackets | 6 no. 4" brass hinges | 3 no. 3" metal hooks | 3 no 1 1/2" metal screw eyes | various screws and nails | approximately 200 bricks

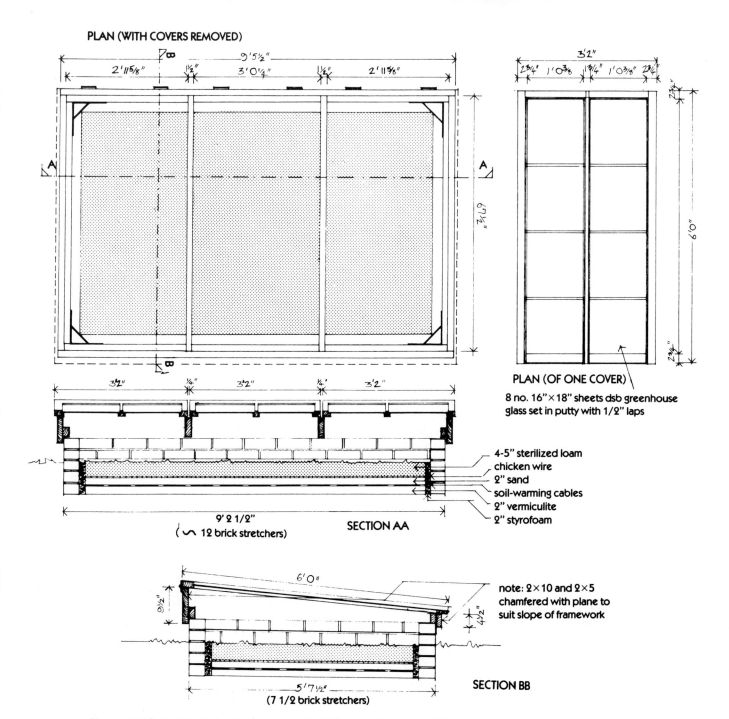

PLAN (WITH COVERS REMOVED)

PLAN (OF ONE COVER)

8 no. 16"×18" sheets dsb greenhouse glass set in putty with 1/2" laps

4-5" sterilized loam
chicken wire
2" sand
soil-warming cables
2" vermiculite
2" styrofoam

SECTION AA

9' 2 1/2"
(⌒ 12 brick stretchers)

note: 2×10 and 2×5 chamfered with plane to suit slope of framework

SECTION BB

5' 7 1/2"
(7 1/2 brick stretchers)

Figure 14.10. Detailed plan for permanent coldframe with glazed timber sash covers.

Timber for the sashes should be of good quality, preferably of redwood or cedar, and planed all around. The ½"×⅜" rabbets in the sashes can easily be cut on a bench saw, or your timber supplier can usually do it for you at a small charge. (You might also ask them to rip diagonally through the 2"×10"s which form the sides of the framework.) The joints of the sashes should be half-lapped, glued and screwed (use 1¼" brass screws) as shown in Figure 14.11. This provides a fairly rigid joint without too much elaborate chiseling.

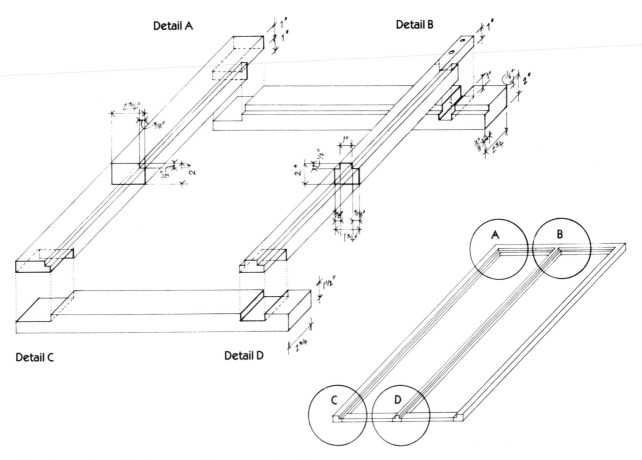

Figure 14.11. Details of half-lapped joints used in making timber sash.

Once put together, the sashes should be glazed with 16"×18" panes of double-strength greenhouse glass. The panes are lapped over each other by ½" and set in putty at each side, where they fit into the rabbets in the framework. A brass hook should be screwed into the center of the bottom rail of each sash for later use in securing the sash on windy days.

To put the framework together, rest the two intermediate rails (c) in position on the masonry walls. Place the back side (a, with f and g attached) so that the intermediate rails fit into position between the ledges. C and f and g should all be resting on the masonry walls. With one person putting his weight on part c, someone else can hammer home a couple of 3" nails, through a into c. Repeat this procedure to secure the front side (d) to the intermediate rails. Finally, fit the sides

(b) between the front and back pieces, nailing through a into b, and then through d into b.

The nails act only as temporary fixings. For a rigid framework, install metal brackets inside each corner. Either shelf brackets or ordinary steel angles may be used, but they should be galvanized or "japanned" (a black protective enamel used on metal fixings) to prevent them from rusting. Each leg of the bracket should be at least 6", and preferably 9", long. The longer the leg, the more rigid the frame will be. The brackets should be secured to the ledge pieces (e and f) with 2¼" brass or galvanized screws.

Attaching the covers. The wooden framework should now be complete, resting on the masonry walls, and ready to fix the covers to. Fix two hinges to the top of each sash. Then lay the sash in place on the framework and screw the other side of each hinge to the back rail (a) of the frame as shown in Figure 14.8. Use 4" brass door butt hinges with ¾" brass or galvanized screws.

Props for covers. The coldframe is now ready for use, but a prop for holding each sash open will make the coldframe easier to use. The props can easily be made by drilling ½" holes at 4" intervals along a piece of 2" x 1" timber. A peg, which can be moved from hole to hole to vary its height, forms a support for the sash when it needs to be opened for ventilation. A piece of string tied through the hook in the end of the sash and the hook in the top mortar joint of the masonry wall will hold the sash firmly down against the peg even on windy days.

Figure 14.12. A lightweight mobile coldframe, made of 2" by 1" timber framework, covered with flat fiberglass sheeting.

A Design for a Mobile Coldframe

This lightweight mobile coldframe has a timber framework consisting entirely of 2"×1"s covered with fiberglass sheets. The material costs are minimal and it should be possible to put the frame together in less than a day if you have everything on hand.

Assemble the ends, sides and covers separately according to the plan given in Figure 14.14. The covers and the sides are each put together with half-lapped joints, using two 1¼" brass or galvanized screws in each joint. The ends should have fully lapped joints and diagonal braces, which add to rigidity.

Attach the sides to the ends of the frame by screwing through the vertical members of the ends (see Figure 14.13). Use three screws to connect each vertical member.

Each cover should be attached by two

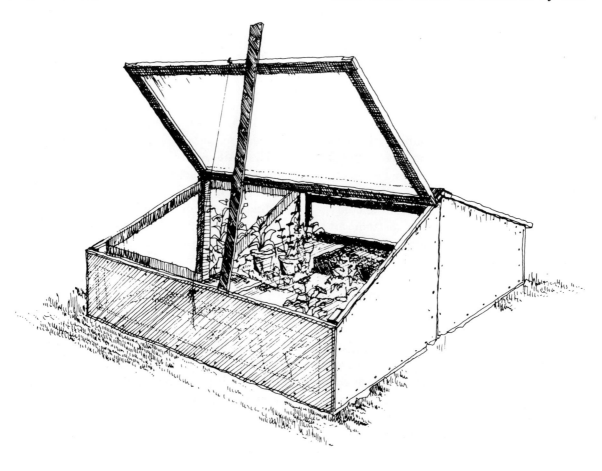

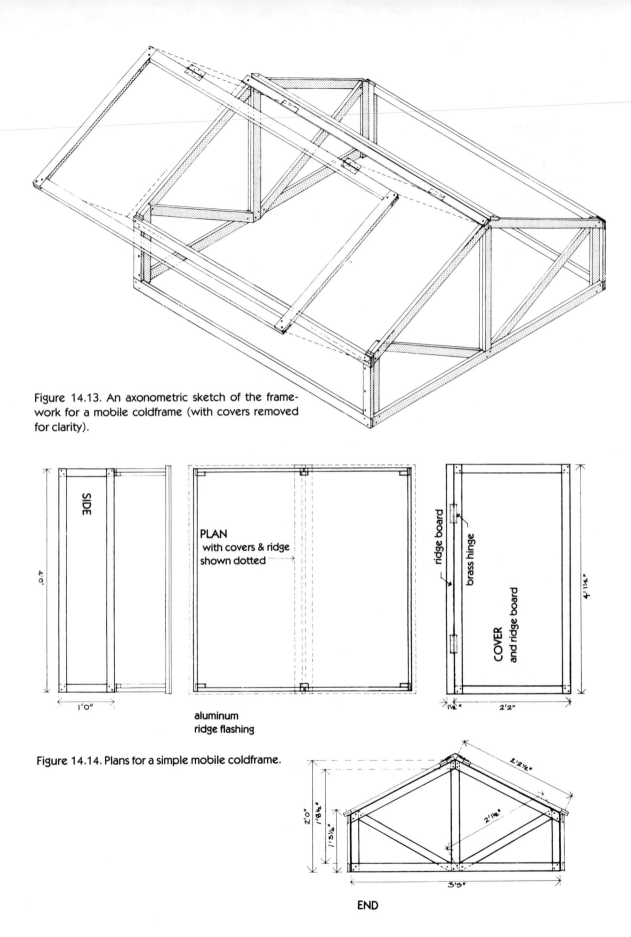

Figure 14.13. An axonometric sketch of the framework for a mobile coldframe (with covers removed for clarity).

SIDE

4'0"

1'0"

PLAN
with covers & ridge shown dotted

aluminum
ridge flashing

ridge board

brass hinge

COVER
and ridge board

4'1½"

1½" 2'2"

Figure 14.14. Plans for a simple mobile coldframe.

END

2'0"
1'8¾"
1'5¼"

2'2¼"

2'1½"

3'9"

Materials Required		
Flat Fiberglass Sheet	Lengths of 2"×1" timber (actual dimension 1-1/2×3/4)	
	4 no.	2'1-1/2"
	4 no.	2'1-1/2"
	4 no.	1'3-1/2"
	2 no.	3'9"
	2 no.	1'8-1/2"
	2 no.	2'0"
	4 no.	4'0"
	4 no.	1'0"
covers	4 no.	4'1-1/2"
	4 no.	2'2"
ridge	2 no.	4'1-1/2"
total area 4' × 9'		

Figure 14.15. A list of materials needed.

hinges to one of the two ridge pieces (see Figure 14.14). Then attach the ridge pieces to the apex of each end of the frame, using one screw for each junction.

Once the framework is complete, cut the fiberglass (with a fine tooth saw or strong shears) to the sizes shown in Figure 14.15. Fix the fiberglass in place on the sides, ends and covers. It can be nailed or even stapled into place, but for a longer-lasting job use screws with rubber washers to protect the ragged edge around the screw hole.

Finally, to make the ridge watertight requires a thin strip of flashing down the space between the two ridge pieces (see Figure 14.14). This can be made of roofing felt, thin aluminum sheeting or even fiberglass. It should form a watertight membrane, overlapping the two ridge pieces from end to end, without interfering with the opening and shutting of the covers.

Figure 14.16. A new idea in coldframes: This model of an insulated coldframe was demonstrated at the third annual Toward Tomorrow Fair at the University of Massachusetts in June, 1978, by a firm called Solar Survival (Box 119, Harrisville, N.H. 03450). It features beadwall insulation particles that can be stored in a cylindrical container at the top during the day, so sunlight can reach the plants inside, and the beads can be dropped by gravity at night into a space between two layers of plastic glazing. A "flip valve" is turned to keep the beadwall in storage or let it drop down. (Plans for the structure, which also can make use of 30-gallon drums of water or used motor oil for temperature stability, are available from the firm for $6.)

The Sunspace in the Home

The principles of passive solar collection discussed in relation to greenhouses can also be applied to house design. The greenhouse can be integrated into the home as a plant "conservatory," as a solar collector, as a sunroom, or as a combination of all three. Passive collection of solar heat through south-oriented windows and greenhouses is simpler and cheaper to install and to run than the active systems which have received more attention in recent years.

Space for plants in the home is not difficult to contrive. A glassed-in porch or the area directly behind a south-facing window both make useful greenhouse-type spaces, as house plant enthusiasts know. Window-box greenhouses and Wardian cases can be used to moderate the environment for plants that require high humidity levels. But the design of a house from scratch requires careful consideration of the implications of direct solar gain, the incorporation of insulating shutters and storage systems, as well as careful planning to allow plants and people to co-exist.

One-Zone and Two-Zone Houses

Passive solar collection through greenhouses and sunspaces can be divided broadly into two types (Figure 15.1). In the first, "one-zone" type, the greenhouse and the home are

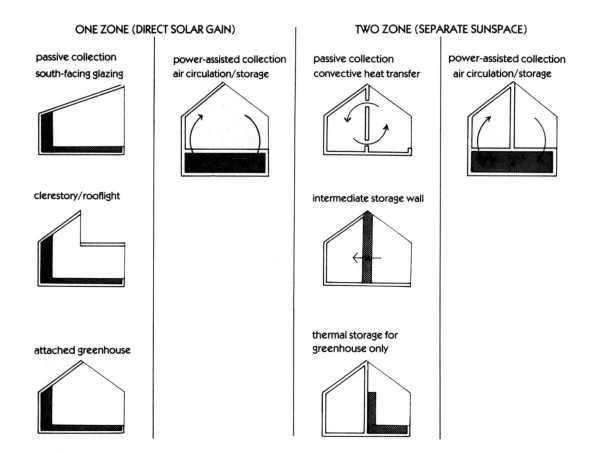

ONE ZONE (DIRECT SOLAR GAIN)

passive collection
south-facing glazing

power-assisted collection
air circulation/storage

clerestory/rooflight

attached greenhouse

TWO ZONE (SEPARATE SUNSPACE)

passive collection
convective heat transfer

power-assisted collection
air circulation/storage

intermediate storage wall

thermal storage for
greenhouse only

Figure 15.1. Diagrams show how passive solar collection can work in various ways in a greenhouse or a sunspace in the home.

one and the same building. Direct solar gain through south-facing vertical glazing, clerestory glazing, or rooflights, allows sunshine to penetrate deep into the structure, to be absorbed by floors and walls, and used by plants and people. In the second, "two-zone" type, the greenhouse or sunspace is a separate room, additional to the main part of the house. This allows the outer zone to be kept at temperature and humidity levels more suitable to plants, or to solar collection, than to humans. The inner zone can then be maintained at human comfort levels while benefitting from heat gain and insulation provided by the greenhouse space in winter.

As a secondary zone, the greenhouse offers many possibilities. It can be a useful additional room at certain times of the day when the temperature range is suitable. It could be

a simple lean-to structure, or it could be the largest space in the home. It could be an extension of the "family" room including a breakfast or dining area, or it could provide a children's play space. An area of greenery adjacent to a study-bedroom might add to one's experience of both work and relaxation. The possibilities are infinite.

The configuration of the greenhouse in relation to the house also offers many possibilities. It could provide a visual link between other rooms of the house. It could wrap around a corner, or fit into a corner. It could wrap around the house or be enclosed by the house on all but the south side. Examples of all these configurations (Figure 15.2) are given in the following pages to show the many available possibilities. There are, however, several problems that can arise with

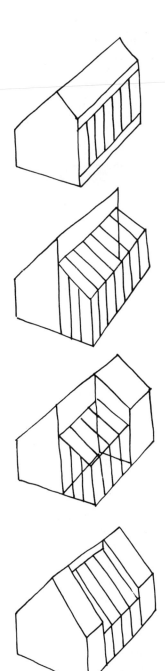

1. South-facing glazing for direct solar gain.

2. Separate sunspace adjoining south wall.

3. Sunspace partially enclosed by house.

the use of greenhouses or sunspaces in the home. These can be summarized as follows:

1. *Glare.* Intense sunlight, and particularly the contrast between dark walls and bright windows, can be a strain to the eyes. Baffles, shades or louvers can prevent this.

2. *Local discomfort.* Extreme differences in temperature, and particularly in radiant heat balance, can be uncomfortable. These can occur at night as well as during the day. To a certain extent they can be accommodated if one is prepared to move in or out of the sun according to one's needs, and can organize life around the changing pattern of solar radiation. Efficient collection and storage systems, high thermal mass, or air circulation, can reduce temperature extremes.

Figure 15.2. Design possibilities are varied when considering the relationship of the greenhouse and the home.

4. House wrapped around sunspace on all but south exposure.

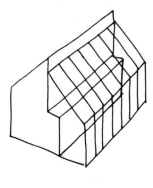

6. Two-story sunspace linking first and second floors of house.

5. Second floor sunspace

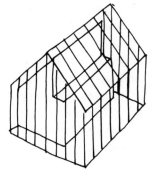

7. Sunspace provides complete outer skin to house

3. *Slow response.* With conventional heating systems, we are used to being able to switch on a furnace and warm up quickly. Conventional frame houses have very little thermal mass: solar-heated homes generally use thermal storage as part of the structure to moderate temperature fluctuations. Auxiliary systems need to be designed to work with the thermal-mass concept, but even so, it would take more time and more energy if for some reason you wanted to increase the temperature in the house using auxiliary heat.

4. *Fabric fading.* Carpets, upholstery and curtains all need to be chosen to withstand strong sunlight. Blinds and shades can be used for protection.

5. *Lack of privacy.* This depends on one's location and one's personal attitudes. Solar windows can be problematical in urban areas. Some people dislike the "feeling" of large expanses of glazing, but there are many ways of softening their effect. The size of panes and the position and type of glazing bars can all help to reduce the sometimes oppressive effect of large "patio" type windows, though of course at the expense of a slight loss of light.

One-Zone Sunspaces

Houses that contain an expanse of south-facing glass are not, of course, technically "greenhouses." Difficulties can result because some plants require higher conditions of humidity than would be acceptable for human comfort. On the whole, however, illumination levels and environmental conditions acceptable for humans are acceptable for most vegetables and house plants. The "one-zone" houses illustrated here are primarily designed for direct-gain passive solar heating. Their ability to provide an environ-ment for plants is secondary, though many of the sunspaces are filled with greenery.

THE SUNSCOOP HOUSE

David Wright has designed and built many houses that are highly efficient as solar collectors. By using large areas of south-facing glazing with ingenious shuttering systems, he has created greenhouse-homes that absorb and retain solar heat within the mass of the building. His first house in Santa Fe, New Mexico, now a classic in the field of passive solar houses, was designed around the deceptively simple idea of a glazed facade to an insulated adobe building (Figure 15.3). The adobe wall forming the rear of the building, the floor, and a row of 55-gallon water-filled drums buried in the window seating, all act like a massive heat sink. The external walls are insulated on the outside with three inches of sprayed urethane foam, covered with a layer of adobe cement. The floor consists of two feet of rock storage, insulated from below and covered with a thin concrete slab. Altogether, there are more than 30,000 pounds of adobe and rocks and 500 gallons of water to store heat. This means that the daily temperature fluctuations in northern New Mexico are dampened considerably as the mass of the building absorbs and releases solar heat. The shutters on the south-facing glazed wall consist of a series of urethane foam panels that are covered and hinged with burlap. They are raised and lowered by means of a simple winch. Unwanted summer sun is cut out by overhanging eaves at the front of the building.

The house is now more than three years old and has therefore been thoroughly tested. When Wright himself lived there he kept a complete record of its thermal performance and concluded that it worked well in the cold winter conditions that prevail there. With only a small wood-burning stove as a backup source of heat, the minimum temperature at night during the first winter was 47 degrees

Figure 15.3. Photo and floor plans describe David Wright's first passive solar house in Santa Fe, New Mexico, now considered a classic. Designed around an adobe wall, with a glazed south facade, it stores and releases heat through 30,000 pounds of adobe and rocks and 500 gallons of stored water.

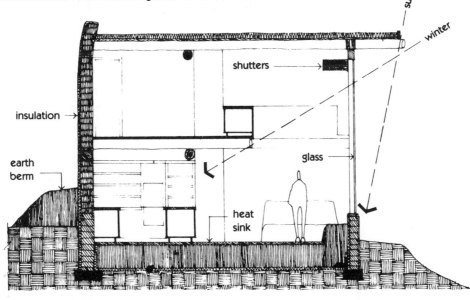

cross section

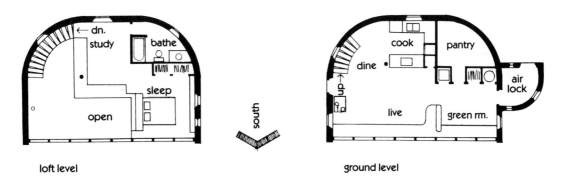

loft level   south   ground level

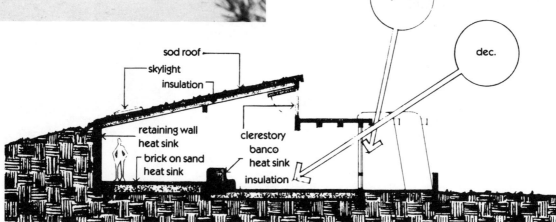

Fahrenheit when outside the thermometer went down to minus 10. One of the advantages of the simple open-plan design is that the sleeping loft remains the warmest part of the house throughout the night because it is open to the room below and the warmth given off from floor and walls gradually finds its way upstairs.

The internal surfaces of the house are fairly dark earth colors, which absorb solar heat and cut down on glare. Wright admits that some patches of the house become uncomfortable in the full sunlight, but then, as he says, it is quite easy to move one's chair! One has to learn to live with a house like this, to learn which parts are most comfortable at various times of day, and which are most suitable for different kinds of plants. The whole building is a complete organism that needs occasional tuning to the climatic conditions. The simple shutter system replaces a conventional thermostat as the basic means of control.

Buried in the ground. Wright used the same principles in two other houses in Santa Fe. They are heavily insulated adobe buildings with large south-facing glazed areas. They have both the light and airy aspects of a greenhouse and the dark, warm feeling of being inside a cave. They use the plastic qualities of adobe to the full as well as its heat-retaining qualities. Wright's third house, nicknamed "The Sun Cave," is actually buried in the ground, thus benefitting from the insulating qualities of the earth around it (Figure 15.4). Even the roof is insulated with earth, so that the whole house disappears into the dry New Mexico landscape and is well protected from cold winds and winter storms. This house has a south-facing clerestory window to admit direct sunlight deep into the structure. The clerestory is closed with a simple flap shutter during the night; the shutter opens against the sloping ceiling during the day.

Wright has further developed these ideas since his move to California. At Sea Ranch (Figure 15.5) he has constructed for himself a house that is almost wholly buried in the ground for protection from strong coastal winds. A sunken courtyard south of the house

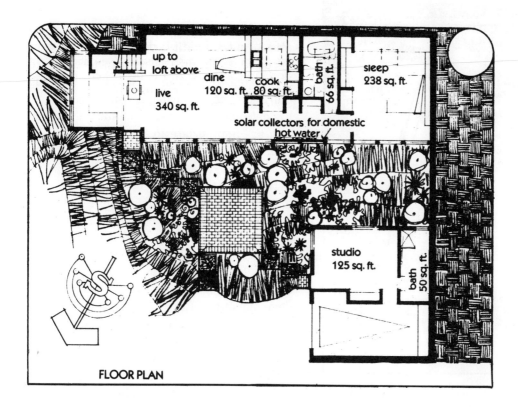

FLOOR PLAN

up to loft above
dine 120 sq. ft.
cook 80 sq. ft.
bath 66 sq. ft.
sleep 238 sq. ft.
live 340 sq. ft.
solar collectors for domestic hot water
studio 125 sq. ft.
bath 50 sq. ft.

Figure 15.5. Further developing his ideas, Wright utilized a sunken courtyard and moved further into the earth's protection at Sea Ranch, California. These diagrams show how the sun penetrates (or is deflected) and how the orientation is a bit more to the southeast.

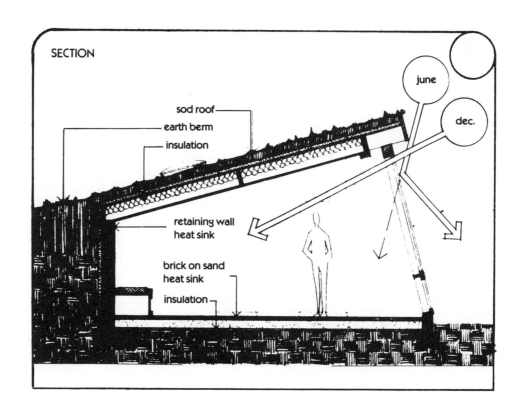

SECTION

sod roof
earth berm
insulation
june
dec.
retaining wall heat sink
brick on sand heat sink
insulation

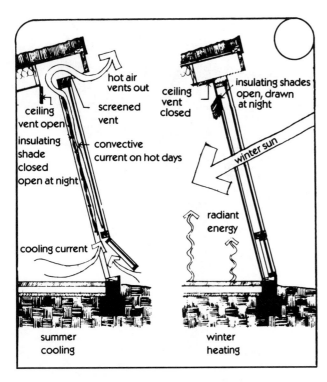

hot air vents out

ceiling vent open

screened vent

ceiling vent open

insulating shade closed open at night

convective current on hot days

cooling current

summer cooling

insulating shades open, drawn at night

ceiling vent closed

winter sun

radiant energy

winter heating

Figure 15.5 (cont'd). Detail of summer cooling and winter heating, Wright house, Sea Ranch.

creates a wind-protected area and allows the sloping glazed facade to receive full winter sunlight. In California, the sun is more welcome for a longer period of the year than it is in New Mexico and only in a few months during the summer is any cooling required. The glazed facade of the building is therefore at a 70-degree incline, which allows more sunlight to penetrate the building during spring and fall. Again, a simple shutter system is used along the whole south-facing glazed facade to retain winter heat and repel summer sun.

Wright's houses are not specifically designed for plants, yet they are in a sense environmentally conditioned greenhouses, creating a trap for solar heat and admitting enough light for most plants to thrive. His original D-shaped house in Santa Fe had a large area that was entirely devoted to plants and acted like a wall of foliage at the entrance to the living area. For a more serious plant enthusiast it might be necessary to separate a section of one's house specifically

for plants, to be able to maintain temperature and humidity more suited to their needs, but Wright's basic attitudes toward increasing the thermal mass of the building and reducing its heat loss, and particularly his detailed consideration of shuttered glazing, are appropriate to the design of greenhouses or homes.

Heat-recovery system. Malcolm Wells is another architect with long experience in the design of passive solar homes, and who has a particular interest in underground dwellings. His own office in New Jersey is completely buried underground. One of his most ambitious housing projects to date is the development at Raven Rocks, Ohio, (Figure 15.6), which is a large multi-family housing and office project buried in a south-facing hillside. The lower floor contains south-facing greenhouses, and south-facing glazing at upper levels admits light deep into the building and traps solar heat which is stored in the massive concrete structure. A heat-recovery system draws warm air from the top of the building down into a rock bed under the lowest floor. Power is provided by wind generators built into the roof and housed in shrouds which intensify the wind pressure on the vanes. This elaborate project will ultimately house nineteen people who have already started the construction work, most of which they intend to do themselves.

An interesting aspect of this building is its deep plan which, together with the fact that it is buried in the hillside, reduces the exposed surface area of the house to an absolute minimum. The deep plan is made possible by a stepped section and the use of double-story open space to get light into the innermost rooms. In summer the warm air rises through the double-story space and is vented at the top. In winter it is recirculated to the bottom of the house to conserve energy.

Row-house application. Another interesting approach to deep planning in a very different context is Ian Steen's house in

Figure 15.6. Architect Malcolm Wells's ambitious underground, passive solar multi-family housing and office project at Raven Rocks, Ohio. The exterior shows it from the south; the interior cross-section shows how shrouds channel winds into generating units at the upper level. Heat is stored in rocks under the building, and the lowest level supports a greenhouse.

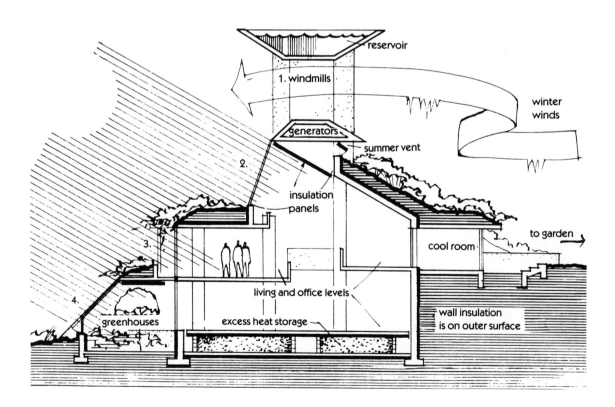

Cambridge, England (Figures 15.7 and 15.8). Steen bought a nineteenth-century row house in need of repair and completely rebuilt the back end, extending the 30-degree roof pitch right down to the ground on one side. Small row houses like this one are common in England. They were built at the end of the last century at a density of around ten to twelve houses per acre and they generally suffer from being cramped and dark inside. Any rear extensions make the internal rooms of the house even darker, as well as cutting off neighbors' light. Steen overcame these problems with an extension that creates a feeling of spaciousness and light throughout the house. His sloping double-glazed roof also acts as a heat collector on sunny days and is protected against heat loss at night by an ingenious system of accordion shutters. The glazed roof consists of three panels, two of which are counterbalanced against each other and can slide open in summer to provide ventilation top and bottom. The lowest panel covers a greenhouse area used for growing tomatoes and squash during the summer. In England there is not usually enough warmth to grow vegetables such as these out of doors very successfully.

Figure 15.7. Architect's drawings show the floor plans and a cross-section of Ian Steen's nineteenth-century English row house in which the roof line has been extended to the ground, providing a sunroom and greenhouse space.

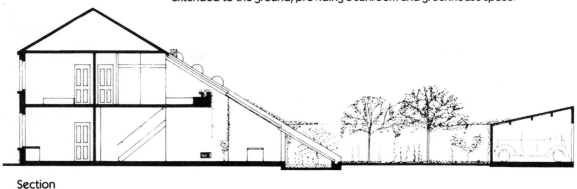

Section

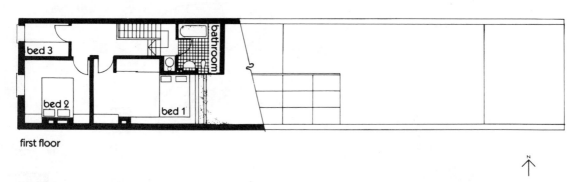

first floor

ground floor

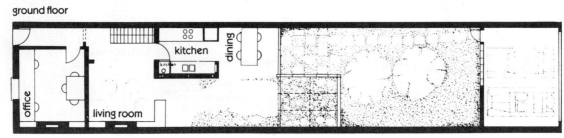

Figure 15.8. Photographs of the Ian Steen row house show what some imagination can do with the most mundane of homes. The greenhouse space is especially useful in the English climate, where summers are not usually warm enough to grow tomatoes or squash.

This ambitious conversion has not been without its problems. Steen has done most of the work himself and regards it as a continuing experiment. Air leakage at the junction of the sliding panels had to be solved by inserting complex draft-proof gaskets. Expansion of the aluminum angles which form the runners for the sliding panels also caused a problem that was overcome by fitting them loosely with slotted screws and incorporating an expansion joint.

Steen's house demonstrates the potential for attached greenhouses in the city, by permitting natural light and solar heat into deep plan, high-density houses. Roof spaces in particular, often underused in cities, could become potential locations for plant houses or hydroponic beds.

Recycled glazing. Carl Pucci's house for Linda McNichol in Vermont (Figure 15.9) uses a roof-light greenhouse to illuminate the center of the house and unite the seven different levels of rooms that surround it. The house itself, built with improvisation, uses a hundred or so recycled windows from a demolished hospital wing. These were spread around the house fairly liberally and were also used as the roof of the greenhouse, the only special precaution being to build up the glazing compound at the bottom of each pane of glass so that water would not collect there. Being made from around $3,000 worth of recycled materials, the house also required a lot of attention to caulking, battening and weatherstripping, to deal with those places where the second-hand materials didn't fit too well.

A central space opens up into a cupola in the roof for summer ventilation. The conservatory is one day to have thermal blankets between the window supports, though, as with many owner-built homes on a tight budget, such details tend to get delayed.

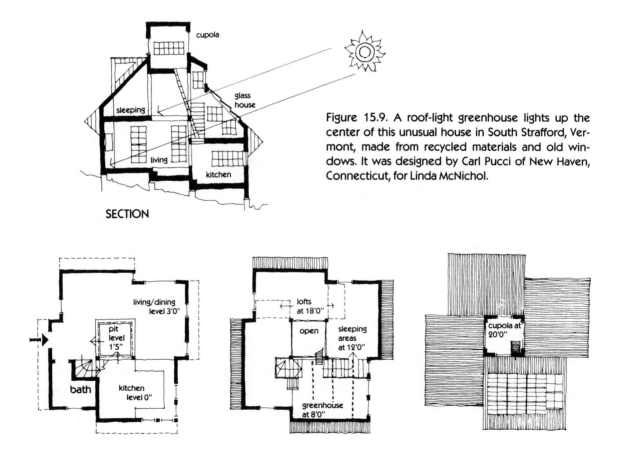

SECTION

Figure 15.9. A roof-light greenhouse lights up the center of this unusual house in South Strafford, Vermont, made from recycled materials and old windows. It was designed by Carl Pucci of New Haven, Connecticut, for Linda McNichol.

Front View

Side View

Cutaway View

Figure 15.10. The "solar cave" designed by John Hix in Caledon, Ontario, is built so deeply into the side of a hillock that from the north it is scarcely distinguishable from the pasture that surrounds it. It has triple glazing with a thermal curtain, a heat pump, and a heat-circulating fireplace.

Heat pump systems. John Hix is a Canadian architect with a long interest in low-energy housing design. He was the architect for the Provident House in Aurora, Canada, a totally solar-heated building with year-round heat storage. This house has fairly complex and expensive mechanical systems which are out of range for the average homeowner. Like many architects working in the field of solar energy, Hix has become disillusioned with complex active collection systems. His most recent work uses simple large areas of vertical south-facing glazing which act like solar collectors. Some heat is trapped in the floor and exposed masonry surfaces of the house. Eventually the space itself begins to overheat, and an air-to-water heat pump comes into operation to cool the

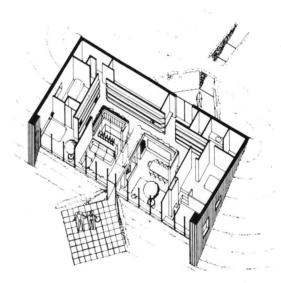

space and transfer the heat to a water storage tank. The stored heat is released by reversing the circulation of the heat pump at night. The solar house at Caledon, Ontario, incorporates such a system (Figure 15.10). The south-facing windows are triple glazed and have insulating curtains. The house is half buried in the earth. The resultant building is therefore similar to Wright's house at Sea Ranch, California, though additional glazing and insulation and the incorporation of a heat pump to upgrade the solar energy are all necessary for the more severe climate (7,000 degree days).

Calculations show that around 53 percent of the heat requirement of the house will be provided directly or indirectly by the sun, 11 percent being direct passive solar gain, and 42 percent being via the heat-pump system. The glazed south wall of this house is used for growing garden seedlings in late winter, and the intention is to use Wardian cases for species that require higher humidity.

The Solsearch Arks. The Solsearch architectural practice in Cambridge, Massachusetts, was founded in 1974 by David Bergmark and Ole Hammerlund. They were architects to the New Alchemy Institute for its "Arks" at Prince Edward Island and Cape Cod, and they have also designed a simple domestic-scale version of the Ark, one of which has been constructed at Washington, Connecticut (Figure 15.11). In this house the

Figure 15.11. The Solsearch architectural firm of Cambridge, Massachusetts, built this "ark" in Washington, Connecticut, which features a glass-covered sunspace all along its south side. It has a sophisticated glazing system, and rock storage underneath.

kitchen, dining area and living areas are all in a glass-roofed sunspace that runs along the south side. There is a half basement with utility rooms and bedrooms, and on a half level up from the greenhouse are further bedrooms. The glazing system in the sunspace roof is quite sophisticated. The outer layer is of Acrylite SDP double-glazing panels, on rafters at four-foot centers. There is an inner layer of Teflon film which creates an additional dead airspace in the glazing with very little loss in solar transmission. Beneath the glazing is a series of fixed horizontal polished aluminum louvers spanning between the rafters. These allow the sun to be admitted during winter when its altitude is low, but cut out most of the direct sunlight in summer. They also reduce the amount of glare from a bright sky, and the aluminum reduces radiative heat loss at night. The louvers form a kind of staircase up the main rafters, the risers of the staircase being blocked with another layer of glazing to further reduce heat loss.

The air in the sunspace is continually circulated on sunny winter days through rock storage underneath it. Two major ducts draw air down from the apex of the sunspace and through the rock bed. Return air is drawn through a continuous plenum at the cool side of the rock bed near the center of the house and back out into the sunspace to prevent its overheating. When heat is required from storage, a secondary fan system draws air through the warm side of the rock bed nearest the south-facing glazing.

In summer the sunspace is ventilated at the apex through a continuous vent panel. Collection fans that circulate the air through the rock bed can be used at night to cool the rocks and the slab above them and provide a source of cool intake air during the day to replace the warm air exhausted through the roof vent. The vast thermal mass of the building (the Ark 2 uses a four-foot-deep rock storage bed under the whole greenhouse floor area) is vitally necessary to maintain a relatively smooth thermal equilibrium while admitting an otherwise uncomfortably high percentage of solar radiation. The thermal mass works to one's advantage in summer as well as winter.

Planters are provided alongside the front wall of the Ark next to the double-glazed windows, which also provide a view from the living area. Here they receive maximum illumination in winter and are heated by night by the air drawn out of the storage bed. In summer, the windows can be opened to allow maximum ventilation to the plants.

Louvers for solar control. Peter Calthorpe, working with the Farallones Institute in California, has developed a system similar to the Solsearch Ark design, using a louvered double-glazing system and underfloor rock storage. The "louver" cabin at the Farallones Institute was constructed in an attempt to resolve a number of shortcomings that were noticed in the four original cabins (Figure 12.10) built to monitor the performance of simple passive solar heating systems. It uses a vertically charged rock bed, with radiant heat distribution, as described in Chapter 12. The addition of a simple venetian blind between a layer of double glazing on the outside and single glazing on the inside allows indirect light into the cabin while intercepting most of the direct radiation. The blind is flat black on one side and specular aluminum on the other. During periods of solar collection, the black side absorbs incoming radiation and a small fan draws air downwards between layers of glazing to remove the heat. The heated air then passes through the rock bed, at input temperatures of about 100° F., and is returned to the room, having lost its heat to the rocks, at around 60°F. On days without direct solar radiation, the blind can be drawn up to allow diffuse radiation into the room, and at night the blind can be shut to provide a specular reflective barrier to thermal radiation from the inside of the cabin.

Though louvers would reduce the amount of solar radiation incident on the plants, they do allow more flexibility in controlling direct solar radiation. A research project at the Uni-

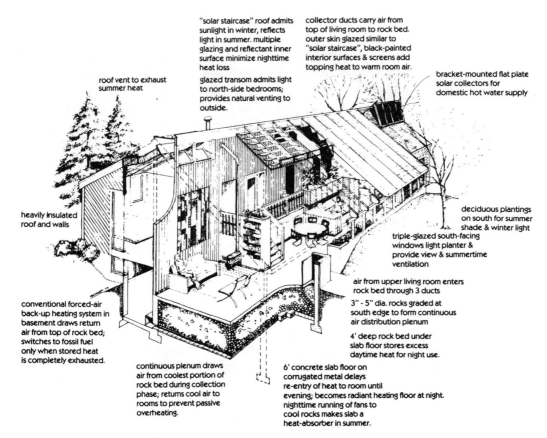

"solar staircase" roof admits sunlight in winter, reflects light in summer. multiple glazing and reflectant inner surface minimize nighttime heat loss

collector ducts carry air from top of living room to rock bed. outer skin glazed similar to "solar staircase", black-painted interior surfaces & screens add topping heat to warm room air.

roof vent to exhaust summer heat

glazed transom admits light to north-side bedrooms; provides natural venting to outside.

bracket-mounted flat plate solar collectors for domestic hot water supply

heavily insulated roof and walls

deciduous plantings on south for summer shade & winter light

triple-glazed south-facing windows light planter & provide view & summertime ventilation

conventional forced-air back-up heating system in basement draws return air from top of rock bed; switches to fossil fuel only when stored heat is completely exhausted.

air from upper living room enters rock bed through 3 ducts

3" - 5" dia. rocks graded at south edge to form continuous air distribution plenum

4' deep rock bed under slab floor stores excess daytime heat for night use.

continuous plenum draws air from coolest portion of rock bed during collection phase; returns cool air to rooms to prevent passive overheating.

6' concrete slab floor on corrugated metal delays re-entry of heat to room until evening; becomes radiant heating floor at night. nighttime running of fans to cool rocks makes slab a heat-absorber in summer.

Figure 15.12. A cutaway perspective of Solsearch's "Ark Two" on Prince Edward Island, Canada, describes details of the heating system and concepts.

versity of Arizona has used louver blinds on the vertical sidewalls of an attached solar greenhouse. The transparent roof of the greenhouse provides most of the illumination necessary for plants, and the sidewalls act like solar collectors feeding a rock storage bed, using a patented "clear-view" louver system.

Two-Zone Sunspaces

The houses discussed so far fall into the "one-zone" category with the greenhouse or sunspace as an indispensible part of the house. The separation of the greenhouse from the living areas of the house provides more flexibility both in use and in maintaining different environmental conditions. Some of the options are illustrated in the following examples. They include greenhouses designed to

act like buffer zones to the house, moderating its heat loss, and sunspaces designed to collect direct solar radiation passively, providing excess heat for the house for most of the heating seaon while requiring auxiliary heat from the house in midwinter. With an air-circulation rock-storage system, the sunspace can be designed to collect and save a substantial amount of the heat required by the house.

A prefabricated lean-to. Doug Kelbaugh's house in Princeton, New Jersey (Figure 15.13) has an attached greenhouse which is clearly a separate zone from the main house, though it is divided only by a heavy curtain at night. The house itself is based on the "Trombe wall" principle so the facade of the house is taken up mainly by one large solar collector and storage unit. This consists of thermopane glass, fixed on the

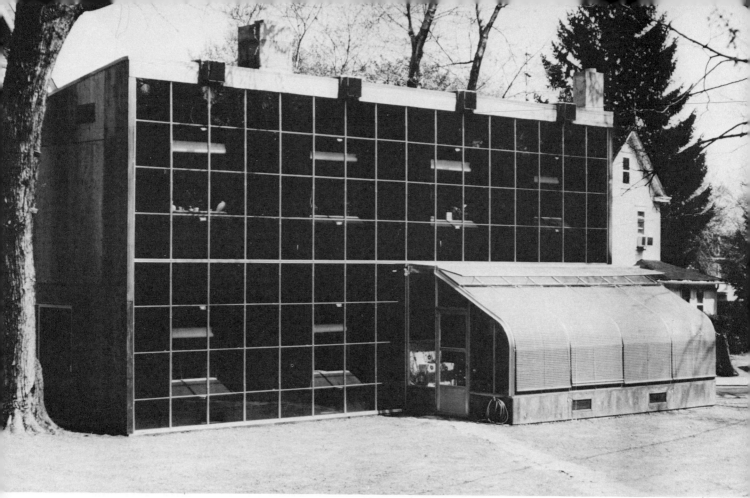

Figure 15.13. A two-zone principle is employed in the Doug Kelbaugh house in Princeton, New Jersey, where a heavy curtain is drawn at night to separate the greenhouse from the rest of the home.

outside of the thick concrete wall that forms both the structure of the house as well as a heat sink. The Kelbaugh House, like many other solar houses, has collectors and windows that are in direct competition for south light. In these circumstances, the greenhouse can be used to great effect because it provides a sunny, open environment which, because of the solar collector wall, is lacking in the main body of the house.

During the first winter the house performed well, costing only about $100 in space-heating bills. It was the greenhouse that turned out to be the least efficient part of the system (Figure 15.14). Its temperature swung from 75 degrees on a sunny winter's day to 50 degrees or below at night. This was much more than the maximum swing in temperature of 6 degrees in the main body of the house. This fault was remedied by placing water-filled oil drums in the greenhouse

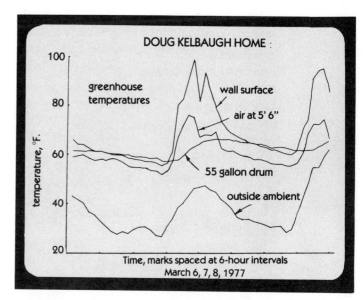

Figure 15.14. A temperature fluctuation chart in the Kelbaugh greenhouse shows a swing from 75 degrees on a sunny winter day to less than 50 at night.

to add to its thermal mass and moderate the temperature fluctuation.

Another problem was the direct heat loss through the greenhouse. Kelbaugh used a standard Lord and Burnham lean-to model with curved eaves. The detailing matched the glazed wall of the house, but the greenhouse itself was not designed to the high-insulation specification required for a low-energy house. The hourly heat loss in the greenhouse alone was 32,000 Btu's at zero degrees outside temperature. This amounted to almost half the total heat loss of the house. It was decided to double glaze the greenhouse, which proved a complex and expensive operation. The manufacturers offered assistance in this, even though the model was not designed specifically for double glazing. The result was a reduction in heat loss of about 12,000 Btu's, which saved a noticeable amount of fuel.

Blinds are required to shade the greenhouse in summer. Kelbaugh used the standard Lord and Burnham slatted roller blind and painted it bright red, which adds a splash of color to the otherwise somber concrete and glass facade of the building.

Seasonal sunspaces. In Denmark, several experimental house have been built using greenhouses as additional living spaces. Three houses built at Skive, Felsted, and Kokkedal are straightforward examples of the two-zone house (Figures 15.15 and 15.16). Each consists of a highly insulated conventional brick house for year-round use, and a large greenhouse attached to the south wall for intermittent seasonal use. The houses are heated by a combination of solar energy and earth-to-air heat pumps. Solar collectors, placed at first-floor level in the greenhouse, provide domestic water heating, with excess heat stored either in a swimming pool (at Felsted and Kokkedal) or in the earth beneath the house (at Skive). The latter is an experimental system of heat storage designed to work with the heat pump which retrieves stored heat from the earth in winter.

The solar collectors and heat pump have so far managed to supply all the heat needed by the house, though requiring a lot of extra equipment and a high electricity bill. The combination of solar collectors, greenhouse and heat pump seems to produce an efficient well-balanced system for the Danish climate. The incident solar energy on the collectors is obviously reduced by reflection off the greenhouse roof, but this appears to be more than compensated for by the increase in collector efficiency due to protection from wind and from external temperature. The greenhouse

Arkitektur Magazine

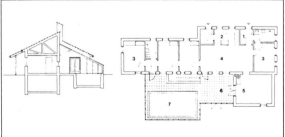

Figure 15.15. The south facade of a solar-energy home in Kokkedal, Denmark, which features a swimming pool that functions as a heat accumulator, in addition to a heat pump and greenhouse-sunroom. In the diagram numbers, 1 is a hall, 2 the kitchen, 3, 4, and 5 are living and working areas, 6 is the sunroom, and 7 the pool.

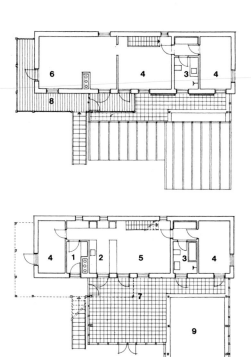

Arkitektur Magazine

Figure 15.16. A balcony gives access to the living room and study on the first floor of this solar-energy house at Felsted, Denmark. Numbers in the diagram refer to: 1, a hall; 2, kitchen; 3, bath; 4, 5, and 6, living and working spaces; 7, the sunroom; 8, balcony, and 9, swimming pool.

areas themselves have proved to be the preferred living spaces for a long period of the year. In Denmark, winter and summer are very short, and the intermediate seasons when the glasshouse comes into its own are much longer. The heated, enclosed swimming pool which stores solar heat is an added bonus. A row of vents is provided along the top of each greenhouse for use in summer.

The use of a large lean-to greenhouse affects the planning of the house. It implies a linear plan with the main rooms stretched out behind the greenhouse. It also gives the opportunity, as in the two-story house at Felsted, of having the upstairs rooms look out onto a balcony in the greenhouse, which thereby provides a vertical as well as a horizontal connection among various rooms.

At Skive, a row of fourteen low-energy demonstration houses has been built, funded by various companies and government agencies, to illustrate various possibilities offered by renewable energy sources. Most of the houses are fitted with solar collectors, and one is surmounted by a large windmill. Many derive benefit from the passive collection and storage of solar energy in greenhouses. The

street is appropriately called "Solhaven" (Sun Haven). Number 18 Solhaven, designed by Hougaard Nielsens, has an interesting greenhouse attachment which incorporates focusing solar collectors in the glass roof (Figure 15.17). These are used for domestic water heating during summer, and in the winter any energy they collect is connected into the earth-to-air heat-pump system that provides space heating for the house. The heat pump can be reversed in summer.

At Number 14 Solhaven, a less conventional-looking house uses the principle of an unheated sunroom which is partially covered with solar collectors (Figure 15.18). On this house, the collectors are of the flatplat type, which absorb both direct and diffused radiation, and they are inclined at a steeper angle to the horizontal to be more efficient during winter months. The solar energy collected is used for space heating. The house is constructed of thick brick walls and has fairly small windows. The sunroom therefore provides a light and open living room in contrast to the more enclosed, heated and well-insulated sections of the house. It is estimated that solar energy, together with heat reclaimed

from waste water, accounts for about half of the space heating required.

The Danish experimental houses have demonstrated the viability of combined greenhouses and solar-heating applications in cool climates. Many parts of the northern U.S. have a similar climate to Denmark, though in many areas it would be necessary to apply shades to the greenhouse in summer. Inland areas of northern U.S. have colder winters to contend with, but they also have a more reliable supply of sunshine during winter, when the greenhouse could be expected to perform well.

Figure 15.17. At Number 18 Solhaven ("Sun Haven") in the Danish town of Skive is this greenhouse attachment to a house incorporating focusing solar collectors in the glass roof. The "trough" collectors are also used to supply domestic hot water in the summer; and in winter they are connected to the terrestrial heat system.

Arkitektur Magazine

Arkitektur Magazine

Figure 15.18. A less-conventional house is Number 14 Solhaven at Skive, Denmark, in which flat-plate collectors are pitched at a more severe angle for winter efficiency. A sunroom provides a light and open living room, as the interior photo shows, in contrast to the more enclosed and well-insulated rooms that are heated.

Arkitektur Magazine

Architects' Journal

Flexible vacation home. A small vacation home designed by the English architects Colquhoun and Miller is another example of the two-zone principle used to great effect (Figure 15.19). The larger zone is in this case a glazed conservatory. The upper section of the conservatory is separated by a series of sliding partitions from a more enclosed kitchen and dining area. The lower section opens off an enclosed area which can be divided up with more partitions into two or three bedrooms, as required. The sliding screens allow the whole of the upper and lower areas to become one space. The rear section of the house can be completely isolated to reduce the volume of the house when artificial heating is required. The house is built almost entirely of man-made materials: a steel

Figure 15.19. Pillwood House, a small vacation home near Cornwall, England, designed by English architects Colquhoun and Miller, is shown in photos, cross-section, floor plans, and an axonometric sketch. It embodies the two-zone principle, the larger zone being a glazed conservatory, and the smaller, or rear area, can be partitioned off according to heating needs. The closeup photo shows a detail of the mechanism for interior roller blinds that are drawn to minimize the summer's heat. Louvered windows also provide ventilation. The concrete floor is a heat sink, absorbing radiation by day, releasing it by night.

Architects' Journal

Architects' Journal

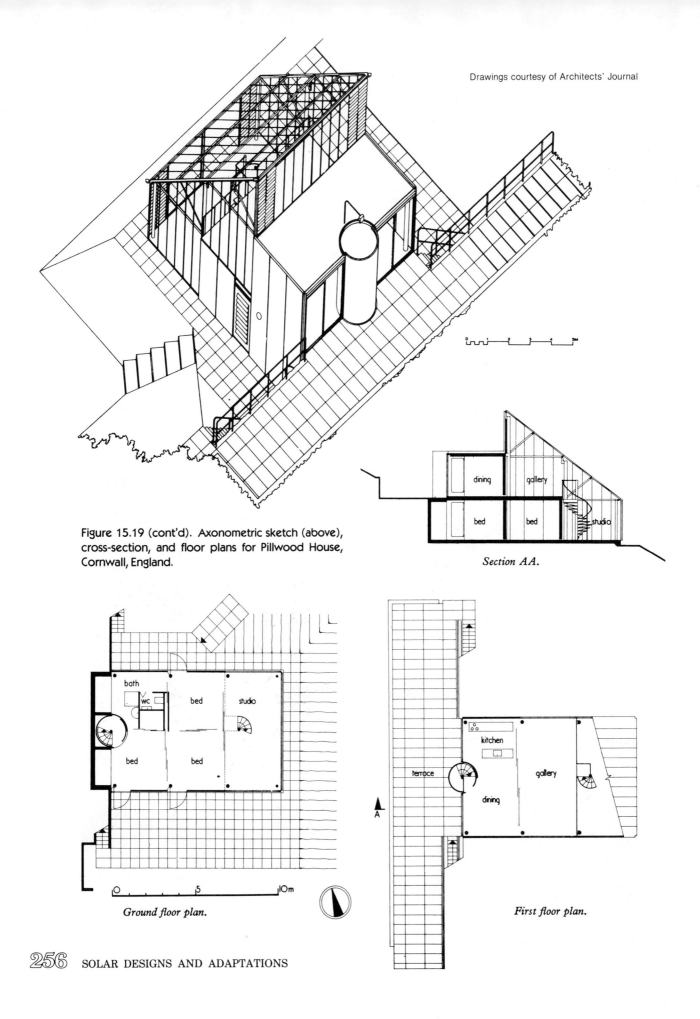

Drawings courtesy of Architects' Journal

Figure 15.19 (cont'd). Axonometric sketch (above), cross-section, and floor plans for Pillwood House, Cornwall, England.

dining   gallery

bed   bed   studio

Section AA.

bath
wc
bed   studio
bed   bed

Ground floor plan.

0 ____ 5 ____ 10m

kitchen
terrace
dining   gallery

A

First floor plan.

framework, aluminum patent-glazing bars, glass, and white insulated glass-reinforced plastic (GRP) wall panels. Even the spiral staircases are made of GRP. The concrete floor slabs act like a heat sink, absorbing radiation during the day and releasing it in the evening. In winter months, under-floor heating provides a backup source of heat for the rear living area. The intention is to install a wood-burning stove in the kitchen-dining area, which would be cheaper to run than the existing heating system. Internal roller blinds are used for shading in summer, and louvered windows at the top of the conservatory provide ventilation.

The pristine quality of this particular design is set off by the natural beauty of its surroundings. Careful attention to detail in the building has turned what otherwise might have been an overgrown aluminum greenhouse into a piece of sculpture. The house is located on the south coast of England in an area where decorative Victorian conservatories are widespread. The architects have taken the principle of a glazed living area and fashioned it to suit a particular taste and a particular setting. It shows how precise detailing and attention to quality can really affect the appearance of a building.

Reflective surfaces. James Lambeth is another architect with an obvious flair for crisp detailing. His design for the Coombes house in Springdale, Arkansas, is dominated by a central south-facing glasshouse (Figure 15.20). The glasshouse forms a partial enclosure for a swimming pool and a central focus for all other rooms. Much of Lambeth's work includes the use of reflective surfaces to concentrate solar energy. In this case, an outward-sloping reflective glass panel above the greenhouse directs solar heat down into the pool during spring and fall. In midwinter, the reflector casts sunlight onto the deck floor of the pool, where it is stored in a concrete floor.

The greenhouse in the Coombes residence is protected from heat loss on all except the

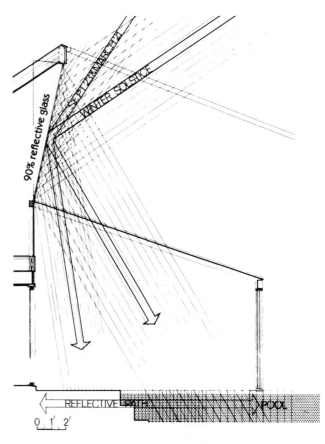

Figure 15.20. Architect James Lambeth devoted much attention to using a reflective surface for focusing the sun's rays when he designed the Coombes house in Springdale, Arkansas. Here, the glass panel above a swimming pool concentrates the rays on a heat-storing concrete deck during winter, and on the pool itself in spring and fall.

south side by the house itself, which forms a concave heat trap around it. It receives winter sun throughout the day, but in early morning and late evening the side walls block off the summer sun that would otherwise penetrate deep into the building and cause overheating.

Adobe and glass. Unit One, First Village, near Santa Fe, New Mexico, was the first passive solar home constructed with solar-demonstration program federal funds. It was a speculative house designed and built by

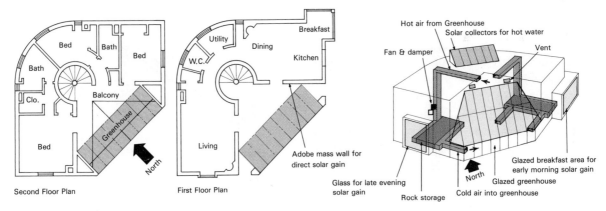

Second Floor Plan

First Floor Plan

Bed · Bath · Bed
Bath · Clo. · Balcony · Greenhouse · Bed · North

Utility · W.C. · Dining · Breakfast · Kitchen · Living

Adobe mass wall for direct solar gain

Glass for late evening solar gain

Hot air from Greenhouse · Solar collectors for hot water
Fan & damper · Vent
Glazed breakfast area for early morning solar gain
North · Glazed greenhouse
Rock storage · Cold air into greenhouse

Figure 15.21. Floor plans for the Unit One House built for Communico, Santa Fe County, New Mexico. The south-facing greenhouse wall is 276 sq. feet. The north wall is constructed of natural adobe bricks 14 inches thick at the first floor, tapering to 10 inches at the second. The adobe mass stores heat for use at night. Additional heat storage is provided by rock beds under living room and dining room floors, served by fans that circulate heated air from the greenhouse roof. Electric baseboard heaters provide auxiliary heating; summer overheating is relieved by vents in the greenhouse roof.

Wayne and Susan Nichols. Like the Coombes residence, it is built around the concept of a two-story greenhouse enclosed by the house on all except the south side. The greenhouse is not intended as a day-round living area, though its present owner, Doug Balcomb, testifies that it is in fairly regular use. There are fourteen-inch-thick adobe walls which separate the greenhouse from rooms behind. These walls act as one component of the solar-heating system, absorbing incoming radiation during the day and gradually releasing it to the interior at night. Every room has a frontage on the greenhouse walls. The second component of the heating system consists of two under-floor rock beds on each side of the house. Each bed holds about twenty-four cubic yards of rocks, and a one-third h.p. fan is used to circulate air from the top of the greenhouse, horizontally through the rock beds and back out into the greenhouse. Backdraft dampers are necessary to prevent heat from traveling back out through the vertical intake duct when the fans are not operating. Distribution of heat from the rock bed is by the release of radiant heat through the floor. Slab temperatures range from 85°F. on

a sunny winter's day to 78 after a cold night, sinking to 70 after a sunless day. The two systems together keep the house very comfortable, the high mean radiant temperatures allowing comfortable conditions at lower air temperatures. Balcomb estimates the savings from the solar heating system amount to around $500 per year. Maintenance costs are, of course negligible, and the fans add little to the electricity bill.

An inflatable conservatory. On the other side of Santa Fe is Hal Migel's home. This is a one-story house stretched out behind a south-facing greenhouse covered with two sheets of polyethylene film. The sheets are held in place by a "zip-lock" aluminum fastening system, and an electric fan maintains a continuous air pressure between the two layers of film, producing an inflatable transparent wall. During the heating season, this wall forms a continuous conservatory along the south face of Migel's adobe house. The warm air in the conservatory is circulated through a rock-storage bed under the house which provides radiant under-floor heating during winter. The conservatory also

Figure 15.22. The one-story Migel home in Santa Fe, New Mexico, is made of adobe with a south-facing greenhouse covered with two sheets of polyethylene that have an inflated air space in between. Warm air in the greenhouse in winter circulates into a rock-storage bed beneath the house, providing radiant under-floor heating for the home. Vegetables are grown all winter in the greenhouse. In summer, the plastic is removed, providing an outdoor garden space as well as more ventilation in the house. The owner says that 80 percent of his heating is provided by the greenhouse. The interior photo shows a piece of the air hose that keeps the polyethylene layers inflated.

provides an additional living space, links various rooms of the house together, and grows vegetables throughout the winter. In summer the inflatable covers can be stripped off, making the space into an outdoor garden and allowing direct ventilation into the house. The polyethylene has to be replaced fairly frequently, but the advantages of having a demountable airtight conservatory are obviously great, and Migel estimates that 80 percent of the space heating for his 2,500-square-foot home is provided by the 400-square-foot conservatory.

Low-cost/fast payback. Near Atlantic City, New Jersey, where the climate is less conducive to allowing solar heating to pay for itself, Donald Watson has built a house that uses a similar sunspace and rock-bed system. Compared with New Mexico, New Jersey has only a moderate winter-heating require-

ment, and a moderate amount of winter sunshine. Investments in solar energy must be kept low in cost to achieve a reasonable payback. Watson designed a system that added less than $1,500 to the cost of the house. This represented the installed cost of the insulated rock bed, dampers, fans, and wiring. Another $1,250 was spent on additional insulation, high-quality windows and internal glazed doors between sunspace and living area. The contribution toward the heat loss of the house, calculated according to the amount of fuel used during the first eight months, and compared to a comparably insulated house, was 66 percent. This represents a payback of between five and seven years for a reasonably modest investment.

The distribution of heat from the rock bed is simply tied in to the auxiliary forced-air system. Air is drawn from the house, through the rock bed, and back out into the house.

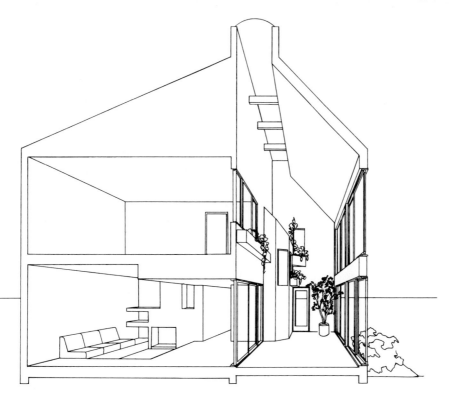

Figure 15.23. The concept of the "sunspace in the home" is typified in this house near Atlantic City, New Jersey, designed by Donald Watson, author of Designing & Building a Solar House. The cutaway perspective shows how the sunspace is built into the house but separated from it by glass doors. The diagram details workings of the rock storage system underneath, and how it is tied into the home's forced-air heating system.

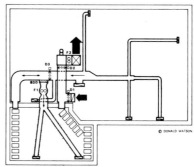

Robert Perron photo

When the heat in the storage is insufficient, the auxiliary burner comes on to heat the house directly. By using separate fans for collection and distribution, the system benefits from thermal stratification while simplifying both the ducting and the damper controls, which can otherwise become very complex and expensive.

Though relatively untested so far, this kind of two-fan system seems to be the simplest answer to sunspace/rock-storage heating. It ought to be easy to retrofit existing homes having forced-air distribution systems, even if the rock bed only provides preheating for the house most of the time.

The holistic approach. Dan Scully's design work at Total Environmental Action is, as the name of the group suggests, concerned with a holistic approach toward reducing energy consumption. TEA, located in Harrisville, New Hampshire, has been responsible for much work in the forefront of the passive-solar-energy movement, designing

buildings that use solar energy generally through a combination of different systems.

The Cook house, designed for upstate New York, is buried into a south-facing sloping hillside. There is a formal entry that leads up around a sunken greenhouse and into the main living area in the center of the house (Figure 15.24). Beyond this is a two-story bedroom zone. The two major light and heat traps are the greenhouse itself, which has a

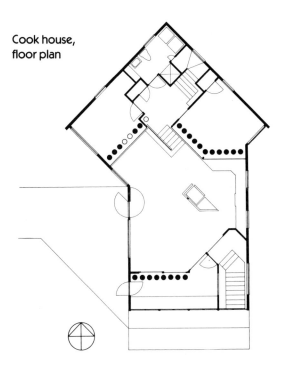

Cook house, floor plan

Figure 15.24. Dan Scully's Cook house in upstate New York is designed along a north-south axis, with the greenhouse along the south (see floor plan).

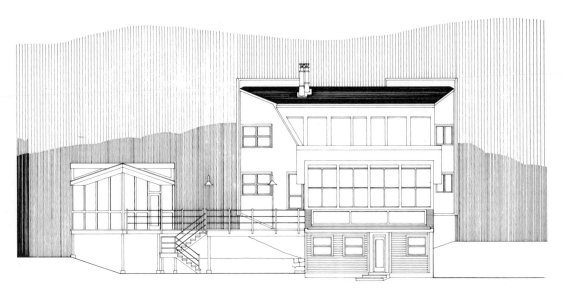

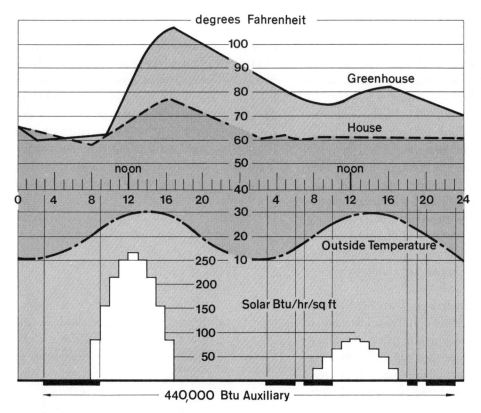

Figure 15.24 (cont'd). Chart of temperature variations in house, greenhouse, and outside over sunny winter day (left) and cloudy winter day (right). Auxiliary heater use and solar produced Btu's are shown at bottom.

concave glazed facade with insulating shutters to prevent nighttime heat loss plus an overhanging roof to cut out summer sun, and a clerestory light shaft between living and bedroom areas. The clerestory is protected by beadwall insulation at night. Divisions between the zones are made with water walls of Kalwall storage tubes painted dark colors. Incorporating thermal mass vertically in this way not only means that it is more directly exposed to the sun, but also that it will not be covered by rugs and furniture which often cause problems with thermal storage in floors.

There is a total storage capacity of 42 Btu's per degree Fahrenheit for every square foot of south-facing glass, which according to simulation tests on a two-day period in the middle of winter should enable the house to utilize 55 percent of the available solar energy. The tests showed that with the use of insulat-

ing shutters the greenhouse would remain about 15°F. warmer than the house throughout the cloudy day despite the use of auxiliary heating inside the house.

Many solar-heated buildings are built on an east-west linear plan with a series of rooms stretched out behind collectors or south-facing glazing. This can lead to problems with ventilation and obstruction of views from the center of the house. The Cook house is stretched out along a north-south axis, which means that the main living area can have cross ventilation and windows to east and west as well as a view through the greenhouse to the south. Nevertheless, the design manages to incorporate a south-facing glazed collection area equal to 23 percent of the floor area of the house. This arrangement also protects the main living area with buffer areas to the north and south where temperature control is not as crucial.

The Double-Skin Principle

In most of the houses so far illustrated, the greenhouse area is seen as a buffer zone on the south side of the building. In the Coombes house, the insulated zone is wrapped around the greenhouse to form a sheltered micro-climate. Another alternative to the two-zone approach is to wrap the greenhouse all around the insulated zone forming, in effect, a house within a house. This has been attempted by a number of architects, among them Frei Otto, in his own house which is built into a hillside in a village near Stuttgart, Germany. The house consists of an outer glazed skin, artificially heated to enclose an environment of semi-tropical plants. Within this are enclosed flat-roofed bedrooms and living rooms which can be separately ventilated to the outside if necessary. It requires a great deal of artificial heat during the winter, but in summer a large area of the roof slides open to provide adequate ventilation.

In Cambridge, England, in the late 1960s, John Hix, the architect now working in Canada, built an experimental house within the framework of a commercial greenhouse. The external glazed skin was modified with polystyrene sheets that fitted under the glass to produce an insulated but translucent roof. Most of the side walls were also insulated. The basic idea behind the house was to demonstrate that "off the shelf" industrial components could be used to provide cheap, flexible housing. Within the glasshouse framework, heated by a commercial greenhouse air heater, bedrooms, bathrooms and internal living spaces were created using a simple partitioning system. Hix's glasshouse was cheap to build but expensive to heat. Like the Frei Otto house, it was built in the days of cheap energy. But the basic principles still deserve consideration. Conventional green-houses are still cheap to erect and glazing is also relatively cheap. An *external* skin, which provides protection against rain and can temper the winter heat loss, allows the *internal* skin to be built to a lower specification than usual. The main problems to be overcome are the possibility of overheating in summer, and the difficulty of ventilating internal rooms. Without expensive environmental control equipment, these problems become severe in any climate where greenhouses have to be permanently shaded or ventilated in summer. In cold climates, however, the concept of a transparent outer skin is worth further investigation.

Underground cooling. One architect who has started to develop the double-skin principle to suit a number of different climates is Lee Porter Butler, president of ekose'a, a San Francisco-based firm of architects and energy-conservation engineers.

Butler designed a house for his family in Tennessee in 1968 which incorporated a vast 3,000-square-foot greenhouse that includes a swimming pool. He was impressed with the stable temperatures that were maintained in the greenhouse, and with the success of an underground cooling system he also incorporated. Similar features went into the Jackson house, built in 1975 in western Tennessee. This house contains a 360-square-foot sunroom which acts like a heat collector for the 1,440 square feet of the main house behind. Heat storage is primarily in the floor of the greenhouse, which has a four-inch concrete slab and 18 inches of dirt below, insulated underneath with a two-inch layer of urethane foam. Theoretically, the storage capacity of the concrete and dirt is about 50,000 Btu's over a 10-degree temperature rise. The main means of heat distribution consists of simply opening sliding glass doors and windows between the sunspace and the rooms behind. In the mild Tennessee winters (3,200 degree days), the sun provides almost all the heat the home requires.

Summer cooling is in fact more of a problem because external conditions are both hot and humid. The greenhouse helps in cooling the house because hot air rises to the top and is vented through a kind of thermal chimney at the top of the house (Figure 15.25). This pulls air through the rooms below and, in turn, outside air is pulled in through an underground duct. In the duct, the humid external air releases some of its moisture, thus eventually lowering the humidity inside the house. The cool air not only enters the rooms but also blows through the subfloor area and around the walls, removing heat from the structure as well as the rooms themselves.

The sunroom itself is shaded by deciduous trees in summer so that overheating is minimized, and the overhanging roof prevents any direct sunlight from entering the house itself.

Natural circulation. In a further development of the double-skin idea, Butler built a house at Lake Tahoe, Nevada, which uses a natural circulation loop between the building's two skins. During winter days, hot air rises to the top of the greenhouse, pulling in cooler air through subfloor ducts. This in turn draws the heated air down the north side of the house. The greenhouse in this case is two and a half stories high, and the extra height helps to accelerate the thermosiphoning effect.

In summer, vents at the top of the building exhaust the hot air that rises through the greenhouse and draw in cooler air through underground ducts similar to the Jackson house. The advantages of naturally controlled heating and cooling systems are obviously great in that they eliminate both the noise and the cost of fan-driven systems. Duct sizing is more important, as is an understanding of how natural air circulation works. An important feature of Butler's houses is that not only are they well insulated, but also well sealed against infiltra-

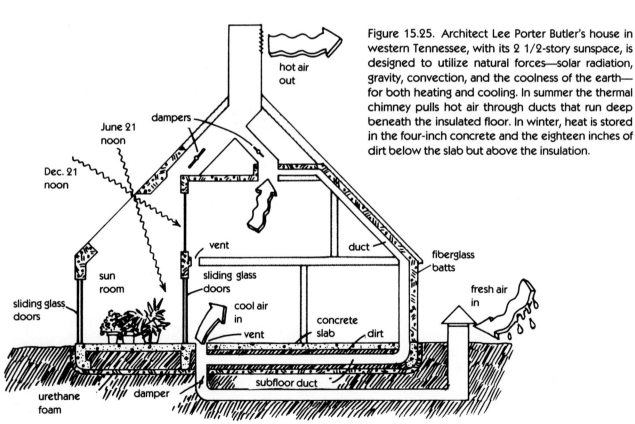

Figure 15.25. Architect Lee Porter Butler's house in western Tennessee, with its 2 1/2-story sunspace, is designed to utilize natural forces—solar radiation, gravity, convection, and the coolness of the earth—for both heating and cooling. In summer the thermal chimney pulls hot air through ducts that run deep beneath the insulated floor. In winter, heat is stored in the four-inch concrete and the eighteen inches of dirt below the slab but above the insulation.

From The Solar Home Book by Bruce Anderson, Cheshire Books, Harrisville, NH, 1976. Reprinted with permission.

tion so the natural air circulation patterns can be more easily controlled.

The sunroom collector. The designs discussed in this chapter illustrate several different approaches to incorporating a greenhouse area into the home. At a time when active solar-energy systems are still out of the range of most incomes, the interest in passive solar collection is increasing. These attached greenhouses demonstrate that with careful attention to design and climate, the conventional sunroom can become a useful solar collector. The delightful advantage of using a greenhouse as a solar collector is that it is a simple structure requiring few if any elaborate controls. It is something one can build oneself with only a basic knowledge of construction, and it can provide satisfaction in several ways in a short time.

It would be a great shame if, in response to the energy crisis, we go back to a domestic architecture of small rooms with tiny windows. Glass and the transparent substitutes for it are some of the most exciting building materials we have to work with. We must not be dominated by blanket-style building codes that limit the use of glass simply because it has a high thermal transmittance. The intelligent use of glass should be one of the major determinants in the style of houses built now that the illusion of an energy glut is past.

Having a greenhouse in the home also serves to emphasize to us our dependence on the food chains that are powered by solar energy. The therapeutic effects of gardening, both indoors and outdoors, are well known. Having a food-production unit as part of one's home is a constant reminder that man plays only a small part in the energy cycles that keep the planet alive. The art of plant husbandry is essentially one of recognizing and maintaining the delicate balances necessary for growth. Creating one's own microclimate and simulating the important elemental cycles that keep the world in balance can increase our awareness of our part in maintaining the natural order.

Designers of projects discussed in Chapter 15 (listed alphabetically).

Arkitektgruppen i Arhus Aps
Sondergade 1A
8000 Arhus C.
Denmark

Lee Porter Butler
3375 Clay St.
San Francisco, California 94118

Peter Calthorpe
The Farallones Institute
15290 Coleman Valley Road
Occidental, California 95465

Colquhoun & Miller
23 Neal St.
London WC2H 9PU
England

John Hix
207 Queens Way West
Toronto 117
Canada

Doug Kelbaugh
70 Pine St.
Princeton, New Jersey 08540

James Lambeth
1891 Clark St.
Fayetteville, Arkansas 72701

Wayne Nichols
Route 3, Box 81D
Santa Fe, New Mexico 87501

Carl Pucci
415 Temple St.
New Haven, Connecticut 06511

Dan Scully
Total Environmental Action
Church Hill
Harrisville, New Hampshire 03450

Solsearch, Architects
1430 Massachusetts Ave.
Cambridge, Massachusetts 02138

Ian Steen
10 Trafalgar Road
Cambridge, England

Donald Watson, AIA
Box 401
Guilford, Connecticut 06437

Malcolm Wells
Box 183
Cherry Hill, New Jersey 08002

David Wright, AIA
Box 49
The Sea Ranch, California 95497

References

Most of the information and photographs were provided through the courtesy of the designers involved. The following references will give further information and examples of the use of greenhouses and sunspaces as part of the house.

The Proceedings of a Conference on Solar Energy for Heating Greenhouses and Greenhouse-Residential Combinations. March, 1977, Cleveland and Wooster, Ohio. Available at $5 from the Department of Agricultural Engineering, OARDC, Wooster, Ohio 44691.

"A Survey of Passive Solar Building." 1978. Prepared by the AIA Research Corporation, 1735 New York Avenue Northwest, Washington, D.C. 20006. Contains useful summary sheets of at least 100 passive solar building, including many based on sunspace principles.

"Passive Solar Heating and Cooling." Conference workshop proceedings, May, 1976, Albuquerque, New Mexico. Available from the National Technical Information Service, U.S. Department of Commerce, Springfield, Virginia 22161, for $10.50.

Proceedings of the Second National Passive Solar Conference. March, 1978, Philadelphia.

30 Energy-Efficient Houses You Can Build, by Alex Wade and Neal Ewenstein, Rodale Press. 1977. $8.95. Detailed design ideas on passive solar heating, the intelligent use of windows, skylights, greenhouses, etc.

"Six Low Energy Houses," *Arkitektur* magazine. Issue no. 7 (July 1977) discusses the Danish houses covered in this chapter.

Appendix

HEAT AVAILABLE FOR
COLLECTION

The heat that is trapped by a greenhouse depends on the amount of sunlight available, the type and number of layers of glazing, and the efficiency with which the greenhouse heat collection system works.

A simple formula for calculating the heat available each month is given in the equation

$$Qg = HG \times PA \times DM \times GA \times SC \times CE$$

Where

QG = Heat collected by the glasshouse in any one month.

HG = Heat gained through each square foot of glazing in Btu's/sq. ft./day

PA = The percentage of actual sunshine available.

DM = The number of days per month.

GA = The glazed area in square feet.

SC = The shading coefficient of the glass.

CE = The efficiency of the collection system.

HEAT GAINED THROUGH
GLASS

Table I gives values of the average amount of heat passing through a single layer of glazing for each month of the year, at three different latitudes. Heat gain values for glazing at four different angles are given. These have been computed according to information in Reference 1. Interpolation is possible between the various latitudes and the angles of glazing given. For simplicity, the values of heat gain for equivalent months each side of the solstices (i.e., January and November, February and October, etc.) are assumed to be equal. In reality, the amount of heat gained in the latter half of the year will be up to 5 percent lower than in the first six months.

For horizontal and angled glazing, no allowance has been made for ground reflectance, though for glazing tilted at 60 degrees or more, ground reflectance could increase the amount of sunlight available by 10 to 20 percent. For vertical glazing, a ground reflectance factor of 20 percent is included, though in conditions of snow cover the value given could be increased by as much as 50 percent due to reflection.

The values in Table I should be modified by the sky clearness factors shown in Figure 1 that take into account altitude, haziness and air pollution, which continually affect the amount of solar radiation available.

Figure 2 gives some indication of the reduction in the amount of solar energy available when the greenhouse is oriented away from due south. The values of solar heat gain in Table 1 should be multiplied by the appropriate percentage reduction factors as shown in Figures 1 and 2.

AVAILABLE ENERGY

Table 2 gives the average percentage of sunshine available in major cities located throughout the

U.S.A. For more accurate information you could consult your nearest weather station. Airports and state weather bureaus often record such information also.

GLAZED AREA

The area of glazing should be measured for each plane of glass (roof and walls). The net area of glazing will be significantly less than the overall area when the shading effect of the mullions is taken into account. For lightweight metal-framed greenhouses, the structure will reduce the overall glazed area by around 5 percent. With a timber-framed structure, the glazed area could be reduced by as much as 15 or 20 percent if deep structural members are used.

THE SHADING COEFFICIENT
OF THE GLAZING

The values in Table 1 are for the solar energy transmitted by double-strength clear window glass. This is assumed to have a shading coefficient of 1.0, corresponding to a maximum solar transmittance of around 93 percent. The effect of double glazing, shades, or curtains will reduce solar-heat gain by the amount shown in Figure 3. In addition, the accumulation of dirt on the glass can reduce solar-heat transmission by 10 percent or so in areas with high atmospheric pollution.

Table 1. Values of the average amount of heat passing through a single layer of glazing for each month of the year, at three different latitudes, and at different angles. These were computed according to information in the ASHRAE Handbook of Fundamentals and ASHRAE Handbook of Applications.

| | LAT. 32° | | | | | LAT. 40° | | | | | LAT. 48° | | | | |
| | Solar radiation measured normal to the sun's rays and on a horizontal plane | | Solar heat gain in Btus/sq. ft./day through glazing tilted at an angle of: | | | Solar radiation measured normal to the sun's rays and on a horizontal plane | | Solar heat gain in Btus/sq. ft./day through glazing tilted at an angle of: | | | Solar radiation measured normal to the sun's rays and on a horizontal plane | | Solar heat gain in Btus/sq. ft./day through glazing tilted at an angle of: | | |
	NORMAL	HORIZ.	30°	60°	90°	NORMAL	HORIZ.	30°	60°	90°	NORMAL	HORIZ.	30°	60°	90°
DEC.	2348	1136	1649	1907	1690	1978	782	1298	1635	1560	1444	446	905	1215	1250
JAN/NOV	2458	1288	1762	1953	1655	2182	948	1464	1767	1615	1710	596	1086	1414	1395
FEB/OCT	2872	1724	2035	1921	1530	2640	1414	1827	1943	1600	2330	1080	1556	1804	1575
MAR/SEPT	3012	2084	2127	1786	1215	2916	1852	2035	1908	1360	2870	1578	1620	1918	1500
APR/AUG	3076	2390	2090	1371	770	3092	2274	2108	1643	960	3076	2106	2085	1801	1190
MAY/JULY	3112	2582	2032	1134	535	3160	2552	2108	1421	700	3254	2482	2153	1608	955
JUNE	3084	2634	1953	1010	470	3180	2648	2082	1316	620	3312	2626	2192	1494	870

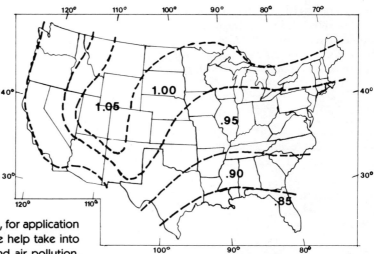

Figure 1. Winter sky clearness factors, for application to the values listed in Table 1. These help take into account factors of altitude, haze and air pollution, which all affect the amount of solar radiation available.

Figure 2. Variations in solar radiation on vertical walls as a function of the orientation away from due south.

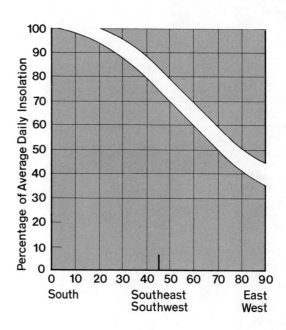

COLLECTION EFFICIENCY

For a well-designed solar greenhouse with adequate heat-storage capacity and an efficient exchange of heat from the collecting surfaces, all of the heat trapped by the glazing should be usable. In these ideal conditions, temperatures would not rise high enough to necessitate ventilation and therefore waste of heat. Rarely, however, will a system prove so efficient. Little data is available on the efficiency of the greenhouse as a heat collector. In a greenhouse full of plants, a substantial proportion of the incident radiation is used in plant transpiration and is converted into latent heat, resulting in increased humidity. Most of this heat is lost through ventilation and condensation on the glazing. In winter, a greenhouse full of plants will convert about 30 percent of the incoming energy into latent heat; in summer this figure may increase to exceed 50 percent.

Research at Cornell University showed that a double-glazed quonset-type greenhouse with an air-circulation and rock-storage system could achieve an average winter collection efficiency of around 25 percent. In a sunroom with less planting, the efficiency would obviously be greater. The Delta Solar house, built by Cedric Green in Suffolk, in England, with a simple south-facing conservatory and convective heat distribution, was

SHADING COEFFICIENTS

Glazing	No Shade	With Light Drapes	With Dark Drapes
1/8" clear glass	1.0	0.56	0.70
1/4" clear glass	0.93	0.56	0.70
"Thermopane" glass (2 1/8" layers with 1/4" airspace)	0.87	0.50	0.58

Figure 3. Shading coefficients: the amounts by which double glazing, shades, or curtains will reduce solar-heat gain.

fully monitored and had a collection efficiency of 53 percent (Reference 7.) Watson (Reference 3) quotes system efficiencies of 80 percent for solar-oriented windows with exposed masonry surfaces on the inside of the house, and 100 percent for solar windows with low-temperature heat-storage systems. Figure 4 gives some idea of collection efficiencies that could be expected for different types of solar greenhouse.

Table 2. The average monthly percentage of sunshine available in cities throughout the United States.

MEAN PERCENTAGE OF POSSIBLE SUNSHINE FOR SELECTED LOCATIONS

STATE AND STATION	YEARS	JAN.	FEB.	MAR.	APR.	MAY	JUNE	JULY	AUG.	SEPT.	OCT.	NOV.	DEC.	ANNUAL
ALA. BIRMINGHAM	56	43	49	56	63	66	67	62	65	66	67	58	44	59
MONTGOMERY	49	51	53	61	69	73	72	66	69	69	71	64	48	64
ALASKA, ANCHORAGE	19	39	46	56	58	50	51	45	39	35	32	33	29	45
FAIRBANKS	20	34	50	61	68	55	53	45	35	31	28	38	29	44
JUNEAU	14	30	32	39	37	34	35	28	30	25	18	21	18	30
NOME	29	44	46	48	53	51	48	32	26	34	35	36	30	41
ARIZ. PHOENIX	64	76	79	83	88	93	94	84	84	89	88	84	77	85
YUMA	52	83	87	91	94	97	98	92	91	93	93	90	83	91
ARK. LITTLE ROCK	66	44	53	57	62	67	72	71	73	71	74	58	47	62
CALIF. EUREKA	49	40	44	50	53	54	56	51	46	52	48	42	39	49
FRESNO	55	46	63	72	83	89	94	97	97	93	87	73	47	78
LOS ANGELES	63	70	69	70	67	68	69	80	81	80	76	79	72	73
RED BLUFF	39	50	60	65	75	79	86	95	94	89	77	64	50	75
SACRAMENTO	48	44	57	67	76	82	90	96	95	92	82	65	44	77
SAN DIEGO	68	68	67	68	66	60	60	67	70	70	70	76	71	68
SAN FRANCISCO	64	53	57	63	69	70	75	68	63	70	70	62	54	66
COLO. DENVER	64	67	67	65	63	61	69	68	68	71	71	67	65	67
GRAND JUNCTION	57	58	62	64	67	71	79	76	72	77	74	67	58	69
CONN. HARTFORD	48	46	55	56	54	57	60	62	60	57	55	46	46	56
D. C. WASHINGTON	66	46	53	56	57	61	64	64	62	62	61	54	47	58
FLA. APALACHICOLA	26	59	62	62	71	77	70	64	63	62	74	66	53	65
JACKSONVILLE	60	58	59	66	71	71	63	62	63	58	58	61	53	62
KEY WEST	45	68	75	78	78	76	70	69	71	65	65	69	66	71
MIAMI BEACH	48	66	72	73	73	68	62	65	67	62	62	65	65	67
TAMPA	63	63	67	71	74	75	66	61	64	64	67	67	61	68
GA. ATLANTA	65	48	53	57	65	68	68	62	63	65	67	60	47	60
HAWAII. HILO	9	48	42	41	34	31	41	44	38	42	41	34	36	39
HONOLULU	53	62	64	60	62	64	66	67	70	70	68	63	60	65
LIHUE	9	48	48	48	46	51	60	58	59	67	58	51	49	54
IDAHO, BOISE	20	40	48	59	67	68	75	89	86	81	66	46	37	66
POCATELLO	21	37	47	58	64	66	72	82	81	78	66	48	36	64
ILL. CAIRO	30	46	53	59	65	71	77	82	79	75	73	56	46	65
CHICAGO	66	44	49	53	56	63	69	73	70	65	61	47	41	59
SPRINGFIELD	59	47	51	54	58	64	69	76	72	73	64	53	45	60
IND. EVANSVILLE	48	42	49	55	61	67	73	78	76	73	67	52	42	64
FT. WAYNE	48	38	44	51	55	62	69	74	69	64	58	41	38	57
INDIANAPOLIS	63	41	47	49	55	62	68	74	70	68	64	48	39	59
IOWA. DES MOINES	66	56	56	56	59	62	66	75	70	64	64	53	48	62
DUBUQUE	54	48	52	52	58	60	63	73	67	61	55	44	40	57
SIOUX CITY	52	55	58	58	59	63	67	75	72	67	65	53	50	63
KANS. CONCORDIA	52	60	60	62	63	65	73	79	76	72	70	64	58	67
DODGE CITY	70	67	66	68	68	68	74	78	78	76	75	70	67	71
WICHITA	46	61	63	64	64	66	73	80	77	73	69	67	59	69
KY. LOUISVILLE	59	41	47	52	57	64	68	72	69	68	64	51	39	59
LA. NEW ORLEANS	69	49	50	57	63	66	64	58	60	64	70	60	46	59
SHREVEPORT	18	48	54	58	60	69	78	79	80	79	77	65	60	69
MAINE, EASTPORT	58	45	51	52	52	51	53	55	57	54	50	37	40	50
MASS. BOSTON	67	47	56	57	56	59	62	64	63	61	58	48	48	57
MICH. ALPENA	45	29	43	52	56	59	64	70	64	52	44	24	22	51
DETROIT	69	34	42	48	52	58	65	69	66	61	54	35	29	53
GRAND RAPIDS	56	26	37	48	54	60	66	72	67	58	50	31	22	49
MARQUETTE	55	31	40	47	52	53	56	63	57	47	38	24	24	47
S. STE. MARIE	60	28	44	50	54	54	59	63	58	45	36	21	22	47
MINN. DULUTH	49	47	55	60	58	58	60	68	63	53	47	36	40	55
MINNEAPOLIS	45	49	54	55	57	60	64	72	69	60	54	40	40	56
MISS. VICKSBURG	66	46	50	57	64	69	73	69	72	74	71	60	45	64
MO. KANSAS CITY	69	55	57	59	60	64	70	76	73	70	67	59	52	65
ST. LOUIS	68	48	49	56	59	64	68	72	68	67	65	54	44	61
SPRINGFIELD	45	48	54	57	60	63	69	77	72	71	65	58	48	63
MONT. HAVRE	55	49	58	61	63	63	65	78	75	64	57	48	46	62
HELENA	65	46	55	58	60	59	63	77	74	63	57	48	43	60
KALISPELL	50	28	40	49	57	58	60	77	73	61	50	28	20	53
NEBR. LINCOLN	55	57	59	60	60	63	69	76	71	67	66	59	55	64
NORTH PLATTE	53	63	63	64	62	64	72	78	74	72	70	62	58	68
NEV. ELY	21	61	64	68	65	67	79	79	81	81	73	67	62	72
LAS VEGAS	19	74	77	78	81	85	91	84	86	92	84	83	75	82
RENO	51	59	64	69	75	77	82	90	89	86	76	68	56	76
WINNEMUCCA	53	52	60	64	70	76	83	90	90	86	75	62	53	74
N. H. CONCORD	44	48	53	55	53	51	56	57	58	55	50	43	43	52
N. J. ATLANTIC CITY	62	51	57	58	59	62	65	67	66	65	54	58	52	60

MEAN PERCENTAGE OF POSSIBLE SUNSHINE FOR SELECTED LOCATIONS

STATE AND STATION	YEARS	JAN.	FEB.	MAR.	APR.	MAY	JUNE	JULY	AUG.	SEPT.	OCT.	NOV.	DEC.	ANNUAL
N. MEX. ALBUQUERQUE	28	70	72	72	76	79	84	76	75	81	80	79	70	76
ROSWELL	47	69	72	75	77	76	80	76	75	74	74	74	69	74
N. Y. ALBANY	63	43	51	53	53	57	62	63	61	58	54	39	38	53
BINGHAMTON	63	31	39	41	44	50	56	54	51	47	43	29	26	44
BUFFALO	49	32	41	49	51	59	67	70	67	60	51	31	28	53
CANTON	43	37	47	50	48	54	61	63	61	54	45	30	31	49
NEW YORK	83	49	56	57	59	62	65	66	64	64	61	53	50	59
SYRACUSE	49	31	38	45	50	58	64	67	63	56	47	29	26	50
N. C. ASHEVILLE	57	48	53	56	61	64	63	59	59	62	64	59	48	58
RALEIGH	61	50	56	59	64	67	65	62	62	63	64	62	52	61
N. DAK. BISMARCK	65	52	58	56	57	58	61	73	69	62	59	49	48	59
DEVILS LAKE	55	53	60	59	60	59	62	71	67	59	56	44	45	58
FARGO	39	47	55	56	58	62	63	73	69	60	57	39	46	59
WILLISTON	43	51	59	60	63	66	66	78	75	65	60	48	48	63
OHIO, CINCINNATI	44	41	46	52	56	62	69	72	68	68	60	46	39	57
CLEVELAND	65	29	36	45	52	61	67	71	68	62	54	32	25	50
COLUMBUS	65	36	44	49	54	63	68	71	68	66	60	44	35	55
OKLA. OKLAHOMA CITY	62	57	60	63	64	65	74	78	78	74	68	64	57	68
OREG. BAKER	46	41	49	56	61	63	67	83	81	74	62	46	37	60
PORTLAND	69	27	34	41	49	52	55	70	65	55	42	28	23	48
ROSEBURG	29	24	32	40	51	57	59	79	77	68	42	28	18	51
PA. HARRISBURG	60	43	52	55	57	61	65	68	63	62	58	47	43	57
PHILADELPHIA	66	45	56	57	58	61	62	64	61	62	61	53	49	57
PITTSBURGH	63	32	39	45	50	57	62	64	61	62	54	39	30	51
R. I. BLOCK ISLAND	48	45	54	47	56	58	60	62	62	60	59	50	44	56
S. C. CHARLESTON	61	58	60	65	72	73	70	66	66	67	68	68	57	66
COLUMBIA	55	53	57	62	68	69	68	63	65	64	68	64	51	63
S. DAK. HURON	62	55	62	60	62	65	68	76	72	66	61	52	49	63
RAPID CITY	53	58	62	63	62	61	66	73	73	69	66	58	54	64
TENN.-KNOXVILLE	62	42	49	53	59	64	66	64	59	64	64	53	41	57
MEMPHIS	55	44	51	57	64	68	74	73	74	70	69	58	45	64
NASHVILLEE	63	42	47	54	60	65	69	69	68	69	65	55	42	59
TEX. ABILENE	14	64	68	73	66	73	86	83	85	73	71	72	66	73
AMARILLO	54	71	71	75	75	75	82	81	81	79	76	76	70	76
AUSTIN	33	46	50	57	60	62	72	76	79	70	70	57	49	63
BROWNSVILLE	37	44	49	51	57	65	73	78	78	67	70	54	44	61
DEL RIO	36	53	55	61	63	60	66	75	80	69	66	58	52	63
EL PASO	53	74	77	81	85	87	87	78	78	80	82	80	73	80
FT. WORTH	33	56	57	65	66	67	75	78	78	74	70	63	58	68
GALVESTON	66	50	50	55	61	69	76	72	71	70	74	62	49	63
SAN ANTONIO	57	48	51	56	58	60	69	74	75	69	67	55	49	62
UTAH, SALT LAKE CITY	22	48	53	61	68	73	78	82	82	84	73	56	49	69
VT. BURLINGTON	54	34	43	48	47	53	59	62	59	51	43	25	24	46
VA. NORFOLK	60	50	57	60	63	67	66	66	66	63	64	60	51	62
RICHMOND	56	49	55	59	63	67	66	65	62	63	64	58	50	61
WASH. NORTH HEAD	44	28	37	42	48	48	48	50	46	48	41	31	27	41
SEATTLE	26	27	34	42	48	53	48	62	56	53	36	28	24	45
SPOKANE	62	26	41	53	63	64	68	82	79	68	53	28	22	58
TATOOSH ISLAND	49	26	36	39	45	47	46	48	44	47	38	26	23	40
WALLA WALLA	44	24	35	51	63	67	72	86	84	72	59	33	20	60
YAKIMA	18	34	49	62	70	72	74	86	86	74	61	38	29	65
W. VA. ELKINS	55	33	37	42	47	55	55	56	53	55	51	41	33	48
PARKERSBURG	62	30	36	42	49	56	60	63	60	60	53	37	29	48
WIS. GREEN BAY	57	44	51	55	56	58	64	70	65	58	52	40	40	55
MADISON	59	44	49	52	53	58	64	70	66	60	56	41	38	56
MILWAUKEE	59	44	48	53	56	60	65	73	67	62	56	44	39	57
WYO. CHEYENNE	63	65	66	64	61	59	68	70	68	69	69	65	63	66
LANDER	57	66	70	71	66	65	74	76	75	72	67	61	62	69
SHERIDAN	52	56	61	62	61	61	67	76	74	67	60	53	52	64
YELLOWSTONE PARK	35	39	51	55	57	56	63	73	71	65	57	45	38	56
P. R. SAN JUAN	57	64	69	71	66	59	62	65	67	61	63	63	65	65

COLLECTION EFFICIENCY

	Greenhouse with full planting	Sunspace with no plants
Double-glazed conventional greenhouse with air circulation and rock storage	25%	65%
Double-glazed solar-oriented greenhouse with adequate water storage capacity in direct sun	35%	75%
Double-glazed solar-oriented greenhouse with air circulation and rock storage	45%	85%

Figure 4. Collection efficiencies for different types of solar greenhouses.

CALCULATING HEAT LOSS

To calculate the monthly heat loss of a greenhouse, one first has to make an estimate of the hourly heat loss. This can be divided into two components: the heat lost by conduction through the walls, floor and roof, and the heat lost by ventilation and infiltration. Thus:

$$Qhl = Qhc + Qhv$$

Where

Qhl = The total hourly heat loss of the building in Btu's/hour/° Fahrenheit.

Qhc = the heat loss by conduction in Btu's per hour/° Fahrenheit.

Qhv = the heat loss by ventilation and infiltration in Btu's/hour/° Fahrenheit.

HEAT LOSS BY CONDUCTION

$$Qhc = U_1 \times A_1 + U_2 \times A_2 + U_3 \times A_3 ...$$

Where

U_1 U_2 and U_3 are the U values of the different wall constructions used, and A_1, A_2 and A_3 are their respective areas.

The U values of various types of construction are given in Chapter 10. These values vary according to exposure and orientation, and are therefore only approximate. Further, more detailed values, can be obtained from References 1 and 3. To take into account the U values of movable insulation over glazing, it is necessary to estimate the number of hours the insulation will be used. Thus if one assumes in midwinter that the glazing would be covered for 16 hours of the day and uncovered for 8 hours, then the average daily U value would be

$$16/24 \times Uig + 8/24 \times Ug$$

Where

Uig = the U value of the insulated glazing and

Ug = the U value of the uninsulated glazing.

HEAT LOSS BY VENTILATION AND INFILTRATION

$$Qhv = N \times V \times 0.02$$

Where

N = the number of air changes per hour.

V = the volume of the building in cubic feet.

0.02 = the volumetric heat capacity of air, in Btu's per cubic foot/°F.

The number of air changes per hour will vary from 0.5 for a tightly sealed plastic film enclosure, to around 4.0 for an old leaky greenhouse with lapped-glass joints. An appropriate air-change rate for a well-constructed solar greenhouse might be around 1.5.

MONTHLY HEAT LOSS

To estimate the monthly heat loss of a building that is to be heated to room temperature (70°F.) the Degree Day formula can be used:

$$Qml = Qhl \times 24 \times DDm$$

Where

Qml = the monthly heat loss of the building in Btu's

Qhl = the hourly heat loss in Btu's/hour

24 = the number of hours per day

DDm = the number of Degree Days per month.

Degree Days for various locations are given in Table 3. Your local weather station will have more accurate monthly data available.

Where it is not necessary to maintain a temper-

STATE AND STATION	JULY	AUG.	SEP.	OCT.	NOV.	DEC.	JAN.	FEB.	MAR.	APR.	MAY	JUNE	ANNUAL
ALA. BIRMINGHAM	0	0	6	93	363	555	592	462	363	108	9	0	2551
HUNTSVILLE	0	0	12	127	426	663	694	557	434	138	19	0	3070
MOBILE	0	0	0	22	213	357	415	300	211	42	0	0	1560
MONTGOMERY	0	0	0	68	330	·527	543	417	316	90	0	0	2291
ALASKA ANCHORAGE	245	291	516	930	1284	1572	1631	1316	1293	879	592	315	10864
ANNETTE	242	208	327	567	738	899	949	837	843	648	490	321	7069
BARROW	803	840	1035	1500	1971	2362	2517	2332	2468	1944	1445	957	20174
BARTER IS.	735	775	987	1482	1944	2337	2536	2369	2477	1923	1373	924	19862
BETHEL	319	394	612	1042	1434	1866	1903	1590	1655	1173	806	402	13196
COLD BAY	474	425	525	772	918	1122	1153	1036	1122	951	791	591	9880
CORDOVA	366	391	522	781	1017	1221	1299	1086	1113	864	660	444	9764
FAIRBANKS	171	332	642	1203	1833	2254	2359	1901	1739	1068	555	222	14279
JUNEAU	301	338	483	725	921	1135	1237	1070	1073	810	601	381	9075
KING SALMON	313	322	513	908	1290	1606	1600	1333	1411	966	673	408	11343
KOTZEBUE	381	446	723	1249	1728	2127	2192	1932	2080	1554	1057	636	16105
MCGRATH	208	338	633	1184	1791	2232	2294	1817	1758	1122	648	258	14283
NOME	481	496	693	1094	1455	1820	1879	1666	1770	1314	930	573	14171
SAINT PAUL	605	539	612	862	963	1197	1228	1168	1265	1098	936	726	11199
SHEMYA	577	475	501	784	876	1042	1045	958	1011	885	837	696	9687
YAKUTAT	338	347	474	716	936	1144	1169	1019	1042	840	632	435	9092
ARIZ. FLAGSTAFF	46	68	201	558	867	1073	1169	991	911	651	437	180	7152
PHOENIX	0	0	0	22	234	415	474	328	217	75	0	0	1765
PRESCOTT	0	0	27	245	579	797	865	711	605	360	158	15	4362
TUCSON	0	0	0	25	231	406	471	344	242	75	6	0	1800
WINSLOW	0	0	6	245	711	1054	1054	770	601	291	96	0	4782
YUMA	0	0	0	0	148	319	363	228	130	29	0	0	1217
ARK. FORT SMITH	0	0	12	127	450	704	781	596	456	144	22	0	3292
LITTLE ROCK	0	0	9	127	465	716	756	577	434	126	9	0	3219
TEXARKANA	0	0	0	78	345	561	626	468	350	105	0	0	2533
CALIF. BAKERSFIELD	0	0	0	37	282	502	546	364	267	105	19	0	2122
BISHOP	0	0	42	248	576	797	874	666	539	306	143	36	4227
BLUE CANYON	34	50	120	347	579	766	865	781	791	582	397	195	5507
BURBANK	0	0	6	43	177	301	366	277	239	138	81	18	1646
EUREKA	270	257	258	329	414	499	546	470	505	438	372	285	4643
FRESNO	0	0	0	78	339	558	586	406	319	150	56	0	2492
LONG BEACH	0	0	12	40	156	288	375	297	267	168	90	18	1711
LOS ANGELES	28	22	42	78	180	291	372	302	288	219	158	81	2061
MT. SHASTA	25	34	123	406	696	902	983	784	738	525	347	159	5722
OAKLAND	53	50	45	127	309	481	527	400	353	255	180	90	2870
POINT ARGUELLO	202	186	162	205	291	400	474	392	403	339	298	243	3595
RED BLUFF	0	0	0	53	318	555	605	428	341	168	47	0	2515
SACRAMENTO	0	0	12	81	363	577	614	442	360	216	102	6	2773
SANDBERG	0	0	30	202	480	691	778	661	620	426	264	57	4209
SAN DIEGO	6	0	15	37	123	251	313	249	202	123	84	36	1439
SAN FRANCISCO	81	78	60	143	306	462	508	395	363	279	214	126	3015
SANTA CATALINA	16	0	9	50	165	279	353	308	326	249	192	105	2052
SANTA MARIA	99	93	96	146	270	391	459	370	363	282	233	165	2967
COLO. ALAMOSA	65	99	279	639	1065	1420	1476	1162	1020	696	440	168	8529
COLORADO SPRINGS	9	25	132	456	825	1032	1128	938	893	582	319	84	6423
DENVER	6	9	117	428	819	1035	1132	938	887	558	288	66	6283
GRAND JUNCTION	0	0	30	313	786	1113	1209	907	729	387	146	21	5641
PUEBLO	0	0	54	326	750	986	1085	871	772	429	174	15	5462
CONN. BRIDGEPORT	0	0	66	307	615	986	1079	966	853	510	208	27	5617
HARDFORT	0	6	99	372	711	1119	1209	1061	899	495	177	24	6172
NEW HAVEN	0	12	87	347	648	1011	1097	991	871	543	245	45	5897
DEL. WILMINGTON	0	0	51	270	588	927	980	874	735	387	112	6	4930
FLA. APALACHICOLA	0	0	0	16	153	319	347	260	180	33	0	0	1308
DAYTONA BEACH	0	0	0	0	75	211	248	190	140	15	0	0	879
FORT MYERS	0	0	0	0	24	109	146	101	62	0	0	0	442
JACKSONVILLE	0	0	0	12	144	310	332	246	174	21	0	0	1239
KEY WEST	0	0	0	0	0	28	40	31	9	0	0	0	108
LAKELAND	0	0	0	0	57	164	195	146	99	0	0	0	661
MIAMI BEACH	0	0	0	0	0	40	56	36	9	0	0	0	141
ORLANDO	0	0	0	0	72	198	220	165	105	6	0	0	766
PENSACOLA	0	0	0	19	195	353	400	277	183	36	0	0	1463
TALLAHASSEE	0	0	0	28	198	360	375	286	202	36	0	0	1485
TAMPA	0	0	0	0	60	171	202	148	102	0	0	0	683
WEST PALM BEACH	0	0	0	6	65	87	64	31	0	0	0	0	253
GA. ATHENS	0	0	12	115	405	632	642	529	431	141	22	0	2929
ATLANTA	0	0	18	127	414	626	639	529	437	168	25	0	2983
AUGUSTA	0	0	0	78	333	552	549	445	350	90	0	0	2397
COLUMBUS	0	0	0	87	333	543	552	434	338	96	0	0	2383
MACON	0	0	0	71	297	502	505	403	295	63	0	0	2136
ROME	0	0	24	161	474	701	710	577	468	177	34	0	3326
SAVANNAH	0	0	0	47	246	437	437	353	254	45	0	0	1819
THOMASVILLE	0	0	0	25	198	366	394	305	208	33	0	0	1529
IDAHO BOISE	0	0	132	415	792	1017	1113	854	722	438	245	81	5809
IDAHO FALLS 46W	16	34	270	623	1056	1370	1538	1249	1085	651	391	192	8475
IDAHO FALLS 42NW	16	40	282	648	1107	1432	1600	1291	1107	657	388	192	8760
LEWISTON	0	0	123	403	756	933	1063	815	694	426	239	90	5542
POCATELLO	0	0	172	493	900	1166	1324	1058	905	555	319	141	7033
ILL. CAIRO	0	0	36	164	513	791	856	680	539	195	47	0	3821
CHICAGO	0	0	81	326	753	1113	1209	1044	890	480	211	48	6155
MOLINE	0	9	99	335	774	1181	1314	1100	918	450	189	39	6408
PEORIA	0	6	87	326	759	1113	1218	1025	849	426	183	33	6025
ROCKFORD	6	9	114	400	837	1221	1333	1137	961	516	236	60	6830
SPRINGFIELD	0	0	72	291	696	1023	1135	935	769	354	136	18	5429
IND. EVANSVILLE	0	0	66	220	606	896	955	767	620	237	68	0	4435
FORT WAYNE	0	9	105	378	783	1135	1178	1028	890	471	189	39	6205
INDIANAPOLIS	0	0	90	316	723	1051	1113	949	809	432	177	39	5699
SOUTH BEND	0	6	111	372	777	1125	1221	1070	933	525	239	60	6439
IOWA Burlington	0	0	93	322	768	1135	1259	1042	859	426	177	33	6114
DES MOINES	0	9	99	363	837	1231	1398	1165	967	489	211	39	6808
DUBUQUE	12	31	156	450	906	1287	1420	1204	1026	546	260	78	7376
SIOUX CITY	0	9	108	369	867	1240	1435	1198	989	483	214	39	6951
WATERLOO	12	19	138	428	909	1296	1460	1221	1023	531	229	54	7320

STATE AND STATION	JULY	AUG.	SEP.	OCT.	NOV.	DEC.	JAN.	FEB.	MAR.	APR.	MAY	JUNE	ANNUAL
KANS. CONCORDIA	0	0	57	276	705	1023	1163	935	781	372	149	18	5479
DODGE CITY	0	0	33	251	666	939	1051	840	719	354	124	9	4986
GOODLAND	0	6	81	381	810	1073	1166	955	884	507	236	42	6141
TOPEKA	0	0	57	270	672	980	1122	893	722	330	124	12	5182
WICHITA	0	0	33	229	618	905	1023	804	645	270	87	6	4620
KY. COVINGTON	0	0	75	291	669	983	1035	893	756	390	149	24	5265
LEXINGTON	0	0	54	239	609	902	946	818	685	325	105	0	4683
LOUISVILLE	0	0	54	248	609	890	930	818	682	315	105	9	4660
LA. ALEXANDRIA	0	0	0	56	273	431	471	361	260	69	0	0	1921
BATON ROUGE	0	0	0	31	216	369	409	294	208	33	0	0	1560
BURRWOOD	0	0	0	0	96	214	298	218	171	27	0	0	1024
LAKE CHARLES	0	0	0	19	210	341	381	274	195	39	0	0	1459
NEW ORLEANS	0	0	0	19	192	322	363	258	192	39	0	0	1385
SHREVEPORT	0	0	0	47	297	477	552	426	304	81	0	0	2184
MAINE CARIBOU	78	115	336	682	1044	1535	1690	1470	1308	858	468	183	9767
PORTLAND	12	53	195	508	807	1215	1339	1182	1042	675	372	111	7511
MD. BALTIMORE	0	0	48	264	585	905	936	820	679	327	90	0	4654
FREDERICK	0	0	66	307	624	955	995	876	741	384	127	12	5087
MASS. BLUE HILL OBSY	0	22	108	381	690	1085	1178	1053	936	579	267	69	6368
BOSTON	0	9	60	316	603	983	1088	972	846	513	208	36	5634
NANTUCKET	12	22	93	332	573	896	992	941	896	621	384	129	5891
PITTSFIELD	25	59	219	524	831	1231	1339	1196	1063	660	326	105	7578
WORCESTER	6	34	147	450	774	1172	1271	1123	998	612	304	78	6969
MICH. ALPENA	68	105	273	580	912	1268	1404	1299	1218	777	446	156	8506
DETROIT (CITY)	0	0	87	360	738	1088	1181	1058	936	522	220	42	6232
ESCANABA	59	87	243	539	924	1293	1445	1296	1203	777	456	159	8481
FLINT	16	40	159	465	843	1212	1330	1198	1066	639	319	90	7377
GRAND RAPIDS	9	28	135	434	804	1147	1259	1134	1011	579	279	75	6894
LANSING	6	22	138	431	813	1163	1262	1142	1011	579	273	69	6909
MARQUETTE	59	81	240	527	936	1268	1411	1268	1187	771	468	177	8393
MUSKEGON	12	28	120	400	762	1088	1209	1100	995	594	310	78	6696
SAULT STE. MARIE	96	105	279	580	951	1367	1525	1380	1277	810	477	201	9048
MINN. DULUTH	71	109	330	632	1131	1581	1745	1518	1355	840	490	198	10000
INTERNATIONAL FALLS	71	112	363	701	1236	1724	1919	1621	1414	828	443	174	10606
MINNEAPOLIS	22	31	189	505	1014	1454	1631	1380	1166	621	288	81	8382
ROCHESTER	25	34	186	474	1005	1438	1593	1366	1150	630	301	93	8295
SAINT CLOUD	28	47	225	549	1065	1500	1702	1445	1221	666	326	105	8879
MISS. JACKSON	0	0	0	65	315	502	546	414	310	87	0	0	2239
MERIDIAN	0	0	0	81	339	518	543	417	310	81	0	0	2289
VICKSBURG	0	0	0	53	279	462	512	384	282	69	0	0	2041
MO. COLUMBIA	0	0	54	251	651	967	1076	874	716	324	121	12	5046
KANSAS	0	0	39	220	612	905	1032	818	682	294	109	0	4711
ST. JOSEPH	0	6	60	285	708	1039	1172	949	769	348	133	15	5484
ST. LOUIS	0	0	60	251	627	936	1026	848	704	312	121	15	4900
SPRINGFIELD	0	0	45	223	600	877	973	781	660	291	105	6	4561
MONT. BILLINGS	6	15	186	487	897	1135	1296	1100	970	570	285	102	7049
GLASGOW	31	47	270	608	1104	1466	1711	1439	1187	648	335	150	8996
GREAT FALLS	28	53	258	543	921	1169	1349	1154	1063	642	384	186	7750
HAVRE	28	53	306	595	1065	1367	1584	1364	1181	657	338	162	8700
HELENA	31	59	294	601	1002	1265	1438	1170	1042	651	381	195	8129
KALISPELL	50	99	321	654	1020	1240	1401	1134	1029	639	397	207	8191
MILES CITY	6	6	174	502	972	1296	1504	1252	1057	579	276	99	7723
MISSOULA	34	74	303	651	1035	1287	1420	1120	970	621	391	219	8125
NEBR. GRAND ISLAND	0	6	108	381	834	1172	1314	1089	908	462	211	45	6530
LINCOLN	0	6	75	301	726	1066	1237	1016	834	402	171	30	5864
NORFOLK	9	0	111	397	873	1234	1414	1179	983	498	233	48	6979
NORTH PLATTE	0	6	123	440	885	1166	1271	1039	930	519	248	57	6684
OMAHA	0	12	105	357	828	1175	1355	1126	939	465	208	42	6612
SCOTTSBLUFF	0	0	138	459	876	1128	1231	1008	921	552	285	75	6673
VALENTINE	9	12	165	493	942	1237	1395	1176	1045	579	288	84	7425
NEV. ELKO	9	34	225	561	924	1197	1314	1036	911	621	409	192	7433
ELY	28	43	234	592	939	1184	1308	1075	977	672	456	225	7733
LAS VEGAS	0	0	0	78	387	617	688	487	335	111	6	0	2709
RENO	43	87	204	490	801	1026	1073	823	729	510	357	189	6332
WINNEMUCCA	0	34	210	536	876	1091	1172	916	837	573	363	153	6761
N. H. CONCORD	6	50	177	505	822	1240	1358	1184	1032	636	298	75	7383
MT. WASH. OBSY.	493	536	720	1057	1341	1742	1820	1663	1652	1260	930	603	13817
N. J. ATLANTIC CITY	0	0	39	251	549	880	936	848	741	420	133	15	4812
NEWARK	0	0	30	248	573	921	983	876	729	381	118	0	4859
TRENTON	0	0	57	264	576	924	989	885	753	399	121	12	4980
N. MEX. ALBUQUERQUE	0	0	12	229	642	868	930	703	595	288	81	0	4348
CLAYTON	0	6	66	310	699	899	986	812	747	429	183	21	5158
RATON	9	28	126	431	825	1048	1116	904	834	543	301	63	6228
ROSWELL	0	0	18	202	573	806	840	641	481	201	31	0	3793
SILVER CITY	0	0	6	183	525	729	791	605	518	261	87	0	3705
N. Y. ALBANY	0	19	138	440	777	1194	1311	1156	992	564	239	45	6875
BINGHAMTON (AP)	22	65	201	471	810	1184	1277	1154	1045	645	313	99	7286
BINGHAMTON (PO)	0	28	141	406	732	1107	1190	1081	949	543	229	45	6451
BUFFALO	19	37	141	440	777	1156	1256	1145	1039	645	329	78	7062
CENTRAL PARK	0	0	30	233	540	902	986	885	760	408	118	9	4871
J. F. KENNEDY INTL.	0	0	36	248	564	933	1029	935	815	480	167	12	5219
LAGUARDIA	0	0	27	223	528	887	973	879	750	414	124	6	4811
ROCHESTER	9	31	126	415	747	1125	1234	1123	1014	597	279	48	6748
SCHENECTADY	0	22	123	422	756	1159	1283	1131	970	543	211	30	6650
SYRACUSE	6	28	132	415	744	1153	1271	1140	1004	570	248	45	6756
N.C. ASHEVILLE	0	0	48	245	555	775	784	683	592	273	87	0	4042
CAPE HATTERAS	0	0	0	78	273	521	580	518	440	177	25	0	2612
CHARLOTTE	0	0	6	124	438	691	691	582	481	156	22	0	3191
GREENSBORO	0	0	33	192	513	778	784	672	552	234	47	0	3805
RALEIGH	0	0	21	164	450	716	725	616	487	180	34	0	3393
WILMINGTON	0	0	0	74	291	521	546	462	357	96	0	0	2347
WINSTON SALEM	0	0	21	171	483	747	753	652	524	207	37	0	3595
N. DAK. BISMARCK	34	28	222	577	1083	1463	1708	1442	1203	645	329	117	8851
DEVILS LAKE	40	53	273	642	1191	1634	1872	1579	1345	753	381	138	9901
FARGO	28	37	219	574	1107	1569	1789	1520	1262	690	332	99	9226
WILLISTON	31	43	261	601	1122	1513	1758	1473	1262	681	357	141	9243

Table 3 (Continued).

STATE AND STATION	JULY	AUG.	SEP.	OCT.	NOV.	DEC.	JAN.	FEB.	MAR.	APR.	MAY	JUNE	ANNUAL
OHIO AKRON	0	9	96	381	726	1070	1138	1016	871	489	202	39	6037
CINCINNATI	0	0	54	248	612	921	970	837	701	336	118	9	4806
CLEVELAND	9	25	105	384	738	1088	1159	1047	918	552	260	66	6351
COLUMBUS	0	6	84	347	714	1039	1088	949	809	426	171	27	5660
DAYTON	0	6	78	310	696	1045	1097	955	809	429	167	30	5622
MANSFIELD	9	22	114	397	768	1110	1169	1042	924	543	245	60	6403
SANDUSKY	0	6	66	313	684	1032	1107	991	868	495	198	36	5796
TOLEDO	0	16	117	406	792	1138	1200	1056	924	543	242	60	6494
YOUNGSTOWN	6	19	120	412	771	1104	1169	1047	921	540	248	60	6417
OKLA. OKLAHOMA CITY	0	0	15	164	498	766	868	664	527	189	34	0	3725
TULSA	0	0	18	158	522	787	893	683	539	213	47	0	3860
OREG. ASTORIA	146	130	210	375	561	679	753	622	636	480	363	231	5186
BURNS	12	37	210	515	867	1113	1246	988	856	570	366	177	6957
EUGENE	34	34	129	366	585	719	803	627	589	426	279	135	4726
MEACHAM	84	124	288	580	918	1091	1209	1005	983	726	527	339	7874
MEDFORD	0	0	78	372	678	871	918	697	642	432	242	78	5008
PENDLETON	0	0	111	350	711	884	1017	773	617	396	205	63	5127
PORTLAND	25	28	114	335	597	735	825	644	586	396	245	105	4635
ROSEBURG	22	16	105	329	567	713	766	608	570	405	267	123	4491
SALEM	37	31	111	338	594	729	822	647	611	417	273	144	4754
SEXTON SUMMIT	81	81	171	443	666	874	958	809	818	609	465	279	6254
PA. ALLENTOWN	0	0	90	353	693	1045	1116	1002	849	471	167	24	5810
ERIE	0	25	102	391	714	1063	1169	1081	973	585	288	60	6451
HARRISBURG	0	0	63	298	648	992	1045	907	766	396	124	12	5251
PHILADELPHIA	0	0	60	291	621	964	1014	890	744	390	115	12	5101
PITTSBURGH	0	9	105	375	726	1063	1119	1002	874	480	195	39	5987
READING	0	0	54	257	597	939	1001	885	735	372	105	0	4945
SCRANTON	0	19	132	434	762	1104	1156	1028	893	498	195	33	6254
WILLIAMSPORT	0	9	111	375	717	1073	1122	1002	856	468	177	24	5934
R. I. BLOCK IS.	0	16	78	307	594	902	1020	955	877	612	344	99	5804
PROVIDENCE	0	16	96	372	660	1023	1110	988	868	534	236	51	5954
S. C. CHARLESTON	0	0	0	59	282	471	487	389	291	54	0	0	2033
COLUMBIA	0	0	0	84	345	577	570	470	357	81	0	0	2484
FLORENCE	0	0	0	78	315	552	552	459	347	84	0	0	2387
GREENVILLE	0	0	0	112	387	636	648	535	434	120	12	0	2884
SPARTANBURG	0	0	15	130	417	667	663	560	453	144	25	0	3074
S. DAK. HURON	9	12	165	508	1014	1432	1628	1355	1125	600	288	87	8223
RAPID CITY	22	12	165	481	897	1172	1333	1145	1051	615	326	126	7345
SIOUX FALLS	19	25	168	462	972	1361	1544	1285	1082	573	270	78	7839
TENN. BRISTOL	0	0	51	236	573	828	828	700	598	261	68	0	4143
CHATTANOOGA	0	0	18	143	468	698	722	577	453	150	25	0	3254
KNOXVILLE	0	0	30	171	489	725	732	613	493	198	43	0	3494
MEMPHIS	0	0	18	130	447	698	729	585	456	147	22	0	3232
NASHVILLE	0	0	30	158	495	732	778	644	512	189	40	0	3578
OAK RIDGE (CO)	0	0	39	192	531	772	778	669	552	228	56	0	3817
TEX. ABILENE	0	0	0	99	366	586	642	470	347	114	0	0	2624
AMARILLO	0	0	18	205	570	797	877	664	546	252	56	0	3985
AUSTIN	0	0	0	31	225	388	468	325	223	51	0	0	1711
BROWNSVILLE	0	0	0	0	66	149	205	106	74	0	0	0	600
CORPUS CHRISTI	0	0	0	0	120	220	291	174	109	0	0	0	914
DALLAS	0	0	0	62	321	524	601	440	319	90	6	0	2363
EL PASO	0	0	0	84	414	648	685	445	319	105	0	0	2700
FORT WORTH	0	0	0	65	324	536	614	448	319	99	0	0	2405
GALVESTON	0	0	0	0	138	270	350	258	189	30	0	0	1235
HOUSTON	0	0	0	6	183	307	384	288	192	36	0	0	1396
LAREDO	0	0	0	0	105	217	267	134	74	0	0	0	797
LUBBOCK	0	0	18	174	513	744	800	613	484	201	31	0	3578
MIDLAND	0	0	0	87	381	592	651	468	322	90	0	0	2591
PORT ARTHUR	0	0	0	22	207	329	384	274	192	39	0	0	1447
SAN ANGELO	0	0	0	68	318	536	567	412	288	66	0	0	2255
SAN ANTONIO	0	0	0	31	207	363	428	286	195	39	0	0	1549
VICTORIA	0	0	0	6	150	270	344	230	152	21	0	0	1173
WACO	0	0	0	43	270	456	536	389	270	66	0	0	2030
WICHITA FALLS	0	0	0	99	381	632	698	518	378	120	6	0	2832
UTAH MILFORD	0	0	99	443	867	1141	1252	988	822	519	279	87	6497
SALT LAKE CITY	0	0	81	419	849	1082	1172	910	763	459	233	84	6052
WENDOVER	0	0	48	372	822	1091	1178	902	729	408	177	51	5778
VT. BURLINGTON	28	65	207	539	891	1349	1513	1333	1187	714	353	90	8269
VA. CAPE HENRY	0	0	0	112	360	645	694	633	536	246	53	0	3279
LYNCHBURG	0	0	51	223	540	822	849	731	605	267	78	0	4166
NORFOLK	0	0	0	136	408	698	738	655	533	216	37	0	3421
RICHMOND	0	0	36	214	495	784	815	703	546	219	53	0	3865
ROANOKE	0	0	51	229	549	825	834	722	614	261	65	0	4150
WASH. NAT'L. AP.	0	0	33	217	519	834	871	762	626	288	74	0	4224
WASH. OLYMPIA	68	71	198	422	636	753	834	675	645	450	307	177	5236
SEATTLE	50	47	129	329	543	657	738	599	577	396	242	117	4424
SEATTLE BOEING	34	40	147	384	624	763	831	655	608	411	242	99	4838
SEATTLE TACOMA	56	62	162	391	633	750	828	657	657	474	295	159	5145
SPOKANE	9	25	168	493	879	1082	1231	980	834	531	288	135	6655
STAMPEDE PASS	273	291	393	701	1008	1178	1287	1075	1085	855	654	483	9283
TATOOSH IS.	295	279	306	406	534	639	713	613	645	525	431	333	5719
WALLA WALLA	0	0	87	310	681	843	986	745	589	342	177	45	4805
YAKIMA	0	12	144	450	828	1039	1163	868	713	435	220	69	5941
W. VA. CHARLESTON	0	0	63	254	591	865	880	770	648	300	96	9	4476
ELKINS	9	25	135	400	729	992	1008	896	791	444	198	48	5675
HUNTINGTON	0	0	63	257	585	856	880	764	636	294	99	12	4446
PARKERSBURG	0	0	60	264	606	905	942	826	691	339	115	6	4754
WIS. GREEN BAY	28	50	174	484	924	1333	1494	1313	1141	654	335	99	8029
LA CROSSE	12	19	153	437	924	1339	1504	1277	1070	540	245	69	7589
MADISON	25	40	174	474	930	1330	1473	1274	1113	618	310	102	7863
MILWAUKEE	43	47	174	471	876	1252	1376	1193	1054	642	372	135	7635
WYO. CASPER	6	16	192	524	942	1169	1290	1084	1020	657	381	129	7410
CHEYENNE	19	31	210	543	924	1101	1228	1056	1011	672	381	102	7278
LANDER	6	19	204	555	1020	1299	1417	1145	1017	654	381	153	7870
SHERIAN	25	31	219	539	948	1200	1355	1154	1054	642	366	150	7683

ature of 70°F., an estimate must be made of the average monthly temperature difference between inside and out. Thus the formula becomes:

$$Qml = Qhl \times 24 \times Dm \times (To - Tr)$$

Where

Qhl = the hourly heat loss of the building in Btu's/hour.
24 = the number of hours per day
Dm = the number of days per month
To = the average monthly outdoor temperature in °F.
Ti = the average monthly indoor temperature in °F.

Average outdoor temperatures for each month are given in Figure 5, though more accurate data are available from weather stations. The average indoor temperature will depend on what plants you wish to grow in the greenhouse. For a cool greenhouse growing leafy vegetables throughout the winter, one should aim for an average daily temperature of around 45°F.

These calculation procedures are based on a number of simplistic assumptions and do not take into account the dynamics of the greenhouse environment. More sophisticated calculation procedures which allow detailed consideration of temperature variations throughout the day as well as taking into account the effect of solar heat storage, are explained in References 5 and 6.

Figure 5. Average daily temperatures for the week that includes the 21st day of each month, from the Climatic Atlas of the United States (Reference 4).

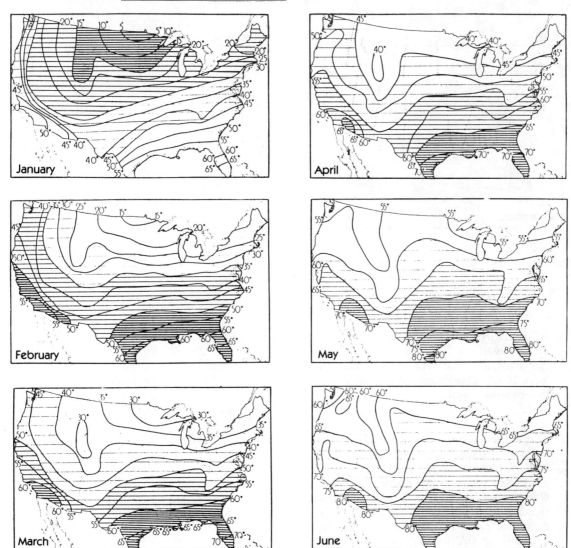

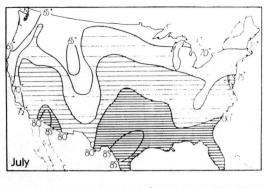

July

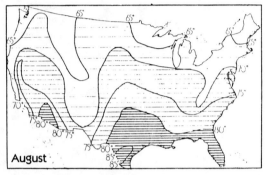

August

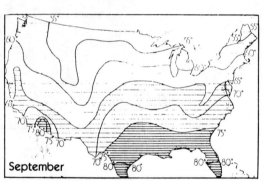

September

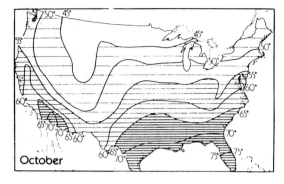

October

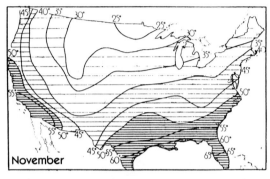

November

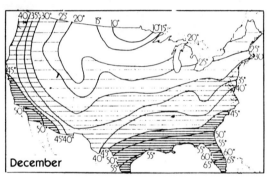

December

References

1. *ASHRAE Handbook of Fundamentals* (1977) and *Handbook of Applications* (1974). ASHRAE, 345 East 47th St., New York, New York 10017. These standard engineering texts give detailed calculation procedures and design data.

2. "Experimental Results of a Greenhouse Solar Collector and Modular Gravel Storage System" by R.W. Langhans et al., in *The Proceedings of a Conference on Solar Energy for Heating Greenhouses and Greenhouse Residential Combinations,* March, 1977, Cleveland, Ohio. Available from the Department of Agricultural Engineering, OARDC, Wooster, Ohio 44691.

3. *Designing and Building a Solar House,* by Donald Watson. Garden Way Publishing, Charlotte, Vermont 05445. This book contains detailed but simple calculation procedures for estimating the performance of active and passive solar-heating systems.

4. *Climatic Atlas of the United States.* U.S. Department of Commerce. 1968. Available from the Government Printing Office, Washington D.C.

5. "Glazed Area Insulation and Thermal Mass in Passive Solar Design," by Charles Michel. Published in the *Proceedings of the First Annual*

Conference of the New England Solar Energy Association. July, 1976. Amherst, Massachusetts.

6. *Predicting the Performance of Passive Solar Heated Buildings,* by Mazria, Baker and Wessling. 1977. Available from the Center for Environmental Research, University of Oregon, Eugene, Oregon. 75 cents.

7. "The Delta Solar House," an article in *Building Design* (May 4, 1978). Morgan-Grampian Press, London.

Index